A COMPANION
TO THE MOVIES

A COMPANION
TO THE MOVIES

Roy Pickard

FREDERICK MULLER LIMITED
LONDON

First published in Great Britain in 1972 by
Lutterworth Press, London.

Revised and updated edition published in
Great Britain in 1979 by Frederick Muller Limited,
London, NW2 6LE

British Library Cataloguing in Publication Data

Pickard, Roy
    A companion to the movies. — Revised and
    updated ed.
    1. Moving-pictures — United States — Biography
    2. Moving-pictures — Great Britain — Biography
    I. Title
    791.43'092'2   PN1998.A2

    ISBN 0 — 584 — 10359 — X

Typeset by Texet, Leighton Buzzard, Bedfordshire
Printed in Great Britain by
The Anchor Press, Tiptree, Essex

ACKNOWLEDGEMENTS

Grateful acknowledgement is made to the following organizations for supplying photographs for this book: Paramount; Twentieth Century-Fox; United Artists; Warner Bros; MGM; Columbia; Universal; Richard Williams Studios.

FOR JOAN AND CLAIRE, AGAIN

CONTENTS

PREFACE

This volume is an updated and extensively revised version of my book, first published in 1972. Its purpose now, as it was then, is to provide the film enthusiast with a handy reference guide to all the main genres of entertainment in the English speaking cinema.

Each genre is dealt with in a separate chapter which is divided into two parts, the first dealing in chronological order with outstanding films selected for their critical importance or box-office success, the second with a 'Who's Who' of those actors, directors, writers, cameramen, etc. who have worked with distinction in the genre under discussion.

One of the most interesting aspects of the updating has been the discovery of how tastes have changed in the last seven years. In 1972, westerns were most definitely 'in' and comedy 'out'. That situation has now reversed itself thanks to Woody Allen, Mel Brooks and company.

Science-fiction (included here under Fantasy) is another genre that has at last received its due recognition thanks to the two blockbusters *Star Wars* and *Close Encounters Of The Third Kind*. The popularity of musicals has increased, horror and war films continue to hold their own as does the romantic movie of which there have been any number of fine examples during the 70s. Even swashbucklers and epics (in their new guise of disaster spectaculars) have enjoyed a comeback.

A section on Animation has been included in this new edition which I hope will add to the book's value. There are also comprehensive check lists of art directors, costume designers and editors to go alongside the existing lists of cameramen, composers and writers.

A Companion To The Movies still remains the only film book to explore in detail the various popular genres of the cinema. The first edition was described by 'The Hollywood Reporter' as being "a valuable addition to film reference books. Because of the unique approach the author has taken it should become a staple for film libraries."

Hopefully, in its revised form, the book will become so again and be both useful and entertaining, not only to those already acquainted with its pages but to new readers as well.

Roy Pickard,
August, 1979

COMEDY

THE GOLD RUSH   1925

This comedy of a lone gold prospector in the Klondyke at the turn-of-the-century has become one of the enduring masterpieces of the silent cinema. A satire on man's greed, it is perhaps the most perfect of Chaplin's feature works and contains extraordinary scenes at both ends of the emotional scale, e.g. the New Year's Eve party sequence in which Charlie waits alone for the girl who never comes and the celebrated scene when Chaplin and fellow prospector Mack Swain fight it out in a log cabin, teetering on the edge of a cliff. Most of Chaplin's work falls into the classic category, yet only rarely was his touch so sure and the result of his labours so perfectly balanced as in this film.

Production Company:	United Artists
Production and Direction:	Charles Chaplin
Screenplay:	Charles Chaplin
Assistant Directors:	Charles Riesner and
	H. d'Abbadie d'Arrast
Photography:	R. H. Totheroh

Leading Players: Charles Chaplin, Mack Swain, Georgia Hale, Tom Murray, Henry Bergman, Malcolm Waite, Betty Morrissey

Note: Shot in Hollywood and on location in Nevada, spring, 1924 — summer, 1925. Premiered in New York at the Strand Theatre, August 16, 1925.

THE GENERAL   1926

Brilliant stunt work and perfect timing are the key factors in this Buster Keaton comedy about a Southern engine driver who, together with his beloved locomotive 'The General', gets caught up with both sides during the American Civil War. A strong case can be made that the film is the funniest of all time (it is certainly the best train film ever made), yet strangely the story is based on a tragic real-life incident, when a group of Union spies broke through the Confederate lines, stole a train and drove it back towards the north, destroying the tracks and bridges on the way. Just ten miles from the border they were captured and hanged. They were later posthumously awarded the first Congressional Medal of Honour in American history.

Production Company:	United Artists
Direction:	Buster Keaton and Clyde Bruckman
Adaptation:	Al Boasberg and Charles Smith

Photography: Bert Haines and J. D. Jennings
Technical Direction: Fred Gabourie
Leading Players: Buster Keaton, Marion Mack, Glen Cavender,
   Jim Farley, Frederick Vroom, Charles Smith, Frank Barnes,
   Frank Hagney

BRINGING UP BABY   1938

The film in which Cary Grant and Katharine Hepburn become involved
with two Brazilian leopards, a small town sheriff (Walter Catlett), a
drunken Irish gardener (Barry Fitzgerald) and a big-game hunter
(Charles Ruggles), whilst searching for a missing bone from the skeleton
of a dinosaur. If the story sounds crazy, then that is only the half of it.
From the opening scenes on the golf course and in the restaurant, when
Miss Hepburn loses the back of her dress, to the final sequence when
everybody, including the leopards, finish up in gaol, this is the zaniest,
fastest and most inspired American comedy of the thirties. It is a movie
of which it really is true to say: "They don't make them like that any
more."

Production Company: RKO Radio
Production and Direction: Howard Hawks
Screenplay: Dudley Nichols, Hager Wilde
   from a story by Hager Wilde
Photography: Russell Metty
Music: Roy Webb
Leading Players: Cary Grant, Katharine Hepburn, Charles Ruggles,
   Walter Catlett, Barry Fitzgerald, May Robson, Fritz Feld

THE CAT AND THE CANARY   1939

This was one of the best of Bob Hope's early comedies. Set in a ghostly
mansion in the Louisiana swamps, it centres on the relatives of a long-
dead eccentric who foregather ten years after his death to hear the
midnight reading of the will. The ghost sequences — the film is full
of sliding panels, clutching hands and underground passages — are
imaginatively conceived and at times hold as much terror as those in a
genuine horror film. With Hope around, however, the tension never
lasts for long, especially when he answers the question "Don't big,
empty houses scare you?" with the wisecrack "Not me, I used to be in
vaudeville." George Zucco appears as the family lawyer and Gale
Sondergaard as a sinister housekeeper.

Production Company: Paramount
Direction: Elliott Nugent
Screenplay: Walter De Leon and Lynn Starling
   from the play by John Willard
Photography: Charles Lang
Leading Players: Bob Hope, Paulette Goddard, John Beal, Douglass
   Montgomery, Gale Sondergaard, Nydia Westman, George Zucco,
   Willard Robertson, Elizabeth Patterson

THE PALM BEACH STORY   1942

In many ways the zaniest of all Preston Sturges' comedies. The plot, such as it is, concerns a scatter-brained wife (Claudette Colbert) who becomes involved with a multi-millionaire and his much-married sister whilst trying to raise 99,000 dollars to finance her husband's new invention. The film is enlivened most by the sudden appearance of the Ale and Quail Club, a group of ageing sportsmen who, together with their guns and dogs, burst into the film for no other apparent reason than to accompany Miss Colbert on one of the most riotous train journeys ever filmed. Sheer nonsense, but brilliantly done.

Production Company: Paramount
Associate Producer: Paul Jones
Direction and Screenplay: Preston Sturges
Photography: Victor Milner
Music: Victor Young
Leading Players: Claudette Colbert, Joel McCrea, Mary Astor, Rudy Vallee, Sig Arno, Robert Warwick, Arthur Stuart Hull, Torben Meyer, Jimmy Conlin, Victor Potel, William Demarest, Jack Horton, Robert Greig, Roscoe Ates, Dewey Robinson, Chester Conklin, Sheldon Jeff, Franklin Pangborn

Note: Filmed in Hollywood, December, 1941 — February 1942.

WOMAN OF THE YEAR   1942

The first, and arguably the best, of the nine Tracy/Hepburn movies, built around the experiences of a down-to-earth baseball correspondent who finds his life shattered when he takes for a wife an international columnist who works for the same newspaper. The direction, screenplay and superb professionalism of the players all contribute to the film's overall success, as they do to the film's most memorable scene, when Miss Hepburn, watched in amazement by the unobserved Tracy, tries to cook him a decent breakfast.

Production Company: Metro-Goldwyn-Mayer
Production: Joseph L. Mankiewicz
Direction: George Stevens
Original Screenplay: Ring Lardner Jr., and
                              Michael Kanin
Photography: Joseph Ruttenberg
Music: Franz Waxman
Leading Players: Spencer Tracy, Katharine Hepburn, Fay Bainter, Reginald Owen, Minor Watson, William Bendix

Note: Filmed in Hollywood, September-November, 1941.

EVERYBODY DOES IT   1949

There are so many amusing moments in this film that it is a pity that it has been neglected for so long. In retrospect, it seems one of the funniest American comedies of the post-war decade. Paul Douglas features as an amiable business man married to a society girl (Celeste Holm) who is always singing but has no vocal talent. In trying to dissuade her, he finds that he has a magnificent baritone voice himself and proceeds to embark on a nation-wide tour with ravishing *prima donna*, Linda Darnell. Nunnally Johnson's screenplay bristles with witty repartee, especially in the first half, and there is a gloriously farcical climax when a drunken Douglas makes a disastrous attempt at Wagnerian opera.

Production Company:	Twentieth Century-Fox
Production:	Nunnally Johnson
Direction:	Edmund Goulding
Screenplay:	Nunnally Johnson
Photography:	Joseph LaShelle
Music Direction:	Alfred Newman
Leading Players:	Paul Douglas, Celeste Holm, Linda Darnell, Charles Coburn, Millard Mitchell, Lucile Watson

Note: Filmed in Hollywood, March-April, 1949

THE MAN IN THE WHITE SUIT   1951

The central figure in Mackendrick's film is a young research chemist (Alec Guinness) who works at a Northern textile factory trying to invent a material that will never stain or wear out. When, eventually, he succeeds, he finds that his invention causes chaos among management and labour, both of whom see the cloth as a dangerous threat to their livelihood. The satire is generally on the mild side, but occasionally the film cuts deeper; the final sequence in a dark, rainy street when the white suit disintegrates and the young inventor is left alone outside the factory gates, is worthy of Chaplin in its pathos. Not the most characteristic of Ealing films, but in many ways the most imaginative and perfectly realized.

Production Company:	Ealing Studios
Production:	Michael Balcon
Direction:	Alexander Mackendrick
Screenplay:	Roger MacDougall, John Dighton and Alexander Mackendrick
Photography:	Douglas Slocombe
Music:	Benjamin Frankel
Leading Players:	Alec Guinness, Joan Greenwood, Cecil Parker, Michael Gough, Ernest Thesiger, Howard Marion Crawford, Vida Hope

Note: Filmed at Ealing Studios and on location in Bromley, December, 1950-March, 1951.

GENEVIEVE   1953

An amusing little trifle about the week-end adventures of two young couples — a young barrister (John Gregson) and his unenthusiastic wife (Dinah Sheridan), and a playboy (Kenneth More) and his equally bored girlfriend (Kay Kendall) — who enter their respective cars in the annual veteran car run from London to Brighton. The performances are good, but not surprisingly it is the two cars — the 1904 Darracq (Genevieve) and the rival 1904 Spiker — that steal the show. The film proved to be the sleeper of the early fifties and one of the biggest box-office successes of the decade.

Production Company:	Sirius
Production and Direction:	Henry Cornelius
Screenplay:	William Rose
Photography (Technicolor):	Christopher Challis
Music:	Larry Adler

Leading Players: John Gregson, Dinah Sheridan, Kenneth More, Kay Kendall, Geoffrey Keen, Harold Siddons, Joyce Grenfell

SOME LIKE IT HOT   1959

The funniest of all Billy Wilder's comedies, with Jack Lemmon and Tony Curtis as two jazz musicians who find themselves on the run, masquerading as members of an all-girl dance band after witnessing a gang-land massacre in Prohibition Chicago. Wilder is brilliantly served by his two male leads and by Marilyn Monroe (as the band's vocalist, Sugar Kane), although the success of the film can be attributed more to the continuously witty screenplay, and to its unashamed vulgarity, which Wilder cheerfully and with great skill exploits to the full.

Production Company:	A Mirisch Co. Presentation/ United Artists
Production and Direction:	Billy Wilder
Screenplay:	Billy Wilder and
suggested from a story by R. Thoeren and M. Logan	I. A. L. Diamond
Photography:	Charles B. Lang
Music:	Adolph Deutsch

Leading Players: Marilyn Monroe, Tony Curtis, Jack Lemmon, George Raft, Pat O'Brien, Joe E. Brown, Nehemiah Persoff, Joan Shawlee

Note: Filmed at the Goldwyn Studios in Hollywood, on location near San Diego, at the Coronado Beach Hotel and in downtown Los Angeles, August-November, 1958.

THE ODD COUPLE   1968

Wilder also wanted to film this screen version of Neil Simon's Broadway hit but even allowing for his mastery of the genre it is difficult to see how he could have improved on the end result. The film is essentially a piece for two actors — Jack Lemmon, whose wife has just left him and is seeking a divorce, and Walter Matthau, his already divorced sports-writer friend who invites him to stay in his apartment during the traumatic 'after period'. Lemmon is meticulous, tidy and a hypochon-driac, Matthau the All-American slob, good natured and trailing garbage all over his eight-room apartment. The result is a conflict that is both amusing and not a little pathetic as it reveals the human failings that make people, no matter what sex, impossible to live with. Lemmon ('so nervous that he wears a seat belt at a drive-in movie') and Matthau (always fantasising about the girls upstairs) just about tie in the acting stakes.

Production Company:	Paramount
Production:	Howard W. Koch
Direction:	Gene Saks
Screenplay:	Neil Simon
based on his own play	
Photography (Technicolor/	
Panavision):	Robert B. Hauser
Music:	Neal Hefti

Leading Players: Jack Lemmon, Walter Matthau, John Fiedler, Herbert Edelman, David Sheiner, Larry Haines, Monica Evans

SILENT MOVIE   1976

Mel Brooks is rather like Jacques Tati. You either roll in the aisles or you remain completely unmoved. But there is no doubting his ingenuity, especially in this movie. He plays a famous film director who plans a comeback in order to save a bankrupt studio from a takeover. His answer to the problem is a film without sound which is just what this movie is — silent, aided by titles, musical accompaniment and sound effects. Not all of it works but the crazy gags pile up so fast that the weak spots are quickly forgotten and the film moves frenziedly on to the next set of comic routines. Several Hollywood stars (Burt Reynolds, James Caan, Paul Newman, Liza Minnelli) guest briefly as themselves. None is better than Anne Bancroft (Mrs. Mel Brooks) whose cross-eyed dancing of a tango in a night club is the high spot of the movie.

Production Company:	Twentieth Century-Fox
Production:	Michael Hertzberg
Direction:	Mel Brooks
Screenplay:	Mel Brooks, Ron Clark, Rudy De Luca and Barry Levinson
Story:	Ron Clark
Photography:	Paul Lohmann
(De Luxe Color)	
Music:	John Morris

Leading Players: Mel Brooks, Marty Feldman, Dom DeLuise, Bernadette Peters, Sid Caesar.

ANNIE HALL 1977

Annie Hall is invariably referred to as a comedy with tragic undertones. For many, a more apt appraisal would be a tragedy with comic undertones. But whichever way one views this little gem of a film, it contains some deliciously humorous moments as Woody Allen chronicles the relationship between melancholy night club comedian Alvy Singer (Allen) and neurotic young vocalist Annie Hall (Diane Keaton). The 'nervous romance' is complicated, banal, despairing, riotous, fraught, pretentious and eventually wearing to both contestants. Annie finally opts for a smarter life in Hollywood (referred to by Allen as munchkinland) and Alvy stays in New York, as introspective as ever. Not much to it thematically but sheer delight during the actual viewing.

Production Company: United Artists
Production: Charles H. Joffe
Direction: Woody Allen
Screenplay: Woody Allen and
                        Marshall Brickman
Photography: Gordon Willis
  (De Luxe Color)
Leading Players: Woody Allen, Diane Keaton, Tony Roberts, Carol Kane, Paul Simon, Shelley Duvall

COMEDY: WHO'S WHO

ABBOTT, BUD (1895-1974) AND COSTELLO, LOU (1906-1959). Ex-vaudeville team who worked in low-budget double features at MGM and Universal for more than two decades. At their peak during the 40s, they attempted to fill the gap left by Laurel and Hardy, but never succeeded in replacing that immortal pair in the public's affection. Over 35 films together, including *One Night in the Tropics* (their first) (40), *Buck Privates* (40), *In the Navy* (41), *Rio Rita* (42), *Lost in a Harem* (44), *In Society* (44), *Abbott and Costello in Hollywood* (45), *The Time of Their Lives* (46), *The Wistful Widow of Wagon Gap* (47), *Abbott and Costello Meet Frankenstein* (48), *Abbott and Costello Meet the Invisible Man* (51), *Abbott and Costello Meet the Mummy* (55), *Dance With Me Henry* (their last) (56).

ALLEN, WOODY (1935-). Bespectacled night club comedian who has brought a new lease of life to wisecracking screen humour during the 70s. Invariably cast as the outsider — the little guy at odds with the conventions of society — he has parodied science fiction (*Sleeper*), historical drama (*Love And Death*) and everything from horror films to TV panel games (*Everything You Always Wanted To Know About Sex But Were Afraid To Ask*). An Oscar winner for his script and direction of *Annie Hall*. Comedies: *What's New Pussycat* (65) (scripted), *What's Up Tiger Lily?* (66) (co-scripted), *Casino Royale* (67) (as 007's nephew Jimmy Bond), *Take The Money And Run* (69) (directed and co-scripted), *Bananas* (71) (directed and co-scripted), *Play It Again Sam* (72) (scripted), *Everything You Always Wanted To Know About Sex But Were Afraid To Ask* (72) (directed and scripted), *Sleeper* (74) (directed and co-scripted), *Love And Death* (75) (directed and scripted), *Annie Hall* (77) (directed and co-scripted), *Manhattan* (79) (directed and co-scripted).

ARDEN, EVE (1912-). American actress, seen mostly in supporting roles during the 40s. As good with the wisecrack as any comedienne the cinema has produced. Key comedy films: *The Doughgirls* (44), *Voice of the Turtle* (47), *Three Husbands* (50), *We're Not Married* (52), *Our Miss Brooks* (56).

AXELROD, GEORGE (1922-). American playwright/screenwriter/ director, best-known in the comedy genre for his Broadway (and later film) success *The Seven Year Itch* (55), Screenplays include *Phffft* (54), *Breakfast at Tiffany's* (61), *Paris When it Sizzles* (64), *How to Murder Your Wife* (65), *Lord Love a Duck* (66) (also directed), *The Secret Life of an American Wife* (68) (also directed).

BALL, LUCILLE (1910-). One of the most talented comediennes to emerge from the American cinema during the 40s, Lucille Ball never quite received the parts she deserved on the big screen. Her most notable comedy appearances were usually in Bob Hope movies, e.g. *Sorrowful Jones* (49), *Fancy Pants* (50), *The Facts of Life* (60), *Critic's Choice* (63). Since the mid-50s she has starred in the TV shows 'I Love Lucy' and 'The Lucy Show'. Films include *Miss Grant Takes Richmond* (49), *The Fuller Brush Girl* (50), *The Long, Long Trailer* (54), *Forever Darling* (56).

BOULTING, JOHN and ROY (both 1913-). Twin brothers who started in British films in the late 30s working mainly on dramatic material, e.g. *Thunder Rock* (42), *Brighton Rock* (47), *Seven Days To Noon* (50). During the 50s they turned to comedy, producing and direct- ing a series of successful films with Ian Carmichael, Peter Sellers and Richard Attenborough. Most famous picture: *I'm All Right Jack* (59), a lightly satirical look at labour relations during the 'never had it so good' period. Others: *Private's Progress* (56), *Lucky Jim* (57), *Brothers In Law* (57), *Happy Is The Bride* (57), *Carlton-Browne Of The F.O.* (59), *A French Mistress* (60), *Heavens Above* (63), *Rotten To The Core* (65), *There's A Girl In My Soup* (70), *Soft Beds And Hard Battles* (73).

BRACKETT, CHARLES (1892-1969). American writer/producer, in partnership with Billy Wilder, 1938-1950. Later worked at Fox, mainly in a production capacity. Comedy films include *Bluebeard's Eighth Wife* (38), *Midnight* (39), *Ninotchka* (39), *Ball of Fire* (41), (all co-scripted with Wilder), *The Major and the Minor* (42), *A Foreign Affair* (48) (both produced and co-scripted with Wilder), *The Mating Season* (51), *The Model and the Marriage Broker* (52) (both produced and co-scripted at Fox).

BROOKS, MEL (1927-). Along with Woody Allen the major force in American screen comedy in recent years. Something of a specialist in parodying established genres e.g. westerns (*Blazing Saddles*), horror films (*Young Frankenstein*) and Hitchcockian thrillers (*High Anxiety*). His comedies range from the vulgar to the visually inspired and invariably include a stock company of favourite actors — Gene Wilder, Marty Feldman, Dom De Luise, Madeleine Kahn. Films, all of which he has written and directed: *The Producers* (68),

The Twelve Chairs (70), *Blazing Saddles* (74), *Young Frankenstein* (74), *Silent Movie* (76), *High Anxiety* (77).

CAPRA, FRANK (1897-). Sicilian-born director, famous for his American social comedies of the Depression 30s. Won Oscars for *It Happened One Night* (34), *Mr. Deeds Goes To Town* (36), *You Can't Take It With You* (38). Other comedy films, many scripted by Robert Riskin, include *Platinum Blonde* (32), *Lady for a Day* (33), *Mr. Smith Goes to Washington* (39), *Arsenic and Old Lace* (44), *State of the Union* (48), *Here Comes the Groom* (51), *A Hole in the Head* (59), *A Pocketful of Miracles* (61).

CARMICHAEL, IAN (1920-). British actor who excelled in 'Silly Ass' roles in British comedies of the 50s. At his peak in the Boulting satires *Lucky Jim* (57) and *I'm All Right Jack* (59). Others: *Private's Progress* (56), *Brothers In Law* (57), *Happy Is The Bride* (57), *Left Right And Centre* (59), *School For Scoundrels* (60). *Heavens Above* (63), *Smashing Time* (67).

CHAPLIN, CHARLES (1889-1977). Brilliant British comedian whose little tramp figure remains one of the screen's immortal creations. A superb mime, he brought to his films a pathos and compassion that few of his contemporaries could equal, and in *The Gold Rush* (25), *City Lights* (31) and *Modern Times* (36) created three enduring comic masterpieces. Over 60 one and two-reelers and nine features, including *A Dog's Life* (18), *Shoulder Arms* (18), *The Kid* (21), *The Pilgrim* (23), *The Circus* (28), *The Great Dictator* (40), *Monsieur Verdoux* (47), *Limelight* (52), *A King in New York* (57), *A Countess from Hong Kong* (67).

CLARKE, T. E. B. (1907-). British scriptwriter who authored many of Ealing's post-war comedies, e.g. *Hue and Cry* (46), *Passport to Pimlico* (49), *The Lavender Hill Mob* (51), *The Titfield Thunderbolt* (53), *Barnacle Bill* (57).

CORNELIUS, HENRY (1913-58). Underrated British director of two charming post-war comedies: *Passport to Pimlico* (49) and *Genevieve* (53). Also *The Galloping Major* (51), *Next to No Time* (57), *Law and Disorder* (58) (co-directed).

CRICHTON, CHARLES (1910-). British director, famous in the genre for *Hue and Cry* (46) — the film that began the Ealing cycle — and the engaging *The Lavender Hill Mob*, one of the brightest of all British post-war comedies. Others: *The Titfield Thunderbolt* (53), *Law and Disorder* (58) (co-directed), *Battle of the Sexes* (59).

CUKOR, GEORGE (1899-). Well-known for his expert direction of women performers, Cukor has also earned a considerable reputation in the comedy genre, directing nearly twenty comedy movies during his long career. If *The Philadelphia Story* (40) remains his most famous film, his most inventive are those he made from Garson Kanin/Ruth Gordon scenarios during the late 40s and early 50s, e.g. *Adam's Rib* (49), *The Marrying Kind* (52), *Pat And Mike* (52), *It Should Happen To You* (54). Other comedies include: *Holiday* (38), *The Women* (39), *Born Yesterday* (50), *The Model And The Marriage Broker* (52), *The Actress* (53), *Travels With My Aunt* (72), *Love Among The Ruins* (TV) (75).

DIAMOND, I. A. L. (1915-). American scriptwriter, Billy Wilder's regular associate since 1957. Films with Wilder — *Love In The Afternoon* (57), *Some Like It Hot* (59), *The Apartment* (60), *One, Two, Three* (61), *Irma La Douce* (63), *Kiss Me Stupid* (64), *The Fortune Cookie* (66), *The Private Life Of Sherlock Holmes* (70), *Avanti* (72), *The Front Page* (74), *Fedora* (78). Other comedies include *Let's Make It Legal* (51), *Love Nest* (51), *Monkey Business* (52), *Cactus Flower* (69).

EDWARDS, BLAKE (1922-). American writer/director whose *Breakfast At Tiffany's* (61), an adaptation of Truman Capote's novella with Audrey Hepburn as Holly Golightly, remains his best work in the comedy genre. His more recent comedies have included the long line of successful *Pink Panther* movies starring Peter Sellers. Films include *Operation Petticoat* (59), *The Pink Panther* (64), *A Shot In The Dark* (64), *The Great Race* (65), *What Did You Do In The War, Daddy?* (66), *The Party* (68), *The Return Of The Pink Panther* (75), *The Pink Panther Strikes Again* (76), *Revenge Of The Pink Panther* (78), *IO* (79).

FELDMAN, MARTY (1933-). British comedian of the bulging eyes, formerly on TV. A favourite Mel Brooks performer since appearing as the hunchbacked Igor in *Young Frankenstein* (74). Films: *Every Home Should Have One* (69), *The Adventures Of Sherlock Holmes' Smarter Brother* (75), *Silent Movie* (76), *The Last Remake Of Beau Geste* (77) (also directed and co-scripted).

FIELDS, W. C. (1879-1946). Bulbous-nosed, ex-vaudeville performer who frequently authored his own scripts, using such bizarre pen-names as Mahatma Kane Jeeves, Charles Bogle and Otis Criblecobis. His favourite character was the alcoholic, resentful cynic, constantly at odds with society. Appeared at Paramount during the 30s and at Universal in the final stages of his career. Films include *Million Dollar Legs* (32), *If I Had a Million* (32), *Mrs. Wiggs of the Cabbage Patch* (34), *It's a Gift* (34), *The Man on the Flying*

Trapeze (35), *Poppy* (36), *You Can't Cheat an Honest Man* (39), *My Little Chickadee* (40), *The Bank Dick* (40), *Never Give a Sucker and Even Break* (41). Played Micawber in Cukor's 1935 version of *David Copperfield*.

FRANK, MELVIN (1917-   ). Veteran American comedy writer/director /producer. In partnership with Norman Panama during the 40s and 50s but in recent years has worked solo, reaching his creative and commercial peak with the Glenda Jackson-George Segal comedy *A Touch Of Class*. Recent work as writer-producer-director: *Buona Sera Mrs. Campbell* (68), *A Touch Of Class* (73), *The Prisoner Of Second Avenue* (75) (produced and directed only), *The Duchess And The Dirtwater Fox* (76), *Lost And Found* (78).

GRANT, CARY (1904-   ). British-born actor, a regular in the genre since appearing with Mae West in *She Done Him Wrong* (33). Many comedies for Hawks (four), Stevens, McCarey, Cukor, etc. Among his best roles: the timid zoology professor in *Bringing Up Baby* (38), the newspaper editor in *His Girl Friday* (40), and the advertising executive trying to find a home in the country in *Mr. Blandings Builds His Dream House* (48). Also: *Topper* (37), *The Awful Truth* (37), *Holiday* (38), *The Philadelphia Story* (40), *Talk Of The Town* (42), *Once Upon A Honeymoon* (42), *Arsenic And Old Lace* (44), *I Was A Male War Bride* (49), *Monkey Business* (52), *Indiscreet* (58), *Operation Petticoat* (59), *The Grass Is Greener* (60), *That Touch Of Mink* (62), *Father Goose* (64), *Walk Don't Run* (66).

GUINNESS, ALEC (1914-   ). British stage and screen actor who appeared in many memorable Ealing comedies during the post-war period, e.g. *Kind Hearts And Coronets* (as all eight members of the ill-fated d'Ascoyne family) (49), *A Run For Your Money* (49), *The Lavender Hill Mob* (51), *The Man In The White Suit* (51), *The Ladykillers* (55). Others: *The Card* (52), *Barnacle Bill* (57), *The Horse's Mouth* (58), *Hotel Paradiso* (66), *Murder By Death* (76).

HACKETT, ALBERT (1900-   ). American scriptwriter. Many comedies, all written with his wife Frances Goodrich, including *It's a Wonderful Life* (46), *Father of the Bride* (50), *Father's Little Dividend* (51), *The Long, Long Trailer* (53).

HAMER, ROBERT (1911-63). British writer/director, best remembered for his stylish black comedy, *Kind Hearts and Coronets* (49). Also: *His Excellency* (52), *To Paris with Love* (54), *School for Scoundrels* (60).

HAWKS, HOWARD (1896-1977). Although he worked in the genre only infrequently, Hawks must be rated as one of the top American comedy directors. His fast-talking, fast-moving screw ball comedies, *Bringing up Baby* (38), and *His Girl Friday* (40), are perfect examples of their kind and *Ball of Fire* (41), with Barbara Stanwyck and Gary Cooper, remains one of the most neglected comedies of the 40s. Others: *Twentieth Century* (34), *I Was a Male War Bride* (49), *Monkey Business* (52), *Man's Favourite Sport* (63).

HAWN, GOLDIE (1945-   ). The closest equivalent to Judy Holliday in contemporary American cinema — blonde, scatterbrained, vivacious. Awarded an Oscar for her performance in *Cactus Flower* (69) she has several notable dramatic performances to her name — *The Sugarland Express* (74), *Shampoo* (75) — but has yet to fulfill the immense comedy promise of her 'Laugh-In' years on TV. Comedy movies: *Cactus Flower* (69), *There's A Girl In My Soup* (70), *The Duchess And The Dirtwater Fox* (76), *Foul Play* (78).

HAY, WILL (1888-1949). British music-hall comedian, very popular on the big screen during the 30s and 40s. Often cast as a seedy, hopelessly incompetent schoolmaster, but best remembered perhaps for his hilarious station-master of Buggleskelly in *Oh! Mr. Porter* (37). Films include *Boys Will Be Boys* (35), *Where There's a Will* (36), *Good Morning Boys* (37), *Convict 99* (38), *Ask a Policeman* (39), *The Ghost of St. Michael's* (41), *The Goose Steps Out* (42).

HEPBURN, KATHARINE (1907-   ). Perhaps the most talented actress the American cinema has produced. Her best comedy roles e.g. Tracy Lord in *The Philadelphia Story* (40), the lawyer wife of Spencer Tracy in *Adam's Rib* (49), and the tennis champion in *Pat And Mike* (52) have invariably been in films directed by George Cukor, although she was equally splendid for George Stevens in *Woman Of The Year* (42) and Howard Hawks in *Bringing Up Baby* (38). Also: *Holiday* (38), *State Of The Union* (48), *The Iron Petticoat* (56), *The Desk Set* (57), *Guess Who's Coming To Dinner* (67), *Love Among The Ruins* (TV) (75).

HOLLIDAY, JUDY (1923-65). American stage and screen actress who perfected the role of the dumb blonde in Cukor's film version of the stage hit, *Born Yesterday* (50). Others: *Adam's Rib* (49), *The Marrying Kind* (52), *It Should Happen to You* (54), *Phffft!* (54), *Full of Life* (56), *The Solid Gold Cadillac* (56).

HOPE, BOB (1903-   ). Wise-cracking comedian who began in films in 1934 after a career in vaudeville. Best period: 1939-49 when he made over twenty pictures for Paramount, including several 'Road' comedies, *The Cat and the Canary* (39), *Monsieur Beaucaire* (46) and *The Paleface* (48). Co-starred with Lucille Ball in four films, including the much-underrated *Sorrowful Jones* (49), an adaptation of one of Damon Runyon's Broadway short stories. Major films; *Road to Singapore* (40), *The Ghost Breakers* (40), *Caught in the Draft* (41), *Road to Zanzibar* (41), *My Favourite Blonde* (42), *Road to Morocco* (42), *Road to Utopia* (45), *My Favourite Brunette* (47), *Road to Rio* (48), *Fancy Pants* (50), *The Lemon Drop Kid* (51), *My Favourite Spy* (51), *Son of Paleface* (52), *Road to Bali* (53), *Off Limits* (53), *Beau James* (57), *The Facts of Life* (60), *Bachelor in Paradise* (61), *Road to Hong Kong* (62), *Critic's Choice* (63), *I'll Take Sweden* (65), *How to Commit Marriage* (69), *Cancel My Reservation* (72).

HORNE, JAMES V. (1880-1942). American director of numerous Laurel and Hardy comedies: *Big Business* (29), *Chickens Come Home* (31), *Laughing Gravy* (31), *Our Wife* (31), *Come Clean* (31), *One Good Turn* (31), *Beau Chumps* (31), *Any Old Port* (32), *Thicker Than Water* (35), *Bonnie Scotland* (35), *The Bohemian Girl*, (36), *Way Out West* (37).

HUDSON, ROCK (1925-   ). American leading man who showed an unexpected flair for comedy after several years in Universal action pictures. Comedies, many with Doris Day, include: *Pillow Talk* (59), *Come September* (61), *Lover Come Back* (62), *Send Me No Flowers* (64), *Man's Favourite Sport* (64), *Strange Bedfellows* (65), *A Very Special Favour* (65). Recent career mainly on TV in the 'family detective series' *McMillan And Wife* (1971-76).

JOHNSON, NUNNALLY (1897-1977). Veteran American writer/director/producer, a columnist and short story writer before entering films in 1933. Comedy films (all produced and scripted) include *Casanova Brown* (44), *Everybody Does It* (49), *We're Not Married* (52), *How to Marry a Millionaire* (53), *How to be Very, Very Popular* (also directed) (55), *Oh, Men! Oh, Women!* (also directed) (57), *Take Her She's Mine* (63), *The World of Henry Orient* (64).

KANIN, GARSON (1912-   ). American playwright/scriptwriter, who, in collaboration with his actress wife Ruth Gordon, wrote some of the best original screen comedies of the post-war period. Five films for Cukor: *Adam's Rib* (49), *Born Yesterday* (50), *The Marrying Kind* (52), *Pat And Mike* (52) and *It Should Happen To You* (54). Others, as director, *Bachelor Mother* (39), *My Favourite Wife* (40), *Tom, Dick And Harry* (41), *Where It's At* (also scripted) (69), *Some Kind Of A Nut* (also scripted) (70).

KAYE, DANNY (1913-   ). Talented American entertainer with outstanding powers of mimicry and timing. His early pictures (all with Goldwyn) were fast and often very funny, but after his break with the producer his comedies became less distinguished. Key period: 1944-52. Main films: *Up in Arms* (44), *The Kid From Brooklyn* (46), *The Secret Life of Walter Mitty* (47), *The Inspector General* (49), *On the Riviera* (51), *Hans Christian Andersen* (52), *Knock on Wood* (53), *The Court Jester* (56), (the best of his later films), *Me and the Colonel* (57), *The Five Pennies* (59), *The Man from the Diners' Club* (63).

KEATON, BUSTER (1895-1966). Brilliant American comedian, known affectionately as "The Great Stone Face". Made his first appearance in *The Butcher Boy* in 1917, then went on to make eleven superb features during the 20s including the masterpieces *Sherlock Junior* (24) and *The General* (27). Like Harry Langdon, declined into oblivion during the 30s, but now held in higher critical esteem than Chaplin. Feature comedies include *The Three Ages* (23), *Our Hospitality* (23), *The Navigator* (24), *Seven Chances* (25), *Go West* (25), *Battling Butler* (26), *College* (27), *Steamboat Bill Junior* (28), *The Cameraman* (28).

KEATON, DIANE (1949-   ). American actress who has risen to prominence and become an Oscar winner (*Annie Hall*) through a long series of comedies with Woody Allen. Tends to go straight and get involved in much rougher company (the *Godfather* films, *Looking For Mr. Goodbar*) when away from Allen's influence. Films: *Play It Again Sam* (72), *Sleeper* (74), *Love And Death* (75), *Harry And Walter Go To New York* (76), *I Will, I Will . . . For Now* (76), *Annie Hall* (77), *Manhattan* (79).

KENDALL, KAY (1927-59). Sophisticated, red-headed actress who gave a number of delicious comedy performances during her tragically short career, e.g. as Kenneth More's bored, trumpet-playing girl friend in *Genevieve* (53), the television personality in *Simon and Laura* (55) and the bewildered society mother in Minnelli's *The Reluctant Debutante* (58). Also: *Doctor in the House* (54), *The Constant Husband* (54), *Once More with Feeling* (59).

KRASNA, NORMAN (1909-   ). American playwright, a Hollywood scriptwriter since 1932. Academy Award for the screenplay of *Princess O'Rourke* (43). Other comedies: *Bachelor Mother* (39), *The Devil and Miss Jones* (41), *Practically Yours* (44), *The Ambassador's Daughter* (56), *Indiscreet* (58), *Who Was That Lady?* (60), *Sunday in New York* (64).

LANGDON, HARRY (1884-1944). Sad-faced, considerably under-rated American comedian who worked in the same period as Chaplin and Keaton and contributed three of the best comedies of the silent era, i.e. *Tramp, Tramp, Tramp* (26), *The Strong Man* (26), *Long Pants* (27). Made 68 shorts and 24 features during his career. Sound comedy roles only routine.

LAUREL, STAN (1890-1965) and **HARDY, OLIVER** (1892-1957). Famous comedy team, first paired in *Putting Pants on Philip* in 1927. Over 60 two- and three-reelers and some 20 features during their twenty-five years together. Among their most famous roles: the Christmas-tree salesmen in *Big Business* (29) and the piano removal men in *The Music Box* (32). Top features include *Bonnie Scotland* (35), *Way Out West* (37), *Blockheads* (38) and *A Chump at Oxford* (40).

LEISEN, MITCHELL (1898-1972). American director, former set designer, who made a number of excellent Paramount comedies from Wilder/Brackett screenplays during the late 30s. Key films: *Easy Living* (37), *Midnight* (39), *Remember The Night* (40), *Arise My Love* (40), *Take A Letter, Darling* (42), *Practically Yours* (44), *Suddenly It's Spring* (47), *The Mating Season* (51).

LEMMON, JACK (1925-). One of the most reliable of contemporary American comedians and a regular performer in Billy Wilder movies during the 60s. Among his most accomplished portrayals: the bass-player in *Some Like It Hot* (59), the insurance clerk in *The Apartment* (60) and the crippled TV cameraman in *The Fortune Cookie* (66). Four films with Wilder, six with Richard Quine. Other comedy films: *It Should Happen To You* (54), *Phffft!* (54), *Mister Roberts* (55), *Operation Mad Ball* (57), *It Happened To Jane* (59), *The Notorious Landlady* (62), *Irma La Douce* (63), *How To Murder Your Wife* (65), *The Great Race* (65), *The Odd Couple* (68), *The Out-Of-Towners* (70), *Kotch* (directed only) (71), *The War Between Men And Women* (72), *Avanti* (72), *The Front Page* (74), *The Prisoner Of Second Avenue* (75).

LEWIS, JERRY (1926-). American actor/writer/director who made nearly twenty films with crooner Dean Martin before branching out on his own in 1956. Later work, both under his own and Frank Tashlin's direction, not undistinguished, but has faded from the scene during the 70s. Films include *My Friend Irma* (49), *At War With The Army* (50), *That's My Boy* (51), *The Caddy* (53), *Living It Up* (54), *Artists And Models* (55), *Hollywood Or Bust* (56), *The Sad Sack* (57), *The Bellboy* (59), *Cinderfella* (60), *Visit To A Small Planet* (60), *The Ladies Man* (61), *The Errand Boy* (61), *It's Only Money* (62), *The Nutty Professor* (63), *Who's Minding The Store?*

(64), *The Patsy* (65), *The Disorderly Orderly* (65), *Boeing Boeing* (66), *Way . . . Way Out* (67), *Hook, Line And Sinker* (70).

LLOYD, HAROLD (1893-1971). Bespectacled American comedian, who although not possessing the subtlety of Chaplin or Keaton was equally popular at the box office. Excelled in acrobatic tricks, usually on top of high buildings. Most famous film: *Safety Last* (23), in which he plays a store clerk who accepts a bet of 1,000 dollars to climb the outside of a skyscraper. Main features: *A Sailor-Made Man* (21), *Grandma's Boy* (22), *The Freshman* (25), *For Heaven's Sake* (26), *Speedy* (28), *Feet First* (30), *Movie Crazy* (32), *The Milky Way* (36), *Professor Beware* (38), *Mad Wednesday* (*The Sin of Harold Diddlebock*) (46).

LUBITSCH, ERNST (1892-1947). German producer/director, in Hollywood from 1923. Excelled in both the sophisticated comedy and musical comedy fields during the 20s and 30s but suffered something of a decline towards the end of his career. Major comedies: *The Marriage Circle* (24), *Forbidden Paradise* (24), *Trouble in Paradise* (32), *Design for Living* (33), *Bluebeard's Eighth Wife* (38), *Ninotchka* (39), *To Be or Not To Be* (42), *Heaven Can Wait* (43), *Cluny Brown* (46), *That Lady in Ermine* (completed by Otto Preminger after Lubitsch's death) (48).

MACKENDRICK, ALEXANDER (1912-). Former scriptwriter who became one of the top Ealing comedy directors of the post-war period. Films include *Whisky Galore* (48), *The Man In The White Suit* (51), *The Maggie* (54), *The Ladykillers* (55); in USA, *Don't Make Waves* (67).

MANKIEWICZ, JOSEPH L. (1909-). American writer/director whose best comedies e.g. *A Letter to Three Wives* (49) and *All About Eve* (50) are distinguished by sharp, witty dialogue, the like of which is rarely heard nowadays. Won Academy Awards for his writing and direction of both the aforementioned films. Other comedies include *The Late George Apley* (46), and *The Honey Pot* (67).

MARSHALL, GEORGE (1891-1975). Prolific American director of Bob Hope and Jerry Lewis vehicles, including *My Friend Irma* (49), *Fancy Pants* (50), *Off Limits* (53), *Scared Stiff* (53), *Money from Home* (53), *The Sad Sack* (57), *Boy, Did I Get a Wrong Number* (66), *Hook, Line and Sinker* (70).

MARX BROTHERS: CHICO (1891-1961), HARPO (1893-1964),

GROUCHO (1895-1977). Zany trio of American comedians at their best at Paramount during the early 30s when they appeared in such films as *Animal Crackers* (30), *Monkey Business* (31), *Horse Feathers* (32), and *Duck Soup* (33). Later comedies at Metro less noteworthy although *A Night at the Opera* (35) with its famous ship's cabin sequence and riotous climax in the Opera House has its splendid moments. Other comedies: *The Cocoanuts* (29), *A Day at the Races* (37), *Room Service* (38), *At the Circus* (39), *Go West* (40), *The Big Store* (41), *A Night in Casablanca* (46), *Love Happy* (49).

MATTHAU, WALTER (1920-   ). American actor who began his career in minor roles (usually as a heavy) before graduating to comedy leads in the mid-60s. Superb as the shyster lawyer in *The Fortune Cookie* (66) and as the bored film star in Axelrod's *The Secret Life Of An American Wife* (68). Also: *Goodbye Charlie* (64), *A Guide For The Married Man* (67), *The Odd Couple* (68), *Candy* (69), *Cactus Flower* (69), *Kotch* (71), *A New Leaf* (71), *Plaza Suite* (71), *The Front Page* (74), *The Sunshine Boys* (75), *The Bad News Bears* (76), *House Calls* (78), *California Suite* (78), *Little Miss Marker* (79).

MONROE, MARILYN (1926-1962). Pin-up girl of the 50s, best remembered for her dance-band singer, Sugar Kane, in Billy Wilder's *Some Like it Hot* (59) and her innocent, wide-eyed companion of Tom Ewell in the same director's *The Seven Year Itch* (55). Other comedies include *We're Not Married* (52), *Monkey Business* (52), *How to Marry a Millionaire* (53), *The Prince and the Showgirl* (57).

MORE, KENNETH (1914-   ). British stage and screen actor, extremely popular with cinema audiences during the 50s when he gave likeable comedy performances as the 'old crock' fanatic in *Genevieve* (53) and the medical student in *Doctor in the House* (54). Also: *Brandy for the Parson* (52), *Raising a Riot* (54), *The Admirable Crichton* (57), *The Sheriff of Fractured Jaw* (58), *Man in the Moon* (60), *The Spaceman And King Arthur* (79).

NIVEN, DAVID (1909-   ). British actor, the epitome of the debonair Englishman, likeable in just about any kind of role but most at home in comedy thanks to a deftness of touch and impeccable delivery. His personality alone has frequently saved even the most mediocre of films from disaster. Comedies: *Bluebeard's Eighth Wife* (38), *Bachelor Mother* (39), *Appointment With Venus* (52), *The Moon Is Blue* (53), *Oh Men, Oh Women!* (57), *The Little Hut* (57), *My Man Godfrey* (57), *Ask Any Girl* (59), *Please Don't Eat The Daisies* (60), *The Pink Panther* (64), *Bedtime Story* (64), *Prudence And The Pill* (68), *Murder By Death* (76), *Candleshoe* (78).

PANAMA, NORMAN (1914-). American writer/director/producer, in films since 1942. With Melvin Frank, wrote the screenplays for several Bob Hope movies including *The Road To Utopia* (45), *That Certain Feeling* (56) (co-directed), *The Facts Of Life* (60), *Road To Hong Kong* (62) (directed). Best achievement: the screenplay for H. C. Potter's brilliant domestic comedy *Mr. Blandings Builds His Dream House* (48). Recent work (not with Frank) — *Not With My Wife You Don't* (66) (script and direction), *How To Commit Marriage* (69) (direction), *I Will, I Will . . . For Now* (76) (script and direction).

PARROTT, JAMES (1892-1939). American director, best-known for his work on Laurel and Hardy two-reelers. Twenty shorts for the famous pair, including the classic *Big Business* (29) and *The Music Box* (32).

QUINE, RICHARD (1920-). Underrated American comedy director who, like his associate Blake Edwards, gained experience in the genre by scripting Frankie Laine musical comedies at Columbia during the 50s. Six films with Jack Lemmon. Main comedies: *The Solid Gold Cadillac* (56), *Bell, Book and Candle* (58), *The Notorious Landlady* (62), *Sex and the Single Girl* (64), *How to Murder Your Wife* (65), *The Prisoner Of Zenda* (79).

REYNOLDS, BURT (1936-). Former stunt man and TV actor who made it to the top in crime and rugged adventure movies but in recent years has shown a talent for easy throwaway humour especially of the self deprecating kind. A hillbilly Robin Hood in *W. W. and the Dixie Dancekings* (75), a football player in *Semi-Tough* (77), a stunt man in *Hooper* (78). Also: *Fuzz* (72), *Lucky Lady* (75), *Nickleodeon* (76), *Silent Movie* (76) (guest spot), *Smokey And The Bandit* (77), *The End* (78) (also directed).

RISKIN, ROBERT (1897-1955). American scriptwriter, associated with director Frank Capra for over twenty years. Films include *Lady for a Day* (33), *It Happened One Night* (AA) (34), *Mr. Deeds Goes to Town* (36), *You Can't Take It With You* (38), *Meet John Doe* (41), *Riding High* (50), *Here Comes the Groom* (51).

ROACH, HAL (1892-). American producer who began in films as a five-dollar-a-day extra. Worked with Chaplin, Lloyd and Harry Langdon in the silent period and during the mid-20s formed the popular 'Our Gang' series which starred Mary Kornman, Joe Cobb, Jackie Condon and others. Most of his later work in the genre was undistinguished although the Topper ghost comedies of the late 30s were not without their bright moments.

ROSE, WILLIAM (1918-). American scriptwriter who has authored some of the most original British and American comedies of recent years, including *Genevieve* (53), *The Maggie* (54), *The Lady-killers* (55), *The Smallest Show On Earth* (57), *It's A Mad, Mad, Mad, Mad World* (63), *The Russians Are Coming, The Russians Are Coming* (66), *The Flim-Flam Man* (67), *Guess Who's Coming To Dinner* (67).

ROSS, HERBERT (1927-). Former choreographer who has specialized in comedies and musicals since making his debut as a director in 1969 with *Goodbye Mr. Chips*. Draws frequently from the Broadway stage for his comedy work, especially from the plays of Neil Simon — *The Sunshine Boys* (75), *The Goodbye Girl* (77), *California Suite* (78). Also: *The Owl And The Pussycat* (70), *Play It Again Sam* (72).

SEGAL, GEORGE (1934-). American actor who hit stardom as one of the meanest movie characters of the 60s — the double-dealing P.O.W. in *King Rat* — but who, like Burt Reynolds, has subsequently proved himself to be a comedy performer of the most reliable kind. Memorable when suffering from back trouble during a love making session with Glenda Jackson in *A Touch Of Class* (73). Comedies: *Bye Bye Braverman* (68), *Loving* (70), *The Owl And The Pussycat* (70), *Where's Poppa?* (70), *The Hot Rock* (72), *Blume In Love* (73), *The Black Bird* (75) (as Sam Spade Jr.) *The Duchess And The Dirtwater Fox* (76), *Fun With Dick And Jane* (77), *Lost And Found* (78), *Too Many Chefs* (78).

SELLERS, PETER (1925-). Versatile British actor, in films from the mid-50s after radio experience in the Goon Show. Early in his screen career was known as a comedian of many faces e.g. the spiv in *The Ladykillers* (55), the ageing cinema projectionist in *The Smallest Show On Earth* (57) and trade union leader Fred Kite in *I'm All Right Jack* (59). More recently has settled for recreating the accident-prone Inspector Clouseau in the long line of popular *Pink Panther* films. Comedies: *Carlton-Browne Of The F.O.* (59), *The Mouse That Roared* (59), *Two-Way Stretch* (59), *The Million-airess* (60), *Mr. Topaze* (61), *Only Two Can Play* (61), *The Waltz Of The Toreadors* (62), *Lolita* (62), *The Wrong Arm Of The Law* (62), *Heavens Above* (63), *The Pink Panther* (64), *Dr. Strangelove* (64), *A Shot In The Dark* (64), *The World Of Henry Orient* (64), *What's New Pussycat* (65), *The Party* (68), *I Love You Alice B. Tolkas* (68), *There's A Girl In My Soup* (70), *Soft Beds And Hard Battles* (73), *The Return Of The Pink Panther* (75), *The Pink Panther Strikes Again* (76), *Murder By Death* (76), *Revenge Of The Pink Panther* (78), *The Prisoner Of Zenda* (79).

SENNETT, MACK (1880-1960). American producer and founder of the Keystone studios. During the silent era produced many hundreds of comedy shorts and discovered stars of the calibre of Charles Chaplin, Chester Conklin, Mabel Normand and the inimitable Keystone Kops. In 1937 received a special Academy Award "for his lasting contribution to the comedy technique of the screen".

SHAPIRO, STANLEY (1925-). American producer/screenwriter. Several Universal comedies of the early 60s, including *Pillow Talk* (59) (AA), *Operation Petticoat* (59), *Come September* (61), *Lover Come Back* (62), *That Touch Of Mink* (62). Most recently, part-authored the screenplays for *How To Save A Marriage . . . And Ruin Your Life* (68) and *For Pete's Sake* (74).

SHAVELSON, MELVILLE. (1971-). American writer/director who has partnered producer Jack Rose on numerous Hollywood comedies since the mid-40s. Many screenplays for Danny Kaye, Jerry Lewis, Bob Hope, etc., including *Wonder Man* (45), *The Kid From Brooklyn* (46), *Sorrowful Jones* (49), *The Great Lover* (49), *Living It Up* (54). Also: *It's A Great Feeling* (49), *Room For One Moore* (52), *The Seven Little Foys* (55), (also directed), *Beau James* (57) (also directed), *Houseboat* (58) (also directed), *It Happened In Naples* (also directed) (60), *Yours, Mine and Ours* (68) (also directed), *The War Between Men And Women* (also directed) (72), *Mixed Company* (also directed) (74).

SIM, ALASTAIR (1900-1976). Scottish-born comedy actor, at his peak during the post-war years when he appeared as the timid writer of detective stories in *Hue And Cry* (47) and the headmaster at odds with Margaret Rutherford in *The Happiest Days Of Your Life* (50). Other comedies include *Laughter In Paradise* (51), *Folly To Be Wise* (52), *Innocents In Paris* (53), *The Belles Of St. Trinians* (54), *The Green Man* (56), *Left Right And Centre* (59), *School For Scoundrels* (60), *The Millionairess* (60), *The Ruling Class* (72).

SIMON, NEIL (1927-). Broadway playwright who has adapted the greater part of his work to the movie screen and established himself as the one contemporary writer whose wit and polish can be compared with Billy Wilder, Preston Sturges, etc. Has recently begun writing comedy directly for the screen — *Murder By Death* (76), *The Cheap Detective* (78). Films: *Come Blow Your Horn* (63), *Barefoot In The Park* (67), *The Odd Couple* (68), *The Out-of-Towners* (70), *Plaza Suite* (71), *Last Of The Red Hot Lovers* (72), *The Prisoner Of Second Avenue* (75), *The Sunshine Boys* (75), *The Goodbye Girl* (77), *California Suite* (78).

STREISAND, BARBRA (1942-   ). The one surefire 'bankable' female star of the 70s, equally at home in zany comedy as in musicals as she has consistently proved since debuting in *Funny Girl* in 1968. Top portrayals: her foul-mouthed call girl with hiccups in *The Owl And The Pussycat* (70) and her eccentric drifter set on Ryan O'Neal in *What's Up Doc?* (72). Also: *Up The Sandbox* (72), *For Pete's Sake* (74), *The Main Event* (79).

STURGES, PRESTON (1898-1959). American writer/director and leading satirist of the early war years. Most notable films: *The Great McGinty* (40), a comic investigation into the corruption in American politics, *Sullivan's Travels* (42), a satire on Hollywood and the zany *The Palm Beach Story* (see page 3). Others: *The Lady Eve* (41), *The Miracle of Morgan's Creek* (44), *Hail the Conquering Hero* (44), *Mad Wednesday* (*The Sin of Harold Diddlebock*) (46), *Unfaithfully Yours* (48), *The Diary of Major Thompson* (56).

TASHLIN, FRANK (1913-1972). American writer/director, former cartoonist. Several excellent comedies with Jayne Mansfield and Jerry Lewis during the 50s but later work uninspired. Films include *Susan Slept Here* (54), *Artists And Models* (55), *The Girl Can't Help It* (57), *Will Success Spoil Rock Hunter?* (57), *Cinderfella* (60), *It's Only Money* (62), *The Man From The Diner's Club* (63), *The Alphabet Murders* (65), *The Glass Bottom Boat* (66), *Caprice* (67), *The Private Navy Of Sgt. O'Farrell* (68).

TAUROG, NORMAN (1899-1978). American director responsible for many of the early Martin and Lewis comedies at Paramount, e.g. *Jumping Jacks* (52), *The Stooge* (53), *The Caddy* (53), *Living It Up* (54), *You're Never Too Young* (55), *Pardners* (56).

TRACY, SPENCER (1900-67). A major Hollywood star, many of whose best-known roles were in the comedy genre, e.g. the sports reporter in *Woman of the Year* (42), the lawyer husband of Katharine Hepburn in *Adam's Rib* (49) and the harassed father of Elizabeth Taylor in *Father of the Bride* (50) and *Father's Little Dividend* (51). Also: *Libeled Lady* (36), *State of the Union* (48), *Pat and Mike* (52), *It's a Mad, Mad, Mad, Mad World* (63), *Guess Who's Coming To Dinner* (67).

WILDER, BILLY (1906-   ). Austrian-born director, long in America, whose comedy movies are marked by a bitter cynicism and an enjoyable bad taste. A scriptwriter for Lubitsch, Leisen, Hawks, etc. before turning to directing in 1942 with *The Major And The Minor* (42). Comedies (all directed and co-scripted) include *A Foreign Affair* (48), *Sabrina* (54), *The Seven Year Itch* (55), *Love In*

The Afternoon (57), *Some Like It Hot* (59), *The Apartment* (60), *One, Two, Three* (61), *Irma La Douce* (63), *Kiss Me Stupid* (64), *The Fortune Cookie* (66), *The Private Life Of Sherlock Holmes* (70), *Avanti* (72), *The Front Page* (74).

WILDER, GENE (1934-). American actor who has come to the fore via Mel Brooks' hit comedies of the 70s. He has since branched out on his own but has proved considerably less effective when away from Brooks. Films: *The Producers* (68), *Start The Revolution Without Me* (69), *Everything You Always Wanted To Know About Sex But Were Afraid To Ask* (72), *Blazing Saddles* (74), *Young Frankenstein* (74), *The Adventures Of Sherlock Holmes' Smarter Brother* (75), (also directed and scripted), *Silver Streak* (76), *The World's Greatest Lover* (77) (also directed and scripted).

FANTASY

FRANKENSTEIN   1931

James Whale's adaptation of Mary Shelley's horror classic, with Colin Clive as the brilliant scientist Baron Frankenstein and Boris Karloff as the grotesque, pitiful monster he creates from the organs of dead bodies. The dark, forbidding Transylvanian sets dominate a powerful film which is marred only by a somewhat overwrought performance by Clive and some unintentionally amusing dialogue. In view of modern transplant surgery, a less fantastic story than it used to be.

Production Company: Universal
Direction: James Whale
Screenplay: Garrett Fort
    Francis Edward Faragoh and
    Robert Florey
      from the novel by Mary Shelley
      and the play by Peggy Webling
Photography: Arthur Edeson
Leading Players: Colin Clive, Mae Clarke, John Boles, Boris
    Karloff, Edward Van Sloan, Dwight Frye

Note: Universal originally cast Bela (Dracula) Lugosi as the monster and assigned Frenchman Robert Florey to direct. After seeing the camera tests Lugosi refused the part, protesting that the make-up rendered him unrecognizable. The studio started afresh, bringing in Britisher James Whale as director. He tested more than a dozen actors before selecting the unknown Karloff for the monster. During the shooting Karloff spent nearly four hours daily with make-up man Jack Pierce. The plot-twist, in which the monster is given a madman's brain, was not in Shelley's original novel and was devised by Robert Florey.

DR. JEKYLL AND MR. HYDE   1932

Among the most rewarding screen adaptations of a major literary classic, and easily the best version of the Jekyll and Hyde story. Fredric March (Academy Award, best actor 1932) appears as the luckless Jekyll, Miriam Hopkins plays his mistress Champagne Ivy (a character not in Stevenson's original book) and Edgar Norton features as his faithful manservant. The film's most famous sequence is of course the initial transformation of Jekyll into Hyde — a technically superb achievement done without cuts or dissolves. However, a later scene, when Jekyll witnesses a cat devouring a bird in a London park, and finds that the incident starts off a chain reaction which turns him into Hyde without the aid of a drug, is artistically just as rewarding. Impeccable sets, including exteriors of foggy London streets, and outstanding monochrome photography by Karl Struss.

Production Company:	Paramount
Direction:	Rouben Mamoulian
Screenplay:	Samuel Hoffenstein and
from the novel by	Percy Heath
Robert Louis Stevenson	
Photography:	Karl Struss
Art Direction:	Hans Dreier

Leading Players: Fredric March, Miriam Hopkins, Rose Hobart, Holmes Herbert, Halliwell Hobbes, Arnold Lucy, Tempe Piggott, Edgar Norton

KING KONG   1933

A huge, 50-ft. ape is captured on a tropical island of prehistoric monsters and taken to New York where he escapes, runs amok in the streets and is finally destroyed by planes whilst seeking refuge on top of the Empire State Building. This haunting movie is still the most famous fantasy of them all, and is notable not only for the special effects work of Willis O'Brien, but for the 'character' of the luckless beast who remains one of the most sympathetic monsters ever created by a Hollywood studio.

Production Company:	RKO Radio
Direction:	Merian C. Cooper and
	Ernest B. Schoedsack
Screenplay:	James Creelman and
from an original story by	Ruth Rose
Edgar Wallace and	
Merian C. Cooper	
Photography:	Edward Lindon
Special Effects:	Willis O'Brien
Music:	Max Steiner

Leading Players: Fay Wray, Robert Armstrong, Bruce Cabot, Frank Reicher, Sam Hardy, Noble Johnson

Note: King Kong was shot in the spring and summer of 1932. The models of Kong and other prehistoric monsters averaged only 16 inches in height and were made of rubber and sponge material. Edgar Wallace worked on the original story with Merian C. Cooper but died during the preparation of the script.

THE INVISIBLE MAN   1933

An early-Thirties horror thriller, with Claude Rains appearing (if that is the correct word) as a megalomaniac scientist who discovers an Indian drug that renders him invisible. For much of its running time the film is no more than rather ordinary melodrama, but John Fulton's trick-photography continues to fascinate, and the scene in which Rains removes the bandages from his head, and then his clothes, to vanish completely, is still one of the great moments of Hollywood fantasy. Impressive too is the final sequence, when the maniac doctor is tracked down and destroyed as his footprints are discovered in the snow. Based on the novel by H. G. Wells.

Production Company:	Universal
Direction:	James Whale
Screenplay:	R. C. Sheriff and
from the novel by	Philip Wylie
H. G. Wells	(uncredited)
Photography:	Arthur Edeson
	and John Mescall
Special Effects:	John P. Fulton

Leading Players: Claude Rains, Gloria Stuart, William Harrigan, Henry Travers, Una O'Connor, Forrester Harvey

BRIDE OF FRANKENSTEIN   1935

A satirical sequel to Mary Shelley's *Frankenstein*, reuniting Colin Clive with monster Karloff and introducing two new characters — Ernest Thesiger as a necromancer whose hobby is miniaturizing people and imprisoning them in large jars, and Elsa Lanchester as Karloff's terrifying she-mate. Baroque cinema and something of a rarity in that it is one of the few sequels that has proved superior to its prototype.

Production Company:	Universal
Direction:	James Whale
Screenplay:	John L. Balderstone and
	William Hurlbut
based on characters created by	Mary Shelley
Photography:	John D. Mescall
Music:	Franz Waxman

Leading Players: Boris Karloff, Colin Clive, Valerie Hobson, Elsa Lanchester, Ernest Thesiger, O. P. Heggie, Dwight Frye, Una O'Connor

I WALKED WITH A ZOMBIE   1943

One of Val Lewton's earliest productions, an understated, modestly budgeted horror thriller about a young nurse who is employed by a wealthy planter to care for his sick wife on the voodoo-infested island of Haiti. The film is directly derived from the *Jane Eyre* story and, despite its atrocious title, ranks as one of the most artistic horror films of the war years. The climax, when the nurse takes the wife on a nocturnal journey through the sugar plantations to a voodoo ceremony, is unforgettable in its suggestion of impending horror.

Production Company:	RKO Radio

Production: Val Lewton
Direction: Jacques Tourneur
Screenplay: Curt Siodmak and Ardel Wray
    from a story by Inez Wallace
Photography: J. Roy Hunt
Music: Roy Webb
Leading Players: James Ellison, Frances Dee, Tom Conway,
    Edith Barrett, Christine Gordon, James Bell

Note: Filmed at the RKO Studios in Hollywood, November-December, 1942.

THE WAR OF THE WORLDS   1953

H. G. Wells' classic story of an invasion from Mars, updated and transferred from the quiet of the Surrey countryside to post-war Southern California. The striking special effects and miniature work more than compensate for the inadequacy of the playing and ensure the film a place among the best science-fiction movies of the early fifties. High spots: the early scenes when the Martians first arrive and the sequence in a ruined cottage when hero and heroine are attacked by an exposed Martian, the only time in the film that one of the creatures is seen in any detail.

Production Company: Paramount
Production: George Pal
Direction: Byron Haskin
Screenplay: Barré Lyndon
    from the novel by H. G. Wells
Photography (Technicolor):   George Barnes
Music: Leith Stevens
Leading Players: Gene Barry, Ann Robinson, Henry Brandon,
    Les Tremayne, Bob Cornthwaite, Sandro Giglio, Lewis Martin

Note: Filmed at Paramount studios, on location near Phoenix, Arizona and on the freeway in Hollywood, January-March, 1952. The Martian machines which appeared gigantic on the screen were, in actuality, no higher than two feet tall. The destruction of buildings, bridges and complete cities was also done with miniature props. The film was narrated by Cedric Hardwicke.

ROBINSON CRUSOE ON MARS   1964

Byron Haskin's remarkably assured and quite ingenious updating of DeFoe's eighteenth century classic, with the hero recast as a U.S. astronaut marooned on Mars with only a tiny monkey for company. A clever, often valid speculation of the future, beautifully shot by Winton Hoch amid the desolate peaks and canyons of California's Death Valley. Superior in every way to more famous films of its kind.

Production Company: Paramount

Production:	George Pal
Direction:	Byron Haskin
Screenplay:	Ib Melchior and
based on Defoe's	John C. Higgins
'Robinson Crusoe'	
Photography (Techniscope/	Winton C. Hoch
Technicolor):	
Music:	Van Cleave

Leading Players: Paul Mantee, Vic Lundin, Adam West

PLANET OF THE APES   1968

American astronaut Charlton Heston crashlands on an unknown planet after racing through time and space and finds that he has arrived in a society in which humans (all dumb and reduced to animal level) are subservient to apes in a simian civilization. This intriguing, sometimes satirical movie contains some effective set pieces, e.g. the landing of the space-ship and a man-hunt by gorillas, and reaches a quite shattering climax when the astronaut discovers that he has landed on the planet Earth two thousand years hence and that the ape society is a direct result of mankind having destroyed itself by atomic warfare. In these last scenes the anti-bomb message comes across more strongly than in many a more blatant message movie.

Production Company:	APJAC/Twentieth
	Century-Fox
Production:	Arthur P. Jacobs
Direction:	Franklin J. Schaffner
Screenplay:	Michael Wilson and
from the novel 'Monkey Planet'	Rod Serling
by Pierre Boulle	
Photography (Panavision/	Leon Shamroy
DeLuxe colour):	
Music:	Jerry Goldsmith

Leading Players: Charlton Heston, Roddy McDowall, Kim Hunter, Maurice Evans, James Whitmore, James Daly

Note: Filmed on location in Utah and Arizona, and at the Twentieth Century-Fox studio and ranch, May-August, 1967.

2001, A SPACE ODYSSEY   1968

A fascinating extension of Arthur C. Clarke's short story 'The Sentinel', about the future of space travel and the discovery of extra-terrestrial intelligence. The film is told in three parts: 'The Dawn of Man', in which early ape men are endowed with their first intelligence by a mysterious black monolith; a middle section dealing with the discovery of a similar monolith on the moon in the twenty-first century; and a final episode when scientists and astronauts make an 18-month journey to Jupiter to find the life-source of the Universe. The technical effects are stunning and the music (drawn from Strauss, Ligeti, Khatchaturian, etc.) exactly right, although in the final analysis it is the climactic 20 minutes when the sole surviving astronaut finds himself lost in another time and dimension that intrigue the most. Without question the best science-fiction film of all time and the only 'religiously-based' movie ever to capture the imagination of a younger mass audience.

Production Company: MGM
Direction: Stanley Kubrick
Screenplay: Stanley Kubrick and
                          Arthur C. Clarke
   from 'The Sentinel' by
   Arthur C. Clarke
Photography (Super Panavision/ Geoffrey Unsworth
Cinerama/Metrocolor):
   Special photographic effects: Stanley Kubrick
Leading Players: Keir Dullea, Gary Lockwood, William Sylvester,
   Daniel Richter, Douglas Rain, Leonard Rossiter

Note: Filmed at MGM's Boreham Wood Studios near London over a period of two years, 1966-67, and released in April, 1968. A ten-minute prologue (filmed in small screen black-and-white) in which space, theology and biology experts were interviewed on extra-terrestrial possibilities was deleted just before the world premiere; a further 19 minutes were cut from the film after its initial Washington, New York and Los Angeles openings. The film was originally titled *Journey Beyond the Stars*.

THE EXORCIST   1973

In this elaborate piece of horror William Friedkin uses sound to un-nerving effect. The howling of dogs and a sudden wind whistling across a dusty expanse of desert, the scuffling of 'something nasty in a Washington attic', the out-of-this-world rasp of a possessed voice, all curdle the blood more than the visual horrors even though the initial head-turning sequence still retains a shock value. Basically, it is an exercise in old-fashioned horror: little girl, possessed by the Devil, has the spirit of Satan exorcised by a young priest who dies in the attempt. That it appears to amount to something rather more is due entirely to style over content, a style most evident in the menacing prologue when Jesuit archaeologist Max von Sydow has a premonition of things to come during excavations in Iraq and the final sequences when the priest crashes to a hair-raising death through a window and down a flight of steps. Detective Lee J. Cobb, more interested in asking for the autograph of the girl's actress mother, brings the only light relief.

Production Company: Warner Bros.
Production: William Peter Blatty
Direction: William Friedkin
Screenplay: William Peter Blatty
   based on his own novel
Photography (Metrocolor):   Owen Roizman

Music: Jack Nitzsche
Leading Players: Ellen Burstyn, Max von Sydow, Lee J. Cobb,
    Kitty Winn, Jack MacGowran, Jason Miller, Linda Blair, William
    O'Malley

STAR WARS   1977

2001 might be the superior film but *Star Wars* has at last made science
fiction box-office. The movie is essentially no more than *Flash Gordon*
revisited. Two young space adventurers and a princess challenge
and defeat the evil would-be-ruler of the Universe. It's as simple as
that but it's been a long, long time since good has won out so handsomely over evil. It's also been a long time since special effects of the
kind seen in this film have so dominated a two hour viewing session.
One shot of a massive spacecraft landing immediately overhead is
breathtaking. Alec Guinness, Mark Hamill, Harrison Ford and Carrie
Fisher star, but it is the effects and boyish enthusiasm of director
George Lucas which make the film an experience instead of just another
night out at the movies.

Production Company: Twentieth Century-Fox
Production: Gary Kurtz
Direction: George Lucas
Screenplay: George Lucas
Photography (Technicolor/
    Panavision):   Gilbert Taylor
Music: John Williams
Leading Players: Mark Hamill, Harrison Ford, Carrie Fisher,
    Peter Cushing, Alec Guinness, Anthony Daniels, Kenny Baker,
    David Prowse

FANTASY: WHO'S WHO

ARNOLD, JACK (1916-). American director who made several interesting, small-scale horror films at Universal during the fifties, including *It Came From Outer Space* (53), a 3-D adaptation of a Ray Bradbury short story and *The Incredible Shrinking Man* (57). Also: *The Creature From The Black Lagoon* (54), *Tarantula* (55), *Revenge Of The Creature* (55), *The Space Children* (58).

ASHER, JACK (1916-). British cameraman. Many Hammer productions, including *The Curse of Frankenstein* (57), *Dracula* (58), *The Revenge of Frankenstein* (58), *The Mummy* (59), *Brides of Dracula* (60), *The Two Faces of Dr. Jekyll* (60).

ATWILL, LIONEL (1885-1946). British stage actor whose most famous horror role was that of the deranged sculptor in Michael Curtiz's *The Mystery of the Wax Museum* (33). Appeared in many other Hollywood horror movies, often as a mad scientist, e.g. *Dr. X* (32), *The Sphinx* (33), *The Vampire Bat* (33), *Son of Frankenstein* (39), *The Gorilla* (39), *Ghost of Frankenstein* (42), *Frankenstein Meets the Wolf Man* (43), *House of Frankenstein* (44), *House of Dracula* (45).

BAKER, ROY WARD (1916-). British director who in the 50s sank submarines (*Morning Departure*) and ocean liners (*A Night To Remember*) but has since turned to the relatively less harmful pursuits of putting vampires and Martian invaders through their paces. Films: *Quatermass And The Pit* (67), *The Anniversary* (68), *Moon Zero Two* (69), *The Vampire Lovers* (70), *The Scars Of Dracula* (70), *Dr. Jekyll And Sister Hyde* (71), *Asylum* (72), *Vault Of Horror* (73), *And Now The Screaming Starts* (73), *The Legend Of The Seven Golden Vampires* (74).

BALDERSTONE, JOHN L. (1889-1954). American screenwriter with several notable horror films among his credits: *The Mummy* (32), *Bride of Frankenstein* (35), *Mad Love* (35), etc.

BLOCH, ROBERT (1917-   ). Since Anthony Perkins raised his terrifying knife outside Janet Leigh's shower in *Psycho* (the film was based on a Bloch story) this American screenwriter has been a formidable figure in the cinema of the macabre. Among his screenplays in the horror genre: *The Cabinet Of Dr. Caligari* (62), *Strait-Jacket* (64), *The Night Walker* (64), *The Skull* (65) (story only), *The Psychopath* (66), *The Deadly Bees* (67), *Torture Garden* (67), *The House That Dripped Blood* (71), *Asylum* (72).

BODEEN, DEWITT (1908-   ). American author/critic/screenwriter. Three films for Lewton during the 40s: *The Cat People* (42), *The Seventh Victim* (43), *Curse of the Cat People* (44).

BRADBURY, RAY (1920-   ). American novelist, short-story writer, arguably the most accomplished science-fiction author of recent times. Several films have been adapted from his work, including *It Came From Outer Space* (53), *The Beast From Twenty-Thousand Fathoms* (53), *Farenheit 451* (66), *The Illustrated Man* (69).

BROWNING, TOD (1882-1962). The first major American director to work consistently in the genre, Browning made several films with Lon Chaney during the 20s and was also responsible for the Bela Lugosi version of *Dracula* in 1931. Two of his lesser known movies — *Freaks* (32), a sadistic tale of circus performers and *The Devil Doll* (36), a story of miniaturization — belong with his best work. Also: *The Unholy Three* (25), *The Unknown* (27), *London After Midnight* (27), *The Mark of the Vampire* (35), *Miracles for Sale* (39).

CARRADINE, JOHN (1906-   ). American character actor who has appeared in over 170 feature films including twenty in the horror genre. Mad doctors and fanatics have invariably been his forte, usually in second rate productions, but his Count Dracula in Universal's *House Of Frankenstein* (44) and *House Of Dracula* (45) is not without distinction. Appeared recently for Michael Winner in *The Sentinel* (77). Pictures include: *The Invisible Man* (33), *The Black Cat* (34), *Bride Of Frankenstein* (35), *The Invisible Man's Revenge* (44), *The Mummy's Ghost* (44), *The Unearthly* (57), *Billy The Kid vs Dracula* (66) (again as Count Dracula), *Terror In The Wax Museum* (73).

CASTLE, WILLIAM (1914-1977). American producer/director, for years associated with cheap low-grade horror movies but who subsequently astounded the industry by producing one of the horror classics of contemporary cinema — *Rosemary's Baby* (68). After completing his first horror flick, *Macabre* (57), he insured each member of the audience for 1000 dollars with Lloyds of London against death by fright! Films: *The House On Haunted Hill* (58), *The Tingler* (59), *Homicidal* (61), *The Old Dark House* (63), *Strait-Jacket* (64), *The Night Walker* (64), *Project X* (68), *Bug* (75).

CHANEY, LON (1883-1930). American actor, known as the man of a thousand faces. A master of the macabre, he appeared in several horror films during the 20s, including *The Monster* (25), *The Unholy Three* (25), *The Unknown* (27), *London After Midnight* (27). His best-known role in the genre was Erik the Phantom in Rupert Julian's silent version of *The Phantom of the Opera* (25).

CHANEY, LON Jun. (1912-1973). The son of the silent actor, who followed his father into horror movies. Films, mostly double features at Universal, included *The Wolf Man* (41), *The Ghost Of Frankenstein* (42) (succeeding Karloff as the monster), *The Mummy's Tomb* (42), *Son Of Dracula* (43), *Frankenstein Meets The Wolf Man* (43), *The Mummy's Ghost* (44), *House Of Frankenstein* (44), *The Mummy's Curse* (44), *House Of Dracula* (45), *The Haunted Palace* (63).

CLIVE, COLIN (1898-1937). British stage and screen actor, famous for his portrayal of Baron Frankenstein in Whale's 1931 version of Shelley's classic. Appeared also in the sequel, *Bride of Frankenstein* (35), and in Karl Freund's *Mad Love* (35), an adaptation of Maurice Renard's 'The Hands of Orlac'.

CORMAN, ROGER (1926-). Prolific young American director (almost fifty films since 1955), best-known for the horror movies he made from the works of Edgar Allan Poe during the 60s. His horror 'repertory company' included actors Vincent Price, Peter Lorre and Boris Karloff, cameraman Floyd Crosby, set-designer Daniel Haller and composer Les Baxter. Main films: *The House Of Usher* (60), *The Pit And The Pendulum* (61), *The Premature Burial* (61), *Tales Of Terror* (62), *Tower Of London* (62), *The Raven* (63), *The Terror* (63), *X — The Man With X-Ray Eyes* (63), *The Haunted Palace* (63), *The Masque Of The Red Death* (64), *The Tomb Of Ligeia* (65), *Gas-s-s-s!* (70).

CROSBY, FLOYD (1900-). Veteran American cameraman who worked with Roger Corman during the 60s. Main films: *The House of Usher* (60), *The Pit and the Pendulum* (61), *The Premature Burial* (61), *Black Zoo* (62), *Tales of Terror* (62), *The Raven* (63), *X — The Man With X-Ray Eyes* (63), *The Haunted Palace* (63).

CURTIZ, MICHAEL (1888-1962). Hungarian-born director, in Hollywood from 1928. Three horror films at the Warner studio: *Dr. X* (32), *The Mystery of the Wax Museum* (33), *The Walking Dead* (36).

CUSHING, PETER (1913-). British actor, in horror films since 1957 when Hammer revived Mary Shelley's original 'Frankenstein' novel under the title *The Curse of Frankenstein*. During the last fifteen years has also driven a stake through Dracula's heart, revived the Egyptian mummy Imhotep and appeared in several Frankenstein sequels. Main films include *Dracula* (58), *The Revenge Of Frankenstein* (58), *The Mummy* (59), *Brides Of Dracula* (60), *The Gorgon* (64), *The Evil Of Frankenstein* (64), *The Skull* (65), *Dr. Who And The Daleks* (65), *Daleks — Invasion Earth 2150 A.D.* (66), *Frankenstein Created Woman* (67), *Torture Garden* (67), *Frankenstein Must Be Destroyed* (70), *Scream And Scream Again* (70), *The Vampire Lovers* (70), *I, Monster* (71), *The House That Dripped Blood* (71), *Dracula A.D. 72* (72), *Dr. Phibes Rises Again* (72), *Tales From The Crypt* (72), *Asylum* (72), *The Creeping Flesh* (73), *And Now The Screaming Starts* (73), *The Satanic Rites Of Dracula* (74), *Frankenstein And The Monster From Hell* (74), *From Beyond The Grave* (74), *The Beast Must Die* (74), *Horror Express* (74), *Madhouse* (74), *The Legend Of The Seven Golden Vampires* (74), *The Ghoul* (75), *Legend Of The Werewolf* (75), *The Uncanny* (77), *Star Wars* (77).

D'AGOSTINO, ALBERT S. (1893-1970). RKO art director who collaborated with Walter Keller on all Lewton's horror movies of the 40s. Also designed the sets for Howard Hawks' science-fiction fantasy, *The Thing From Another World* (51). Lewton films: *The Cat People* (42), *I Walked With a Zombie* (43), *The Leopard Man* (43), *The Seventh Victim* (43), *Curse of the Cat People* (44), *Isle of the Dead* (45), *The Body Snatcher* (45), *Bedlam* (46).

DAVIS, BETTE (1908-). Hands on hips, her head thrown back and a loud rasping cackle emerging from her lips. Not quite the Bette Davis of the tearjerking 40s but no less effective. Her first venture into horror territory was in Robert Aldrich's *Whatever Happened To Baby Jane?* (62) in which she played a demented ex-child star. Subsequent excursions have included *Hush, Hush . . . Sweet Charlotte* (64), *The Nanny* (65), *The Anniversary* (68), *Burnt Offerings* (76).

DE PALMA, BRIAN (1944-). The director who has probably frightened more people in one single moment — the climax of *Carrie* (76) when a hand reaches up from the charred earth — than any other contemporary film-maker. A director of considerable style he is capable of producing great visual excitement, especially when working in the horror/thriller genre i.e. *Sisters* (73), *The Phantom Of The Paradise* (74), *Carrie* (76), *The Fury* (78).

EDESON, ARTHUR (1891-1970). American cinematographer who did outstanding work at Universal during their golden period of the early 30s. Films in the genre include *The Bat* (26), *The Gorilla* (27), *Frankenstein* (31), *The Old Dark House* (32), *The Invisible Man* (33).

FISHER, TERENCE (1904-). Hammer Films' leading director of horror fantasies. Nearly twenty films in the genre since the cycle began in 1957, including *The Curse Of Frankenstein*, the film that started the revival, and *Dracula* (58) with Christopher Lee. Also: *Revenge Of Frankenstein* (58), *The Mummy* (59), *Brides Of Dracula* (60), *The Two Faces Of Dr. Jekyll* (60), *The Curse Of The Werewolf* (61), *The Phantom Of The Opera* (62), *The Gorgon* (64), *The Skull* (65), *Dracula, Prince Of Darkness* (65), *Frankenstein Created Woman* (67), *The Devil Rides Out* (68), *Frankenstein Must Be Destroyed* (70), *Frankenstein And The Monster From Hell* (74).

FLOREY, ROBERT (1900-1979). French-born writer/director whose work, although limited, has been of considerable interest. His *The Beast With Five Fingers* (47), a macabre story about a severed hand, briefly reinstated the genre after the war. Also: *Frankenstein* (co-scripted only) (31), *Murders in the Rue Morgue* (32).

FRANCIS, FREDDIE (1917-). British director, former cameraman. Has worked almost exclusively in the horror genre since gaining director status in the early 60s, even though he lensed just one classic horror film, *The Innocents* (61) as a cameraman. Films: *Paranoiac* (63), *Nightmare* (64), *The Evil Of Frankenstein* (64), *Dr. Terror's House Of Horrors* (65), *The Skull* (65), *The Psychopath* (66), *The Deadly Bees* (67), *They Came From Beyond Space* (67), *Torture Garden* (67), *Dracula Has Risen From The Grave* (68), *Trog* (70), *Tales From The Crypt* (72), *Tales That Witness Madness* (73), *The Creeping Flesh* (73), *The Ghoul* (75), *Legend Of The Werewolf* (75).

FREUND, KARL (1890-1969). Czech-born cameraman who did distin-guished work for Tod Browning (*Dracula*) and Robert Florey (*Murders in the Rue Morgue*) during the early 30s. After a brief, successful attempt at directing — *The Mummy* (32), *Mad Love* (35) — he returned to cinematography and remained as lighting cameraman for the rest of his career.

FUEST, ROBERT (1927-). Talented British director who deserves praise if only for bringing to celluloid life the bizarre Dr. Phibes of Vincent Price, a disfigured musical genius who sets about revenging himself on the surgical team who failed to save his wife on the operating table. Films: *The Abominable Dr. Phibes* (71), *Dr. Phibes Rises Again* (72) (also co-scripted), *The Final Programme* (73) (also scripted), *The Devil's Rain* (76).

GERSTAD, MERRITT B. Tod Browning's regular cameraman of the late 20s. Films include *The Unknown* (27), *London After Midnight* (27), *The Thirteenth Chair* (29), *Freaks* (32).

GOLDSMITH, JERRY (1930-). American composer with several horror and science-fiction films to his credit. Won an Oscar for his 1976 score of Richard Donner's *The Omen*. Films: *The Satan Bug* (65), *Seconds* (66), *Planet Of The Apes* (68), *The Illustrated Man* (69), *Escape From The Planet Of The Apes* (71), *The Mephisto Waltz* (71), *The Other* (72), *The Reincarnation Of Peter Proud* (75), *Logan's Run* (76), *Damnation Alley* (77), *Coma* (78), *Damien-Omen II* (78), *Capricorn One* (78), *Magic* (78), *Alien* (79).

GOODMAN, JOHN B. (1901-). American art director, many years at Universal. Academy Award for his colour designs of *The Phantom Of The Opera* (43). Others: *Frankenstein Meets The Wolf Man* (43), *Flesh And Fantasy* (43), *The Climax* (44), *House Of Frankenstein* (44), *House Of Dracula* (45).

GRANT, ARTHUR (1915-1972). British cinematographer who took over from Jack Asher as Hammer's leading colour cameraman. Films: *The Curse of the Werewolf* (61), *The Phantom of the Opera* (62), *Frankenstein Created Woman* (67), *The Mummy's Shroud* (67), *Dracula Has Risen From the Grave* (68), *The Devil Rides Out* (68), *Taste the Blood of Dracula* (70), *Blood from the Mummy's Tomb* (71).

HALLER, DANIEL (1929-). Roger Corman's regular set designer on his Poe adaptations. Films: *The House Of Usher* (60), *The Pit And The Pendulum* (61), *The Premature Burial* (61), *Tales Of Terror* (62), *The Raven* (63), *The Terror* (63), *The Haunted Palace* (63). Has subsequently turned to direction e.g. *Die, Monster, Die* (65), *The Dunwich Horror* (70), *Buck Rogers In The 25th Century* (79).

HARRYHAUSEN, RAY (c.1920-). An expert in photographic special effects and trick photography. Films mostly in the fantasy category: *The Beast From Twenty Thousand Fathoms* (53), *It Came From*

Beneath The Sea (55), *20 Million Miles To Earth* (57), *The Seventh Voyage Of Sinbad* (58), *The Three Worlds Of Gulliver* (60), *Mysterious Island* (61), *Jason And The Argonauts* (63), *First Men In The Moon* (64), *One Million Years B.C.* (67), *The Valley Of Gwangi* (69), *The Golden Voyage Of Sinbad* (73), *Sinbad And The Eye Of The Tiger* (77).

HASKIN, BYRON (1899-   ). Underestimated American director who began in films in 1918 and worked as a cameraman before reaching director status. His science-fiction movies are among the most rewarding of recent times, and include the beautifully realized *Robinson Crusoe on Mars* (64), (see page 28). Others: *The War of the Worlds* (53), *The Naked Jungle* (54), *Conquest of Space* (55), *From the Earth to the Moon* (58), *The Power* (67).

HERRMANN, BERNARD (1911-1975). American composer, most famous for his scores for Hitchcock (see thrillers) but equally as effective when accompanying the fantasy adventures of Ray Harryhausen's monsters: *The Seventh Voyage Of Sinbad* (58), *The Three Worlds Of Gulliver* (60), *Mysterious Island* (61), *Jason And The Argonauts* (63). Also: *The Day The Earth Stood Still* (51), *Journey To The Centre Of The Earth* (59), *Fahrenheit 451* (66).

KARLOFF, BORIS (1887-1969). British-born actor (real name William Pratt), forever associated with Frankenstein's monster, whom he played in three Universal horror movies of the thirties: *Frankenstein* (31), *Bride of Frankenstein* (35), *Son of Frankenstein* (39). Over thirty horror films during his career, including several for Lewton and Corman. Major films: *The Mummy* (as Imhotep) (32), *The Mask of Fu Manchu* (32), *The Ghoul* (33), *The Black Cat* (34), *The Raven* (35), *The Walking Dead* (36), *The Invisible Ray* (36), *Tower of London* (39), *House of Frankenstein* (44), *The Climax* (44), *The Body Snatcher* (45), *Isle of theDead* (45), *Bedlam* (46), *The Black Castle* (52), *Frankenstein 1970* (58), *The Terror* (63), *The Raven* (63), *The Sorcerers* (67), *Curse of the Crimson Altar* (68).

KENTON, ERLE C. (1896-   ). American director, mostly of undistinguished B pictures although *The Island of Lost Souls* (32), an adaptation of a minor H. G. Wells novel is not without interest. Others: *The Ghost of Frankenstein* (42), *The House of Frankenstein* (44), *The House of Dracula* (45).

KNEALE, NIGEL (1922-   ). British playwright/scriptwriter, best known as the author of the original TV Quatermass stories. Story only on *The Quatermass Experiment* (55). Co-scripted, with Val Guest, the second film in the series *Quatermass II* (57) and authored the screenplay of the third, *Quatermass And The Pit* (67). Also scripted *The Abominable Snowman* (57), *First Men In The Moon* (64), *The Witches* (66).

LANG, CHARLES (1902-). Paramount cameraman whose lighting of Hollywood's 'first serious ghost film', *The Uninvited* (44), was as imaginative as any to be found in the genre during the 40s. Also: *The Cat and the Canary* (39), *The Ghost Breakers* (40).

LEE, CHRISTOPHER (1922-). British actor, a specialist in horror movies since 1957. Has played both Frankenstein's monster and the vampire Count Dracula on the screen, appearing in the latter role on many occasions since 1958. Main films include *The Curse Of Frankenstein* (57), *Dracula* (58), *The Mummy* (59), *The Two Faces Of Dr. Jekyll* (60), *The Terror Of The Tongs* (61), *The Gorgon* (64), *Dr. Terror's House Of Horrors* (65), *The Skull* (65), *Dracula — Prince Of Darkness* (65), *Rasputin — The Mad Monk* (66), *The Devil Rides Out* (68), *Curse Of The Crimson Altar* (68), *Dracula Has Risen From The Grave* (68), *The Oblong Box* (69), *The Scars Of Dracula* (70), *Scream And Scream Again* (70), *Taste The Blood Of Dracula* (70), *I, Monster* (71), *Dracula A.D. 72* (72), *The Creeping Flesh* (73), *The Wicker Man* (73), *Horror Express* (74), *The Satanic Rites Of Dracula* (74), *To The Devil A Daughter* (76).

LENI, PAUL (1885-1929). Talented German-born director who specialized in horror movies during the 20s. After the German classic *Waxworks* (24), made several films in America, including *The Cat and the Canary* (27), *The Chinese Parrot* (27), *The Man Who Laughs* (28), *The Last Warning* (29).

LEWTON, VAL (1904-1951). A master of the low-budget film who has become something of a cult figure in recent years. Produced eight small-scale horror movies at RKO during the 40s working with the same team of directors, writers and cameramen throughout. All eight movies are remarkable for the way they build up horror through atmosphere and suggestion rather than through physical shock. Best achievements: *I Walked with a Zombie* (Tourneur, 43), and *The Body Snatcher* (Wise, 45). Also: *The Cat People* (42), *The Leopard Man* (43), *The Seventh Victim* (43), *Curse of the Cat People* (44), *Isle of the Dead* (45), *Bedlam* (46).

LORRE, PETER (1904-1964). Hungarian-born actor who made several films in the horror genre. One of his least-known but most interesting performances was as the scientist who grafts a murderer's hands on to the arms of a pianist in Karl Freund's *Mad Love* (35). Also: *The Beast With Five Fingers* (47), *Tales of Terror* (62), *The Raven* (63), *The Comedy of Terrors* (63).

LUCAS, GEORGE (1945-   ). American writer/director whose vigorous enthusiasm for the film medium has transmitted itself triumphantly via *Star Wars* (77). Spectacle and special effects were less evident in his earlier *THX 1138* (71), a sober '1984' look into a mechanized society of the future.

LUGOSI, BELA (1882-1956). Hungarian actor, second only to Karloff in popularity during the 30s and 40s. Became famous for his performance as Count Dracula in Tod Browning's 1931 version of the Stoker novel. Over twenty horror movies, including *The Thirteenth Chair* (29), *Island of Lost Souls* (32), *White Zombie* (32), *Murders in the Rue Morgue* (as Dr. Mirakle) (32), *Night of Terror* (33), *The Black Cat* (34), *The Raven* (35), *The Invisible Ray* (36), *Son of Frankenstein* (39), *Dark Eyes of London* (39), *The Gorilla* (39), *The Wolf Man* (41), *The Ghost of Frankenstein* (42), *Return of the Vampire* (44), *The Body Snatcher* (45).

MATHESON, RICHARD (1926-   ). American scriptwriter, numerous films for Corman, e.g. *The House Of Usher* (60), *The Pit And The Pendulum* (61), *Tales Of Terror* (62), *The Raven* (63). Also scripted Jack Arnold's *The Incredible Shrinking Man* (57), *Master Of The World* (61), *Burn, Witch, Burn* (62), *The Comedy Of Terrors* (63), *Fanatic* (65), *The Devil Rides Out* (68), *The Legend Of Hell House* (73). His novel 'I am Legend' has been filmed twice as *The Last Man On Earth* (64), and *The Omega Man* (71).

MEREDITH, BURGESS (1908-   ). A sly smile, an 'I know something you don't know' expression and an unnerving presence. Just three factors that have made this American character actor a regular 'Devil' in recent years. Pictures include *Torture Garden* (67), *Burnt Offerings* (76), *The Sentinel* (77), *Magic* (78), *The Manitou* (78).

MESCALL, JOHN (1899-   ). American cameraman, one of a trio of talented photographers (Edeson and Freund were the others) who worked at Universal during the 30-35 period. Films: *The Invisible Man* (33), *The Black Cat* (34), *Bride of Frankenstein* (35).

MILLAND, RAY (1905-   ). Popular Paramount performer of the 40s who appeared in Lewis Allen's sedate little ghost film, *The Uninvited* (44). More recently has become something of a specialist in the horror genre e.g. *The Premature Burial* (61), *Panic In Year Zero* (62), *X — The Man With X-Ray Eyes* (63), *The Thing With Two Heads* (72), *Frogs* (72), *Terror In The Wax Museum* (74).

MOHR, HAL (1894-1974). Veteran American cameraman who won an Academy Award for his colour photography of Arthur Lubin's remake of *The Phantom of the Opera* (43). Also: *The Last Warning* (29), *The Cat Creeps* (30), *The Walking Dead* (36), *The Climax* (44).

MUSURACA, NICHOLAS (1908-). The most talented of RKO's cinematographers. Four films for Val Lewton: *The Cat People* (42), *The Seventh Victim* (43), *The Curse of the Cat People* (44), *Bedlam* (46).

O'BRIEN, WILLIS (1886-1962). American special effects expert, famous for his creation of the giant ape King Kong. Films include: *The Lost World* (25), *King Kong* (33), *Son of Kong* (33), *Mighty Joe Young* (49), *The Animal World* (56), *The Black Scorpion* (57).

PAL, GEORGE (1908-). A former puppeteer, Hungarian-born producer George Pal has become a specialist in science-fiction movies and, apart from Lewton, is the only producer to have made a creative contribution to the fantasy genre. In 1950 he began the post-war science-fiction cycle with *Destination Moon*, a sober and fairly intelligent forecast of space travel. Others: *When Worlds Collide* (51), *The War Of The Worlds* (53), *The Naked Jungle* (54), *Conquest Of Space* (55), *The Time Machine* (60), *Robinson Crusoe On Mars* (64), *The Power* (67), *Dog Savage — The Man Of Bronze* (75).

PIERCE, JACK (1889-1968). The king of make-up at Universal studios during the golden age of Karloff, Lugosi and company, Pierce was responsible for the appearance of just about every monster on the studio lot — werewolves, mummies, wolf men! He remains best-known, however, for his stunning make-up work on Boris Karloff in the 1931 *Frankenstein*, a make-up that was subsequently handed down to a succession of Karloff-like monsters.

POLANSKI, ROMAN (1933-). Madness, horror and tension have always been part of this Polish director's work but never were they more in evidence than in *Rosemary's Baby* (68), a frighteningly realistic probe into witchcraft in modern day New York. Mia Farrow's slow decline into madness seemed simply a continuation of the fate suffered by Catherine Deneuve in an earlier Polanski nightmare *Repulsion* (65). Also: *Dance Of The Vampires* (67), *The Tenant* (76).

PRICE, VINCENT (1911-   ). Distinguished American actor, the man most associated with contemporary horror movies. Over twenty films in the genre, including Andre de Toth's *House Of Wax* (53), a remake of *The Mystery Of The Wax Museum* (Price had the Atwill role) and *The Masque Of The Red Death* (64), perhaps the best of all Roger Corman's Poe adaptations. Also: *The Mad Magician* (54), *The Fly* (58), *The House On Haunted Hill* (58), *Return Of The Fly* (59), *The House Of Usher* (60), *The Pit And The Pendulum* (61), *Master Of The World* (61), *Tales Of Terror* (62), *Tower Of London* (62), *The Raven* (63), *Diary Of A Madman* (63), *The Comedy Of Terrors* (63), *The Haunted Palace* (63), *The Last Man On Earth* (64), *The Tomb Of Ligeia* (65), *City Under The Sea* (65), *The Oblong Box* (69), *Scream And Scream Again* (70), *Cry Of The Banshee* (70), *The Abominable Dr. Phibes* (71), *Dr. Phibes Rises Again* (73), *Theatre Of Blood* (73), *Madhouse* (74).

RAINS, CLAUDE (1890-1967). Cultured British performer, in Hollywood from 1932. Several films in the genre, including *The Invisible Man* (33), in which he was seen only in the last reel, and *The Phantom of the Opera* (43).

ROBINSON, BERNARD (1912-   ). British art director whose imaginative Transylvanian sets have been one of the most rewarding features of the Hammer series. Films include: *Dracula* (58), *The Revenge of Frankenstein* (58), *The Mummy* (59), *Brides of Dracula* (60), *The Two Faces of Dr. Jekyll* (60), *The Curse of the Werewolf* (61), *The Gorgon* (64), *Dracula, Prince of Darkness* (65), *The Devil Rides Out* (68), *Dracula Has Risen from the Grave* (68), *Frankenstein Must Be Destroyed* (70).

ROBSON, MARK (1913-1978). American director, former cutter at the RKO Studio. Three quality horror films for Lewton during the 40s. Films: *The Seventh Victim* (43), *Isle of the Dead* (45), *Bedlam* (46).

SANGSTER, JIMMY (1925-   ). Hammer scriptwriter. Numerous screenplays since 1957, e.g. *The Curse Of Frankenstein* (57), *Dracula* (58), *The Mummy* (59), *Brides Of Dracula* (60), *The Nanny* (65), *The Horror Of Frankenstein* (70) (direction only), *Lust For A Vampire* (71) (direction only), *Fear In The Night* (72) (direction and screenplay).

SASDY, PETER. Stylish, Hungarian-born director who handled several of Hammer's horror movies of the early 70s. Films: *Taste The Blood Of Dracula* (70), *Countess Dracula* (71), *Hands Of The Ripper* (71), *Doomwatch* (72), *Nothing But The Night* (73), *I Don't Want To Be Born* (75).

SCHOEDSACK, ERNEST B. (1893-　). American director who, with Merian C. Cooper, filmed the classic *King Kong* (33). Apart from *The Most Dangerous Game* (*The Hounds of Zaroff*) (32), other films in similar vein undistinguished. Also: *Son of Kong* (33), *Dr. Cyclops* (40), *Mighty Joe Young* (49).

SIODMAK, CURT (1902-　). German writer/director, in Hollywood from 1937. Many horror films since the early 40s, but only one — Jacques Tourneur's *I Walked With A Zombie* (43) which he co-scripted — of any lasting quality. Other screenplays: *The Wolf Man* (41), *Frankenstein Meets The Wolf Man* (43), *The Climax* (44), *The Beast With Five Fingers* (47), *The Magnetic Monster* (53) (also directed), *Riders To The Stars* (54), *Creature With The Atom Brain* (55). His novel 'Donovan's Brain' has been filmed on three occasions — in 1944, 53 and 63.

STEINER, MAX (1888-1972). Steiner's early compositions at RKO included several in the fantasy genre, most notably the brilliant *King Kong* (33). He later scored the sequel *Son of Kong* (33), *The Most Dangerous Game* (32), *She* (35). After the war composed *The Beast with Five Fingers* (47) at Warners.

STRUSS, KARL (1890-　). American cinematographer, with Paramount during the 30s. Provided some brilliant trick photography for Rouben Mamoulian on *Dr. Jekyll And Mr. Hyde* (32). Also *Island Of Lost Souls* (32), *Rocketship XM* (50), *Kronos* (57), *The Fly* (58).

SUBOTSKY, MILTON (1921-　). American writer/producer who, with Max Rosenburg, formed Amicus Productions in Britain in the 60s, a company which became famous for its anthology horror films: *Torture Garden* (67), *Tales From The Crypt* (72), *Asylum* (72). Others from the same stable: *Dr. Terror's House Of Horrors* (65), *The Skull* (65), *Dr. Who And The Daleks* (65), *The Psychopath* (66), *Daleks — Invasion Earth 2150 A.D.* (66), *Scream And Scream Again* (70), *I, Monster* (71), *The House That Dripped Blood* (71), *Vault Of Horror* (73), *From Beyond The Grave* (74), *Madhouse* (74).

TOURNEUR, JACQUES (1904-1977). Possibly the most talented of the three directors who worked for Lewton in the 40s. *The Cat People* (42), and *I Walked with a Zombie* (43) are both minor horror classics and his later, *Night of the Demon* (57), an updating of M. R. James' 'Casting the Runes', belongs with the most underrated films in the whole fantasy genre. Also: *The Leopard Man* (43), *The Comedy of Terrors* (63), *City Under The Sea* (65).

VON SYDOW, MAX (1929-   ). This distinguished Swedish actor seems to have been grappling with the Devil for most of his screen career, especially in his movies with Ingmar Bergman. Considering the quality of his apprenticeship one would have thought he would have learned a thing or two. Not so. As Father Merrin in Friedkin's *The Exorcist* (73) he came up against a demoniacal Linda Blair and lost six-love. He subsequently repeated his role in *Exorcist II — The Heretic* (77).

WAXMAN, FRANZ (1906-1967). German composer, in Hollywood from 1934. Composed the music for Whale's *Bride of Frankenstein* (35) and also for a number of subsequent films in the genre, including *The Invisible Ray* (36), *The Devil Doll* (36), *Dr. Jekyll and Mr. Hyde* (41).

WEBB, ROY (1888-   ). RKO's leading composer of the 40s and 50s, scoring most of their major films of the period as well as the Lewton B pictures *The Cat People* (42), *I Walked with a Zombie* (43), *The Leopard Man* (43), *The Seventh Victim* (43), *The Curse of the Cat People* (44), *The Body Snatcher* (45), *Bedlam* (46).

WHALE, JAMES (1896-1957). British director, prominent in the theatre before entering films in 1930. Most famous for the horror movies he directed at Universal, particularly *Frankenstein* (31) and the satirical sequel *Bride of Frankenstein* (35). Also: *The Old Dark House* (32), *The Invisible Man* (33).

WILLIAMS, JOHN. The composer who brought back dash and romance to film scores with his sweeping themes for *Star Wars* (77). Now associated more with fantasy and science-fiction than any other genre: *Close Encounters Of The Third Kind* (77), *The Fury* (78), *Superman* (78), *Dracula* (79).

WISE, ROBERT (1914-   ). American director who, like his RKO colleague Mark Robson, graduated to the director's chair via the studio's cutting rooms. His horror movies include the Lewton productions *The Curse of the Cat People* (44) and *The Body Snatcher* (45), and *The Day the Earth Stood Still* (51), one of the most intelligent films in the science-fiction cycle of the 50s. Others: *The Haunting* (63), *The Andromeda Strain* (71), *Audrey Rose* (77), *Star Trek — The Motion Picture* (79).

WRAY, FAY (1907-   ). The genre's favourite heroine of the early 30s, encountering, in the space of just two years, the giant ape *King Kong* (33), Count Zaroff's hounds in *The Most Dangerous Game*

(32) and the mad sculptor in *The Mystery of the Wax Museum* (33). Also featured in *Dr. X* (32) and *The Vampire Bat* (33).

THRILLERS AND CRIME

SCARFACE   1932

Director Howard Hawks has said that his intention in *Scarface* was to treat the story of the Al Capone family as if they were the Borgias set down in Chicago during the Twenties. This certainly seems apparent when the film is viewed today, yet for most people it is simply one of the best gangster movies ever made and remembered, both for Paul Muni's excellent portrayal of Capone and George Raft's early appearance as the coin-tossing bodyguard, Rinaldo. The screenplay was written in eleven days and adapted from books, newspapers and the experiences of Chicago reporters.

Production Company:	United Artists
Production:	Howard Hughes and
	Howard Hawks
Direction:	Howard Hawks
Screenplay:	Ben Hecht
from the novel by Armitage Trail	
Adaptation and Dialogue:	Seton I. Miller
	John Lee Mahin and
	W. R. Burnett
Photography:	Lee Garmes and
	L. William O'Connell
Music:	Adolph Tandler and
	Gus Arnheim

Leading Players: Paul Muni, Ann Dvorak, Karen Morley,
    Osgood Perkins, Boris Karloff, C. Henry Gordon, George Raft

THE ROARING TWENTIES   1939

Ostensibly a gangster melodrama, this movie is more important historically for its portrait of life in Prohibition America, when the after-effects of World War I brought unemployment to millions of returning soldiers and one absurd government law allowed many of the jobless to drift into crime through bootlegging. James Cagney is at the top of his form as a man trapped by the events of his time, although in retrospect it is the depth of the writing (unusual in a film of this kind) and Raoul Walsh's brilliant re-creation of the period that impress the most.

Production Company:	Warner Bros./
	First National
Executive Producer:	Hal B. Wallis

Direction: Raoul Walsh
Screenplay: Jerry Wald,
                                        Richard Macaulay
                                        and Robert Rossen
      from a story by Mark Hellinger
Photography: Ernest Haller
Music: Heinz Roemheld
                                        and Ray Heindorf
Leading Players: James Cagney, Priscilla Lane, Humphrey Bogart,
      Gladys George, Jeffrey Lynn, Frank McHugh

HIGH SIERRA   1941

With this absorbing movie Raoul Walsh brought to an end the Warner
gangster cycle that had begun more than a decade earlier with *Little
Caesar*. Based on a novel by W. R. Burnett, *High Sierra* features
Humphrey Bogart as 'the last of the Dillinger gang' who is sprung
from jail in order to carry out one last hold-up at a luxury desert resort.
From the opening sequences, when the doomed criminal becomes
involved with a young crippled girl, to the flight across the desert and
the final shoot-out in the mountains, the film is directed and performed
with a skill that is rare in the genre. Indeed it often seems to be working
on what can only be described as a near tragic level. Together with
Angels With Dirty Faces and *The Roaring Twenties*, it belongs with
the most successful crime movies ever produced at the Warner studio.

Production Company: Warner Bros.
Executive Producer: Hal B. Wallis
Associate Producer: Mark Hellinger
Direction: Raoul Walsh
Screenplay: John Huston and
                                        W. R. Burnett
      suggested from a novel by W. R. Burnett
Photography: Tony Gaudio
Music: Adolph Deutsch
Leading Players: Humphrey Bogart, Ida Lupino, Alan Curtis,
      Arthur Kennedy, Joan Leslie, Henry Hull, Henry Travers,
      Jerome Cowan

THE KILLERS   1946

Adapted by Anthony Veiller and John Huston (uncredited) from the
Hemingway short story, this neglected Siodmak thriller opens with
the murder of 'The Swede', then relates in flashback the events that
led to the killing. If the extension of Hemingway's ten-page story is
not completely successful this is probably because no scriptwriter,
other than Hemingway himself, could have sustained the quality of
the original. Yet when this has been said the film is far from being a
'hack' job and for much of its length carries conviction, especially in
the opening scenes in the restaurant car and the later robbery sequences,
all of which bear the mark of a true craftsman.

Production Company:	Universal
Production:	Mark Hellinger
Direction:	Robert Siodmak
Screenplay:	Anthony Veiller and
from the story by	John Huston
Ernest Hemingway	
Photography:	Woody Bredell
Music:	Miklos Rozsa

Leading Players: Burt Lancaster, Ava Gardner, Edmond O'Brien, Albert Dekker, Sam Levene, William Conrad, Charles McGraw

Note: Filmed in Hollywood, May-July, 1946.

THE THIRD MAN   1949

Perhaps the most memorable moment in *The Third Man* comes when Joseph Cotten shouts drunkenly at a cat stalking along the wet streets of Vienna. The cat stops suddenly and rubs his head against a foot in a darkened doorway. A neighbour, irritated with Cotten's continual shouting, turns on the light of his bedroom. For a brief second the face of Orson Welles as Harry Lime is illuminated on the screen and a film that has been simmering slowly since the opening scene suddenly bursts into a crescendo of excitement. Based on a Graham Greene original about racketeering in post-war Vienna, the movie is still one of the truly classic thrillers to come from a British studio, not the least of its attributes being Carol Reed's imaginative use of the war-ravaged streets of Vienna and the haunting zither music of Anton Karas. Also in the cast: Trevor Howard as the head of the British Military Police and Valli as Lime's mistress.

Production Company:	London Films
Production and Direction:	Carol Reed
Screenplay:	Graham Greene
Photography:	Robert Krasker
Music:	Anton Karas

Leading Players: Joseph Cotten, Trevor Howard, Valli, Orson Welles, Bernard Lee, Wilfred Hyde White

Note: Filmed on location in Vienna and at Isleworth studios, England, November 1948-March 1949.

FIVE FINGERS   1952

One of the most neglected of spy thrillers, *Five Fingers* is based on fact and set in Turkey during the early days of World War II. James Mason plays an Albanian valet (code name Cicero) at the British Embassy in Ankara who gains access to important allied war documents, photographs them and then sells them to the enemy. The astonished Germans, unable to believe their good fortune, pay him in counterfeit money and fail to act on the information he provides. The film's main assets are Michael Wilson's witty script, the playing of Mason and, in a minor role, John Wengraf as Von Papen, and a thrilling manhunt through Istanbul; an additional quality in view of more recent developments in the cinema is the almost total absence of violence.

Production Company: Twentieth Century-Fox
Production: Otto Lang
Direction: Joseph L. Mankiewicz
Screenplay: Michael Wilson
from the book 'Operation Cicero'
  by L. C. Moyzish
Photography: Norbert Brodine
Music: Bernard Herrmann
Leading Players: James Mason, Danielle Darrieux, Michael
  Rennie, Walter Hampden, Oscar Karlweis, Herbert Berghof,
  John Wengraf

Note: Filmed in Hollywood and on location in Ankara and Istanbul, August-October, 1951.

REAR WINDOW   1954

Perhaps the finest example of Hitchcock's talent; a taut, and in the the last twenty minutes, desperately exciting thriller about a magazine photographer recovering from a broken leg in his Greenwich Village apartment who suspects that a murder has been committed in the apartment building opposite. The confined setting — only one ingenious set is used throughout — enables Hitchcock to wring the utmost tension (and black humour) from the situation and to draw a splendid performance from James Stewart, who was here making the second of his four appearances for the director. Grace Kelly features as Stewart's rich society girl friend, Thelma Ritter as his caustic nurse and Raymond Burr, in his pre-Perry Mason days, appears as the sinister murder suspect Lars Thorwald.

Production Company: Paramount
Production and Direction: Alfred Hitchcock
Screenplay: John Michael Hayes
  from a novelette by
  Cornell Woolrich
Photography (Technicolor): Robert Burks
Music: Franz Waxman
Leading Players: James Stewart, Grace Kelly, Wendell Corey,
  Thelma Ritter, Raymond Burr, Judith Evelyn

Note: Filmed at the Paramount Studio in Hollywood, December, 1953-January, 1954.

CONFIDENTIAL REPORT   1955

Although none of Orson Welles' thrillers have been completely successful, all contain moments that serve to remind audiences of his cinematic genius. This film is no exception. The basic story about a ruthless financier who tracks down and eliminates the characters in his shady past is no more than common-place, but individual scenes, involving Mischa Auer as a flea trainer in Copenhagen, Michael Redgrave as a Polish antique dealer and Katina Paxinou as a retired madame in Mexico are brilliantly executed. The murder of an old dope pedlar in a bombed Munich on Christmas Eve is as thrilling as anything to be found in Hitchcock.

Production Company: Mercury
Direction: Orson Welles
Screenplay: Orson Welles
     from his novel 'Mr. Arkadin'
Photography: Jean Bourgoin
Music: Paul Misraki
Leading Players: Orson Welles, Paolo Mori, Robert Arden, Michael Redgrave, Patricia Medina, Akim Tamiroff, Mischa Auer, Katina Paxinou

Note: Filmed in eight months during 1954 in France, Spain, Germany and Italy.

PSYCHO   1960

Anthony Perkins as the crazed taxidermist, Janet Leigh as his luckless victim and, best of all perhaps, Martin Balsam as the private-eye Arbogast who meets an alarming death as he topples backwards down the now famous flight of stairs. This extraordinary movie is probably Hitchcock's most famous film, although at the time of its first showing it was misunderstood by the critics and attacked for its grisly murder sequences. Hitchcock himself has called it his 'little joke'. A brilliant Herrmann score heightens the atmosphere.

Production Company: Paramount
Production and Direction: Alfred Hitchcock
Screenplay: Joseph Stefano
     from the novel by Robert Bloch
Photography: John L. Russell
Music: Bernard Herrmann
Leading Players: Janet Leigh, Anthony Perkins, Vera Miles, John Gavin, Martin Balsam, John McIntire, Simon Oakland

Note: Filmed at Paramount Studios in Hollywood, December 1959-February 1960.

THE MANCHURIAN CANDIDATE   1962

Arguably the most brilliant thriller of the decade, with Laurence Harvey as a Korean war hero who is brainwashed in Manchuria and returned to the United States with instructions to assassinate a leading Presidential candidate. The plot was thought far-fetched at the time of the film's initial showing, but President Kennedy's subsequent murder proved that the events depicted in the climax were all too easily related to real life. Highlights: the brainwashing sequence when American P.o.W.s are led to believe they are attending an American gardening club and the climax set at a political convention in Madison Square Garden.

Production Company:	M.C./United Artists
Production:	George Axelrod and
	John Frankenheimer
Direction:	John Frankenheimer
Screenplay:	George Axelrod
based on the novel by	
Richard Condon	
Photography:	Lionel Lindon
Music:	David Amram

Leading Players: Frank Sinatra, Laurence Harvey, Janet Leigh, Angela Lansbury, Henry Silva, James Gregory, Leslie Parrish, John McGiver

Note: Filmed in Hollywood and on location at Madison Square Garden, January-April, 1962. The total shooting schedule was 39 days.

FROM RUSSIA WITH LOVE   1963

Most people have their favourite Bond movie. This one, in which Bond is assigned to steal a cipher machine from the Russians in Istanbul, is probably the most accomplished, for it is more feasible than its predecessor *Dr. No* and relies more on characterization than the later movies which were often dwarfed by their gadgets and machines. Robert Shaw as a blond assassin, Lotte Lenya as the sadistic Rosa Klebb and Pedro Armendariz as a Turkish ally, feature in the leading roles. Best moments: A Russian being picked off by telescopic rifle whilst escaping down a giant poster-board and an excitingly staged fight between Shaw and Connery on the Orient Express.

Production Company:	Eon/United Artists
Production:	Harry Saltzman and
	Albert R. Broccoli
Direction:	Terence Young
Screenplay:	Richard Maibaum
from the novel by Ian Fleming	
Photography (Technicolor):	Ted Moore
Music:	John Barry

Leading Players: Sean Connery, Daniela Bianchi, Pedro Armendariz, Lotte Lenya, Robert Shaw, Bernard Lee

BONNIE AND CLYDE   1967

Faye Dunaway as Bonnie Parker and Warren Beatty as Clyde Barrow, two bored products of the Depression who create a reign of terror in the mid-western states during the thirties. Throughout their brief careers they retain a sense of innocence, even though their initial crimes of minor bank robberies are eventually superseded by more violent escapades and murder. Because of its unusual style — Arthur Penn treats his subjects part-seriously, part-humorously — the film was accused of romanticizing violence, but the murder scenes are treated with a horrifying realism and tend to condemn rather than condone violence, especially in the final sequence when the pair's death by gunfire is stressed in slow motion. The acting throughout is magnificent, the period detail beautifully caught and the photography of Burnett Guffey of Academy Award winning calibre.

Production Company: Tatira/Hiller/Warner Bros.
Production: Warren Beatty
Direction: Arthur Penn
Screenplay: David Newman and
      Robert Benton
Photography (Technicolor):   Burnett Guffey
Music: Charles Strouse
Leading Players: Warren Beatty, Faye Dunaway, Michael J. Pollard, Gene Hackman, Estelle Parsons, Denver Pyle, Dub Taylor, Evans Evans

Note: Filmed on location in Dallas, October, 1966-January, 1967.

THE GODFATHER   1972

It's been called the Mafia home movie. For three years it ranked as the most profitable film of all time. It is also, unlike most moneymakers, close to being a masterpiece, telling the inside story of the Don Corleone family which rules supreme over rival Mafia factions in post-war America and is eventually taken over by the Godfther's youngest son, Michael, who emerges as even more ruthless than his father. All of which somewhat over-simplifies 175 minutes of brilliant screen time as Francis Ford Coppola probes deeply into what makes the Mafia tick — or rather, kill — and combines scenes of horrendous violence with those of extreme tenderness i.e. the lengthy wedding sequence at the beginning of the film. Brando is the ageing, cat-stroking Corleone, Al Pacino the heir apparent, Robert Duvall the family lawyer. It may not add up to anything more than an in-depth version of the films Walsh and Curtiz were making at Warners in the 30s, but it is made with style and great skill. And it has class!

Production Company: Paramount
Production: Albert S. Ruddy
Direction: Francis Ford Coppola
Screenplay: Mario Puzo and
      Francis Ford Coppola
    based on the novel by
    Mario Puzo
Photography (Technicolor):   Gordon Willis

Music: Nino Rota
Leading Players: Marlon Brando, Al Pacino, James Caan,
   Richard Castellano, Robert Duvall, Sterling Hayden, John Marley,
   Richard Conte, Diane Keaton, Al Lettieri, Talia Shire

THE GODFATHER PART II   1974

A rarity, a sequel that is superior to its predecessor. In fact, arguably
the American movie of the 70s, following the continuing murderous
career of Michael Corleone (played here with even more authority by
Al Pacino) and at the same time flashing back to the early years of the
century when his father (Robert De Niro) first arrived in New York.
The work of the great American directors — Stevens, Wyler, Hawks,
etc. is reflected in every frame of this film but Coppola has not aped
the masters. He has simply learned from them and adapted accordingly.
Highlights: a frightening assassination attempt through a bedroom
window, the elite panicking in Cuba as Castro comes to power, and
the careful stalking and final murder of a petty gangster.

Production Company: Paramount
Production and Direction: Francis Ford Coppola
Screenplay: Francis Ford Coppola
   based on the novel by   and Mario Puzo
   Mario Puzo
Photography (Technicolor):   Gordon Willis
Music: Nino Rota
Leading Players: Al Pacino, Robert Duvall, Diane Keaton, Robert
   De Niro, John Cazale, Talia Shire, Lee Strasberg, Michael V. Gazzo

CHINATOWN   1974

The classiest private-eye thriller since the heyday of Bogart, with
Jack Nicholson becoming more and more involved with enigmatic
femme fatale Faye Dunaway during a case of murder and double-cross
in the Los Angeles of 1937. Impeccably in period, Polanski's movie
is a model of its kind, so complicated at times that one never trusts
the motives of anyone in the case, not even shamus Nicholson who
at one point has his nose cut open by a knife-happy little thug (played
in a gruesome little cameo by Polanski himself). The only thing one can
be reasonably certain about is that Miss Dunaway will get her come-
uppance. She does, halted by a shower of bullets as she tries for a
getaway on the edge of Chinatown. Director John Huston also hovers
round the edge of the movie, offering a deliciously malevolent portrait
of soft-spoken corruption.

Production Company: Paramount
Production: Robert Evans
Direction: Roman Polanski
Screenplay: Robert Towne
Photography (Technicolor/   John A. Alonzo
Panavision):

Music: Jerry Goldsmith
Leading Players: Jack Nicholson, Faye Dunaway, John Huston,
    Perry Lopez, John Hillerman, Darrell Zwerling, Diane Ladd,
    Roman Polanski

THRILLERS AND CRIME: WHO'S WHO

ALDRICH, ROBERT (1918-   ). American director, a frequent visitor to the seamier side of urban life since the mid-fifties when he turned *Kiss Me Deadly* (55), a pulp private-eye thriller by Mickey Spillane, into a miniature classic. Also remade James Hadley Chase's *No Orchids For Miss Blandish* as *The Grissom Gang* (71) and in *Hustle* (76) proved that the lot of an honest cop is not a happy one in the grim, violent world of the 70s. Others: *World For Ransom* (54), *Twilight's Last Gleaming* (77), *The Choirboys* (78).

ANDREWS, DANA (1912-   ). American actor often cast as a detective or D.A. in Fox thrillers of the 40s. His less than sympathetic cop in Preminger's *Where The Sidewalk Ends* (50) was something of a refreshing change from his usual clean-cut image. Films include *Laura* (44), *Fallen Angel* (45), *Boomerang* (47), *While The City Sleeps* (56), *Beyond A Reasonable Doubt* (56), *The Satan Bug* (65), *Innocent Bystanders* (72).

BACALL, LAUREN (1924-   ). Husky voiced ex-model who epitomized the smart-talking American heroine of the late 40s. Three crime films with husband Humphrey Bogart — *The Big Sleep* (46), *Dark Passage* (47) and *Key Largo* (48), and a later welcome reappearance in the genre in *The Moving Target* (66). In recent years has ventured into Agatha Christie territory as one of the snowbound passenger suspects in *Murder On The Orient Express* (74).

BACON, LLOYD (1889-1955). American director of more than a dozen crime movies, many with Bogart, Robinson, Raft. Best achievement: *A Slight Case of Murder* (38), a satirical Damon Runyon story with Edward G. Robinson as a retired gangster. Main films: *Marked Woman* (37), *San Quentin* (37), *Racket Busters* (38), *Invisible Stripes* (39), *Brother Orchid* (40), *Larceny Inc.* (42).

BANCROFT, GEORGE (1882-1956). Burly American character actor who appeared as the hoodlum Bull Weed in the first major gangster movie *Underworld* (27) and then continued in similar roles, mostly at Warners, during the 30s. Supported Cagney, Bogart and Raft in numerous films including *Angels with Dirty Faces* (38) and *Each Dawn I Die* (39).

BARRY, JOHN (1933-   ). Barry's scores for the Bond films — the 007 theme originated from the first movie *Dr. No* (62) — established him as a leading composer of contemporary film music. *Goldfinger* (64) is perhaps the most enjoyable of all his Bond scores, whilst the haunting *Ipcress File* (65) remains the most impressive of his other films in the genre. Also: *From Russia With Love* (63), *Thunderball* (65), *The Quiller Memorandum* (66), *You Only Live Twice* (67), *Deadfall* (68), *On Her Majesty's Secret Service* (69), *Diamonds Are Forever* (71), *The Tamarind Seed* (74), *The Man With The Golden Gun* (74), *Moonraker* (79).

BENDIX, WILLIAM (1907-64). Best remembered for his dumb villains, e.g. 'White Suit' in Hathaway's *The Dark Corner* (46), Bendix also portrayed a number of sympathetic characters on the right side of the law such as the shell-shocked war veteran in Raymond Chandler's *The Blue Dahlia* (46) and Detective Lou Brady in *Detective Story* (51). Films include *The Glass Key* (42), *Race Street* (48), *The Big Steal* (49), *Macao* (52), *The Rough and the Smooth* (59).

BENNETT, JOAN (1910-   ). One of the genre's favourite bad girls, brilliant as the unscrupulous tramp in Fritz Lang's *Scarlet Street* (45). Several other films for Lang during the 40s, i.e. *Man Hunt* (41), *Woman in the Window* (44), *Secret Beyond the Door* (48). Also: *The Woman on the Beach* (47), *The Reckless Moment* (49).

BERGMAN, INGRID (1915-   ). During her first ten years in Hollywood Ingrid Bergman appeared in several thrillers and established herself as Hitchcock's favourite leading lady of the 40s. Her most famous thriller role and the one for which she won an Academy Award was as the terrified heiress in Cukor's *The Murder In Thornton Square (Gaslight)* (44). Films for Hitchcock: *Spellbound* (45), *Notorious* (46), *Under Capricorn* (49). Also *Murder On The Orient Express* (74) (AA).

BOGART, HUMPHREY (1899-1957). Bogart's long and distinguished career in crime movies came to an end in 1955 when he played the escaped convict Glenn Griffin in Wyler's *The Desperate Hours*. Between 1936 and 1955 he appeared in no fewer than 37 crime thrillers, creating such notorious criminals as Duke Mantee (*The Petrified Forest*) and Roy Earle (*High Sierra*) as well as the private eyes Sam Spade (*The Maltese Falcon*) and Philip Marlowe (*The Big Sleep*). Other films in the genre include *Bullets or Ballots* (36), *Black Legion* (36), *Marked Woman* (37), *Kid Galahad* (37), *San Quentin* (37), *Dead End* (37), *Angels with Dirty Faces* (38), *Invisible Stripes* (39), *The Roaring Twenties* (39), *Brother Orchid* (40), *Across the Pacific* (42), *Conflict* (45), *Dark Passage* (47), *Key Largo* (48), *The Enforcer (Murder Inc.)* (51).

BRANDO, MARLON (1924-   ). Both of Brando's Academy Awards
have been earned for his involvement in screen crime — as the
punch-drunk ex-boxer Terry Malloy in Kazan's *On The Waterfront*
(54) and Mafia chief Don Corleone in *The Godfather* (72). Eighteen
years separated the two films. In between Brando cast his net wide,
appearing in a great variety of movies including an underrated
little kidnapping thriller *The Night Of The Following Day* (69).

BRONSON, CHARLES (1922-   ). The personification of the 'hit, hit
and hit again' type thug hero of the 70s. A man of few words and
even fewer expressions but ranking as one of the most popular
American stars of the decade. Thrillers (many directed by Michael
Winner) are usually slick and very violent. Films: *Machine Gun
Kelly* (58), *The Mechanic* (72), *The Valachi Papers* (72), *The Stone
Killer* (73), *Mr. Majestyk* (74), *Death Wish* (74), *Breakout* (75),
St. Ives (76), *Telefon* (77), *Love And Bullets, Charlie* (79).

BRUCE, NIGEL (1895-1954). Bluff, British-born actor who played
Dr. Watson opposite Rathbone's Sherlock Holmes in more than a
dozen films during the 40s. Films: *The Hound of the Baskervilles*
(39), *The Adventures of Sherlock Holmes* (39), *Sherlock Holmes
and the Voice of Terror* (42), *Sherlock Holmes and the Secret
Weapon* (42), *Sherlock Holmes in Washington* (43), *Sherlock
Holmes Faces Death* (43), *Spider Woman* (44), *The Scarlet Claw*
(44), *Pearl of Death* (44), *House of Fear* (45), *Woman in Green*
(45), *Pursuit to Algiers* (45), *Terror by Night* (46), *Dressed to
Kill* (46).

BURKS, ROBERT (1910-1968). American cameraman, best known for
his long and distinguished association with Alfred Hitchcock.
Films for the director: *Strangers on a Train* (51), *I Confess* (53),
Dial M for Murder (54), *Rear Window* (54), *To Catch a Thief*
(AA) (55), *The Man Who Knew Too Much* (56), *The Trouble with
Harry* (56), *The Wrong Man* (57), *Vertigo* (58), *North by Northwest*
(59), *The Birds* (63), *Marnie* (64).

BURNETT, W. R. (1899-   ). American novelist/scriptwriter who
authored the original novels of *Little Caesar* (31), *High Sierra*
(41), and *The Asphalt Jungle* (50) and collaborated on the
screenplays of *Scarface* (32), *This Gun for Hire* (42), *The Racket*
(51) and *Illegal* (55).

CAGNEY, JAMES (1904-   ). Cagney reigned supreme at Warners for
more than a decade, strutting his way through numerous gangster
movies including *Public Enemy* (31), *G-Men* (35) and the
memorable *Angels with Dirty Faces* (38). Of all his directors, and

he worked with most of the great names on the Warner lot, Raoul Walsh drew the best from him in *The Roaring Twenties* (39), a story of bootlegging in prohibition America (see page 47) and *White Heat* (49). Also: *Smart Money* (31), *Hard to Handle* (33), *The Mayor of Hell* (33), *Each Dawn I Die* (39), *Kiss Tomorrow Goodbye* (50), *Love Me or Leave Me* (55).

CAINE, MICHAEL (1933-). British leading man who has appeared as Len Deighton's intelligence agent, Harry Palmer, in three films i.e. *The Ipcress File* (65), *Funeral In Berlin* (66), *Billion Dollar Brain* (67). Other thrillers: *Gambit* (66), *Deadfall* (68), *Get Carter* (71), *Pulp* (72), *Sleuth* (72), *The Black Windmill* (74), *The Marseilles Contract* (74), *The Wilby Conspiracy* (75), *Peeper* (76), *The Silver Bears* (78).

CARROLL, LEO G. (1892-1972). British character actor, in Hollywood for many years, well known to cinema audiences long before he became popular as Alexander Waverly in the 'Man from Uncle' TV series. His many Hitchcock films include *Rebecca* (40), *Suspicion* (41), *Spellbound* (as Dr. Murchison) (45), *The Paradine Case* (47), *Strangers on a Train* (51), *North by Northwest* (59). Also appeared as the Nazi fifth columnist in Hathaway's *The House on 92nd Street* (45).

CHANDLER, RAYMOND (1889-1962). American novelist, creator of the private-eye Philip Marlowe, a tough cynical detective played with varying degrees of success by Dick Powell in *Farewell My Lovely* (45), Humphrey Bogart in *The Big Sleep* (46), Robert Montgomery in *The Lady In The Lake* (46), George Montgomery in *The High Window* (47) and James Garner in *Marlowe* (69). Of all these actors, Powell came closest to the author's conception of the role. More recent screen Marlowes who have ventured down those mean, dark streets include Elliott Gould in *The Long Goodbye* (73) and Robert Mitchum, twice, in remakes of *Farewell My Lovely* (75) and *The Big Sleep* (78). As a scriptwriter Chandler collaborated on *Double Indemnity* (44), *The Blue Dahlia* (46) and *Strangers On A Train* (51).

COBB, LEE J. (1911-1976). American actor, excellent both as detectives (*Johnny O'Clock* and *Coogan's Bluff*) and gang bosses (*Party Girl*). His waterfront racketeer, Johnny Friendly in Elia Kazan's *On the Waterfront* (54) remains his finest performance in the genre. Films include: *Boomerang* (47), *Johnny O'Clock* (47), *Call Northside 777* (48), *Thieves Highway* (49), *Party Girl* (58), *The Trap* (59), *Coogan's Bluff* (68).

COLMAN, RONALD (1891-1959). British actor, the first talking *Bulldog*

Drummond (29). Appeared in the role a second time in 1934 in *Bulldog Drummond Strikes Back*. Also: *Raffles* (30), *A Double Life* (47) (AA).

CONNERY, SEAN (1930-). The first, and for many people, only James Bond, Connery triumphed over Rosa Klebb, Oddjob, Pussy Galore and co. in five movies before tiring of the role in 1967. He was replaced by George Lazenby in *On Her Majesty's Secret Service* (69) but returned to the part in *Diamonds Are Forever* (71). Films (as Bond): *Dr. No* (62), *From Russia With Love* (63), *Goldfinger* (64), *Thunderball* (65), *You Only Live Twice* (67), *Diamonds Are Forever* (71). Others: *The Anderson Tapes* (71), *The Offence* (72), *Murder On The Orient Express* (74) (as Colonel Arbuthnot), *Ransom* (75), *The Next Man* (76), *The First Great Train Robbery* (78).

CONTE, RICHARD (1919-1975). A regular performer in thrillers during the post-war era, Conte gave excellent performances in what were often only second-rate crime pictures. His best movies, e.g. *Somewhere In The Night* (46), in which he played an amnesiac, and Hathaway's *Call Northside 777* (48) as an innocent man convicted of murder, occurred early in his career. Films: *Cry Of The City* (48), *Thieves Highway* (49), *The Sleeping City* (50), *Hollywood Story* (51), *The Blue Gardenia* (53), *New York Confidential* (55), *The Brothers Rico* (57), *Oceans Eleven* (60), *Tony Rome* (67), *Lady In Cement* (68), *The Godfather* (72).

COOK, ELISHA JUN. (1902-). American supporting actor who produced a series of miniature portraits of small-time hoods during the 40s. Superb as Greenstreet's hireling Wilmer Cook, in Huston's *The Maltese Falcon* (41). Films in the genre include *I Wake Up Screaming* (*Hot Spot*) (41), *Phantom Lady* (44), *Dillinger* (45), *The Big Sleep* (46), *Born To Kill* (47), *Don't Bother To Knock* (52), *The Killing* (56), *Baby Face Nelson* (57), *Johnny Cool* (63), *Electra Glide In Blue* (73), *The Outfit* (74), *The Black Bird* (75), *St. Ives* (76).

COPPOLA, FRANCIS FORD (1939-). American writer/director, arguably the most accomplished film-maker to emerge from the English-speaking post-war cinema. Ripped open the Mafia case-book with his two *Godfather* masterpieces and on a slightly less bloodthirsty but equally unsavoury level, investigated the modern practice of electronic bugging in *The Conversation* (74). Films: *The Godfather* (72), *The Godfather Part II* (74).

CORMAN, ROGER (1926-). American director, best known for his horror films (see page 34). Two major biographical crime movies in recent years, i.e. *The St. Valentine's Day Massacre* (67) and *Bloody Mama* (70).

CREGAR, LAIRD (1916-1944). Heavyweight supporting actor who promised to be as effective a villain for Fox as Greenstreet was for Warners before death cut short his promising career at the tragically early age of twenty-eight. Sixteen films in five years. Best known roles: the psychotic cop in *I Wake Up Screaming* (41), the fifth columnist in *This Gun for Hire* (42) and Jack the Ripper in *The Lodger* (44).

CURTIZ, MICHAEL (1888-1962). Hungarian-born director, proficient in all film genres, not least crime movies which included the boxing melodrama *Kid Galahad* (37) and the Cagney/Bogart vehicle *Angels With Dirty Faces* (38). Others: *20,000 Years In Sing Sing* (33), *The Kennel Murder Case* (33), *Jimmy The Gent* (34), *Front Page Woman* (36), *The Unsuspected* (47), *Flamingo Road* (49), *The Breaking Point* (50).

DASSIN, JULES (1911-). American director, prominent in the genre during the late 40s when he shot the semi-documentary thriller *The Naked City* (48) on location in New York. Also: *Brute Force* (47), *Thieves Highway* (49), *Night And The City* (50), *Topkapi* (64), *Uptight* (68).

DEARDEN, BASIL (1911-1971). British director whose thrillers *Sapphire* (59) and *Victim* (61) combined a detective story element with a more problematical basic theme, i.e. colour prejudice and homosexuality. His best achievement, *The League of Gentlemen* (60), is a partly humourous thriller about a group of ex-commandos who use their army training to rob a London bank. Other films: *The Blue Lamp* (50), *Pool Of London* (51), *The Gentle Gunman* (52), *Violent Playground* (58), *The Secret Partner* (61), *Life For Ruth* (62), *The Mind Benders* (63), *Masquerade* (65), *The Assassination Bureau* (69), *The Man Who Haunted Himself* (70).

DMYTRYK, EDWARD (1908-). Thriller and private-eye movies were among Dmytryk's early output in the 40s, and he returned to the genre with some distinction in 1965 when he directed the intriguing urban drama *Mirage*. His most accomplished works are those he made at RKO, e.g. *Farewell My Lovely* (45), perhaps the most successful version of a Raymond Chandler novel, and *Crossfire* (47), a taut little thriller that also explored the problem of anti-semitism in post-war America. Others: *Cornered* (46), *Obsession* (48), *The Sniper* (52), *The Human Factor* (75).

DUNAWAY, FAYE (1941-   ). American actress invariably hovering
'on the wrong side of the tracks' and in the thick of things when
kidnapping (*The Happening*) (67), murder (*Bonnie And Clyde*)
(67) and robbery (*The Thomas Crown Affair*) (68) occur on screen.
At her best as the double-dealing *femme fatale* in Polanski's private-
eye thriller *Chinatown* (74). Also: *Three Days Of The Condor* (75),
Eyes Of Laura Mars (78).

DURYEA, DAN (1907-1968). American actor who excelled in villainous
roles during the 40s and 50s. Superb as the blackmailers in Fritz
Lang's *The Woman in the Window* (44) and *Scarlet Street* (45)
and as the sneering thug, Silky, in George Sherman's underrated *Larceny* (48). Films: *Ministry of Fear* (44), *Criss Cross*
(49), *One Way Street* (50), *The Underworld Story* (50).

DUVALL, ROBERT (1931-   ). Dependable American character actor.
The Corleone family lawyer in the two *Godfather* films; Dr. Watson
in *The Seven-Per-Cent Solution* (76). Also: *Bullitt* (68), *The
Detective* (68), *Badge 373* (73), *The Outfit* (74), *Breakout* (75),
The Killer Elite (76).

EASTWOOD, CLINT (1930-   ). *The* superstar of the modern cinema.
Began his career in westerns (see page 95) but of late has brought
his rough tough ways to urban America and shown that the 'if
you can't beat 'em join 'em' philosophy works wonders when
applied on the right side of the law. His *Play Misty For Me* (71),
a thriller about a disc jockey pursued by a homicidal listener,
proved that he was not just a rugged face but a director of some
consequence. Films: *Coogan's Bluff* (68), *Dirty Harry* (71),
Magnum Force (73), *Thunderbolt And Lightfoot* (74), *The Eiger
Sanction* (75) (also directed), *The Enforcer* (76), *The Gauntlet*
(77) (also directed), *Every Which Way But Loose* (78), *Escape
From Alcatraz* (79).

FLEISCHER, RICHARD (1916-   ). American director who first gained
the attention of serious film critics with his excellent B thriller,
The Narrow Margin (52). In recent years has directed several films
based on real life murder cases, e.g. *Compulsion* (59), an adaptation of the Leopold/Loeb murder trial with Orson Welles as
Clarence Darrow; *The Girl In The Red Velvet Swing* (55), an
account of the Stanford White killing in turn-of-the-century
America; *The Boston Strangler* (68) with Tony Curtis as Albert
DeSalvo; and *Ten Rillington Place* (71) with Richard Attenborough
as Christie and John Hurt as Timothy Evans. Also: *Bodyguard*
(48), *Trapped* (49), *Armoured Car Robbery* (50), *Violent Saturday*
(55), *Blind Terror* (71), *The Last Run* (71), *The New Centurions* (72),
The Don Is Dead (73), *Mr. Majestyk* (74).

FRANKENHEIMER, JOHN (1930-). A 'wonder boy' director who began his screen career when still in his twenties, but has since had to struggle to retain his early impetus. Classic thrillers such as *The Manchurian Candidate* (62) and *Seven Days In May* (64) placed him in the front rank of American stylists and the genre has also been responsible for his recent comeback e.g. *French Connection II* (75), *Black Sunday* (77).

GARFIELD, JOHN (1913-1952). American stage and screen actor, seen frequently in crime movies during the 40s. Among his best performances in the genre: the lawyer involved in the numbers racket in *Force Of Evil* (48) and the fugitive criminal in John Berry's *He Ran All The Way* (51). Also: *They Made Me A Criminal* (39), *The Postman Always Rings Twice* (46), *We Were Strangers* (49), *Under My Skin* (50), *The Breaking Point* (50).

GILBERT, LEWIS (1920-). Now the number one director of the Bond movies — *You Only Live Twice* (67), *The Spy Who Loved Me* (77), *Moonraker* (79). Earned his reputation by directing several of Britain's flag waving war movies of the 50s, occasionally delving into the more criminal side of things i.e. *Cosh Boy* (53), *The Good Die Young* (54), *Cast A Dark Shadow* (55).

GOLDMAN, WILLIAM (1931-). American novelist/screenwriter, in movies since the mid-60s. Best known for his script of *Butch Cassidy And The Sundance Kid* (69) but much work in the thriller genre i.e. *Masquerade* (65), *The Moving Target* (66), *The Hot Rock* (72), *All The President's Men* (76), *Marathon Man* (76).

GOMEZ, THOMAS (1905-1971). Plump, American actor who spent many years playing crooks and cops in Hollywood crime movies. Appeared as one of Edward G. Robinson's henchmen in *Key Largo* (48) and, most memorably, as the reluctant operator of the New York numbers racket in *Force of Evil* (48). Also *Phantom Lady* (44), *The Dark Mirror* (46), *Singapore* (47), *Ride the Pink Horse* (47), *Macao* (52).

GRANT, CARY (1904-). British-born actor, long associated with Alfred Hitchcock. Films for the director: *Suspicion* (41), *Notorious* (46), *To Catch a Thief* (55), *North by Northwest* (as the luckless advertising executive, Roger Thornhill) (59). Also: *Crisis* (50), *Charade* (63).

GREENSTREET, SYDNEY (1879-1954). Twenty-stone British stage actor who debuted in films as the curio dealer, Casper Gutman, in

Huston's *The Maltese Falcon* (41). Many films at Warners during the 40s, including *Across The Pacific* (42), *The Conspirators* (44), *The Mask Of Dimitrios* (as Mr. Peters) (44), *Conflict* (45), *Three Strangers* (46), *The Verdict* (46), *Flamingo Road* (49).

GUFFEY, BURNETT (1905-   ). Columbia's ace cameraman for many years. Later worked with Arthur Penn on *Bonnie and Clyde* (AA) (67). Films: *Johnny O'Clock* (47), *The Undercover Man* (49), *Convicted* (50), *The Sniper* (52), *The Brothers Rico* (57), *Nightfall* (57), *Let No Man Write My Epitaph* (59), *The Split* (68).

HACKMAN, GENE (1930-   ). A little-known performer until the late 60s, Hackman first created attention when he won a supporting actor nomination for his portrayal of Warren Beatty's brother in *Bonnie And Clyde* (67). In 1971 he won an Oscar for his tough cop tracking down dope smugglers in *The French Connection*, a role he later repeated in *French Connection II* (75). Also: *The Split* (68), *Prime Cut* (72), *Cisco Pike* (72), *The Conversation* (74), *Night Moves* (75), *The Domino Principle* (77).

HAMILTON, GUY (1922-   ). British director, best known in the genre for the excellent *Goldfinger* (64), the third film in the James Bond saga. Other Bonds: *Diamonds Are Forever* (71), *Live And Let Die* (73), *The Man With The Golden Gun* (74). Also: *Funeral In Berlin* (66).

HAMMETT, DASHIELL (1894-1961). American crime writer and former Pinkerton detective whose novels *The Maltese Falcon* (filmed three times), *The Glass Key* (filmed twice) and *The Thin Man*, provided the basis for some of Hollywood's finest thrillers. As a scriptwriter he collaborated on Mamoulian's *City Streets* (31).

HATHAWAY, HENRY (1898-   ). Veteran American director who handled a long series of semi-documentary thrillers for Fox immediately after the war, e.g. *The House on 92nd Street* (45), *13 Rue Madeleine* (46), *Kiss of Death* (47), *Call Northside 777* (48). Also: *Johnny Apollo* (40), *The Dark Corner* (46), *Fourteen Hours* (51), *Diplomatic Courier* (52), *23 Paces to Baker Street* (56), *Seven Thieves* (60).

HAWKS, HOWARD (1896-1977). A master director only given his true place in American cinema in the last decade. Two of his films — *Scarface* (32), a gangster movie based on the criminal career of Al Capone and *The Big Sleep* (46), an adaptation of Chandler's detective novel — are brilliant examples of the American crime film. Also: *The Criminal Code* (31).

HECHT, BEN (1894-1964). American scriptwriter, former newsman and playwright. Screenplays include *Underworld* (AA) (27), *Scarface* (32), *Spellbound* (45), *Notorious* (46), *Ride the Pink Horse* (47), *Kiss of Death* (47), *Whirlpool* (50), *Where the Sidewalk Ends* (50).

HELLINGER, MARK (1903-1947). American newspaper correspondent who entered films as a scriptwriter during the 30s then became a producer on such classic crime films as *The Killers* (46) and *The Naked City* (48). Other films in the genre (as scriptwriter): *The Roaring Twenties* (39). (As producer): *It All Came True* (40), *Brother Orchid* (40), *They Drive By Night* (40), *High Sierra* (41), *Brute Force* (47).

HERRMANN, BERNARD (1911-1975). American composer, eight films for Hitchcock during the 56-64 period: *The Man Who Knew Too Much* (56), *The Trouble With Harry* (56), *The Wrong Man* (57), *Vertigo* (58), *North By Northwest* (59), *Psycho* (60), *The Birds* (63), *Marnie* (64). Other thriller scores: *Hangover Square* (45), *On Dangerous Ground* (51), *Five Fingers* (52), *Cape Fear* (61), *Twisted Nerve* (69), *Sisters* (75), *Obsession* (75).

HITCHCOCK, ALFRED (1899-   ). The master of the suspense thriller and the only director to work continuously in the same genre throughout his career. Two peak creative periods, i.e. the 30s when he filmed such British thrillers as *The Thirty-Nine Steps* (35) and *The Lady Vanishes* (38) and the 50s when he worked at Warners, Paramount and Metro on a brilliant series of thrillers, including *Strangers on a Train* (51), *I Confess* (53), *To Catch a Thief* (55) and *The Man Who Knew Too Much* (56). *Psycho* (60) is perhaps the most perfectly realized of all his works yet *Rear Window* (54), *Vertigo* (58) and *North by Northwest* (59) all have their supporters among contemporary critics. Among his most famous scenes: the windmills turning the wrong way in *Foreign Correspondent* (40), the attempted assassination in the Albert Hall in *The Man Who Knew Too Much* (34) (56), Cary Grant alone on a prairie road in *North by Northwest* (59) and the crows gathering in the school playground in *The Birds* (63). Other major films: *The Lodger* (26), *Blackmail* (29), *The Secret Agent* (36), *Sabotage* (36), *Young and Innocent* (37), *Jamaica Inn* (39), *Rebecca* (40), *Suspicion* (41), *Saboteur* (42), *Shadow of a Doubt* (43), *Lifeboat* (44), *Spellbound* (45), *Notorious* (46), *The Paradine Case* (47), *Rope* (48), *Dial M for Murder* (54), *The Trouble with Harry* (56), *The Wrong Man* (57), *Marnie* (64), *Torn Curtain* (66), *Topaz* (70), *Frenzy* (72), *Family Plot* (76).

HOFFMAN, DUSTIN (1937-   ). American actor, memorable as the college innocent in *The Graduate* (67). Has since operated in murkier waters i.e. violent Cornwall in *Straw Dogs* (71), a corrupt Washington in *All The President's Men* (76) and a spy-ridden New York in *Marathon Man* (76). In the latter suffered the agonizing torture of having his teeth drilled — through the front — by ex-Nazi Laurence Olivier. Also: *Straight Time* (78), *Agatha* (79).

HUNT, PETER (1928-   ). British director, former editor, associated with several British thrillers of the 60s including the Bond and Harry Palmer movies. Films (as editor and 2nd unit director): *Dr. No* (62), *From Russia with Love* (63), *Goldfinger* (64), *Thunderball* (65), *The Ipcress File* (65), *You Only Live Twice* (67). (As director): *On Her Majesty's Secret Service* (69).

HUSTON, JOHN (1906-   ). Before his recent sad decline Huston was one of the most vigorous and inventive of American directors, making a masterpiece with his first Hollywood film *The Maltese Falcon* (41), and a near classic robbery movie with *The Asphalt Jungle* (50). Since the 50s he has worked only infrequently in the genre. Others: *Key Largo* (48), *The List Of Adrian Messenger* (63), *The Kremlin Letter* (70), *The Mackintosh Man* (73), *Chinatown* (74) (actor only), *Breakout* (75) (actor only), *Winter Kills* (79) (actor only).

KARLOFF, BORIS (1887-1969). British actor best known for his horror roles (see page 38). Also appeared in several American crime films of the 30s (he was a mobster in Hawks' *Scarface*) and in a series of minor detective films about an Oriental sleuth named Mr. Wong. Films include: *The Criminal Code* (31), *Smart Money* (31), *Scarface* (32), *Mr. Wong Detective* (38), *The Mystery of Mr. Wong* (39), *Mr. Wong in Chinatown* (39), *The Fatal Hour* (40), *Doomed to Die* (40).

KEIGHLEY, WILLIAM (1889-   ). American director who handled some of Warner's more routine gangster pieces of the 30s. Not to be compared with the films of Walsh or Curtiz, his movies are nonetheless not without a professional gloss and the Cagney vehicles especially are still viewable today. Films: *Journal of a Crime* (34), *G-Men* (35), *Special Agent* (35), *Bullets or Ballots* (36), *Each Dawn I Die* (39), *Street with no Name* (48).

KELLY, GRACE (1928-   ). Self-possessed, blonde American actress who played the lead in three Hitchcock movies of the early 50s, i.e. *Dial M for Murder* (54), *Rear Window* (54), *To Catch a Thief* (55). Made her début in a small part in Hathaway's semi-documentary thriller, *Fourteen Hours* (51).

KRASNER, MILTON (1898-   ). American cinematographer who has enjoyed distinguished careers at several Hollywood studios, including Universal, Fox and MGM, where he collaborated regularly with Vincente Minnelli. Thrillers include: *The Woman In The Window* (44) and *Scarlet Street* (45) both for Lang, *The Dark Mirror* (46) for Siodmak, *No Way Out* (50), *Deadline U.S.A.* (52), *The Girl In The Red Velvet Swing* (55), *23 Paces To Baker Street* (56), *The St. Valentine's Day Massacre* (67).

LADD, ALAN (1913-1964). One of the most popular of the screen's tough guys, often cast opposite 'peek-a-boo' leading lady Veronica Lake during the 40s. First major role: the hired assassin, Raven, in Graham Greene's *This Gun for Hire* (42). Films, mostly at Paramount, include: *The Glass Key* (42), *Lucky Jordan* (43), *The Blue Dahlia* (46), *Calcutta* (47), *Saigon* (48), *Chicago Deadline* (49), *Appointment with Danger* (51), *Hell on 'Frisco Bay* (55).

LANG, FRITZ (1890-1976). Brilliant German director noted for his cold, bleak American thrillers of the 40s and 50s. Outstanding achievements in the genre: the unrelenting, pessimistic *Scarlet Street* (45) and *The Big Heat* (53), one of the most accomplished gangster movies of the decade. Also: *You Only Live Once* (37), *Man Hunt* (41), *Hangmen Also Die* (43), *The Woman in the Window* (44), *The Ministry of Fear* (44), *Cloak and Dagger* (46), *Secret Beyond the Door* (48), *The Blue Gardenia* (53), *While the City Sleeps* (56), *Beyond a Reasonable Doubt* (56).

LA SHELLE, JOSEPH (1903-   ). American cameraman who won an Oscar for his monochrome photography of Preminger's *Laura* (44). Numerous other films for the director, including the thrillers *Fallen Angel* (45), *Where the Sidewalk Ends* (50), *The Thirteenth Letter* (51).

LAUGHTON, CHARLES (1899-1962). British actor who tried his hand at most film genres during his 35-year career. Excelled as the publishing tycoon in *The Big Clock* (48) and the barnstorming barrister in Wilder's *Witness for the Prosecution* (57). In 1950 appeared as Maigret in *The Man on the Eiffel Tower*. Also: *Payment Deferred* (32), *The Suspect* (44), *The Paradine Case* (47), *The Bribe* (48).

LAWRENCE, MARC (1910-   ). A familiar heavy in Hollywood crime movies, memorable as Edward G. Robinson's gangland crony in Huston's *Key Largo* (48) and as the bookie in the same director's *The Asphalt Jungle* (50). Major films in the genre: *Invisible Stripes* (39), *Johnny Apollo* (40), *This Gun For Hire* (42), *Dillinger* (45),

Cloak And Dagger (46), *Black Hand* (50), *Johnny Cool* (63),
Diamonds Are Forever (71), *Marathon Man* (76), *Foul Play* (78).

LEE, BERNARD (1908-   ). British supporting actor who has played 'M'
in all the Bond movies made to date. Also appeared as Sergeant
Paine in Reed's *The Third Man* (49) and a Scotland Yard detective
in *Father Brown* (54). Bond films: *Dr. No* (62), *From Russia With
Love* (63), *Goldfinger* (64), *Thunderball* (65), *You Only Live Twice*
(67), *On Her Majesty's Secret Service* (69), *Diamonds Are Forever*
(71), *Live And Let Die* (73), *The Man With The Golden Gun* (74),
The Spy Who Loved Me (77), *Moonraker* (79).

LEHMAN, ERNEST (c.1920-   ). Screenwriter for Hitchcock on *North
By Northwest* (59) and *Family Plot* (76). Others in the genre: *The
Sweet Smell Of Success* (57), *The Prize* (63), *Black Sunday* (77)
(co-scripted).

LEROY, MERVYN (1900-   ). Veteran American director whose reputation
in the crime genre rests almost entirely on one film, *Little Caesar*
(31), the story of the rise and fall of a smalltime hoodlum in
Depression America. The movie began the Warner gangster cycle
of the 30s and established Edward G. Robinson as a Hollywood star
of the top rank. Also: *Johnny Eager* (41), *The F.B.I. Story* (59),
Moment to Moment (66).

LITVAK, ANATOLE (1920-1974). Russian-born director who worked
mostly on American productions from 1937. Thrillers include
Confessions of a Nazi Spy (39), a forerunner of the semi-
documentary thrillers of the post-war years and *Sorry, Wrong
Number* (48), the film which earned Barbara Stanwyck an Oscar
nomination as the bed-ridden heiress who hears her own murder
being plotted over the telephone. Also: *The Amazing Dr. Clitterhouse* (38), *Castle on the Hudson* (40), *City for Conquest* (40),
Blues in the Night (41), *Five Miles to Midnight* (63), *The Night of
the Generals* (67), *Lady in the Car with Glasses and a Gun* (70).

LORRE, PETER (1904-1964). Hungarian-born actor, superb as the
hunted child murderer in Fritz Lang's *M* (31), but never given the
opportunity to develop his talent in Hollywood. Apart from *The
Maltese Falcon* (as Joel Cairo) (41), *The Mask of Dimitrios* (44)
and *Three Strangers* (46), his American thrillers were only routine.
Played John P. Marquand's Oriental detective Mr. Moto in several
B films of the late 30s. Pictures include *The Man Who Knew Too
Much* (34), *Secret Agent* (36), *Black Angel* (46), *The Verdict*
(46), *Casbah* (48), *Rope of Sand* (49), *Beat the Devil* (54).

LOY, MYRNA (1905-). American actress, the sophisticated wife of Hammett's private-eye Nick Charles in six 'Thin Man' movies, i.e. *The Thin Man* (34), *After the Thin Man* (36), *Another Thin Man* (39), *Shadow of the Thin Man* (41), *The Thin Man Goes Home* (44), *Song of the Thin Man* (47).

LUMET, SIDNEY (1924-). Versatile American director whose work ranges from Tennessee Williams drama (*The Fugitive Kind*) to large-scale musicals (*The Wiz*) and even takes in, uncharacteristically, Agatha Christie (*Murder On The Orient Express*). Most at home, however, when out and about in the streets of his native New York i.e. *Serpico* (73), *Dog Day Afternoon* (75). Many films with Sean Connery and Al Pacino. Also: *The Deadly Affair* (67), *The Anderson Tapes* (71), *The Offence* (72).

MACDONALD, JOE (1905-1968). American cameraman who shot many location thrillers for Hathaway and Kazan in the late 40s. Films in the genre (mostly at Fox) include: *The Dark Corner* (46), *Call Northside 777* (48), *The Street With No Name* (48), *Panic In The Streets* (50), *Fourteen Hours* (51), *Pickup On South Street* (53), *House Of Bamboo* (55), *The List Of Adrian Messenger* (63), *Mirage* (65), *Blindfold* (66).

McQUEEN, STEVE (1930-). A violent excursion into Peckinpah territory in *The Getaway* (72); an ambitious caper and a seductive game of chess with Faye Dunaway in *The Thomas Crown Affair* (68); best of all, a thrilling car chase at breakneck speed over the hilly streets of San Francisco in *Bullitt* (68). Superstar McQueen may well be a man of few words and a puzzled look but the above movies ensure him a unique place in the history of the genre.

MAIBUM, RICHARD (1909-). American scriptwriter, in films from 1935. Associated in recent years with the James Bond movies, e.g. *Dr. No* (62), *From Russia With Love* (63), *Goldfinger* (64), *Thunderball* (65), *On Her Majesty's Secret Service* (69), *Diamonds Are Forever* (71), *The Man With The Golden Gun* (74), *The Spy Who Loved Me* (77). Also: *They Gave Him A Gun* (37), *O.S.S.* (46). *The Big Clock* (as producer) (48), *Ransom* (56), *The Day They Robbed The Bank Of England* (60).

MANCINI, HENRY (1922-). American composer whose catchy theme tunes have accentuated some of the lighter moments of film thrillers, e.g. *Touch Of Evil* (58), *Experiment In Terror* (*Grip Of Fear*) (62), *Charade* (63), *Arabesque* (66), *Wait Until Dark* (67). He remains best-known for his romantic 'Moon River' song from *Breakfast At Tiffany's* and the infectious *Pink Panther* theme.

MARVIN, LEE (1924-   ). The most popular screen heavy of the last two decades, excellent as the hoods in *The Big Heat* (53), *Violent Saturday* (55) and Siegel's remake of *The Killers* (64), but most impressive as the vengeful criminal in John Boorman's *Point Blank* (67). Also: *Bad Day At Black Rock* (54), *Pete Kelly's Blues* (55), *I Died A Thousand Times* (55), *The Rack* (56), *Prime Cut* (72), *The Klansman* (74), *Avalanche Express* (79).

MATE, RUDOLPH (1898-1964). Polish-born cameraman who did memorable work on Hitchcock's *Foreign Correspondent* (40) and Charles Vidor's *Gilda* (46). Later turned to directing but, like so many other cameramen who changed roles, his work proved only routine. Films (as director): *The Dark Past* (48), *D.O.A.* (50), *Union Station* (50), *The Green Glove* (52), *Second Chance* (53).

MATURE, VICTOR (1915-   ). Thick-set American actor, very popular in gangster movies during the 40-55 period. At his best as the stool-pigeon in Hathaway's *Kiss of Death* (47). Also: *I Wake Up Screaming (Hot Spot)* (41), *Cry of the City* (48), *Gambling House* (50), *The Las Vegas Story* (52), *Violent Saturday* (55).

MEEKER, RALPH (1920-   ). American actor well-known for his portrayal of private-eye Mike Hammer in Aldrich's *Kiss Me Deadly* (55). Also: *Big House U.S.A.* (55), *The St. Valentine's Day Massacre* (as Bugs Moran) (67), *The Detective* (68), *The Anderson Tapes* (71). *Winter Kills* (79).

MITCHUM, ROBERT (1917-   ). American actor, in leading roles since 1946. Excellent as the private detective in Tourneur's *Out Of The Past (Build My Gallows High)* (47) and as the sadistic psychopath in *Cape Fear* (62). Films: *Crossfire* (47), *The Big Steal* (49), *Where Danger Lives* (50), *His Kind Of Woman* (51), *The Racket* (51), *Macao* (52), *Angel Face* (52), *Foreign Intrigue* (56), *The List Of Adrian Messenger* (63), *The Friends Of Eddie Coyle* (73), *The Yakuza* (75), *Farewell My Lovely* (75) (as Philip Marlowe), *The Big Sleep* (78) (as Philip Marlowe), *Agency* (79).

MONTGOMERY, ROBERT (1904-   ). American actor who appeared as private-eye Philip Marlowe in *The Lady in the Lake* (46), a film which he also directed, using the unusual technique of the subjective camera throughout. Also: *Ride the Pink Horse* (directed) (47).

MOORE, ROGER (1928-   ). The TV Saint whose halo eventually slipped and allowed him to kill for queen and country as Ian Fleming's super agent 007. The regular James Bond since Sean Connery vacated the role in 1971. Films (as Bond): *Live And*

Let Die (73), *The Man With The Golden Gun* (74), *The Spy Who Loved Me* (77), *Moonraker* (79). Others: *Crossplot* (69), *The Man Who Haunted Himself* (70).

MOORE, TED (1914-). South African-born cameraman on several James Bond movies: *Dr. No* (62), *From Russia With Love* (63), *Goldfinger* (64), *Thunderball* (65), *Diamonds Are Forever* (71), *Live And Let Die* (73), *The Man With The Golden Gun* (74).

MURPHY, RICHARD (1912-). American scriptwriter at his best when scripting the semi-documentary Fox thrillers of the post-war years, e.g. *Boomerang* (47), *Cry of the City* (48), *Panic in the Streets* (50). Also worked on the screenplay of Fleischer's *Compulsion* (59).

MUSURACA, NICHOLAS (1908-). RKO cameraman responsible for the brilliant photography of Siodmak's gothic thriller *The Spiral Staircase* (46). Also: *Out of the Past (Build My Gallows High)* (47), *Where Danger Lives* (50), *The Blue Gardenia* (53).

NEGULESCO, JEAN (1900-). Rumanian-born director whose best movies were those he directed at Warners in the 40s, e.g. *The Mask of Dimitrios* (44), *The Conspirators* (44) and the undervalued *Three Strangers* (46), a bizarre story of three people drawn together by a sweepstake ticket on the Chinese New Year. Directed several romantic dramas during the 50s (see page 165).

NEWMAN, PAUL (1925-). American actor who has twice portrayed Ross MacDonald's private-eye Lew Harper on screen — in *The Moving Target* (66) and *The Drowning Pool* (75). Also a defecting scientist for Hitchcock in *Torn Curtain* (66), a diamond thief for Huston in *The Mackintosh Man* (73) and a 30s con artist for George Roy Hill in *The Sting* (73).

NOLAN, LLOYD (1903-). One of the screen's most familiar custodians of the law, best remembered perhaps as the F.B.I. man who tracks down the Nazi spies in *The House On 92nd Street* (45). Also: *G-Men* (35), *Johnny Apollo* (40), *The House Across The Bay* (40), *Michael Shayne Private Detective* (41), *Somewhere In The Night* (46), *The Lady In The Lake* (46), *The Street With No Name* (48), *The Double Man* (67).

NORWOOD, EILLE. British actor who appeared as Sherlock Holmes in nearly 50 two-reelers (all directed by Maurice Elvey) during the

20s. Hubert Willis featured as Dr. Watson in all the films which included adaptations of the stories *A Scandal in Bohemia, The Empty House, The Red-Headed League, The Man with the Twisted Lip, The Sign of Four* and *The Final Problem*.

OLAND, WARNER (1880-1938). The best of all the screen Charlie Chans. Sixteen movies in six years, all for Fox, including *Charlie Chan Carries On* (31), *Charlie Chan's Greatest Case* (33), *Charlie Chan in London* (34), *Charlie Chan's Secret* (36). After his death he was succeeded in the role by Sidney Toler (twenty-two films in ten years) and Roland Winters (six films in three years).

PACINO, AL (1939-   ). Distinguished young American actor: Mafia chief Michael Corleone in the two Godfather films, an honest cop exposing police corruption in *Serpico* (73), a bank robber seeking finance for a sex change operation in *Dog Day Afternoon* (75). Not quite so effective when faced with the more tender side of life, i.e. opposite Marthe Keller in *Bobby Deerfield* (77).

PAKULA, ALAN J. (1928-   ). American director, former producer long in association with Robert Mulligan. Leans heavily towards the *film noir* in his work especially in his Kafka-like urban thriller *Klute* (71). Also: *The Parallax View* (74), *All The President's Men* (76).

PALANCE, JACK (1921-   ). American actor, mostly seen in villainous parts. Best used by Elia Kazan as the fugitive plague carrier in *Panic In The Streets* (50). Films: *Sudden Fear* (52), *Second Chance* (53), *Man In The Attic* (54), *I Died A Thousand Times* (55), *The House Of Numbers* (57), *The Man Inside* (58), *Once A Thief* (65), *They Came To Rob Las Vegas* (69).

PECK, GREGORY (1916-   ). American actor who appeared twice for Hitchcock during the 40s — as the amnesiac John Ballantine in *Spellbound* (45), less memorably, as the barrister in *The Paradine Case* (47). Also: *Night People* (54), *Cape Fear* (62), *Mirage* (65), *Arabesque* (66), *The Most Dangerous Man In The World* (69), *I Walk The Line* (70), *The Boys From Brazil* (78).

PECKINPAH, SAM (1926-   ). Most famous for his westerns, Peckinpah has strayed from the wide open spaces of late and ventured into the city steets of contemporary America. But Old West or new cities, the result has inevitably been the same — man proving himself to himself amid violence and slow motion death. Films: *Straw Dogs* (71), *The Getaway* (72), *Bring Me The Head Of Alfredo Garcia* (74), *The Killer Elite* (76).

POWELL, WILLIAM (1892-   ). Polished American actor, famous for his portrayals of the private-eyes Philo Vance and Nick Charles. His performance in *The Thin Man* (34), the first of his six films as Charles, won him an Academy Award nomination as best actor of the year. Films: *The Dragnet* (28), *The Canary Murder Case* (the first of his four appearances as Vance) (29), *The Greene Murder Case* (29), *The Benson Murder Case* (30), *The Kennel Murder Case* (33) (all as Vance), *After The Thin Man* (36), *Another Thin Man* (39), *Shadow Of The Thin Man* (41), *The Thin Man Goes Home* (44), *The Hoodlum Saint* (46), *Song Of The Thin Man* (47).

PREMINGER, OTTO (1906-   ). Austrian director, in Hollywood from 1935, who made a number of interesting small scale thrillers early in his career, including the classic *Laura* (44) and the very much underrated *Fallen Angel* (45). Others: *Whirlpool* (50), *Where The Sidewalk Ends* (50), *The Thirteenth Letter* (51), *Angel Face* (52), *Anatomy Of A Murder* (59), *Bunny Lake Is Missing* (65), *Rosebud* (75), *The Human Factor* (79).

RAFT, GEORGE (1895-   ). Although one of the legendary figures of crime films, Raft rarely received the same opportunities as Bogart Cagney, or Robinson and spent much of his time in stock, inferior roles at the Warner studio. He is best remembered for his coin-tossing bodyguard of Paul Muni in *Scarface* (32) and for his Spats Colombo in Wilder's *Some Like it Hot* (59). Films include: *Quick Millions* (31), *Undercover Man* (33), *The Glass Key* (35), *Each Dawn I Die* (39), *Invisible Stripes* (39), *The House Across the Bay* (40), *They Drive by Night* (40), *Race Street* (48), *Rogue Cop* (54).

RAINS, CLAUDE (1890-1967). British stage and screen actor, expert at playing cunning sophisticated villains, e.g. the Nazi heavy in Hitchcock's *Notorious* (46), and the radio storyteller, Victor Grandison, in *The Unsuspected* (47). Also: *Deception* (46), *Rope of Sand* (49), *Where Danger Lives* (50), *The Man Who Watched Trains Go By* (52).

RATHBONE, BASIL (1892-1967). Tall British actor whose thin chiselled features made him a perfect choice for the role of Sherlock Holmes. After playing the great detective in the full-length features *The Hound of the Baskervilles* (39), and *The Adventures of Sherlock Holmes* (39), he appeared in twelve double features at Universal, most of which were directed by Roy William Neill (for full listing *see* Nigel Bruce).

REED, CAROL (1906-1976). British director of the brilliant *Odd Man Out* (47) and *The Third Man* (49). Other ventures into the genre less memorable: *The Man Between* (53), *Our Man In Havana* (59), *The Running Man* (63).

REYNOLDS, BURT (1936-   ). Virile leading man now most at ease in comedy (see page 19) but for much of his early career seen as a cop, private-eye, moonshiner, etc. in a long string of variable crime thrillers. Notable as police lieutenant Phil Gaines in Aldrich's *Hustle* (76). Also: *Operation C.I.A.* (65), *Fuzz* (72), *Shamus* (73), *White Lightning* (73), *Gator* (76).

ROBINSON, EDWARD G. (1893-1973). American actor famous for his portrayal of the hoodlum Rico Bandello in LeRoy's *Little Caesar* (31). During the 40s appeared in more sympathetic parts, e.g. the University Professor in *The Woman In The Window* (44), the insurance investigator in *Double Indemnity* (44), and the F.B.I. man in Orson Welles' *The Stranger* (46). Major films: *Smart Money* (31), *Bullets Or Ballots* (36), *Kid Galahad* (37), *The Last Gangster* (38), *A Slight Case Of Murder* (38), *The Amazing Dr. Clitterhouse* (38), *Confessions Of A Nazi Spy* (39), *Brother Orchid* (40), *Manpower* (41), *Scarlet Street* (45), *Key Largo* (48), *The Glass Web* (53), *Black Tuesday* (54), *Illegal* (55), *Tight Spot* (55), *Hell On 'Frisco Bay* (55), *Seven Thieves* (60), *The Prize* (63).

ROSSEN, ROBERT (1908-1966). An excellent director, and even better scriptwriter, Rossen made his most effective contribution to the genre in the late 30s when he collaborated on the screenplays of such Warner movies as *Marked Woman* (37), *Dust be my Destiny* (39), *The Roaring Twenties* (39) and *Out of the Fog* (41). Later as a director, he filmed *Johnny O'Clock* (47).

ROZSA, MIKLOS (1907-   ). Hungarian-born composer who scored several Hitchcock and Wilder movies during the 40s. Also many thrillers at Universal. Films include: *Double Indemnity* (44), *Spellbound* (45), *The Killers* (46), *Brute Force* (47), *Naked City* (48), *The Asphalt Jungle* (50), *Crisis* (50), *The Private Life Of Sherlock Holmes* (70), *The Private Files Of J. Edgar Hoover* (78).

RUTHERFORD, MARGARET (1892-1972). Dithering, lovable British character actress. Miss Marple in four films later in her career. *Murder She Said* (62), *Murder At The Gallop* (63), *Murder Most Foul* (63), *Murder Ahoy* (64).

SCHEIDER, ROY (1934-   ). American actor who destroyed the monster shark in *Jaws* (75) (see page 227) but found Laurence Olivier's sleeve knife in *Marathon Man* (76) more than he could handle. Hackman's sidekick cop in *The French Connection* (71). Also: *The Seven Ups* (73), *The Outside Man* (73), *Sorcerer* (77).

SEITZ, JOHN F. (1899-1979). American cameraman, in Hollywood from the silent days (see also page 220). Worked at Paramount during the 40s, lensing among others, *Double Indemnity* (44) for Wilder and *The Big Clock* (48) and *Night Has a Thousand Eyes* (48) for Farrow. Also: *This Gun for Hire* (42), *Lucky Jordan* (43), *Chicago Deadline* (49), *Appointment with Danger* (51), *Rogue Cop* (54), *Hell on 'Frisco Bay* (55).

SIEGEL, DON (1913-   ). American director, a specialist in crime movies since the early 50s. Films include *The Line Up* (58), notable for its remarkable car chase climax and a remake of Hemingway's *The Killers* (64). Others: *The Verdict* (46), *The Big Steal* (49), *Riot In Cell Block 11* (54), *Baby Face Nelson* (57), *Madigan* (68), *Coogan's Bluff* (68), *Dirty Harry* (71), *Charley Varrick* (73), *The Black Windmill* (74), *Telefon* (77), *Escape From Alcatraz* (79).

SILLIPHANT, STIRLING (1918-   ). American screenwriter who scripted the Academy Award-winning *In The Heat Of The Night* (67) for Norman Jewison. Other movies in the genre include *Five Against The House* (55), *The Line-Up* (58), *The Slender Thread* (produced) (66), *Marlowe* (69), *The New Centurions* (72), *Shaft In Africa* (73), *The Killer Elite* (75) (co-scripted), *The Enforcer* (76) (co-scripted), *Telefon* (77) (co-scripted).

SIODMAK, ROBERT (1900-1973). American director who, during the late 40s, created a memorable series of thrillers at the Universal and Fox studios. The opening sequences of *The Killers* (46), which he filmed for Mark Hellinger, represents American film making at its very best. Films: *Phantom Lady* (44), *The Suspect* (44), *The Spiral Staircase* (46), *The Dark Mirror* (46), *Cry Of The City* (48), *Criss Cross* (49), *The File On Thelma Jordan* (49), *Deported* (50), *The Rough And The Smooth* (59).

STANWYCK, BARBARA (1907-   ). Top thriller directors Anatole Litvak and Robert Siodmak both directed Stanwyck in the 40s, although it was Billy Wilder who drew the best from her when he cast her as the blonde *femme fatale* Phyllis Dietrichson in *Double Indemnity* (44). For this performance she deserved an Academy Award, an honour that has always eluded her. Films: *The Strange Love of Martha Ivers* (46), *The Two Mrs. Carrolls* (47), *Cry Wolf* (47), *Sorry Wrong Number* (48), *The File on Thelma Jordan* (49), *Jeopardy* (53), *Witness to Murder* (54), *Crime of Passion* (57).

STEIGER, ROD (1925-   ). American method-actor who, in 1959, gave perhaps the most intelligent and convincing portrayal of Al Capone yet seen on the screen. Films: *On The Waterfront* (as Charlie Malloy, brother of Marlon Brando) (54), *Across The Bridge* (57), *Cry Terror* (58), *Al Capone* (59), *Seven Thieves* (60), *In The Heat Of The Night* (67) (AA), *No Way To Treat A Lady* (68), *Hennessy* (75).

STEWART, JAMES (1909-   ). A favourite Hitchcock performer, at his best as the news photographer in *Rear Window* (54) and the obsessed detective in *Vertigo* (58). Films: *Call Northside 777* (48), *Rope* (48), *The Man Who Knew Too Much* (56), *The F.B.I. Story* (59), *Anatomy of a Murder* (59).

STONE, ANDREW (1902-   ). American writer/producer of small budget thrillers (many produced with his wife Virginia): *Highway 301* (51), *The Steel Trap* (52), *Julie* (56), *Cry Terror* (58), *The Last Voyage* (60).

TIERNEY, GENE (1920-   ). Popular Fox star of the 40s, often cast opposite Dana Andrews. Thrillers include *Laura* (44), *The Iron Curtain* (48), *Whirlpool* (50), *Where The Sidewalk Ends* (50), *Night And The City* (50), *Black Widow* (54).

TIOMKIN, DIMITRI (1899-   ). Prolific Hollywood composer. Numerous films for Hitchcock, including *Shadow Of A Doubt* (43), in which he used the Merry Widow waltz to sinister effect, *Strangers On A Train* (51), *I Confess* (53), *Dial M For Murder* (54). Others: *Dillinger* (45), *Whistle Stop* (46), *The Dark Mirror* (46), *D.O.A.* (50), *The Steel Trap* (52), *Angel Face* (52), *Jeopardy* (53), *A Bullet Is Waiting* (54).

TOMASINI, GEORGE (1910-1965). American editor, long associated with Hitchcock. Cut nine films for the director between 1954 and 1964 — *Rear Window* (54), *To Catch a Thief* (55), *The Man Who Knew Too Much* (56), *The Wrong Man* (57), *Vertigo* (58), *North by Northwest* (59), *Psycho* (60), *The Birds* (63), *Marnie* (64).

TREVOR, CLAIRE (1909-   ). American actress, often seen as a bad girl or gangster's moll during the 30s and 40s. Won an Academy Award for her drunken floosie in Huston's *Key Largo* (48). Also: *The Amazing Dr. Clitterhouse* (38), *I Stole A Million* (39), *Farewell My Lovely* (45), *Johnny Angel* (45), *Crack-Up* (46), *The Velvet Touch* (48), *Borderline* (50), *Hoodlum Empire* (52), *Stop, You're Killing Me* (53).

VAN DYKE, W. S. (1889-1944). MGM director of four of the six 'Thin Man' films: *The Thin Man* (34), *After the Thin Man* (36), *Another Thin Man* (39), *Shadow of the Thin Man* (41).

VON STERNBERG, JOSEF (1894-1969). Austrian-born director of the first major American gangster film, *Underworld* (27). Also: *The Dragnet* (28), *The Docks of New York* (28), *Thunderbolt* (29), *Macao* (52).

WALSH, RAOUL (1889-). One of the most talented directors ever to work on crime movies, Walsh has been responsible for at least three masterworks during his career, i.e. *The Roaring Twenties* (39), *High Sierra* (41), and the extraordinary *White Heat* (49), the film which returned James Cagney to the genre after an absence of ten years. *Murder Inc.* (51) which is credited to Bretaigne Windust was mostly directed by Walsh. Others: *The Bowery* (33), *They Drive by Night* (40), *Salty O'Rourke* (45).

WANGER, WALTER (1894-1968). American producer whose two most important films in the genre deal with the direct result of crime rather than crime itself, i.e. *Riot in Cell Block 11* (54), a savage indictment of prison conditions in America and *I Want to Live* (58), an anti-capital punishment drama hinging on the criminal career of Barbara Graham. Also: *You Only Live Once* (37), *Algiers* (38).

WAXMAN, FRANZ (1906-1967). German composer, several scores for Hitchcock: *Rebecca* (40), *Suspicion* (41), *The Paradine Case* (47), *Rear Window* (54). Also: *Confidential Agent* (45), *The Two Mrs. Carrolls* (47), *Cry Wolf* (47), *Dark Passage* (47), *The Unsuspected* (47), *Sorry Wrong Number* (48), *Night And The City* (50), *He Ran All The Way* (51), *Man On A Tightrope* (53), *I, The Jury* (53).

WELLES, ORSON (1915-). Welles directed and performed in several unusual thrillers of the post-war period, including *The Stranger* (46), *The Lady from Shanghai* (47), and *Confidential Report* (55). His Harry Lime in *The Third Man* (49), remains his most famous role in the genre whilst his corrupt detective Hank Quinlan in *Touch of Evil* (58) is probably the most accomplished of all his later screen performances.

WIDMARK, RICHARD (1915-). American actor who has appeared many times in the genre since playing the giggling psychopath Tommy Udo in Hathaway's *Kiss Of Death* (47). Films: *The Street*

With No Name (48), *Road House* (48), *Night And The City* (50), *Panic In The Streets* (50), *No Way Out* (50), *Pick-up On South Street* (53), *The Trap* (59), *Madigan* (68), *The Moonshine War* (70), *Murder On The Orient Express* (74), *The Sellout* (76), *Twilight's Last Gleaming* (76), *Rollercoaster* (77), *Coma* (78).

WONTNER, ARTHUR (1875-1960). British actor who, in many people's view, was the best of all the screen Sherlock Holmes. Played the detective in five films during the 30s, all of which co-starred Ian Fleming as Watson. Films: *Sherlock Holmes' Final Hour* (31), *The Sign of Four* (32), *The Missing Rembrandt* (33), *The Triumph of Sherlock Holmes* (35), *Silver Blaze* (36).

YOUNG, TERENCE (1915-   ). British director, former scriptwriter, who handled three of the first four Bond movies, namely *Dr. No* (62), *From Russia With Love* (63) and *Thunderball* (65). Also: *Triple Cross* (67), *Wait Until Dark* (67), *The Valachi Papers* (72), *The Klansman* (74), *Bloodline* (79).

WESTERNS

THE IRON HORSE   1924

A large-scale (160 minute) western about the construction of the Union Pacific railroad that relies more on its individual action sequences than its thin story line about the search by a son for his father's murderer. The climax, when hordes of Indians attack a derailed train, is superbly handled and gives ample evidence of the experience gained by John Ford in directing his earlier 48 B westerns, many of which starred Harry Carey, Hoot Gibson and Tom Mix. The film was shot almost entirely on location in the Nevada desert and made use of several real-life props, including Wild Bill Hickok's original vest-pocket Deringer revolver.

Production Company:	Fox
Direction:	John Ford
Screenplay:	Charles Kenyon
from a story by	
Kenyon and John Russell	
Photography:	George Schneiderman and
	Burnett Guffey

Leading Players: George O'Brien, Madge Bellamy, Judge Charles Edward Bull, William Walling, Fred Kohler, Cyril Chadwick, Gladys Hulette, J. Farrell McDonald

STAGECOACH   1939

A splendid, handsomely photographed work and the one western that *everyone* knows and likes. The story about a group of people travelling by stagecoach across Apache-infested country is punctuated by some brilliant scenes, such as Thomas Mitchell as Doc Boone being sobered by black coffee so that he can deliver a premature baby and the final stunningly edited chase by Indians across a stretch of salt flats. The film gave a new lease of life to the genre, which had gone through an unhappy period during the thirties, and made a star of John Wayne.

Production Company:	United Artists
Production and Direction:	John Ford
Executive Producer:	Walter Wanger
Screenplay:	Dudley Nichols
from the story *Stage to*	
Lordsburgh by Ernest Haycox	

Photography:	Bert Glennon
Music:	Richard Hageman, W. Franke Harling, John Leipold, Leo Shuken and Louis Gruenberg

Leading Players: John Wayne, Claire Trevor, John Carradine, Thomas Mitchell, Andy Devine, Donald Meek, Louise Platt, Tim Holt, George Bancroft

Note: Filmed in Monument Valley and other locations in Arizona, Utah, California.

RED RIVER   1948

The best cattle drive western of them all with fierce cattle baron John Wayne and foster son Montgomery Clift at odds every inch of the way as they drive 10,000 head of cattle over the Chisholm Trail from Texas to Abilene. Strikingly photographed in monochrome by Russell Harlan, the film impresses most as a straightforward epic adventure, although the complex male relationship between father and son has caused it to be analysed perhaps more than it need be by devotees of the Hawks' cult of the last decade. One aspect of the film that is rarely discussed is Dimitri Tiomkin's music, one of the finest scores in the western genre.

Production Company:	Monterey Productions/ United Artists
Production and Direction:	Howard Hawks
Screenplay:	Borden Chase and
from the novel 'The Chisholm Trail' by Borden Chase	Charles Schnee
Photography:	Russell Harlan
Music:	Dimitri Tiomkin

Leading Players: John Wayne, Montgomery Clift, Joanne Dru, Walter Brennan, Coleen Gray, John Ireland, Noah Beery, Jr.

Note: Filmed on location at Elgin, Arizona, September-November, 1946.

SHE WORE A YELLOW RIBBON   1949

The central figure in this rich Ford movie is an ageing cavalry officer (John Wayne) who, during the last few days before his retirement, prevents a large-scale Indian uprising following Custer's massacre at the Little Big Horn. The affectionate portrait of service life on an isolated outpost during the 1860's and Wayne's remarkable performance (superior in every way to his Academy Award winning portrayal in *True Grit*) help make the film one of the director's most satisfying works, although it is ultimately prevented from being a masterpiece by its surfeit of sentiment. The marvellous colour photography is a direct result of Ford and his cameramen trying to capture the effect of Frederick Remington's paintings on the screen.

Production Company:	Argosy Pictures — RKO Radio
Production:	John Ford and
	Merian C. Cooper
Direction:	John Ford
Screenplay:	Frank S. Nugent and
from the story 'War Party' by	Laurence Stallings
James Warner Bellah	
Photography (Technicolor):	Winton C. Hoch
Second Unit:	Charles P. Boyle
Music:	Richard Hageman

Leading Players: John Wayne, Joanne Dru, John Agar, Ben Johnson, Harry Carey Jr., Victor McLaglen, Mildred Natwick, George O'Brien, Arthur Shields

Note: Filmed in 31 days on location in Monument Valley, November-December, 1948.

BROKEN ARROW   1950

Rightly considered to be the contemporary cinema's first serious portrayal of the American Indian, this film started James Stewart on his long post-war western career as a U.S. Frontier Scout who tries to bring peace between the Apaches and the white man in Arizona during the 1870's. The film's main strength lies in the performances, especially of Jeff Chandler, who became a star overnight with his sympathetic portrayal of Cochise, and in the honesty of the script which looks closely at the Indians' customs and way of life. The soft Technicolor won veteran cameraman Ernest Palmer an Academy Award nomination.

Production Company:	Twentieth Century-Fox
Production:	Julian Blaustein
Direction:	Delmer Daves
Screenplay:	Michael Blankfort
from the novel 'Blood Brother'	
by Elliott Arnold	
Photography (Technicolor):	Ernest Palmer
Music:	Hugo Friedhofer

Leading Players: James Stewart, Jeff Chandler, Debra Paget, Basil Ruysdael, Will Geer, Arthur Hunnicutt.

Note: Filmed under the title *Arrow*, June-August, 1949.

HIGH NOON   1952

A small mid-western American town. An ageing marshal, just married to a young Quaker bride, learns that an outlaw he has sent to prison has been released and is arriving on the noon train to take revenge. As the killer's three henchmen wait at the station the marshal seeks assistance from the townspeople he has defended for so long. One by one they refuse until he is left alone to fight the four men at noon. The film, which is not so much a western, more a deliberate political allegory of

McCarthyism in the fifties, is remarkable for the tension that Fred Zinnemann and his editor wring from the central situation and for Cooper's Academy Award winning performance as Marshal Will Kane.

Production Company:	United Artists
Production:	Stanley Kramer
Direction:	Fred Zinnemann
Screenplay:	Carl Foreman
Photography:	Floyd Crosby
Music:	Dimitri Tiomkin

Leading Players: Gary Cooper, Thomas Mitchell, Lloyd Bridges, Katy Jurado, Grace Kelly, Otto Kruger, Lon Chaney, Henry Morgan

Note: Filmed in Hollywood, September-November, 1951.

SHANE   1953

A film full of famous moments: the uprooting of the stump in the ranch-yard, the murder of Torrey in the muddy street outside Grafton's, the funeral on the hill and the pulsating climax when Shane rides into town . . . And yet a great film in its own right, for although interlaced with scenes of violence it is never violent for its own sake and reflects more than any other movie an accurate picture of pioneer life in the American West of the 1880s. Visually amongst the most beautiful of all westerns, the film has a tremendous personal style, Stevens making great use of overlapping dialogue, the dissolve and, in the case of Torrey's murder, even a distant thunderstorm.

Production Company:	Paramount
Production and Direction:	George Stevens
Screenplay:	A. B. Guthrie, Jun.
from the novel by Jack Schaefer	
Additional dialogue:	Jack Sher
Photography (Technicolor):	Loyal Griggs
Music:	Victor Young

Leading Players: Alan Ladd, Jean Arthur, Van Heflin, Brandon de Wilde, Jack Palance, Ben Johnson, Edgar Buchanan, Emile Meyer, Elisha Cook, Jr.

Note: Filmed on location in Jackson Hole, Wyoming and at the Paramount studio Hollywood, August-November, 1951. Only the sequences at the Shipstead ranch were shot in the studio.

THE MAGNIFICENT SEVEN   1960

The public's favourite western and the one that spawned Elmer Bernstein's world famous music score. The seven are American outlaws who are hired by Mexican peasants to defend their village against marauding bandits. In the original Japanese film, *Seven Samurai*, on which the movie was based, they were Samurai warriors defending a village against fourteenth-century brigands. Amazingly, the updating of the action into a western setting works to perfection and, although never the masterpiece that Kurosawa's film undeniably was, *The Magnificent Seven* is still one of the few remakes that has proved a satisfying work in its own right. The seven are played by Yul Brynner, Horst Buchholz, Steve McQueen, Charles Bronson, Robert Vaughn, Brad Dexter, James Coburn; the bandit leader by Eli Wallach.

Production Company:	Mirisch-Alpha/United Artists
Production and Direction:	John Sturges
Screenplay:	William Roberts
based on Akira Kurosawa's film *Seven Samurai*	
Photography (DeLuxe Color/ Panavision):	Charles B. Lang, Jun.
Music:	Elmer Bernstein

Leading Players: Yul Brynner, Horst Buchholz, Eli Wallach, Steve McQueen, Charles Bronson, Robert Vaughn, Brad Dexter, James Coburn

THE WILD BUNCH   1969

Hailed as one of the best westerns to come out of Hollywood, this excessively violent film concentrates on the last weeks of a gang of outlaws as they drift from Texas into Mexico in the early years of the twentieth century. The theme of men clinging to a past way of life in a society that has outgrown them is one that has been explored frequently in recent years, so often in fact that the theme itself is in danger of becoming a cliché. But here the tragedy of the men's predicament as they find themselves hopelessly enmeshed with a Mexican guerilla unit and faced with the inventions of the new society, is explored in great depth and with not a little compassion. When, in the end, they decide to die in one last desperate blood bath, one is moved and sorry to see them go.

Production Company:	Warner Bros./Seven Arts
Production:	Phil Feldman
Direction:	Sam Peckinpah
Screenplay:	Walon Green and Sam Peckinpah
Photography (Technicolor/ Panavision 70):	Lucien Ballard
Music:	Jerry Fielding

Leading Players: William Holden, Ernest Borgnine, Robert Ryan, Edmond O'Brien, Warren Oates, Jaime Sanchez, Ben Johnson

Note: Filmed in Parras, Coahuila, Mexico, March-July, 1968.

BUTCH CASSIDY AND THE SUNDANCE KID   1969

The final years of the two leading members of the 'Hole in the Wall' gang who, together with an adventurous schoolteacher, operated in the western United States and Bolivia at the turn-of-the-century. The theme is almost identical to that of *The Wild Bunch*, even to the point of using a machine (a bicycle) to symbolize the approach of civilization, yet the treatment is so different, the direction so much lighter, that the film seems to be dealing with a time and people that are a world apart from those in Sam Peckinpah's film. The end result is the same, however, for when the two outlaws are shot down by the Bolivian army and frozen in the frame there is the same sense of melancholy. A superb achievement, enhanced considerably by Burt Bacharach's quietly tragic theme music.

Production Company:	Campanile Productions/ Twentieth Century-Fox
Production:	Paul Monash
Direction:	George Roy Hill
Screenplay:	William Goldman
Photography (DeLuxe Color/ Panavision):	Conrad Hall
Music:	Burt Bacharach

Leading Players:　Paul Newman, Robert Redford, Katharine Ross, Strother Martin, Henry Jones, Jeff Corey

Note: Filmed at Durango, Colorado, St. George, Utah and the Twentieth Century-Fox ranch, September, 1968-January, 1969.

THE GREAT NORTHFIELD MINNESOTA RAID　1972

The West as it really was — dirty, disease ridden, unfriendly — has been portrayed accurately in only a handful of films. This is one of them. It centres round the fateful raid by the Jesse James gang on the bank of Northfield in 1876. For once the central character is not James but Cole Younger (skilfully played by Cliff Robertson) who cons the townsfolk into transferring their gold to the bank in time for the robbery. The raid itself is filmed to perfection, beginning quietly as the white mackintoshed gang rides slowly through the muddy streets and ending in catastrophe amid gunfire and the perpetual shriek of a calliope, set off by the falling body of the town drunk. A realistic folk ballad of the old West, climaxed by Cole Younger, riddled with bullets, being paraded through the town in a cart and staggering to his feet to take a mock bow!

Production Company:	Universal
Production:	Jennings Lang
Direction:	Philip Kaufman
Screenplay:	Philip Kaufman
Photography (Technicolor):	Bruce Surtees
Music:	David Grusin

Leading Players:　Cliff Robertson, Robert Duvall, Luke Askew, R. G. Armstrong, Dana Elcar, Donald Moffat, John Pearce

THE OUTLAW JOSEY WALES   1976

The film that finally established Clint Eastwood as a major director. From its title no more than a routine 'man with no name' western. In reality a moving saga of a peaceful farmer (Eastwood) who joins a band of Southern guerillas after his wife and children are murdered in the Civil War and who then steadfastly refuses to give himself up at the War's close. As he is hunted down he collects an assorted group of characters along the way — an old Cherokee, an ill-used Indian girl, an old landlady and her granddaughter, a Mexican vaquero and a broken down cowboy. All come to depend on him for survival and eventually become his new 'family' as he settles in a small town near the Mexican border. Eastwood harnesses it all together in a manner which is contagiously exhilarating. The film is violent but the end statement that the farmer turned killer has become farmer again, well worth making.

Production Company: Warner Bros.
Production: Robert Daley
Direction: Clint Eastwood
Screenplay: Philip Kaufman and
                         Sonia Chernus

from the novel 'Gone To Texas'
   by Forrest Carter
Photography (DeLuxe/
   Panavision):   Bruce Surtees
Music: Jerry Fielding
Leading Players: Clint Eastwood, Chief Dan George, Sondra Locke,
   Bill McKinney, John Vernon, Paula Trueman

WESTERNS: WHO'S WHO

ALDRICH, ROBERT (1918-   ). Controversial American director whose first major features were both westerns: *Apache* (54), the true story of an Indian warrior who carried on the fight against the American Cavalry after the surrender of Geronimo, and *Vera Cruz* (54) an adventure with Gary Cooper and Burt Lancaster. Also: *The Last Sunset* (61), *Four for Texas* (63), *Ulzana's Raid* (72).

ANDERSON, BRONCHO BILLY (1883-1971). The first great Western star and the founder of Essanay Studios in 1907. Nearly five hundred one- and two-reelers during his career, many of them centring around the fictional character of 'Broncho Billy'. Made his first film appearance in Edwin S. Porter's *The Great Train Robbery* (1903) and directed the majority of his later films himself.

ARTHUR, JEAN (1905-   ). American actress who featured as Calamity Jane in DeMille's *The Plainsman* (37) and Van Heflin's settler wife in *Shane* (53).

AUTRY, GENE (1907-   ). Singing cowboy of innumerable Republic B westerns, at his peak during the late 30s. Film début in *In Old Santa Fe* and *Mystery Mountain* in 1934; thereafter appeared in more than ninety films, many with Smiley Burnette, the most famous of his many sidekicks. Among his directors: Joseph Kane, Lew Landers, Frank McDonald, William Morgan.

BALLARD, LUCIEN (1908-   ). American cameraman, a specialist in westerns during the 60s. Splendid colour work for Peckinpah on *The Wild Bunch* (69) and Hathaway on *True Grit* (69). Also: *White Feather* (55), *The Proud Ones* (56), *The King And Four Queens* (56), *Buchanan Rides Alone* (58), *Ride The High Country/Guns In The Afternoon* (62), *The Sons Of Katie Elder* (65), *Nevada Smith* (66), *Hour Of The Gun* (67), *Will Penny* (68), *The Ballad Of Cable Hogue* (70), *Breakheart Pass* (76), *From Noon Till Three* (76).

BARRETT, JAMES LEE (1929-   ). American scriptwriter, many westerns for Andrew V. McLaglen. Films: *Shenandoah* (65), *Bandolero* (68), *The Undefeated* (69), *The Cheyenne Social Club* (70), *Something Big* (71), *Smokey And The Bandit* (77) (modern west).

BAXTER, WARNER (1892-1951). Western star of the 30s; the screen's most notable Cisco Kid. Films; *In Old Arizona* (29), *Romance of the Rio Grande* (29), *The Arizona Kid* (30), *The Squaw Man* (31), *The Cisco Kid* (31), *Robin Hood of El Dorado* (36), *The Return of the Cisco Kid* (39).

BELLAH, JAMES WARNER. Screenwriter whose magazine stories 'Massacre', 'War Party' and 'Mission with No Record' inspired John Ford's post-war cavalry trilogy *Fort Apache* (48), *She Wore A Yellow Ribbon* (49) and *Rio Grande* (50). Later worked on the scripts of Ford's *Sergeant Rutledge* (60) and *The Man Who Shot Liberty Valance* (62). Also: *The Command* (54) (co-scripted), *A Thunder Of Drums* (61) (co-scripted).

BERNSTEIN, ELMER (1922-). American composer who achieved world fame for his *Magnificent Seven* score, perhaps the most exhilarating music ever written for a western film. Many other films in the genre: *The Tin Star* (57), *The Comancheros* (61), *The Hallelujah Trail* (65), *The Sons Of Katie Elder* (65), *Return Of The Seven* (66), *The Scalphunters* (68), *True Grit* (69), *Guns Of The Magnificent Seven* (69), *Big Jake* (71), *The Magnificent Seven Ride* (72), *Cahill, United States Marshal* (73), *The Shootist* (76), *From Noon Till Three* (76).

BOETTICHER, BUDD (1916-). Director of a number of stylish westerns, many starring Randolph Scott. Underrated when first shown, his films are now considered by many critics to be among the best produced during the 50s. Westerns: *The Cimarron Kid* (52), *Horizons West* (52), *Seminole* (53), *The Man from the Alamo* (53), *Seven Men from Now* (56), *Decision at Sundown* (57), *The Tall T* (57), *Buchanan Rides Alone* (58), *Ride Lonesome* (59), *Westbound* (59), *Comanche Station* (60).

BOND, WARD (1905-1960). One of John Ford's repertory company of supporting players, three of his best performances coming in the director's *Fort Apache* (48) in which he played a cavalry officer, *Wagonmaster* (50) as a Mormon Elder and *The Searchers* (56) as the two-gun preacher Capt. Rev. Samuel Clayton. Played Morgan Earp, brother of Wyatt in *My Darling Clementine* (46). Also: *The Big Trail* (30), *The Oklahoma Kid* (39), *Dodge City* (39), *Virginia City* (40), *Santa Fe Trail* (40), *Dakota* (45), *Canyon Passage* (46), *Three Godfathers* (48), *The Great Missouri Raid* (51), *Only the Valiant* (51), *Hondo* (53), *Johnny Guitar* (54), *The Halliday Brand* (57), *Rio Bravo* (59).

BOONE, RICHARD (1915-). A western actor (usually a heavy) since the early 50s. Played Sam Houston in Wayne's *The Alamo* (60) but gave perhaps his most satisfying performances as the outlaw figures in *The Tall T* (57) and *Hombre* (67). Films: *City Of Bad Men* (53), *The Siege At Red River* (54), *The Raid* (54), *Man Without A Star* (55), *A Thunder Of Drums* (61), *Rio Conchos* (64), *Big Jake* (71), *The Shootist* (76).

BOYD, WILLIAM (1898-1972). A leading star of the 20s (several films with DeMille) who later achieved even greater fame as Clarence E. Mulford's Hopalong Cassidy, a character he played on 66 occasions between 1935 and 1948. Howard Bretherton, Lesley Selander and George Archainbaud were among his regular directors and George Hayes, Jimmy Ellison, Russell Hayden and Andy Clyde among his co-stars. Last film in the series: *Strange Gamble*, directed by George Archainbaud in 1948.

BOYLE, CHARLES P. Colour cameraman, mostly on double feature Universal westerns and Walt Disney vehicles. Worked on the second unit crews of Ford's *Three Godfathers* (48) and *She Wore A Yellow Ribbon* (49) and also collaborated on the photography of Vidor's *Duel In The Sun* (46). Also: *Saddle Tramp* (50), *Apache Drums* (51), *Tomahawk/Battle Of Powder River* (51), *The Lady From Texas* (51), *The Cimarron Kid* (52), *The Battle At Apache Pass* (52), *Untamed Frontier* (52), *Horizons West* (52), *Gunsmoke* (53), *Column South* (53), *The Stand At Apache River* (53), *Davy Crockett, King Of The Wild Frontier* (55), *The Great Locomotive Chase* (56), *Westward Ho The Wagons!* (57).

BRACKETT, LEIGH (1918-1978). Woman novelist and scriptwriter associated in her later years with the films of Howard Hawks, including the westerns *Rio Bravo* (59), *El Dorado* (67) and *Rio Lobo* (70).

BRANDO, MARLON (1924-). A professional 'regulator' tracking rustlers in Montana in *The Missouri Breaks* (76) and an ex-outlaw bent on revenge in his own *One-Eyed Jacks* (61). Only two major westerns but each, in their own way, exceptional, the latter if only for being one of the most expensive and extravagant in the history of the genre — six months shooting, four million dollars over budget, a four hour running time trimmed to two hours twenty-one minutes! Also: *The Appaloosa* (66).

BRENNAN, WALTER (1984-1974). Veteran American character actor who enjoyed a long career in westerns, winning an Oscar for his portrayal of Judge Roy Bean in Wyler's *The Westerner* (40) and working on numerous occasions with Ford and Hawks. Specialized in grizzled old-timers. Major films: *Law And Order* (32), *Barbary Coast* (35), *Dakota* (45), *My Darling Clementine* (as Old Man Clanton) (46), *Red River* (48), *Along The Great Divide* (51), *The Far Country* (55), *The Proud Ones* (56), *Rio Bravo* (59), *How The West Was One* (63), *Support Your Local Sheriff* (69).

BRONSON, CHARLES (1922-). Like Clint Eastwood an actor who has spent as much time in the saddle as in limousines screeching round street corners. Several Indian portraits among his roles including the renegade Captain Jack of the Modoc tribe in Daves' *Drum Beat* (54) and the Apache half-breed in *Chato's Land* (72). Featured as Wild Bill Hickok in *The White Buffalo* (77). Films: *Apache* (54), *Vera Cruz* (54), *Jubal* (56), *Run Of The Arrow* (57), *Showdown At Boot Hill* (58), *The Magnificent Seven* (60), *A Thunder Of Drums* (61), *Four For Texas* (63), *Villa Rides!* (68), *Guns For San Sebastian* (68), *Once Upor A Time In The West* (69), *Red Sun* (72), *Chino* (76), *Breakheart Pass* (76), *From Noon Till Three* (76).

BROWN, JOHNNY MACK (1904-1974). One of the first actors to play Billy the Kid on the screen and a top star before devoting himself solely to B westerns. Made nearly a hundred and thirty westerns all told, averaging seven pictures a year during the 30s and 40s when he rivalled in popularity Gene Autry, Roy Rogers and William Boyd.

BRYNNER, YUL (1915-). Bald-headed American actor who led Steve McQueen, James Coburn and the rest in defence of the Mexican village in *The Magnificent Seven* (60). Also: *Invitation To A Gunfight* (64), *Return Of The Seven* (66), *Villa Rides!* (68), *Catlow* (71), *Westworld* (73), *Futureworld* (76) — appearing in both of the latter films as the robot Gunslinger.

BUCHANAN, EDGAR (1902-1979). A character performer in westerns since the early 40s, often cast as a crooked banker, mayor or doctor, but equally convincing when in more sympathetic vein, e.g. as the homesteader Lewis in *Shane* (53). Films: *When the Daltons Rode* (40), *Arizona* (40), *Texas* (41), *Buffalo Bill* (44), *The Man From Colorado* (48), *The Great Missouri Raid* (51), *Rawhide* (51), *Destry* (55), *Wichita* (55), *Cimarron* (60), *The Comancheros* (61), *Ride the High Country/Guns in the Afternoon* (62), *McLintock* (63), *Welcome to Hard Times/Killer on a Horse* (67).

BUSCH, NIVEN (1903-). Novelist/screenwriter who authored the original book of *Duel in the Sun* (46). A scriptwriter on numerous westerns since 1940. Films: *The Westerner* (40), *Belle Starr* (41), *Pursued* (47), *Distant Drums* (51), *The Man from the Alamo* (53), *The Treasure of Pancho Villa* (55).

BUTTOLPH, DAVID (1902-   ). Composer, first at Fox, later at Warner Bros. Over twenty western scores, including *Buffalo Bill* (44), *Colorado Territory* (49), *Along the Great Divide* (51), *Lone Star* (52), *The Bounty Hunter* (54), *Westbound* (59), *The Horse Soldiers* (59).

CAMERON, ROD (1912-   ). Star of many Republic westerns, former stunt man for Buck Jones. Films include *Dakota Lil* (50), *Oh! Susanna* (51), *Fort Osage* (52), *San Antone* (53), *Santa Fe Passage* (55), *Requiem for a Gunfighter* (65).

CANUTT, YAKIMA (1895-   ). Veteran second-unit director, former actor and Republic stunt man. Doubled as an Indian in the climax of Ford's *Stagecoach* (39) and performed several other daring stunts during the 30s and 40s. Later worked on the second units of several epics (see page 179) and westerns including *The Great Missouri Raid* (51), *Westward Ho The Wagons!* (57), *Cat Ballou* (65), *Blue* (68), *A Man Called Horse* (70), *Rio Lobo* (70), *Breakheart Pass* (76).

CAREY, HARRY (1880-1947). A major western star of the 1917-1930 period, when he starred in several John Ford movies at Universal. Later became a popular character actor. Last westerns: *Duel in the Sun* (46) and *Red River* (48). Films with Ford: *The Soul Herder* (17), *Cheyenne's Pal* (17), *Straight Shooting* (17), *The Secret Man* (17), *A Marked Man* (17), *Bucking Broadway* (17), *Wild Women* (18), *The Phantom Riders* (18), *Thieves Gold* (18), *The Scarlet Drop* (18), *Hell Bent* (18), *A Woman's Fool* (18), *Three Mounted Men* (18), *Roped* (19), *A Fight for Love* (19), *Riders of Vengeance* (19), *The Outcasts of Poker Flat* (19), *Ace of the Saddle* (19), *Rider of the Law* (19), *A Gunfightin' Gentleman* (19), *Marked Men* (19), *The Freeze Out* (21), *The Wallop* (21), *Desperate Trails* (21).

CAREY, HARRY, JUN. (1921-   ). Actor-son of Harry Carey, also used regularly by Ford, although only in supporting roles. Appeared mostly in cavalry parts in his seven pictures with the director. Films include: *Pursued* (47), *Red River* (48), *Three Godfathers* (48), *She Wore A Yellow Ribbon* (49), *Wagonmaster* (50), *Rio Grande* (50), *The Searchers* (56), *From Hell To Texas* (58), *Rio Bravo* (59), *Two Rode Together* (61), *The Comancheros* (61), *Cheyenne Autumn* (64), *Shenandoah* (65), *The Rare Breed* (66), *Alvarez Kelly* (66), *The Way West* (67), *Bandolero* (68), *The Undefeated* (69), *Death Of A Gunfighter* (69), *Dirty Dingus Magee* (70), *Big Jake* (71), *Something Big* (71), *One More Train To Rob* (71), *Cahill, United States Marshal* (73), *Take A Hard Ride* (75).

CARRADINE, JOHN (1906-   ). Supporting performer, seen in more than twenty westerns since playing assassin Bob Ford in *Jesse James* (39) and the gambler Hatfield in Ford's *Stagecoach* (39). A favourite performer of John Ford, he is to be glimpsed briefly in two of the director's last westerns, *The Man Who Shot Liberty Valance* (62) and *Cheyenne Autumn* (64). Films: *The Return Of Frank James* (40), *Western Union* (41), *Barbary Coast Gent* (44), *Johnny Guitar* (54), *Stranger On Horseback* (55), *The True Story Of Jesse James* (57), *The Proud Rebel* (58), *The Oregon Trail* (59), *The Good Guys And The Bad Guys* (69), *The McMasters* (69), *Five Bloody Graves* (70), *The Gatling Gun* (72), *The Shootist* (76), *The White Buffalo* (77).

CHANDLER, JEFF (1918-1961). Undervalued actor who made more than a dozen westerns during his short career. Appeared three times as the Indian chief Cochise, most memorably in Daves' *Broken Arrow* (50) and later in *Battle at Apache Pass* (52) and *Taza, Son of Cochise* (54). Also: *Two Flags West* (50), *The Great Sioux Uprising* (53), *The Spoilers* (55), *Pillars of the Sky* (56), *Drango* (57), *The Jayhawkers* (59), *The Plunderers* (60).

CHASE, BORDEN (1900-1971). Scriptwriter, author of some of the best westerns of Anthony Mann (three films), Robert Aldrich and Howard Hawks. Films: *Red River* (48), *Montana* (48), *Winchester 73* (50), *Lone Star* (52), *Bend Of The River* (52), *Vera Cruz* (54), *The Far Country* (55), *Man Without A Star* (55), *Backlash* (56), *Night Passage* (57), *Ride A Crooked Trail* (58), *Gunfighters Of Casa Grande* (65), *A Man Called Gannon* (69).

CLOTHIER, WILLIAM H. (1903-). Veteran cameraman who graduated from double-feature westerns to major productions of Wellman, Ford and, most recently, Andrew McLaglen. Achieved particularly striking results on Ford's last western, *Cheyenne Autumn* (64). Main films: *The Horse Soldiers* (59), *The Alamo* (60), *The Comancheros* (61), *The Deadly Companions* (61), *The Man Who Shot Liberty Valance* (62), *McLintock* (63), *Shenandoah* (65), *The Rare Breed* (66), *Stagecoach* (66), *The Way West* (67), *The War Wagon* (67), *Bandolero* (68), *The Undefeated* (69), *Chisum* (70), *The Cheyenne Social Club* (70), *Rio Lobo* (70), *Big Jake* (71), *The Train Robbers* (73).

COBURN, JAMES (1928-). The reluctant, but deadly knife thrower in *The Magnificent Seven* (60); Peckinpah's lawman in *Pat Garrett And Billy The Kid* (73); a contestant in the 700 mile endurance horse race in *Bite The Bullet* (75). The lean, rugged personality of this rangy actor has hovered engagingly over the western scene for some twenty years, since he debuted for Boetticher in *Ride Lonesome* (59). Also: *Major Dundee* (65), *Waterhole No. 3* (67), *The Honkers* (72), *The Last Hard Men* (76).

COOK, ELISHA JUN. (1907-   ). Thin-faced little character actor, best remembered for his portrayal of the sodbuster Torrey in *Shane* (53). Subsequent westerns include *Drumbeat* (54), *The Indian Fighter* (55), *The Lonely Man* (57), *One-Eyed Jacks* (61), *Welcome To Hard Times* (67), *The Great Train Robbery* (69), *El Condor* (70), *The Great Northfield Minnesota Raid* (72), *Pat Garrett And Billy The Kid* (73).

COOPER, GARY (1901-1961). American actor who made his most accomplished westerns during the 50s when he worked with Aldrich on *Vera Cruz* (54), won an Oscar for *High Noon* (52) and appeared for Anthony Mann in the underrated *Man of the West* (58). Made his first major western appearance in *The Winning of Barbara Worth* in 1926. Films: *Nevada* (27), *The Virginian* (29), *The Texan* (30), *The Spoilers* (30), *The Plainsman* (as Wild Bill Hickok) (37), *The Westerner* (40), *Dallas* (50), *Distant Drums* (51), *Springfield Rifle* (52), *Garden of Evil* (54), *The Hanging Tree* (59).

CRONJAGER, EDWARD (1904-1960). Oscar-winning cameraman of Wesley Ruggles' *Cimarron* (31). Westerns include *The Virginian* (29), *The Texas Rangers* (36), *Western Union* (41), *Canyon Passage* (46), *Best of the Badmen* (51), *Powder River* (53), *The Siege at Red River* (54).

CRUZE, JAMES (1884-1942). Director of the first 'epic' western, *The Covered Wagon* (23), a location-shot account of the crossing of America in 1849. Subsequent westerns — *The Pony Express* (25), *Helldorado* (34), *Sutter's Gold* (36) — only routine.

CURTIZ, MICHAEL (1888-1962). Curtiz's westerns were not as assured as some of his work in other genres but they contained some remarkable editing and superbly staged action sequences. The opening sixty minutes of his last film, *The Comancheros* (61), includes some of the best work of his career. Films: *Dodge City* (39), *Virginia City* (40), *Santa Fe Trail* (40), *The Proud Rebel* (58), *The Hangman* (59).

DANIELS, WILLIAM (1895-1970). American cameraman who worked with Anthony Mann on *Winchester 73* (50) and *The Far Country* (55). Also: *The Gal Who Took The West* (49), *War Arrow* (54), *Night Passage* (57), *How The West Was Won* (63) (co-photographed).

DAVES, DELMER (1904-1977). Together with John Ford, John Sturges and Anthony Mann, one of the major western directors of the post-war period. Eight westerns during the 50s including *Broken Arrow* (50) (see page 81) and *3.10 To Yuma* (57), a restricted tension movie in the *High Noon* tradition. Also: *Drumbeat* (54), *Jubal* (56), *The Last Wagon* (56), *Cowboy* (58), *The Badlanders* (58), *The Hanging Tree* (59). Co-scripted *White Feather* (55).

DE CARLO, YVONNE (1924-). Universal western star. Films (mostly double features) include *Black Bart* (48), *Calamity Jane And Sam Bass* (as Calamity Jane) (49), *The Gal Who Took The West* (49), *Tomahawk/Battle Of Powder River* (51), *Silver City* (51), *Border River* (54), *Shotgun* (55), *Raw Edge* (56), *McLintock* (63), *Law Of The Lawless* (64), *Hostile Guns* (67), *Arizona Bushwhackers* (67).

DEHNER, JOHN (1915-). American character actor most of whose western roles have been in routine B and double feature movies. The exceptions are his Pat Garrett in Penn's remarkable *The Left-Handed Gun* (58) and Cooper's outlaw cousin in *Man of the West* (58).

DEMILLE, CECIL B. (1881-1959). Showman director invariably linked with spectaculars (see page 179) and large-scale adventure movies (see page 230). Several enjoyable westerns during his career, including *The Squaw Man* (13), the first major film to be produced in Hollywood and *Union Pacific* (39), an account of the building of the famous Union Pacific Railway. Also: *The Squaw Man* (remade in 1918 and 1931), *The Virginian* (14), *Rose of the Rancho* (14), *The Girl of the Golden West* (14), *A Romance of the Redwoods* (17), *The Plainsman* (37).

DE TOTH, ANDRE (1900-). Hungarian-American director, many films with Randolph Scott, i.e. *Carson City* (52), *The Stranger Wore a Gun* (53), *Riding Shotgun* (54), *The Bounty Hunter* (54). Also: *Ramrod* (47), *Springfield Rifle* (52), *The Indian Fighter* (55), *Day of the Outlaw* (59). Co-authored the original story of King's *The Gunfighter* (50).

DEVINE, ANDY (1905-1977). A bumbling sheriff, stage coach driver or deputy in innumerable B westerns. Also worked for Ford on such ambitious productions as *Stagecoach* (39), *Two Rode Together* (61) and *The Man Who Shot Liberty Valance* (62). Among his other western features: *Geronimo* (40), *When the Daltons Rode* (40), *Canyon Passage* (46), *How the West Was Won* (63), *The Ballad of Josie* (68), *Ride a Northbound Horse* (69).

DIETRICH, MARLENE (1904-). German actress who made memorable western appearances for George Marshall in *Destry Rides Again* (as Frenchie) (39) and Fritz Lang in *Rancho Notorious* (52). Also played the female lead in Ray Enright's 1942 version of *The Spoilers*.

DIX, RICHARD (1894-1949). Early western star, best known for his performances as the Indian hero of *The Vanishing American* (26) and Yancey Cravat in the Oscar winning *Cimarron* (31). Also featured as real-life western figures in *Man of Conquest* (as Sam Houston) (39), *Badlands of Dakota* (as Wild Bill Hickok) (41) and *Tombstone, the Town Too Tough to Die* (as Wyatt Earp) (42).

DMYTRYK, EDWARD (1908-). American director with some very efficient westerns among his later work, especially the under-valued *Broken Lance* (54), with Spencer Tracy as a 'King Lear' of the prairies. Also: *Warlock* (59), *Alvarez Kelly* (66), *Shalako* (68).

DOUGLAS, GORDON (1909-). Director of several efficient westerns. Filmed the Jesse James story under the title *The Great Missouri Raid* (51) and remade Ford's *Stagecoach* in 1966. Also: *The Nevadan* (50), *Only the Valiant* (51), *The Iron Mistress* (52), *The Charge at Feather River* (53), *Yellowstone Kelly* (59), *Rio Conchos* (64), *Chuka* (67).

DOUGLAS, KIRK (1916-). A western performer since the early 50s when he appeared as the frontier adventurer Jim Deakins in Hawks' *The Big Sky* (52) and as the consumptive Doc Holliday in *Gunfight At The O.K. Corral* (57). Later made a memorable appearance as the fugitive cowboy in *Lonely Are The Brave* (62). Films: *Along The Great Divide* (51), *Man Without A Star* (55), *The Indian Fighter* (55), *Last Train From Gun Hill* (59), *The Last Sunset* (61), *The Way West* (67), *The War Wagon* (67), *There Was A Crooked Man* (70), *A Gunfight* (71), *Posse* (75) (also directed), *The Villain* (79).

DRU, JOANNE (1923-). A heroine in three major post-war westerns, i.e. Hawks' *Red River* (48) and Ford's *She Wore a Yellow Ribbon* (49) and *Wagonmaster* (50). Also: *Vengeance Valley* (51), *Outlaw Territory* (53), *The Siege at Red River* (54), *Drango* (57).

DUNING, GEORGE (1908-). A film composer since 1947. Westerns (mostly at Columbia) include *The Man from Laramie* (55), *3.10 to Yuma* (57), *Cowboy* (58), *Gunman's Walk* (58) and *Two Rode Together* (61).

DURYEA, DAN (1907-1968). Popular screen heavy who concentrated on westerns later in his career; particularly impressive as the outlaw Johnny Waco Dean in Mann's *Winchester 73* (50). Others: *Along Came Jones* (45), *Black Bart* (48), *Al Jennings of Oklahoma* (51), *Ride Clear of Diablo* (54), *Rails into Laramie* (54), *Night Passage* (57), *Taggart* (64), *The Bounty Killer* (65).

DUVALL, ROBERT (1931-   ). He rides wounded towards a helpless John Wayne, trapped beneath a fallen horse. Slowly he raises his gun. In the nick of time someone else brings him down but it's the nearest anyone has ever come to killing 'the duke' face to face in a western. The film? *True Grit* (69). The character? Robert Duvall as Ned Pepper, one of the meanest villains in recent westerns. Other Duvall contributions to the genre: *Lawman* (71), *Joe Kidd* (72), *The Great Northfield Minnesota Raid* (72) (as Jesse James).

EASTWOOD, CLINT (1930-   ). The dusty plains or the streets of urban America — it matters little to Clint Eastwood, who has been riding tight-lipped across the prairies for nearly two decades. Strictly a 'shoot first and forget it happened' guy, he made his mark as the man with no name in the spaghetti westerns of Sergio Leone and has since starred in and directed one of the few recent classics in the genre, *The Outlaw Josey Wales* (76). He even had the audacity to combine the horror movie with the western in the disquieting *High Plains Drifter* (73). Films: *A Fistful Of Dollars* (64), *For A Few Dollars More* (65), *The Good, The Bad And The Ugly* (66), *Hang 'Em High* (68), *Two Mules For Sister Sara* (70), *The Beguiled* (71), *Joe Kidd* (72).

ELAM, JACK (1917-   ). American supporting actor, a specialist in western villains since the 50s. Early roles only minor (he enjoyed one scene as the drunkard released from jail in Cooper's *High Noon*) but later established himself as a leading character actor, e.g. the preacher in *The Way West* (67), outlaw John Wesley Hardin in *Dirty Dingus Magee* (70) and the half-crazy old rancher in Hawks' *Rio Lobo* (70). Has worked with many leading western directors, including Hathaway, Mann and Sturges. Films: *Rawhide* (51), *Rancho Notorious* (52), *Vera Cruz* (54), *The Far Country* (55), *Man Without A Star* (55), *Wichita* (55), *The Man From Laramie* (55), *Jubal* (56), *Gunfight At The O.K. Corral* (57), *The Last Sunset* (61), *The Comancheros* (61), *The Rare Breed* (66), *Firecreek* (67), *Support Your Local Sheriff* (69), *The Wild Country* (71), *Hannie Caulder* (72), *Pat Garrett And Billy The Kid* (73), *Pony Express Rider* (76), *Grayeagle* (77).

ELLIOTT, 'WILD BILL' (1906-1965). Former rodeo rider who became a popular star in B westerns during the 30s and 40s. Over seventy westerns all told, many directed by Lambert Hillyer.

FLIPPEN, JAY C. (1899-1971). Veteran character actor whose good-natured, hard-bitten western characters were often a welcome contrast to the heavies of Dan Duryea and Jack Elam. Excellent as the old half-breed in Fuller's *Run of the Arrow* (57). Played his later roles in a wheel-chair after suffering a leg amputation. Major westerns: *Winchester 73* (50), *Two Flags West* (50), *Bend of the River* (52), *The Far Country* (55), *Man Without a Star* (55), *The Halliday Brand* (57), *From Hell to Texas* (58), *How the West Was Won* (63), *Cat Ballou* (65), *Firecreek* (67).

FLYNN, ERROL (1909-1959). Top box office star of the 40s; westerns only routine but always fast-moving and enjoyable. Films: *Dodge City* (39), *Virginia City* (40), *Santa Fe Trail* (40), *They Died With Their Boots On* (as General Custer) (41), *San Antonio* (45), *Silver River* (48), *Montana* (50), *Rocky Mountain* (50).

FONDA, HENRY (1905-). Leading western star who has made several films for John Ford, including *My Darling Clementine* (as Wyatt Earp) (46) and *Fort Apache* (as Colonel Owen Thursday, a character closely based on General Custer) (48). Appeared as the buffalo-hunter Jethro Stuart in the all-star *How The West Was Won* (63). Films: *Jesse James* (as Frank James) (39). *The Return Of Frank James* (as Frank) (40), *The Ox-Bow Incident* (42), *The Tin Star* (57), *Warlock* (59), *A Big Hand For The Little Lady* (66), *Welcome To Hard Times* (67), *Firecreek* (68), *Once Upon A Time In The West* (69), *The Cheyenne Social Club* (70), *There Was A Crooked Man* (70).

FORD, GLENN (1916-). Canadian-born actor, in westerns since 1941 when he appeared with William Holden in George Marshall's *Texas*. Later starred in three films for Delmer Daves — *Jubal* (56), *3.10 To Yuma* (57), *Cowboy* (58) — and played Yancey Cravatt in Mann's remake of *Cimarron* (60). Recent westerns: *The Long Ride Home* (67), *Pistolero Of Red River* (67), *Day Of The Evil Gun* (68), *Heaven With A Gun* (69), *Smith!* (69), *Santee* (73).

FORD, JOHN (1895-1973). The undisputed master of the western film. Over fifty films in the genre since first working in Hollywood in 1914, including at least three master works: *Stagecoach* (39), *She Wore a Yellow Ribbon* (49), *Wagonmaster* (50) — and several of near classic quality. Most of his early pictures starred Harry Carey and Tom Mix, most of his later ones John Wayne, Henry Fonda and James Stewart. Main pictures since *Stagecoach* (39): *My Darling Clementine* (46), *Fort Apache* (48), *Three Godfathers* (48), *She Wore a Yellow Ribbon* (49), *Wagonmaster* (50), *Rio Grande* (50), *The Searchers* (56), *The Horse Soldiers* (59), *Sergeant Rutledge* (60), *Two Rode Together* (61), *The Man Who Shot Liberty Valance* (62), *How the West Was Won* (Civil War Episode) (63), *Cheyenne Autumn* (64).

GABLE, CLARK (1901-1960). A Hollywood star for most of his career, Gable appeared in just half-a-dozen westerns, most of which were only routine. *The Tall Men* (55), however, with its wonderful cattle drive sequences is a remarkable film by any standards and one of the most accomplished westerns of the 50s. Also: *Across the Wide Missouri* (51), *Lone Star* (52), *The King and Four Queens* (56).

GARNER, JAMES (1928-). Former TV (*Maverick*) performer seen in several westerns in recent years. Played Wyatt Earp in John Sturges' underrated *Hour Of The Gun* (67), a sequel to the same director's earlier success *Gunfight At The O.K. Corral* (57). Also: *Duel At Diablo* (66), *Support Your Local Sheriff* (69), *A Man Called Sledge* (70), *Support Your Local Gunfighter* (71), *One Little Indian* (73), *The Castaway Cowboy* (74).

GLENNON, BERT (1895-1967). Cameraman who shot many John Ford westerns. Films: *Stagecoach* (39), *They Died With Their Boots On* (41), *San Antonio* (45), *Wagonmaster* (50), *Rio Grande* (50), *Sergeant Rutledge* (60).

GOLDSMITH, JERRY. American composer, active since the early 60s. Westerns: *Lonely Are The Brave* (62), *Rio Conchos* (64), *Stagecoach* (66), *Hour Of The Gun* (67), *Bandolero* (68), *100 Rifles* (69), *The Ballad Of Cable Hogue* (70), *Rio Lobo* (70), *The Wild Rovers* (71), *The Culpepper Cattle Company* (72), *One Little Indian* (73), *Take A Hard Ride* (75), *The Last Hard Men* (76), *Breakheart Pass* (76).

GRANT, JAMES EDWARD (1902-1966). American screenwriter, associated with westerns since 1947 when he wrote (and directed) *The Angel and the Badman*. Films (many for John Wayne): *California Passage* (50), *Hondo* (53), *The Last Wagon* (56), *Three Violent People* (56), *The Sheepman* (58), *The Alamo* (60), *The Comancheros* (61), *McLintock* (63).

GRIES, TOM (1922-1977). Writer/director who, with *Will Penny* (68), created one of the most authentic and realistic westerns of the post-war period. Also: *100 Rifles* (69) (also scripted), *Breakheart Pass* (76).

GUTHRIE, A. B. JUN. Distinguished American novelist chosen by George Stevens to author the screenplay of *Shane* (53). Also scripted Burt Lancaster's only directorial venture to date, *The Kentuckian* (55). Western novels inlude 'The Big Sky', 'These Thousand Hills' and 'The Way West'.

HAGEMAN, RICHARD (c.1882-1966). Composer, best known for his scores for John Ford westerns, i.e. *Stagecoach* (39), *Fort Apache* (48), *Three Godfathers* (48), *She Wore A Yellow Ribbon* (49), *Wagonmaster* (50).

HALL, CONRAD (1927-   ). Academy Award winning cameraman of *Butch Cassidy And The Sundance Kid* (69). Also: *The Professionals* (66) for Richard Brooks and *Tell Them Willie Boy Is Here* (69) for Polonsky.

HART, WILLIAM S. (1870-1946). The most legendary of the silent western stars, Hart was a Broadway actor before entering films in 1914. He appeared in a long series of two-reel and feature length westerns, directing many himself, and bringing to each film a realism that had been missing from the earlier efforts of Broncho Billy Anderson. Major films: *Hell's Hinges* (16), *The Narrow Trail* (17), *The Silent Man* (17), *Breed of Men* (19), *The Money Corral* (19), *Wagon Tracks* (19), *The Toll Gate* (20), *O'Malley of the Mounted* (20), *White Oak* (21), *Wild Bill Hickok* (23), *Tumbleweeds* (25).

HATHAWAY, HENRY (1898-   ). Veteran film maker who began his career in the early 30s directing Randolph Scott westerns at Universal. His handling of *True Grit* (69) has been one of the revelations of recent years. Films: *Heritage of the Desert* (32), *Wild Horse Mesa* (32), *Under the Tonto Rim* (33), *Sunset Pass* (33), *Man of the Forest* (33), *To the Last Man* (33), *The Thundering Herd* (33), *The Last Round-Up* (34) — all with Scott. Also: *Rawhide* (51), *Garden of Evil* (54) *From Hell to Texas* (58), *North to Alaska* (60), *How the West Was Won* (the sequences on the rivers, the plains and the outlaws) (63), *The Sons of Katie Elder* (65), *Nevada Smith* (66), *Five Card Stud* (68), *Shootout* (71).

HAWKS, HOWARD (1896-1977). A director of westerns since 1948 when he filmed the epic *Red River*, one of the most accomplished cattle drive movies of all time. Later directed the underrated *The Big Sky* (52), a pioneer story of the 1830s and *Rio Bravo* (59) with John Wayne and Dean Martin. Also: *El Dorado* (67), *Rio Lobo* (70).

HAYES, GEORGE (GABBY) (1885-1969). Grizzled, bewhiskered old-timer, a sidekick of Roy Rogers in more than forty movies. Over 170 westerns, many with William Boyd and John Wayne.

HEFLIN, VAN (1910-1971). Excellent actor whose western roles were few but notable, i.e. frontier scout Jim Bridger in *Tomahawk* (51), rancher Joe Starrett in *Shane* (53) and the farmer who escorts Glenn Ford to jail in *3.10 to Yuma* (57). Others: *Santa Fe Trail* (40), *Wings of the Hawk* (53), *The Raid* (54), *Gunman's Walk* (58), *Stagecoach* (66).

HESTON, CHARLTON (1924-   ). One of the most intelligent of contemporary screen actors, especially good as the vengeful Yankee major in Peckinpah's *Major Dundee* (65) and the roaming cow hand in *Will Penny* (68). Also: *The Savage* (52), *Pony Express* (as Buffalo Bill) (53), *Arrowhead* (53), *Three Violent People* (56), *The Big Country* (58), *The Last Hard Men* (76), *Wind River* (79).

HOCH, WINTON C. (1906-1979). Ford's colour cameraman on *Three Godfathers* (48), *She Wore A Yellow Ribbon* (49) and *The Searchers* (56). Also: *Tap Roots* (48), *The Sundowners* (50), *The Redhead From Wyoming* (52), *The Young Land* (59), *Sergeants Three* (62).

HOLDEN, WILLIAM (1918-   ). Top Hollywood star of the 50s. Western roles only routine until his performance as Pike, the leader of Sam Peckinpah's *The Wild Bunch* (69). Films: *Arizona* (40), *Texas* (41), *The Man from Colorado* (48), *Streets of Laredo* (49), *Escape from Fort Bravo* (53), *The Horse Soldiers* (59), *Alvarez Kelly* (66), *The Wild Rovers* (71), *The Revengers* (72).

HUFFAKER, CLAIR. Western novelist and screenwriter. Films: *Flaming Star* (60), *The Comancheros* (61), *Rio Conchos* (64), *The War Wagon* (67), *100 Rifles* (69), *Chino* (76).

HUNNICUTT, ARTHUR (1911-   ). Bearded character actor, especially good at portraying frontier scouts and western pioneers. Appeared as Davy Crockett in Frank Lloyd's *The Last Command* (55). Films: *Broken Arrow* (50), *Two Flags West* (50), *Distant Drums* (51), *The Big Sky* (52), *The Tall T* (57), *Cat Ballou* (65), *El Dorado* (67), *Shootout* (71), *The Revengers* (72), *The Spikes Gang* (74), *Winterhawk* (75).

INCE, THOMAS H. (1882-1924). Pioneer film maker associated, mostly as a producer but sometimes as a director, with over 150 films during his career. Produced many of Hart's early westerns and directed such one- and two-reelers as *Across the Plains/War on the Plains* (12), *The Raiders* (12), *The Renegade* (12), *Girl of the Golden West* (12), *Indian Massacre* (12), *Blazing the Trail* (12), *The Heart of an Indian* (13), *Days of 1849* (13).

IVES, BURL (1909-   ). Folk singer turned actor who won an Oscar for his portrayal of the outlaw cattleman in Wyler's *The Big Country* (58). Westerns: *Station West* (48), *Sierra* (50), *Day of the Outlaw* (59), *The McMasters* (69).

JOHNSON, BEN (1919-   ). Former stunt man, a western performer since the mid-40s. Appeared as cavalrymen in Ford's *Fort Apache* (48) and *She Wore A Yellow Ribbon* (49), one of Rykker's hired guns in *Shane* (53) and a member of Heston's punitive patrol in *Major Dundee* (65). Also: *Three Godfathers* (48), *Wagonmaster* (50), *Rio Grande* (50), *One-Eyed Jacks* (61), *The Rare Breed* (66), *The Wild Bunch* (69), *The Undefeated* (69), *Chisum* (70), *Something Big* (71), *The Train Robbers* (73), *Kid Blue* (73), *Bite The Bullet* (75), *Breakheart Pass* (76), *Grayeagle* (77).

JONES, BUCK (1891-1942). Popular star of B westerns. Over one hundred movies during the 20s and 30s, many directed by Lambert Hillyer, Ray Taylor and Howard Bretherton.

KANE, JOSEPH (1904-1975). Director of many Gene Autry and Roy Rogers vehicles at Republic. Later films at the studio more ambitious — *California Passage* (50), *Oh! Susanna* (51), *Jubilee Trail* (54) — but few in the top rank.

KENNEDY, ARTHUR (1914-   ). American actor, well used by Fritz Lang, Anthony Mann and Nicholas Ray during the 50s. At his best as the vengeful westerner in *Rancho Notorious* (52). Appeared briefly as Doc Holliday in Ford's *Cheyenne Autumn* (64). Also: *They Died With Their Boots On* (41), *Cheyenne* (47), *Red Mountain* (51), *Bend of the River* (52), *The Man From Laramie* (55), *The Rawhide Years* (56), *Nevada Smith* (66), *Day of the Evil Gun* (68).

KENNEDY, BURT (1923-   ). Apart from Andrew V. McLaglen and Sam Peckinpah, the only contemporary American director to concentrate almost exclusively on the western. Worked on Boetticher scripts before graduating to director status on *The Canadians* (61). Films: *Mail Order Bride* (also screen.) (64), *The Rounders* (also screen.) (65), *Return Of The Seven* (66), *Welcome To Hard Times* (also screen.) (67), *The War Wagon* (67), *Support Your Local Sheriff* (69), *The Good Guys And The Bad Guys* (69), *Young Billy Young* (also screen.) (69), *Dirty Dingus Magee* (70), *Support Your Local Gunfighter* (71), *Hannie Caulder* (72), *The Train Robbers* (also screen.) (73).

KENNEDY, GEORGE (1927-   ). Character actor, seen in many westerns during the 60s. Took over from Yul Brynner as the leader of the outlaw gang in *Guns Of The Magnificent Seven* (69). Films: *Lonely Are The Brave* (62), *Shenandoah* (65), *The Sons Of Katie Elder* (65), *The Ballad Of Josie* (68), *Bandolero* (68), *The Good Guys And The Bad Guys* (69), *Dirty Dingus Magee* (70), *Cahill, United States Marshal* (73).

KING, HENRY (1896-). Not a western director in the true sense of the word but the maker of *The Gunfighter* (50), one of the first of the realistic westerns and the movie which gave Gregory Peck one of his best ever roles as Jimmy Ringo, an ageing outlaw who attempts to live down his past. Also: *The Winning of Barbara Worth* (26), *Jesse James* (39), *The Bravados* (58).

LADD, ALAN (1913-1964). Former tough guy actor (see page 67), who became a popular western star towards the end of his career. Magnificent in the title role in Stevens' classic *Shane* (53). Others: *Whispering Smith* (49), *Branded* (50), *Red Mountain* (51), *The Iron Mistress* (as Jim Bowie) (52), *Drumbeat* (54), *The Proud Rebel* (58), *The Badlanders* (58), *Guns of the Timberland* (60).

LANCASTER, BURT (1913-). Like Richard Widmark, Kirk Douglas and Robert Mitchum, one of the major stars to emerge after the end of World War II. Western roles somewhat varied, the best occurring in the early 50s when he played Masai in Robert Aldrich's *Apache* (54) and the smiling outlaw Joe Erin in the same director's *Vera Cruz* (54). Also appeared as Wyatt Earp in *Gunfight At The O.K. Corral* (57). Films: *Vengeance Valley* (51), *The Kentuckian* (also directed) (55), *The Unforgiven* (60), *The Hallelujah Trail* (65), *The Professionals* (66), *The Scalphunters* (68), *Lawman* (71), *Valdez Is Coming* (71), *Ulzana's Raid* (72), *Buffalo Bill And The Indians* (76) (as Ned Buntine), *Cattle Annie And Little Britches* (79).

LANG, CHARLES B., JUN. (1902-). One of the most accomplished cameramen ever to work in Hollywood. Achieved some remarkable results during the 50s and 60s, especially on the Brando western *One-Eyed Jacks* (61), which contains some of the finest Technicolor ever seen in an American film. Westerns include *Copper Canyon* (50), *Branded* (50), *Red Mountain* (51), *The Man From Laramie* (55), *Gunfight at the O.K. Corral* (57), *Last Train from Gun Hill* (59), *The Magnificent Seven* (60), *How the West Was Won* (co-phot.) (63), *The Stalking Moon* (69).

LANG, FRITZ (1890-1976). German director of just three westerns, among them *Rancho Notorious* (52), a brutal story of revenge notable for its haunting '*Chuck-a-Luck*' ballad and the performance of Marlene Dietrich. Worked briefly on *Winchester 73* (50) before relinquishing the film to Anthony Mann. Others: *The Return of Frank James* (40), *Western Union* (41).

LAWTON, CHARLES. Columbia cameraman who did distinguished work for Ford and particularly Daves — *Jubal* (56), *3.10 to Yuma* (57), *Cowboy* (58) — after a long career on double feature westerns. Other major films: *The Tall T* (57), *Gunman's Walk* (58), *Two Rode Together* (61).

LEMAY, ALAN (1899-1964). Novelist/screenwriter, long associated with the western genre. Screenplays include *San Antonio* (45), *Cheyenne* (47), *The Walking Hills* (49), *High Lonesome* (also dir.) (50), *Rocky Mountain* (50). Western novels: 'The Searchers', 'The Unforgiven'.

LYLES, A. C. (1918-   ). American producer who has revived the double feature western in recent years often including as many as six former stars in his productions. Howard Keel, Jane Russell, Broderick Crawford, Yvonne de Carlo, Brian Donlevy and Virginia Mayo are among those who have played in his films which include *Young Fury* (65), *Apache Uprising* (66), *Waco* (66), *Red Tomahawk* (67), *Fort Utah* (67), *Hostile Guns* (67), *Arizona Bushwhackers* (68), *Buckskin* (68).

MACDONALD, JOE (1906-1968). Fox cameraman, at his peak during the late 40s when he photographed *My Darling Clementine* (46) for Ford and the desert western *Yellow Sky* (48) for Wellman. Later worked on several westerns for Edward Dmytryk including *Broken Lance* (54), *Warlock* (59) and *Alvarez Kelly* (66). Also: *The True Story of Jesse James* (57), *Rio Conchos* (64), *Invitation to a Gunfighter* (64), *Mackenna's Gold* (69).

MALDEN, KARL (1913-   ). Benevolent as a TV cop in *Streets Of San Francisco* but out West this talented method actor has often been a man to avoid, especially in *Nevada Smith* (66) as one of the rapist murderers hunted down by Steve McQueen and *One-Eyed Jacks* (61) when he clubs Brando's gun hand to a pulp and whips him to within an inch of his life. Westerns: *The Gunfighter* (50), *The Hanging Tree* (59), *How The West Was Won* (63), *Cheyenne Autumn* (64), *Blue* (68), *Wild Rovers* (72).

MCCREA, JOEL (1905-   ). American actor who reached stardom as a dramatic and comedy performer during the 30s then later turned to western roles. Played several real-life western characters during his career, including William Cody in *Buffalo Bill* (44), Wyatt

Earp in *Wichita* (55), Sam Houston in *The First Texan* (56) and
Bat Masterson in *The Gunfight at Dodge City* (59). Came out of
retirement in 1962 to play opposite Randolph Scott in Peckinpah's
Ride the High Country/Guns in the Afternoon. Also: *Wells Fargo*
(37), *Union Pacific* (39), *The Virginian* (46), *Ramrod* (47), *South of
St. Louis* (49), *Colorado Territory* (49), *The Outriders* (50), *Saddle
Tramp* (50), *Cattle Drive* (51), *Border River* (54), *Stranger on
Horseback* (55), *Cattle Empire* (58), *Mustang Country* (76).

MCLAGLEN, ANDREW V. (1920-   ). British-born director who has
developed as the natural successor to John Ford after working as
his assistant during the 50s. The Civil War drama, *Shenandoah*
(65), with James Stewart is perhaps the most accomplished of his
westerns to date. Films: *McLintock* (63), *The Rare Breed* (66),
The Way West (67), *The Ballad Of Josie* (68), *Bandolero* (68),
The Undefeated (69), *Chisum* (70), *Something Big* (71), *One More
Train to Rob* (71), *Cahill, United States Marshal* (73), *The Last
Hard Men* (76).

MCLAGLEN, VICTOR (1886-1959). Irish-born actor, father of Andrew.
Several films for Ford, including the Cavalry trilogy *Fort Apache*
(48), *She Wore a Yellow Ribbon* (49) and *Rio Grande* (50).

MANN, ANTHONY (1907-1967). Talented director who switched to
westerns after making a number of accomplished B thrillers early
in his career. During the 50s enjoyed a nine picture association
with James Stewart, many of their films together falling into the
western category. *Winchester 73* remains the most accomplished of
all his westerns. Films (with Stewart): *Winchester 73* (50), *Bend
of the River* (52), *The Naked Spur* (53), *The Far Country* (55),
The Man from Laramie (55). Others: *Devil's Doorway* (50), *The
Furies* (50), *The Last Frontier* (56), *The Tin Star* (57), *Man of the
West* (58), *Cimarron* (60).

MARSHAL, GEORGE (1891-1975). Veteran director whose *Destry
Rides Again* (39) with James Stewart and Marlene Dietrich was
the best known spoof western before the production of *Cat Ballou*
in 1965. Several Tom Mix movies early in his career. Main films:
When the Daltons Rode (40), *Texas* (41), *Destry* (55), *Pillars of
the Sky* (56), *The Sheepman* (58), *How the West Was Won* (the
railroad sequences) (63).

MARTIN, DEAN (1917-   ). Crooner, ex-partner of Jerry Lewis, who
has given a number of interesting western performances since
appearing as John Wayne's drunken deputy in *Rio Bravo* (59).
Films: *Four for Texas* (63), *The Sons of Katie Elder* (65), *Texas*

Across the River (66), *Rough Night in Jericho* (67), *Bandolero* (68), *Five Card Stud* (68), *Something Big* (71), *Showdown* (73).

MARTIN, STROTHER (1920-   ) Supporting actor. Minor roles in many westerns including *The Wild Bunch* (as one of Robert Ryan's posse) (69) and *Butch Cassidy And The Sundance Kid* (as the foreman of the silver mine) (69). Others: *The Deadly Companions* (61), *The Man Who Shot Liberty Valance* (62), *McLintock* (63), *Invitation To A Gunfighter* (64), *The Sons Of Katie Elder* (65), *Shenandoah* (65), *True Grit* (69), *The Ballad Of Cable Hogue* (70), *Hannie Caulder* (72), *Rooster Cogburn* (75), *Great Scout And Cathouse Thursday* (76), *The Villain* (79).

MARVIN, LEE (1924-   ). American actor who featured as a supporting heavy for more than ten years before winning an Oscar for his drunken gunfighter Kid Shelleen in *Cat Ballou* (65), Appeared briefly but memorably as the half-scalped gun runner in *The Comancheros* (61) and the outlaw Liberty Valance in Ford's *The Man Who Shot Liberty Valance* (62). More recently starred as the ageing cowboy *Monte Walsh* (70). Also: *Duel At Silver Creek* (52), *Seminole* (53), *Gun Fury* (53), *Seven Men From Now* (56), *The Professionals* (66), *The Spikes Gang* (74), *Great Scout And Cathouse Thursday* (76).

MEYER, EMILE (1903-   ). American character actor whose performance as the cattle baron Ryker in *Shane* (53) started him on a long career in westerns. Main films: *White Feather* (55), *Stranger on Horseback* (55), *The Tall Men* (55), *The Maverick Queen* (56), *Young Jesse James* (60), *Taggart* (64).

MITCHELL, THOMAS (1895-1962). One of Hollywood's most talented character actors, Mitchell won an Academy Award for his drunken Doc Boone in Ford's classic *Stagecoach* (39) and later featured for Howard Hughes as Sheriff Pat Garrett in *The Outlaw* (46). Also: *Buffalo Bill* (44), *Silver River* (48), *High Noon* (52), *Destry* (55).

MITCHUM, ROBERT (1917-   ). American actor who began in Gene Autry's 'Hopalong Cassidy' westerns of the early 40s. Appeared for Howard Hawks in *El Dorado* (67) when he repeated Dean Martin's *Rio Bravo* role. Major films: *Pursued* (47), *Rachel and the Stranger* (48), *Blood on the Moon* (48), *River of No Return* (54), *Bandido* (56), *The Wonderful Country* (59), *The Way West* (67), *Five Card Stud* (68), *Young Billy Young* (69), *The Good Guys and the Bad Guys* (69).

MIX. TOM (1881-1940). Top western star of the 20s renowned for his magnificent riding abilities and stunt work. A former cowboy, rodeo rider, sheriff and Texas ranger before entering films. Over 130 movies all told, many of which were photographed by veteran cameraman, Daniel B. Clark.

MOROSS, JEROME. Composer of the memorable score for Wyler's *The Big Country* (58). Others in the genre: *The Proud Rebel* (58), *The Jayhawkers* (59).

MURPHY, AUDIE (1924-1971). Famed World War II hero who became one of Universal's biggest box-office stars of the 50s. Over thirty double feature westerns, many directed by Nathan Juran, Jesse Hibbs and George Marshall. Major westerns: *Texas Kid Outlaw* (50), *Kansas Raiders* (50), *The Cimarron Kid* (52), *Duel at Silver Creek* (52), *Destry* (55), *Walk the Proud Land* (56), *Night Passage* (57), *The Unforgiven* (60), *Six Black Horses* (62), *The Texican* (66).

NEWMAN, ALFRED (1901-1970). Composer of the magnificent scores for *How the West Was Won* (63) and *Nevada Smith* (66). Earlier westerns mostly at Fox: *Belle Starr* (41), *Yellow Sky* (48), *The Gunfighter* (50).

NEWMAN, PAUL (1925-   ). Leading American actor whose performance as Butch in *Butch Cassidy And The Sundance Kid* (69) is one of the best western characterizations of recent years. Excellent also as Billy the Kid in Arthur Penn's *The Left-Handed Gun* (58) the half-breed in Martin Ritt's *Hombre* (66) and William F. Cody in Altman's *Buffalo Bill And The Indians* (76). Also: *The Life And Times Of Judge Roy Bean* (72).

NICHOLS, DUDLEY (1895-1960). Celebrated screenwriter, many films for John Ford including *Stagecoach* (39). Later worked on Hathaway's underrated *Rawhide* (51) and Hawks' *The Big Sky* (52). Others: *The Tin Star* (57), *The Hangman* (59), *Heller in Pink Tights* (60).

NUGENT, FRANK S. (1908-1965). Another of Ford's regular screenwriters. Several films in the western genre, including the first two movies in the director's cavalry trilogy, *Fort Apache* (48), and *She Wore a Yellow Ribbon* (49). Also: *Three Godfathers* (48), *Wagonmaster* (50), *Two Flags West* (50), *The Tall Men* (55), *The Searchers* (56), *Gunman's Walk* (58), *Two Rode Together* (61).

OATES, WARREN (1932-   ). A favourite performer of Sam Peckinpah and Burt Kennedy. Played one of William Holden's doomed outlaw gang in *The Wild Bunch* (69). Westerns: *Yellowstone Kelly* (59), *Ride The High Country/Guns In The Afternoon* (62), *Mail Order Bride* (64), *Major Dundee* (65), *The Shooting* (66), *Return Of The Seven* (66), *Welcome To Hard Times* (67), *There Was A Crooked Man* (70), *Kid Blue* (73).

O'BRIEN, GEORGE (1900-   ). Western star of Ford's *The Iron Horse* (24) and numerous Zane Grey westerns of the 30s. Later featured in character roles for Ford in *Fort Apache* (48), *She Wore A Yellow Ribbon* (49) and *Cheyenne Autumn* (64).

O'HARA, MAUREEN (1920-   ). A favourite leading lady of John Ford and Andrew McLaglen, frequently cast opposite John Wayne. Westerns: *Buffalo Bill* (44), *Rio Grande* (50), *The Deadly Companions* (61), *McLintock* (63), *The Rare Breed* (66), *Big Jake* (71).

PALANCE, JACK (1920-   ). American actor who achieved lasting fame as the hired gunfighter Wilson in Steven's classic *Shane* (53). Later parts less than memorable, although his cowhand-turned-storekeeper in *Monte Walsh* (70) ranks as one of the most thoughtful of recent performances in the genre. Films include *Arrowhead* (53), *The Lonely Man* (57), *The Professionals* (66), *The Desperados* (69), *The McMasters* (69), *Chato's Land* (72).

PECK, GREGORY (1916-   ). Leading American performer, more successful in straight drama than in westerns but outstanding as the ageing outlaw Jimmy Ringo in King's *The Gunfighter* (50). Also: *Duel In The Sun* (46), *Yellow Sky* (48), *Only The Valiant* (51), *The Bravados* (58), *The Big Country* (58), *How The West Was Won* (63), *The Stalking Moon* (69), *MacKenna's Gold* (69), *Shootout* (71), *Billy Two Hats* (74).

PECKINPAH, SAM (1926-   ). The most exciting director to work in the genre since Ford. One masterwork, *Ride The High Country/Guns In The Afternoon* (62), and two near classics, *Major Dundee* (65) and *The Wild Bunch* (69), during his spectacular career. Others: *The Deadly Companions* (61), *The Glory Guys* (screenplay only) (65), *The Ballad Of Cable Hogue* (70), *Pat Garrett And Billy The Kid* (73).

PORTER, EDWIN S. (1869-1941). The producer, director, writer and cameraman of the first western movie, *The Great Train Robbery* (03), a nine-minute film that started Broncho Billy

Anderson on his long career. Nearly twenty westerns during the 1904-10 period, including *Rounding Up and Branding Cattle* (04), *The Western Stage* (04), *Trapped by Nat Pinkerton* (04), *The Hold-Up of the Leadville Stage* (04), *The Train Wreckers* (05), *The Life of an American Cowboy* (06), *Daniel Boone* (07), *On the Western Frontier* (09), *Pony Express* (09), *The Luck of Roaring Camp* (10).

POWER, TYRONE (1914-1958). American leading man, the most famous of all screen actors to play *Jesse James* (39). Other westerns: *Rawhide* (51), *Pony Soldier* (52).

QUINN, ANTHONY (1915-   ). Mexican actor who started in DeMille's Paramount westerns *The Plainsman* (37) and *Union Pacific* (39). Often cast as an Indian early in his career but later roles e.g. Henry Fond's crippled sidekick in *Warlock* (59) and the cattle baron in *Last Train from Gun Hill* (59), more ambitious. Films: *They Died with their Boots On* (41), *The Ox-Bow Incident* (42), *Buffalo Bill* (44), *Black Gold* (47), *Seminole* (53), *Ride Vaquero!* (53), *The Man from Del Rio* (56), *The Ride Back* (57), *Heller in Pink Tights* (60).

RENNAHAN, RAY (1898-   ). The most important of the early Hollywood cameramen to work with the Technicolor process. Shot numerous westerns at Fox and Paramount during the 40s and 50s, including *Belle Starr* (41), *California* (46), *Duel in the Sun* (co-(phot.) (46), *The Paleface* (48), *Whispering Smith* (49), *Streets of Laredo* (49), *The Great Missouri Raid* (51), *Warpath* (51), *Pony Express* (53), *Arrowhead* (53), *The Halliday Brand* (57).

ROGERS, ROY (1912-   ). One of the best known of the singing cowboys, Rogers began in minor parts in Gene Autry pictures then superseded that performer in popularity during the 40s. Nearly ninety B westerns, many with Dale Evans and George 'Gabby' Hayes. Famous for his association with the horse 'Trigger'.

ROSENBERG, AARON (1912-   ). A Universal producer for many years; three films for Anthony Mann, i.e., *Winchester 73* (50), *Bend of the River* (52), *The Far Country* (55). Also: *Cattle Drive* (51), *The Man from the Alamo* (53), *Saskatchewan* (54), *Man Without a Star* (55), *Backlash* (56), *Night Passage* (57), *The Badlanders* (58), *Smoky* (66).

RUGGLES, WESLEY (1889-1972). American director of *Cimarron* (31), still the only western to date to be named Best Film of the

Year by The Academy of Motion Picture Arts and Sciences. Later filmed *Arizona* (40) with Jean Arthur and William Holden.

RUSSELL, JANE (1921-   ). Actress who has appeared as two of the West's most famous real-life characters, i.e., Calamity Jane in the Bob Hope comedy *The Paleface* (48) and Belle Starr in *Montana Belle* (52). Also: *The Outlaw* (46), *Son of Paleface* (52), *The Tall Men* (55), *Johnny Reno* (66), *Waco* (66).

RYAN, ROBERT (1913-1973). American performer whose western roles include the Sundance Kid in *Return of the Bad Men* (48) and Ike Clanton in Sturges' *Hour of the Gun* (67). Superb as the leader of the posse, Deke Thornton, in Peckinpah's *The Wild Bunch* (69). Films: *Trail Street* (47), *The Naked Spur* (53), *The Tall Men* (55), *The Proud Ones* (56), *Day of the Outlaw* (59), *The Professionals* (66) *Custer of the West* (68), *Lawman* (71).

SCOTT, RANDOLPH (1903-   ). Veteran actor who appeared in scores of routine but enjoyable westerns before achieving respectability with the critics as the ageing outlaw in Sam Peckinpah's *Ride the High Country/Guns in the Afternoon* (62). Over sixty westerns, many for Boetticher, including *Jesse James* (39), *Frontier Marshal* (as Wyatt Earp) (39), *Virginia City* (40), *When the Daltons Rode* (40), *Western Union* (41), *Belle Starr* (41), *The Spoilers* (42), *Badman's Territory* (46), *Trail Street* (as Bat Masterson) (47), *Canadian Pacific* (49), *Colt 45* (50), *Santa Fe* (51), *Carson City* (52), *The Bounty Hunter* (54), *Seven Men from Now* (56), *The Tall T* (57), *Decision at Sundown* (57), *Buchanan Rides Alone* (58), *Ride Lonesome* (59), *Westbound* (59), *Comanche Station* (60).

SHERMAN, GEORGE (1908-   ). Competent director of Gene Autry B westerns and double feature productions at Universal. Best achievement: *Tomahawk* (51), one of the earliest films to portray the American Indian in a sympathetic light. Universal pictures include *Black Bart* (48), *Calamity Jane and Sam Bass* (49), *Comanche Territory* (50), *The Battle of Apache Pass* (52), *Dawn at Socorro* (54). Also: *Big Jake* (71).

STANWYCK, BARBARA (1907-   ). A feminine lead in several westerns after playing the legendary sharpshooter *Annie Oakley* in 1936. Films: *Union Pacific* (39), *California* (46), *The Furies* (50), *Cattle Queen of Montana* (54), *The Violent Men* (55), *The Maverick Queen* (56), *Forty Guns* (57).

STEINER, MAX (1888-1972). Austrian-born composer whose work

ranged over many genres. Scored the Academy Award winning *Cimarron* (31) at RKO then worked for more than two decades at Warners. Western scores include *Dodge City* (39), *Virginia City* (40), *Santa Fe Trail* (40), *They Died With their Boots On* (41), *San Antonio* (45), *Pursued* (47), *Cheyenne* (47), *Silver River* (48), *Rocky Mountain* (50), *Dallas* (50), *Distant Drums* (51), *The Last Command* (55), *The Searchers* (56).

STEVENS, GEORGE (1904-1975). Director, former cameraman included here for just one film, *Shane* (53), the most stylish and arguably the greatest western of all time (see page 82).

STEWART, JAMES (1908-). The leading actor in nearly twenty westerns since making his début in the genre as the peace-loving deputy in *Destry Rides Again* (39). Several films for Mann, Daves and Ford, appearing briefly for the latter director as Wyatt Earp in *Cheyenne Autumn* (64). Films: *Winchester 73* (50), *Broken Arrow* (50), *Bend of the River* (52), *The Naked Spur* (53), *The Far Country* (55), *The Man from Laramie* (55), *Two Rode Together* (61), *The Man Who Shot Liberty Valance* (62), *How the West Was Won* (63), *Shenandoah* (65), *The Rare Breed* (66), *Bandolero* (68), *The Cheyenne Social Club* (70), *The Shootist* (76).

STRADLING, HARRY, JUN. Son of the great cameraman Harry Stradling (see page 143) and something of a specialist in westerns in recent years. Shot *Little Big Man* (70) for Arthur Penn as well as several films for Burt Kennedy, i.e. *Support Your Local Sheriff* (69), *Young Billy Young* (69), *The Good Guys And The Bad Guys* (69), *Dirty Dingus Magee* (70). Also: *There Was A Crooked Man* (70), *Something Big* (71), *The Man Who Loved Cat Dancing* (73), *Bite The Bullet* (75), *Rooster Cogburn* (75).

STRODE, WOODY (1923-). Negro actor best known for his performance as the accused soldier in Ford's *Sergeant Rutledge* (60). Also: *The Man Who Shot Liberty Valance* (as Wayne's farmhand, Pompey) (62), *The Professionals* (as the bow and arrow tracker) (66), *Shalako* (68), *The Revengers* (72), *The Gatling Gun* (72), *Winterhawk* (75).

STURGES, JOHN (1911-). Director of *The Magnificent Seven* (60), one of the most popular of all post-war westerns. Portrayed the Earp-Clanton battle in *Gunfight At The O.K. Corral* (57) and the aftermath in the little-known *Hour Of The Gun* (67). Films: *The Walking Hills* (49), *Escape From Fort Bravo* (53) *Backlash* (56), *The Law And Jake Wade* (58), *Last Train From Gun Hill* (59), *The Hallelujah Trail* (65), *Joe Kidd* (72), *Chino* (76).

SURTEES, BRUCE. American cameraman with many westerns among his recent work: *The Hallelujah Trail* (65), *The Beguiled* (71), *The Great Northfield Minnesota Raid* (72), *Joe Kidd* (72), *High Plains Drifter* (73), *The Outlaw Josey Wales* (76), *The Shootist* (76).

TIOMKIN, DIMITRI (1899-   ). Russian-born composer, long in America, at his best when working in the western genre. Academy Awards for his score of *High Noon* (52) and the song 'Do Not Forsake Me Oh My Darling'. Numerous compositions for Hawks, e.g. *Red River* (48), *The Big Sky* (52), *Rio Bravo* (59). Other western scores: *The Westerner* (40). *Duel In The Sun* (46), *The Command* (54), *Gunfight At The O.K. Corral* (57), *Night Passage* (57), *Last Train From Gun Hill* (59), *The Unforgiven* (60), *The Alamo* (60), *The War Wagon* (67).

TOURNEUR, JACQUES (1904-1977). Director, whose few westerns include *Canyon Passage* (46), notable as being one of the best examples of 40s Technicolor, and *Wichita* (55), a small-scale western featuring Joel McCrea as Wyatt Earp. Others: *Way of a Gaucho* (52), *Stranger on Horseback* (55), *Great Day in the Morning* (56).

TREVOR, CLAIRE (1912-   ). A familiar bad girl and saloon hostess since playing Dallas in John Ford's *Stagecoach* (39). Westerns: *The Dark Command* (40), *Texas* (41), *The Desperados* (43), *Best of the Badmen* (51), *Man Without a Star* (55).

VAN CLEEF, LEE (1925-   ). A minor heavy in more than thirty Hollywood movies before achieving fame in Italy in the westerns *For A Few Dollars More* (65) and *The Good, The Bad And The Ugly* (66). Now a major western star in his own right. Films include *High Noon* (as one of the outlaws waiting for the noon train) (52), *The Lawless Breed* (53), *Man Without A Star* (55), *Tribute To A Bad Man* (56), *Gunfight At The O.K. Corral* (57), *The Lonely Man* (57), *The Tin Star* (58), *The Bravados* (58), *The Man Who Shot Liberty Valance* (as Lee Marvin's side-kick) (62), *How The West Was Won* (63), *El Condor* (70), *Captain Apache* (71), *Bad Man's River* (71), *The Magnificent Seven Ride!* (72), *Take A Hard Ride* (75), *The Stranger And The Gunfighter* (76).

VIDOR, KING (1896-   ). The director of Selznick's famous super spectacle, *Duel in the Sun* (46), a bizarre, often crude western but with many brilliant moments, e.g. the Tilly Losch dance in the saloon, the race to the picket fence and the climax on the mountain. Films: *Billy the Kid* (30), *The Texas Rangers* (36), *Man Without a Star* (55).

WALSH, RAOUL (1892-). Director of *In Old Arizona* (29) and *The Big Trail* (30), two of the most important large-scale westerns of the early sound period. Most accomplished work in the genre: *The Tall Men* (55), a cattle drive western starring Clark Gable and Jane Russell. Other westerns (many at Warners): *The Dark Command* (40), *They Died With Their Boots On* (41), *Pursued* (47), *Cheyenne* (47), *Silver River* (48), *Colorado Territory* (49), *Along the Great Divide* (51), *Distant Drums* (51), *The Lawless Breed* (53), *Saskatchewan* (54), *The King and Four Queens* (56), *A Distant Trumpet* (64).

WAYNE, JOHN (1907-1979). The one actor who everyone associates with the western genre. Since his debut in *The Big Trail* in 1930 he featured in eighty westerns, including several for John Ford and Howard Hawks. Among his most famous roles: the Ringo Kid in Ford's *Stagecoach* (39), cattle baron Tom Dunson in *Red River* (48), Captain Nathan Brittles in *She Wore A Yellow Ribbon* (49) and Marshal Rooster Cogburn in *True Grit* (AA) (69). Major films: *The Dark Command* (40), *The Spoilers* (42), *Dakota* (45), *Fort Apache* (48), *Three Godfathers* (48), *Rio Grande* (50), *Hondo* (53), *The Searchers* (56), *Rio Bravo* (59), *The Horse Soldiers* (59), *North To Alaska* (60), *The Alamo* (also dir.) (60), *The Comancheros* (61), *The Man Who Shot Liberty Valance* (62), *How The West Was Won* (63), *McLintock* (63), *The Sons Of Katie Elder* (65), *El Dorado* (66), *The War Wagon* (67), *The Undefeated* (69), *Chisum* (70), *Rio Lobo* (70), *Big Jake* (71), *The Cowboys* (72), *The Train Robbers* (73), *Cahill, United States Marshal* (73), *Rooster Cogburn* (75), *The Shootist* (76).

WEBB, JAMES R. (1912-1974). A western writer since the early 40s when he scripted Roy Rogers B pictures. Later worked with distinction for Aldrich on *Apache* (54), and *Vera Cruz* (54), Wyler on *The Big Country* (58) and Ford on *Cheyenne Autumn* (64). Also wrote the story and screenplay for the multi-starred Cinerama epic *How the West Was Won* (63).

WELLMAN, WILLIAM A. (1896-1975). Veteran film-maker often likened to Howard Hawks in his choice of subject material. Although not strictly a western, his *The Ox-Bow Incident* (42), a savage story of a 19th century lynching, remains the most accomplished of all his works. Westerns include *Robin Hood of El Dorado* (36), *Buffalo Bill* (44), *Yellow Sky* (48), *Across the Wide Missouri* (51), *Westward the Women* (52).

WIDMARK, RICHARD (1915-). Talented American actor who has transferred his bad guy image to numerous westerns, including *Yellow Sky* (48), *Broken Lance* (54), and *The Law and Jake Wade*

(58). Has occasionally portrayed more heroic figures such as Jim Bowie in *The Alamo* (60). Also: *Garden of Evil* (54), *Backlash* (56), *The Last Wagon* (56), *Warlock* (59), *Two Rode Together* (61), *How the West Was Won* (63), *Cheyenne Autumn* (64), *Alvarez Kelly* (66), *The Way West* (67), *Death of a Gunfighter* (69).

WYLER, WILLIAM (1902-). World-famous director who began with several two-reel westerns at Universal; his 1940 production *The Westerner* with Gary Cooper and Walter Brennan as Judge Roy Bean remains the best of his horse operas, although *The Big Country* (58), with its sweeping music score, is still the best-known.

YORDAN, PHILIP (1913-). Western screenwriter, also novelist, playwright and producer. Films (as scriptwriter): *Drums In The Deep South* (51), *Broken Lance* (story) (54), *Johnny Guitar* (54), *The Man From Laramie* (55), *The Bravados* (58), *Day Of The Outlaw* (59), *Captain Apache* (71), *Bad Man's River* (71).

YOUNG, VICTOR (1900-1956). Composer of several western scores, mostly at Paramount. Best known work in the genre: *Shane* (53). Others: *The Dark Command* (40), *Arizona* (40), *The Outlaw* (46), *California* (46), *Streets of Laredo* (49), *Rio Grande* (50), *Johnny Guitar* (54), *Drumbeat* (54), *The Tall Men* (55), *Run of the Arrow* (57).

ZINNEMANN, FRED (1907-). Austrian-born director who has ventured West just once, for the classic, award winning *High Noon* (52) with Gary Cooper and Grace Kelly, (see page 81).

Walter Matthau and Jack Lemmon in the screen version of Neil Simon's Broadway hit *The Odd Couple* (68).

(Above)   A nervous romance. Woody Allen and Diane Keaton in Allen's Oscar-winning comedy *Annie Hall* (77).

(Below)   Smiling but silent. Dom DeLuise, Marty Feldman and Mel Brooks in the 1976 hit *Silent Movie*.

(Above)   Max Von Sydow prepares to take on Satan in Friedkin's *The Exorcist* (73).

(Below)   Just one of the hazards of the planet Tatooine. One of the sandpeople attacks Luke Skywalker (Mark Hamill) in the science-fiction blockbuster *Star Wars* (77).

(Above and below)   The two faces of the Mafia in *The Godfather* (72). James
Caan and Al Pacino enjoy their sister's wedding and a hired heavy meets an abrupt
end through strangulation!

(Above and below)   *Chinatown* (74), the classic private-eye thriller of the 70s. Jack Nicholson finds that nosiness is a dangerous business and femme fatale Faye Dunaway comes to a desperate end.

James Stewart in Delmer Daves' 1950 western *Broken Arrow*.

Disco dance king John Travolta in *Saturday Night Fever* (77).

Holly Golightly (Audrey Hepburn) sets the party alight in Blake Edwards' romantic comedy *Breakfast At Tiffany's* (61).

MUSICALS

LOVE ME TONIGHT   1932

Jeanette MacDonald as a princess, Maurice Chevalier as an impoverished tailor and Myrna Loy (in the role that made her famous) as a countess. This underrated musical fairytale is sometimes attributed to Lubitsch, but was in fact directed by Rouben Mamoulian, one of the most technically advanced directors of the early sound period. Here his genius with the soundtrack is admirably demonstrated, especially in the first sequence when the sounds of early morning Paris are gradually combined with the musical rhythms of the opening number. An advanced film of its day and one that had a lasting effect on the genre during the thirties. The magnificent Rodgers and Hart score includes 'Isn't It Romantic?', 'Mimi' and 'Lover'.

Production Company:	Paramount
Production and Direction:	Rouben Mamoulian
Screenplay:	Samuel Hoffenstein,
	Waldemar Young and
	George Marion, Jr.

based on the play by Leopold
Marchand and Paul Armont

Photography:	Victor Milner
Songs:	Richard Rodgers and
	Lorenz Hart

Leading Players: Maurice Chevalier, Jeanette MacDonald, Myrna Loy, Charlie Ruggles, Charles Butterworth, C. Aubrey Smith

42ND STREET   1933

Perhaps the outstanding example of the 'putting on a show' musical so popular in Hollywood during the early thirties. Warner Baxter features as an overworked director, Dick Powell as the young juvenile lead, Bebe Daniels as the star and Ruby Keeler (Mrs. Al Jolson in real life) as the chorus girl who substitutes for her on opening night. Also on hand: George Brent as Bebe's former vaudeville partner, Guy Kibbee as a Broadway financier and Ginger Rogers and Una Merkel as a couple of veteran showgirls. Top numbers, 'You're Getting to be a Habit with Me', 'Shuffle off to Buffalo', and the climactic '42nd Street', staged by Busby Berkeley with over 100 chorus girls.

Production Company:	Warner Bros.
Direction:	Lloyd Bacon
Screenplay:	James Seymour and
based on a novel by	Rian James
Bradford Ropes	
Photography:	Sol Polito
Songs:	Al Dubin and
	Harry Warren

Leading Players: Warner Baxter, Bebe Daniels, George Brent, Ruby Keeler, Guy Kibbee, Ned Sparks, Dick Powell, Ginger Rogers, Una Merkel

TOP HAT   1935

The third and most delightful of the Astaire-Rogers musicals with the pair involved in the usual romantic misunderstandings in London and on the Italian Riviera. As in all their ten films together the plot is so lightweight it is almost non-existent, but the ease and charm with which the two stars perform, the supporting performances of Edward Everett Horton and Eric Blore (in his usual role of a valet) and, best of all, Berlin's superb score make it the best-loved musical of the decade. Top numbers: 'Top Hat, White Tie and Tails', 'Isn't this a Lovely Day to be Caught in the Rain' and 'The Piccolino'.

Production Company:	RKO Radio
Production:	Pandro S. Berman
Direction:	Mark Sandrich
Screenplay:	Dwight Taylor and
from a story by	Allan Scott
Dwight Taylor	
Photography:	David Abel
Music and Lyrics:	Irving Berlin

Leading Players: Fred Astaire, Ginger Rogers, Edward Everett Horton, Helen Broderick, Erik Rhodes, Eric Blore

MEET ME IN ST. LOUIS   1944

The day-to-day experiences of a middle-class American family (led by lawyer Leon Ames and wife Mary Astor) as they live out a peaceful, non-eventful existence in St. Louis at the turn-of-the-century. Based on New Yorker stories by Sally Benson, the film is little more than a musical family album, yet the exquisite sets and Technicolor and Judy Garland's rendering of 'The Boy Next Door' and 'The Trolley Song' endeared it to millions of war-time moviegoers who regarded it as the first really great Metro musical of the forties. Margaret O'Brien, Lucille Bremer and Joan Carroll feature as Garland's sisters, Marjorie Main as the family maid and Harry Davenport as the grandfather.

Production Company:	Metro-Goldwyn-Mayer
Production:	Arthur Freed
Direction:	Vincente Minnelli

Screenplay:	Irving Brecher and
	Fred F. Finklehoffe
from stories by Sally Benson	
Photography (Technicolor):	George Folsey
Songs:	Hugh Martin and
	Ralph Blane
Musical Direction:	Georgie Stoll

Leading Players: Judy Garland, Margaret O'Brien, Lucille Bremer, Joan Carroll, Mary Astor, Leon Ames, Tom Drake, Marjorie Main, Harry Davenport

Note: Filmed in Hollywood, December, 1943-April, 1944.

ON THE TOWN   1949

Gene Kelly and Stanley Donen directed three of MGM's post-war musicals, with this adaptation of a Leonard Bernstein stage show the best of them. The plot about three sailors (Kelly, Sinatra and Munshin) who embark on a 24-hour shore leave in New York is a simple one, but the imaginative use of natural settings (the film was shot largely on location in New York), together with the exuberance of the numbers, put the film in a class of its own. Even now, some twenty-odd years after it was first made, it is one of the few films that tries to sing and dance for most of its running time. There are so many unforgettable numbers it seems a shame to single out just a few, but the opening 'New York, New York', with its use of montage location shots, 'The Miss Turnstiles Ballet' with Vera-Ellen, and Ann Miller's dynamic 'Prehistoric Joe' are among the best.

Production Company:	Metro-Goldwyn-Mayer
Production:	Arthur Freed
Direction:	Stanley Donen and
	Gene Kelly
Screenplay:	Betty Comden and
from their musical and Jerome	Adolph Green
Robbins' ballet 'Fancy Free'.	
Photography (Technicolor):	Harold Rosson
Music:	Leonard Bernstein

Leading Players: Gene Kelly, Frank Sinatra, Betty Garrett, Ann Miller, Jules Munshin, Vera-Ellen

Note: Filmed at the MGM studios in Hollywood and on location in New York, April-July, 1949.

SINGIN' IN THE RAIN   1952

In many respects this is almost as good a musical as *On the Town*, providing a wide variety of dance routines and some amusing satire on Hollywood in the late twenties when the Talkies were beginning to threaten the careers of some of the silent movie stars. The famous sequence of Kelly dancing alone in the rain is almost matched by such numbers as Donald O'Connor's acrobatic 'Make 'em Laugh', the Kelly/O'Connor duo 'Moses Supposes' and the final 'Broadway Ballet' danced by Kelly and Cyd Charisse. Heading the supporting cast: Jean Hagen as a dumb, squeaky-voiced star of silent films and Millard Mitchell as a Hollywood producer.

Production Company:	Metro-Goldwyn-Mayer
Production:	Arthur Freed
Direction:	Gene Kelly and Stanley Donen
Original Screenplay:	Betty Comden and Adolph Green
Photography (Technicolor):	Harold Rosson
Music:	Nacio Herb Brown and Roger Edens
Lyrics:	Arthur Freed, Al Hoffman, Al Goodhart, Betty Comden and Adolph Green

Leading Players: Gene Kelly, Debbie Reynolds, Jean Hagen, Donald O'Connor, Millar Mitchell, Cyd Charisse, Rita Moreno

Note: Filmed in Hollywood, June-September, 1951.

THE BAND WAGON   1953

This Minnelli musical represented something of a return to form for Fred Astaire who had played in mostly unrewarding parts since the end of the war. He features as a fading Hollywood star, who, although finished in movies, is determined to make a fresh start on Broadway. Jack Buchanan plays the temperamental producer who stages the comeback show, and Oscar Levant and Nanette Fabray provide some bright moments as a couple of stage writers. It is during the musical sequences, however, that the film really comes alive, especially when Astaire and Cyd Charisse perform 'Dancing in the Dark' in Central Park and the 'Girl-Hunt Ballet' finale. Another highlight is the 'Shine on My Shoes' number danced by Astaire with a black shoeshine boy in a New York amusement arcade.

Production Company:	Metro-Goldwyn-Mayer
Production:	Arthur Freed
Direction:	Vincente Minnelli
Screenplay:	Betty Comden and Adolph Green
Photography (Technicolor):	Harry Jackson
Musical Direction:	Adolph Deutsch

Leading Players: Fred Astaire, Cyd Charisse, Jack Buchanan, Oscar Levant, Nanette Fabray

Note: Filmed in Hollywood, October, 1952-January, 1953.

WEST SIDE STORY   1961

The most successful of all Hollywood's stage adaptations of the sixties, with Richard Beymer and Natalie Wood as a modern 'Romeo and Juliet' caught up in adolescent gang wars in Manhattan's Upper West Side. 'The Rumble', played out dramatically against the background of a deserted car lot, and the exhilarating 'America', danced by Rita Moreno and company on a New York rooftop, are memorable numbers. Yet for all their brilliance, it is the opening sequence with its helicopter views of New York and sudden descent into the West Side streets that remains longest in the memory. Academy Award, best film, 1961.

Production Company:	Mirisch-Seven Arts/
	United Artists
Production:	Robert Wise
Direction:	Robert Wise and
	Jerome Robbins
Screenplay:	Ernest Lehman
Photography (Technicolor/	
Panavision 70):	Daniel L. Fapp
Book:	Arthur Laurents
Music:	Leonard Bernstein
Lyrics:	Stephen Sondheim

Leading Players: Natalie Wood, Richard Beymer, Russ Tamblyn, Rita Moreno, George Chakiris, Simon Oakland

Note: Filmed on location in New York and in Hollywood, August, 1960-February, 1961.

THE SOUND OF MUSIC   1965

Condemned by many serious critics for its sweetness and cloying sentimentality, this Academy Award winning musical has become a favourite of millions of people, especially women and children who continue to see it again and again. It stands supreme as the most perfect 'entertainment' ever manufactured at a Hollywood studio, a fact borne out when it became the biggest moneymaker of all time and saved Fox from near bankruptcy after their disaster with *Cleopatra*. Based on the Rodgers and Hammerstein stage musical, it is set in Salzburg during the thirties and concerns a young Austrian nun who renounces her vows to become governess of the seven children of the von Trapp family. The 'Do, Re, Mi' sequence with its brilliant editing is perhaps the most lively of the musical numbers.

Production Company:	Twentieth Century-Fox
Production and Direction:	Robert Wise
Screenplay:	Ernest Lehman
from the stage musical with	Richard Rodgers and
music and lyrics by	Oscar Hammerstein II
Photography (De Luxe color/	
Todd AO):	Ted McCord

Music Supervision: Irwin Kostal
Leading Players: Julie Andrews, Christopher Plummer, Eleanor
   Parker, Richard Haydn, Peggy Wood

Note: Filmed in Hollywood and on location in Salzburg, Austria,
   April-August, 1964.

CABARET   1972

The Sound Of Music's reign as all-time moneymaker lasted for six
years. Screen adaptations of stage musicals have continued unabated,
however, with *Oliver!, Fiddler On The Roof, Jesus Christ Superstar*
and this somewhat less than wholesome story of Berlin night life in
the early 30s during the rise of the Nazi party. In particular it tells of
Sally Bowles (Liza Minnelli), a third rate cabaret artist with an untidy
sex life who lives optimistically from day to day in a brutal, bigotted
society already fraying at the edges and soon to collapse into complete
moral decay. Hardly the stuff of which musicals are made and a long,
long way from *The Sound Of Music*. But the songs have wit and bite,
the performances are outstanding (and in the case of Joel Grey as the
lurid MC of the Kit Kat Klub, brilliant), the camerawork flawless. The
only false note is in the performance of Minnelli. She is simply too
talented for the role of a mediocre cabaret artist but it's a minor flaw
when such songs as 'Money, Money', 'Mein Herr', 'Maybe This Time
I'll Be Lucky' and the title number are to be enjoyed.

Production Company: ABC Pictures Corporation/
                                Allied Artists
Production: Cy Feuer
Direction: Bob Fosse
Screenplay: Jay Presson Allen
   based on the musical play by Joe Masterhoff (book), John
   Kander (music) and Fred Ebb (lyrics), based on the play
   'I Am A Camera' by John Van Druten, adapted from the
   book 'Goodbye To Berlin' by Christopher Isherwood.
Photography (Technicolor):   Geoffrey Unsworth
Music: John Kander
Musical Direction: Ralph Burns
Leading Players: Liza Minnelli, Michael York, Helmut Griem,
   Joel Grey, Fritz Wepper, Marisa Berenson

SATURDAY NIGHT FEVER   1977

A film that will rate high in musical history in that it has brought the
art of dance back to the screen. John Travolta's athletic disco style might
seem far removed from the grace and invention of Astaire and Kelly,
but at least it has enabled the film musical to regain rhythm and visual
excitement. The story — inarticulate New York kid only blossoms when
he gets with it and reigns as dance king on Saturday nights — is at
times strongly reminiscent of Ray's *Rebel Without A Cause* and *West
Side Story*, especially in the scenes of street gangs and youthful daring.
The story, such as it is, is of little consequence, however. The film

really comes alive in the brightly lit, pounding disco sequences which, luckily, are plentiful. Hit numbers: 'Staying Alive', 'How Deep Is Your Love', 'Night Fever'.

Production Company:	Paramount
Production:	Robert Stigwood
Direction:	John Badham
Screenplay:	Norman Wexler
based on a story by Nik Cohn	
Photography (Movielab):	Ralf D. Bode
Music:	The Bee Gees
Additional Music:	David Shire

Leading Players: John Travolta, Karen Lynn Gorney, Barry Miller, Joseph Cali, Paul Pape, Donna Pescow

MUSICALS: WHO'S WHO

ALTON, ROBERT (1903-1957). American choreographer, active at Metro during their golden post-war period. Staged many dance routines for Walters and Sidney and also worked with Minnelli on *Ziegfeld Follies* (46) and *The Pirate* (48). Main films: *Ziegfeld Follies* (46), *Till the Clouds Roll By* (46), *The Pirate* (48), *Easter Parade* (48), *Words and Music* (48), *The Barkleys of Broadway* (49), *Annie Get Your Gun* (50), *Show Boat* (51), *Belle of New York* (52), *Call Me Madam* (53), *There's No Business Like Show Business* (54), *White Christmas* (54).

AMECHE, DON (1908-). Actor-singer, frequently cast opposite Betty Grable in her early musicals at Fox. Starred opposite Alice Faye in *Alexander's Ragtime Band* (38) and featured as composer Stephen Foster in *Swanee River* (39). Films: *Ramona* (36), *You Can't Have Everything* (37), *Hollywood Cavalcade* (39), *Down Argentine Way* (40), *That Night in Rio* (41), *Moon Over Miami* (41), *Greenwich Village* (44), *Slightly French* (49).

ANDREWS, JULIE (1934-). A star from the moment she descended, with umbrella and carpet bag, in *Mary Poppins* (64) and ran up the mountains in *A Sound Of Music* (65). None of her subsequent films has matched the financial success of these first musicals although her best acting performance, despite the film's financial failure, was as Gertrude Lawrence in *Star!* (68). Also: *Thoroughly Modern Millie* (67), *Darling Lili* (70). Much television work in the 70s.

ASTAIRE, FRED (1899-). Together with Gene Kelly, the screen's most celebrated dancer; at his peak during the 30s when he shared innumerable dance routines with co-star Ginger Rogers. *The Band Wagon* (53) in which he performs 'Dancing in the Dark' and 'The Girl-Hunt Ballet' with Cyd Charisse is perhaps the most accomplished of his later films. Worked regularly with Minnelli and Walters during the post-war years at MGM. Main films: *Flying Down To Rio* (33), *The Gay Divorcee* (34), *Roberta* (35), *Top Hat* (35), *Follow The Fleet* (36), *Swing Time* (36), *Shall We Dance?* (37), *Damsel In Distress* (37), *Carefree* (38), *The Story Of Vernon*

And Irene Castle (39), *You'll Never Get Rich* (41), *Holiday Inn* (42), *Yolanda And The Thief* (45), *Ziegfeld Follies* (46), *Blue Skies* (46), *Easter Parade* (48), *The Barkleys Of Broadway* (49), *Three Little Words* (50), *Royal Wedding* (51), *Belle Of New York* (52), *The Band Wagon* (53), *Daddy Long Legs* (55), *Funny Face* (57), *Silk Stockings* (57), *Finian's Rainbow* (68), *That's Entertainment!* (74), *That's Entertainment Part II* (76).

BACON, LLOYD (1889-1955). American director responsible for many of Warner's crime movies (see page 56) and musicals of the 30s. The historic *42nd Street* (33), a backstage story starring Warner Baxter and Ruby Keeler and *Footlight Parade* (33) with James Cagney, are two of his most famous films in the genre. After the war, worked on a series of minor musicals at Fox and Universal. Main films: *The Singing Fool* (28), *Wonder Bar* (34), *Gold Diggers of 1937* (36), *I Wonder Who's Kissing Her Now?* (47), *You Were Meant For Me* (48), *Give My Regards to Broadway* (48), *Call Me Mister* (51), *Golden Girl* (51), *The I Don't Care Girl* (53), *Walking My Baby Back Home* (53).

BEAUMONT, HARRY (1893-1966). Director of *The Broadway Melody* (29), the first musical to be named best picture of the year by the Academy of Motion Picture Arts and Sciences. Later musicals undistinguished.

BERKELEY, BUSBY (1895-1976). The most prominent choreographer/ director of the 30s, Berkeley remained the biggest influence on the musical genre until the advent of Minnelli, Kelly and Donen at MGM. His huge geometric dance routines, many of which featured hundreds of girls, brightened innumerable Warner musicals of the pre-war period. Among his most lavish numbers: 'Remember My Forgotten Man' from *Gold Diggers of 1933* (33), 'By a Waterfall' from *Footlight Parade* (33) and 'Lullaby of Broadway' from *Gold Diggers of 1935* (35).

Main films (as choreographer): *Whoopee* (30), *Palmy Days* (31), *The Kid From Spain* (32), *Roman Scandals* (33), *42nd Street* (33), *Gold Diggers of 1933* (33), *Footlight Parade* (33), *Dames* (34), *Wonder Bar* (34), *Bright Lights* (also dir.) (35), *Gold Diggers of 1935* (also dir.) (35), *Stage Struck* (also dir.) (36), *Gold Diggers of 1937* (36), *Hollywood Hotel* (also dir.) (37), *Gold Diggers in Paris* (38), *Babes in Arms* (also dir.) (39), *Strike Up the Band* (also dir.) (40), *Ziegfeld Girl* (41), *Babes on Broadway* (also dir.) (41), *For Me and My Gal* (also dir.) (42), *Girl Crazy* (43), *The Gang's All Here* (43), (also dir.), *Take Me Out to the Ball Game* (also dir.) (49), *Million Dollar Mermaid* (52), *Easy to Love* (53), *Rose Marie* (54), *Billy Rose's Jumbo* (also second unit dir.) (62).

BERLIN, IRVING (1888-   ). One of the leading American composers of the twentieth century. Films containing his scores include *Mammy* (30), *Top Hat* (35), *Follow the Fleet* (36), *On the Avenue* (37), *Alexander's Ragtime Band* (38), *Carefree* (38), *Holiday Inn* (42), *This is the Army* (43), *Blue Skies* (46), *Easter Parade* (48), *Annie Get Your Gun* (50), *Call Me Madam* (53), *There's No Business Like Show Business* (54), *White Christmas* (54).

BOLGER, RAY (1903-   ). A highly talented dancer whose routines in post-war Warner musicals were somewhat overshadowed by those of Kelly and Astaire at Metro. Best known role: the the scarecrow who accompanies Judy Garland, Bert Lahr (the cowardly lion) and Jack Haley (the tin man) in *The Wizard Of Oz* (39). Also: *Rosalie* (37), *Sweethearts* (38), *Stage Door Canteen* (43), *The Harvey Girls* (46), *Look For The Silver Lining* (49), *Where's Charley?* (52), *April In Paris* (52), *Babes In Toyland* (61).

BRICUSSE, LESLIE (1931-   ). British composer-lyricist. Has worked frequently with Anthony Newley in the theatre and contributed music and lyrics to several screen musicals i.e. *Stop The World — I Want To Get Off* (66), *Doctor Dolittle* (67), *Goodbye, Mr Chips* (69), *Scrooge* (70), *Willy Wonka And The Chocolate Factory* (71). Oscar for the song 'Talk To The Animals' in *Doctor Dolittle*.

BUTLER, DAVID (1894-1979). Director, responsible for many of Shirley Temple's pre-war musicals at Fox and some half-a-dozen of Doris Day's Technicolor vehicles at Warners. Over 40 musicals in all, including *Bright Eyes* (34), *The Little Colonel* (35), *The Littlest Rebel* (35), *Captain January* (36), *Pigskin Parade* (36), *You're a Sweetheart* (37), *If I Had My Way* (40), *Thank Your Lucky Stars* (43), *Shine On Harvest Moon* (44), *It's A Great Feeling* (49), *Look for the Silver Lining* (49), *Tea for Two* (50), *Daughter of Rosie O'Grady* (50), *Lullaby of Broadway* (51), *Where's Charley?* (52), *April in Paris* (52), *By the Light of the Silvery Moon* (53), *Calamity Jane* (53).

CAGNEY, JAMES (1904-   ). American actor who gained fame as a Warner tough guy (see page 58) but who won his Oscar for his portrayal of George M. Cohan in Curtiz's musical biography *Yankee Doodle Dandy* (42). Also memorable as the producer in Bacon's *Footlight Parade* (33). Others: *Blonde Crazy* (31), *Something to Sing About* (37), *West Point Story* (50), *Starlift* (51), *Love Me or Leave Me* (55).

CARON, LESLIE (1931-   ). A ballet dancer with Roland Petit's Ballet des Champs-Elysées before appearing with Kelly in Vincente

Minnelli's *An American in Paris* (51). Achieved her greatest musical success seven years later when she again played under Minnelli's direction in *Gigi* (58). Her orphan girl in Charles Walters' charming *Lili* (53) also ranks with her best musical performances. Others: *The Glass Slipper* (55), *Daddy Long Legs* (55).

CHAMPION, MARGE (1923-). and GOWER (1921-). American dance team who first appeared together on the screen in Bing Crosby's *Mr. Music* (50) at Paramount. Later featured in several musicals at MGM, e.g. *Show Boat* (51), *Lovely to Look At* (52), *Everything I Have is Yours* (52), *Jupiter's Darling* (55), *Three for the Show* (55).

CHAPLIN, SAUL (1912-). American composer-arranger, numerous musicals at Columbia and MGM, e.g. *Louisiana Hayride* (44), *Meet Me On Broadway* (46), *Summer Stock* (50), *An American In Paris* (AA) (51), *Lovely To Look At* (52), *Kiss Me Kate* (53), *Seven Brides For Seven Brothers* (AA) (54), *Jupiter's Darling* (55), *High Society* (56), *West Side Story* (AA) (61). More recently has served in a production capacity on *West Side Story* (61), *The Sound Of Music* (65), *Star!* (68), *Man Of La Mancha* (72) and *That's Entertainment Part II* (76).

CHARISSE, CYD (1923-) One of the most talented dancing stars to emerge from the Metro studio during the late 40s, Cyd Charisse established herself as Astaire's best-ever partner when she accompanied him in Minnelli's *The Band Wagon* (53). She later partnered him for a second time when she starred in Garbo's original Ninotchka role in MGM's *Silk Stockings* (57). MGM films: *Thousands Cheer* (43), *Ziegfeld Follies* (46), *The Harvey Girls* (46), *Till the Clouds Roll By* (46), *Words and Music* (48), *Singin' in the Rain* (52), *Deep in My Heart* (54), *Brigadoon* (54), *It's Always Fair Weather* (55), *Meet Me in Las Vegas* (56), *Black Tights* (59).

CHEVALIER, MAURICE (1887-1972). French star who partnered Jeanette MacDonald in several Lubitsch musicals of the early 30s. Films: *Innocents of Paris* (29), *The Love Parade* (29), *Paramount on Parade* (30), *The Smiling Lieutenant* (31), *Love Me Tonight* (32), *One Hour with You* (32), *The Merry Widow* (34), *Gigi* (58), *Can Can* (60).

COLE, JACK (1914-). American choreographer, former dancer. Films (as choreographer) include: *Cover Girl* (44), *The Jolson Story* (46), *On The Riviera* (51), *The I Don't Care Girl* (53), *Gentlemen Prefer Blondes* (53), *Kismet* (55), *Les Girls* (57), *Let's Make Love* (60).

COMDEN, BETTY (1916-   ) and GREEN, ADOLPH. American writing team. Films (scripts and lyrics): *Good News* (47), *On The Town* (49), *The Barkleys Of Broadway* (49), *Singin' In The Rain* (52), *The Band Wagon* (53), *It's Always Fair Weather* (55), *Bells Are Ringing* (60), *What A Way To Go!* (64).

CROSBY, BING (1901-1977). One of the most legendary of all musical stars, Crosby appeared in nearly sixty top musicals during his career, delivering such immortal songs as 'White Christmas' (*Holiday Inn*), 'Moonlight Becomes You' (*Road to Morocco*), 'In the Cool Cool Cool of the Evening' (*Here Comes the Groom*) and 'True Love' (*High Society*). Although not one of his films can be classified as a major musical, nearly all have their engaging moments, especially *A Connecticut Yankee in King Arthur's Court* (49) with its 'Busy Doing Nothing' number and *Blue Skies* (46) with the Crosby-Astaire duo 'A Couple of Song and Dance Men'.

Main films: *King of Jazz* (30), *Reaching for the Moon* (31), *The Big Broadcast* (32), *College Humour* (33), *We're Not Dressing* (34), *Here is My Heart* (34), *Mississippi* (35), *Anything Goes* (36), *Sing You Sinners* (38), *If I Had My Way* (40), *Rhythm on the River* (40), *Birth of the Blues* (41), *Holiday Inn* (42), *Blue Skies* (46), *Welcome Stranger* (47), *The Emperor Waltz* (48), *A Connecticut Yankee in King Arthur's Court* (49), *Riding High* (50), *Mr. Music* (50), *Here Comes the Groom* (51), *White Christmas* (54), *Anything Goes* (56), *High Society* (56), *High Time* (60), *Robin and the Seven Hoods* (64), *That's Entertainment!* (74).

CUKOR, GEORGE (1899-   ). American director whose musical work includes Garland's *A Star Is Born* (54), and the Oscar-winning *My Fair Lady* (64). Also: *One Hour With You* (co. dir.) (32), *Les Girls* (57), *Let's Make Love* (60), *The Blue Bird* (76).

CUMMINGS, IRVING (1888-1959). Former actor who became the first of Betty Grable's regular directors at Fox. Films include *Down Argentine Way* (40), the film that made Grable a star, *That Night in Rio* (41), *My Gal Sal* (42), *Springtime in the Rockies* (42), *Sweet Rosie O'Grady* (43), *The Dolly Sisters* (45).

CUMMINGS, JACK (1900-   ). American producer responsible for several of Esther Williams' aqua-musicals at MGM. Later worked on two of the studio's top productions of the early 50s: *Kiss Me Kate* (53) and *Seven Brides For Seven Brothers* (54). Films: *Born To Dance* (36), *Broadway Melody Of 1938* (37), *Broadway Melody Of 1940* (40), *I Dood It* (43), *Broadway Rhythm* (43), *Bathing Beauty* (44), *Easy To Wed* (46), *Fiesta* (47), *It Happened In Brooklyn* (47), *Neptune's Daughter* (49), *Three Little Words*

(50), *Texas Carnival* (51), *Lovely To Look At* (52), *Give A Girl A Break* (53), *Can Can* (60), *Viva Las Vegas* (64).

DAILEY, DAN (1915-1978). The Fox studio's leading song and dance man of the post-war era. Frequently teamed with June Haver, Jeanne Crain and Betty Grable (4 films). Musicals: *Ziegfeld Girl* (41), *Lady Be Good* (41), *Mother Wore Tights* (47), *When My Baby Smiles At Me* (48), *You Were Meant for Me* (48), *Give My Regards to Broadway* (48), *My Blue Heaven* (50), *Call Me Mister* (51), *There's No Business Like Show Business* (54), *It's Always Fair Weather* (55), *Meet Me in Las Vegas* (56), *The Best Things in Life are Free* (56).

DARBY, KEN (1909-). Musical arranger who has worked at Paramount (with Crosby), Metro and Fox. Films (as vocal arranger) include *The Wizard of Oz* (39), *Higher and Higher* (43), *Step Lively* (44), *Song of the South* (46), *Oh! You Beautiful Doll* (49), *My Blue Heaven* (50), *With a Song in My Heart* (52), *Call Me Madam* (53), *There's No Business Like Show Business* (54), *Carousel* (56), *The King and I* (56), *South Pacific* (58), *Porgy and Bess* (59), *Flower Drum Song* (61), *State Fair* (62), *Camelot* (67), *Finian's Rainbow* (68).

DAY, DORIS (1924-). American musical star, former dance band singer, whose lively personality helped re-establish Warners as a major musical studio after the war. Her early films were made by Michael Curtiz and David Butler, the latter director guiding her through perhaps her greatest hit at the studio, *Calamity Jane* (53). Major films: *Romance on the High Seas* (48), *My Dream is Yours* (49), *It's a Great Feeling* (49), *Tea For Two* (50), *West Point Story* (50), *Lullaby of Broadway* (51), *On Moonlight Bay* (51), *I'll See You In My Dreams* (52), *April in Paris* (52), *By the Light of the Silvery Moon* (53), *Lucky Me* (54), *Young at Heart* (54), *Love Me or Leave Me* (55), *The Pajama Game* (57), *Billy Rose's Jumbo* (62).

DEL RUTH, ROY (1895-1961). American director whose career in musicals spanned twenty-five years. Worked at Metro for most of the 30s and 40s then turned to Warners where he filmed some of the Doris Day vehicles, e.g. *West Point Story* (50) and *On Moonlight Bay* (51). Earlier films include *The Desert Song* (29), *Gold Diggers of Broadway* (29), *Kid Millions* (34), *Broadway Melody of 1936* (35), *Born to Dance* (36), *Broadway Melody of 1938* (37), *The Chocolate Soldier* (41), *Broadway Rhythm* (43).

DONEN, STANLEY (1924-). After Vincente Minnelli the most

important director on the post-war scene, co-directing with Kelly the classic *On The Town* (49) and *Singin' In The Rain* (52) and working solo on the evergreen *Seven Brides For Seven Brothers* (54). A former choreographer, he worked in this capacity on several MGM movies — *Anchors Aweigh* (45), *Holiday In Mexico* (46), *Take Me Out To The Ball Game* (49), etc., before graduating to the director's chair in 1949. Other musicals: *Royal Wedding* (51), *Give A Girl A Break* (53), *Deep In My Heart* (54), *It's Always Fair Weather* (co. dir.) (55), *Funny Face* (57), *The Pajama Game* (57), *Damn Yankees* (58), *The Little Prince* (74).

DURBIN, DEANNA (1921-   ). Just sixteen when she appeared in her first musical hit *Three Smart Girls* (37), Deanna Durbin joined the ten-year old Shirley Temple and the teenage Judy Garland as one of the most popular stars of the pre-war years. Many of her musicals at Universal were directed by Henry Koster, e.g. *One Hundred Men and a Girl* (37), *Three Smart Girls Grow Up* (38), *First Love* (39), *Spring Parade* (40), *It Started With Eve* (41). Others: *That Certain Age* (38), *It's A Date* (40), *Nice Girl?* (41), *Hers to Hold* (43), *Christmas Holiday* (44), *I'll Be Yours* (47), *Up in Central Park* (48).

EDDY, NELSON (1901-1967). American tenor enormously popular during the 30s when he starred with Jeanette MacDonald in a long series of operettas at MGM. Eight films with MacDonald: *Naughty Marietta* (35), *Rose Marie* (36), *Maytime* (37), *The Girl of the Golden West* (38), *Sweethearts* (38), *New Moon* (40), *Bitter Sweet* (40), *I Married an Angel* (42). Also: *Rosalie* (37), *Balalaika* (39), *The Chocolate Soldier* (41).

EDENS, ROGER (1905-1970). A former pianist and long time associate of Arthur Freed who worked as a musical adaptor, composer and producer at MGM. Films (as musical supervisor) include *The Great Ziegfeld* (36), *Broadway Melody of 1938* (37), *Strike Up the Band* (also comp.) (40), *Ziegfeld Girl* (also comp.) (41), *For Me and My Gal* (42), *Cabin in the Sky* (43), *Meet Me in St. Louis* (44), *Yolanda and the Thief* (45), *The Harvey Girls* (46), *Ziegfeld Follies* (also comp.) (46), *The Pirate* (48), *Easter Parade* (48), *On the Town* (comp. only) (49). Films (as producer or associate producer only) include *Royal Wedding* (51), *Show Boat* (51), *An American in Paris* (51), *The Band Wagon* (53), *Deep in my Heart* (54), *The Unsinkable Molly Brown* (64), *Hello Dolly!* (69).

FAYE, ALICE (1912-   ). Blonde singing and dancing star who made an effective contribution to the Fox musical scene before the War. Eventually replaced as the studio's top musical performer by

Betty Grable with whom she teamed in *Tin Pan Alley* (40).
Musicals, many opposite Don Ameche, John Payne, etc., include
King of Burlesque (35), *Poor Little Rich Girl* (36), *On the Avenue*
(37), *You Can't Have Everything* (37), *Sally, Irene and Mary* (38),
Alexander's Ragtime Band (38), *Rose of Washington Square* (39),
Hollywood Cavalcade (39), *That Night in Rio* (41), *The Great
American Broadcast* (41), *Weekend in Havana* (41), *Hello 'Frisco
Hello* (43), *The Gang's All Here* (43), *State Fair* (62).

FELIX, SEYMOUR (1892-1961). American choreographer, a vaudeville
dancer before entering films in 1929. Academy Award for his
staging of the 'A Pretty Girl is Like a Melody' sequence in *The
Great Ziegfeld* (36). Later films, mostly at Fox, e.g. *Alexander's
Ragtime Band* (38), *Rose of Washington Square* (39), *Tin Pan
Alley* (40), *Three Little Girls in Blue* (46), *Golden Girl* (51), *The
I Don't Care Girl* (53).

FOLSEY, GEORGE J. (1900-). American cameraman, long at MGM.
Many films for Minnelli, Sidney and Berkeley, i.e. *Thousands
Cheer* (43), *Meet Me In St. Louis* (44), *The Harvey Girls* (46),
Ziegfeld Follies (co-phot.)(46), *Take Me Out To The Ball Game* (49).
Others: *The Great Ziegfeld* (36), *Till The Clouds Roll By* (co-phot.)
(46), *Lovely To Look At* (52), *Million Dollar Mermaid* (52), *Seven
Brides For Seven Brothers* (54), *Deep In My Heart* (54), *Hit The
Deck* (55), *That's Entertainment Part II* (76).

FOSSE, BOB (1927-). Dancer/choreographer who has emerged as
one of the most imaginative American directors of the 70s. His
films have usually explored the murkier side of big city night life
i.e. *Sweet Charity* (69) in which Shirley MacLaine played dance
hall hostess Charity Hope Valentine; *Cabaret* (72) with Liza
Minnelli in pre-war Berlin; and the dramatic *Lenny* (74), the
biography of controversial night club entertainer Lenny Bruce.
Films (as actor) include *Kiss Me Kate* (53), *Give A Girl A Break*
(53), *My Sister Eileen* (55), *Damn Yankees* (58), *The Little Prince*
(74) (as 'The Snake') (also choreographer). Films (as choreographer): *My Sister Eileen* (55), *The Pajama Game* (57), *Damn
Yankees* (58), *Sweet Charity* (69) (also directed), *Cabaret* (72)
(also directed).

FREED, ARTHUR (1894-1973). The man who turned MGM into the
greatest musical producing studio of all time. A lyricist on more
than twenty pictures (including *The Broadway Melody*) before
turning producer on *Babes in Arms* in 1939, he helped make stars
of Judy Garland, Mickey Rooney and Gene Kelly and was responsible for some of the most outstanding musicals of the post-war
period. Produced eleven films for Minnelli, between 1942-1958,

i.e. *Cabin in the Sky* (43), *Meet Me in St. Louis* (44), *Yolanda and the Thief* (45), *Ziegfeld Follies* (46), *The Pirate* (48), *An American in Paris* (51), *The Band Wagon* (53), *Brigadoon* (54), *Kismet* (55), *Gigi* (58), *Bells are Ringing* (60).

Others: *Little Nellie Kelly* (40), *Strike Up the Band* (40), *Babes on Broadway* (41), *The Harvey Girls* (46), *Till the Clouds Roll By* (46), *Summer Holiday* (48), *Easter Parade* (48), *Take Me Out to the Ball Game* (49), *On the Town* (49), *Annie Get Your Gun* (50), *Show Boat* (51), *Singin' in the Rain* (52), *It's Always Fair Weather* (55), *Silk Stockings* (57). Song hits include 'Singin' in the Rain' from *Hollywood Revue* (29), 'Temptation' from *Going Hollywood* (33) and 'Good Morning' from *Babes in Arms* (39).

GARLAND, JUDY (1922-1969). The one musical star loved above all others, a superlative singer who first gained attention with her rendering of 'Dear Mr. Gable' in *Broadway Melody of 1938* (37) and the immortal 'Over the Rainbow' in *The Wizard of Oz* (39). At her peak during the 40s when she was associated with her then husband Vincente Minnelli on *Meet Me in St. Louis* (44), *Ziegfeld Follies* (46), and *The Pirate* (48), she is likely to be best remembered for her comeback picture *A Star Is Born* (54), with its memorable 'The Man That Got Away' and 'Born in a Trunk' sequences. Main films: *Babes in Arms* (39), *Little Nellie Kelly* (40), *Strike Up the Band* (40), *Ziegfeld Girl* (41), *Babes on Broadway* (41), *For Me and My Gal* (42), *Presenting Lily Mars* (43), *Girl Crazy* (43), *Thousands Cheer* (43), *The Harvey Girls* (46), *Easter Parade* (48), *Words and Music* (48), *In the Good Old Summertime* (49), *Summer Stock* (50), *I Could Go On Singing* (63).

GARRETT, BETTY (1919-   ). American comedienne/singer, wife of Larry Parks. Screen career short but memorable. Musicals: *Words and Music* (48), *Take Me Out to the Ball Game* (49), *Neptune's Daughter* (49), *On the Town* (as the taxi-driver girl friend of Frank Sinatra) (49), *My Sister Eileen* (55).

GAYNOR, MITZI (1930-   ). Fox musical star of the 50s, best known for her Nellie Forbush in Logan's *South Pacific* (58). Films *My Blue Heaven* (50), *Golden Girl* (51), *The I Don't Care Girl* (53), *There's No Business Like Show Business* (54), *Anything Goes* (56), *Les Girls* (57).

GERSHWIN, GEORGE (1898-1937). Arguably the most talented of all American composers of popular music. Portrayed on the screen by Robert Alda in Warner's biographical *Rhapsody in Blue* (45). Films containing his scores include *Damsel in Distress* (37), *Shall We Dance?* (37), *Goldwyn Follies* (38), *Lady Be Good* (41), *Rhapsody in Blue* (45), *The Barkleys of Broadway* (49), *An American in Paris* (51), *Funny Face* (57), *Porgy and Bess* (59).

GOODRICH, FRANCES (1896-) and HACKETT, ALBERT (1900-).
American writing team who worked on some of the most interesting
of MGM's post-war musicals, notably *The Pirate* (48) and *Seven
Brides for Seven Brothers* (54). Also: *Naughty Marietta* (35), *Rose
Marie* (36), *The Firefly* (37), *Lady in the Dark* (44), *Summer Holiday*
(48), *Easter Parade* (48), *In the Good Old Summertime* (49), *Give
a Girl a Break* (53).

GRABLE, BETTY (1916-1973). World famous musical star (a former
Goldwyn girl) who sang and danced her way through more than
20 Fox musicals during the 40s, earning herself the title of the
GI's favourite 'Pin-Up' Girl. Films mostly routine Irving Cummings
and Walter Lang vehicles, but distinguished by their superb
costumes and handsome Technicolor. Pictures include *Million
Dollar Legs* (33), *Man About Town* (39), *Down Argentine Way*
(40), *Tin Pan Alley* (40), *Moon Over Miami* (41), *Footlight Serenade*
(42), *Song of the Islands* (42), *Springtime in the Rockies* (42),
Coney Island (43), *Sweet Rosie O'Grady* (43), *Pin-Up Girl* (44),
Diamond Horseshoe (45), *The Dolly Sisters* (45), *Mother Wore
Tights* (47), *When My Baby Smiles at Me* (48), *Wabash Avenue*
(50), *My Blue Heaven* (50), *Call Me Mister* (51), *Three for the
Show* (55).

GRAYSON, KATHRYN (1922-). American soprano, best known
for her roles in *Show Boat* (51) and *Kiss Me Kate* (53). Now appears
in night club acts with Howard Keel, the male co-star of many
of her films. Musicals (mostly at MGM) include *Thousands Cheer*
(43), *Anchors Aweigh* (45), *Ziegfeld Follies* (46), *Till the Clouds
Roll By* (46), *Lovely to Look At* (52), *The Grace Moore Story* (53).

GREEN, JOHNNY (1908-). American arranger/composer who won
Oscars for his scoring of *Easter Parade* (48), *An American in Paris*
(51), *West Side Story* (61) and *Oliver!* (68). Other films (musical
direction and supervision): *Bathing Beauty* (44), *Easy To Wed* (46),
Summer Stock (50), *Royal Wedding* (51), *The Great Caruso* (51),
Brigadoon (54), *Invitation to the Dance* (56), *Bye Bye Birdie* (63).

HAVER, JUNE (1926-). Former dance band singer, very active at
Fox and Warner Bros. during the late 40s. Teamed with Betty
Grable in *The Dolly Sisters* (45) and featured as Marilyn Miller
in Butler's *Look for the Silver Lining* (49). Films: *Three Little
Girls in Blue* (46), *Wake Up and Dream* (46), *I Wonder Who's
Kissing Her Now?* (47), *Oh! You Beautiful Doll* (49), *The Daughter
of Rosie O'Grady* (50), *I'll Get By* (50), *The Girl Next Door* (53).

HAYTON, LENNIE. American conductor/arranger (husband of Lena

Horne), in Hollywood from 1941. Academy Award for his scoring of *On The Town* (49). Films (musical direction) include *Yolanda and the Thief* (45), *The Harvey Girls* (46), *Ziegfeld Follies* (46), *Till the Clouds Roll By* (46), *Good News* (47), *Summer Holiday* (48), *The Pirate* (48), *Words and Music* (48), *The Barkleys of Broadway* (49), *Singin' in the Rain* (52), *Star!* (68), *Hello Dolly* (69). (Died 1971).

HAYWORTH, RITA (1918-). The Columbia Studio's answer to Betty Grable at Fox and Judy Garland at MGM. Memorable as the Brooklyn career girl in *Cover Girl* (44). First attracted attention when she partnered Astaire in *You'll Never Get Rich* (41). Films include *My Gal Sal* (42), *You Were Never Lovelier* (42), *Tonight and Every Night* (45), *Down to Earth* (47), *Pal Joey* (57).

HEINDORF, RAY (1910-). The leading conductor/arranger at Warners for more than three decades. Over fifty musicals for the studio since the early 40s, among them *Yankee Doodle Dandy* (AA), (42), *This is the Army* (AA) (43), *Rhapsody in Blue* (45), *Night and Day* (46), *Romance on the High Seas* (48), *My Dream is Yours* (49), *Look for the Silver Lining* (49), *Tea for Two* (50), *Lullaby of Broadway* (51), *April in Paris* (52), *Calamity Jane* (53), *Lucky Me* (54), *A Star is Born* (54), *The Pajama Game* (57), *Damn Yankees* (58), *The Music Man* (AA) (62), *Gypsy* (62), *Finian's Rainbow* (68).

HENIE, SONJA (1913-1969). Norwegian skating star, in many Fox musicals of the war period, i.e. *Sun Valley Serenade* (41), *Iceland* (42), *Wintertime* (43), *It's a Pleasure* (45), *The Countess of Monte Cristo* (48).

HUMBERSTONE, BRUCE (1903-). American director who guided Alice Faye, Betty Grable and Sonja Henie through several musicals at the Fox studio. Later worked at Warner Bros. Films: *Sun Valley Serenade* (41), *Iceland* (42), *Hello 'Frisco Hello* (43), *Pin Up Girl* (44), *Three Little Girls in Blue* (46), *The Desert Song* (53).

HUTTON, BETTY (1921-). A top Paramount star of the 40s who reached her peak at another studio, MGM where she took over the role of Annie Oakley from Judy Garland in *Annie Get Your Gun* (50). Other musicals: *The Fleet's In* (42), *And the Angels Sing* (44), *Incendiary Blonde* (45), *Duffy's Tavern* (45), *Red Hot and Blue* (49), *Somebody Loves Me* (52).

JESSEL, GEORGE (1898-). American producer, former vaudeville performer and actor. Numerous Fox productions during the

1945-1953 period, e.g. *The Dolly Sisters* (45), *I Wonder Who's Kissing Her Now* (47), *When My Baby Smiles at Me* (48), *Oh! You Beautiful Doll* (49), *Golden Girl* (51), *The I Don't Care Girl* (53).

JEWISON, NORMAN (1926-   ). Canadian director, formerly with TV, whose early work at Universal took in several comedies: *Forty Pounds Of Trouble* (63), *Send Me No Flowers* (64), *The Art Of Love* (65) and during the 70s two of the biggest film musicals of the decade, the stage adaptations *Fiddler On The Roof* (71) and *Jesus Christ, Superstar* (73).

JOHNSON, VAN (1916-   ). Capable musical comedy performer. Teamed with Judy Garland and Esther Williams in several MGM musicals. Films: *Easy to Wed* (46), *Till the Clouds Roll By* (46), *In the Good Old Summertime* (49), *The Duchess of Idaho* (50), *Easy to Love* (53), *Brigadoon* (54).

JOLSON, AL (1882-1950). The first great singing star, an ex-vaudeville performer who introduced 'Mammy' in the first talkie, *The Jazz Singer* in 1927, and the equally famous 'Sonny Boy' in *The Singing Fool* (28). Subsequent films less notable, but enjoyed a revival in popularity after World War II when he sang to Larry Parks' miming in *The Jolson Story* (46) and *Jolson Sings Again* (49). Films include *Say it With Songs* (29), *Mammy* (30), *Hallelujah I'm a Bum* (33), *Wonder Bar* (34), *Go Into Your Dance* (35), *Rose of Washington Square* (39), *Swanee River* (39).

JONES, SHIRLEY (1934-   ). American actress who played the feminine leads in the film versions of *Oklahoma!* (55) and *Carousel* (56). Also: *April Love* (57), *Pepe* (60), *The Music Man* (62).

JUNE, RAY (1908-1958). American cameraman with several Metro musicals to his credit, including the Garland vehicles *Babes in Arms* (39), *Strike Up The Band* (40), *Ziegfeld Girl* (41). Later did notable work for Donen on *Funny Face* (57).

KEEL, HOWARD (1919-   ). American singer who featured in nearly a dozen MGM musicals. Several famous performances including Frank Butler in *Annie Get Your Gun* (50), Gaylord Ravenal in *Show Boat* (51), Wild Bill Hickok in *Calamity Jane* (53), and the singing backwoodsman in *Seven Brides for Seven Brothers* (54). Also: *Pagan Love Song* (50), *Texas Carnival* (51), *Lovely to Look At* (52), *Kiss Me Kate* (as Petruchio) (53), *Rose Marie* (54), *Jupiter's Darling* (55), *Kismet* (55).

KEELER, RUBY (1909-). Musical star (formerly married to Al Jolson) of several pleasing Warner entertainments. Often teamed with Dick Powell during the 30s. Films: *42nd Street* (33), *Footlight Parade* (33), *Gold Diggers of 1933* (33), *Dames* (34), *Flirtation Walk* (34), *Go Into Your Dance* (35), *Colleen* (36).

KELLY, GENE (1912-). The outstanding figure on the post-war musical scene. A brilliant dancer/choreographer/director who began opposite Garland in *For Me And My Gal* (42), rose to fame with his 'Alter Ego' number in Columbia's *Cover Girl* (44) and then starred in and directed a long line of outstanding musicals at MGM. Top dance numbers include the 'Mexican Hat Dance' in *Anchors Aweigh* (45), the 'Pirate Ballet' in *The Pirate* (48), 'Slaughter on Tenth Avenue' in *Words And Music* (48), the 'Newspaper Dance' in Walters' underrated *Summer Stock* (50) and the immortal dance in the rain in *Singin' In The Rain* (52).

Other musicals: *DuBarry Was A Lady* (43), *Thousands Cheer* (43), *Ziegfeld Follies* (46), *Take Me Out To The Ball Game* (49), *On The Town* (co-dir.) (49), *An American In Paris* (51), *Brigadoon* (54), *It's Always Fair Weather* (co-dir.) (55), *Invitation To The Dance* (dir.) (56), *Les Girls* (57), *What A Way To Go!* (64), *Les Demoiselles De Rochefort* (66), *Hello Dolly!* (dir.) (69), *That's Entertainment* (74), *That's Entertainment Part II* (76).

KERN, JEROME (1885-1945). American composer, best known perhaps for his score for *Show Boat*, filmed three times by Hollywood; in 1929 with Laura la Plante and Joseph Schildkraut, in 1936 with Irene Dunne, Allan Jones and Paul Robeson and in 1951 with Kathryn Grayson, Howard Keel and Ava Gardner. Film scores: *Sally* (29), *Roberta* (35), *Swing Time* (36), *High, Wide and Handsome* (37), *Lady Be Good* (41), *You Were Never Lovelier* (42), *Cover Girl* (44), *Centennial Summer* (46). Portrayed on the screen by Robert Walker in MGM's 1946 biography *Till the Clouds Roll By*.

KIDD, MICHAEL (1919-). Former ballet dancer who became choreographer at MGM during the 50s. More recently worked on the large-scale Fox productions *Star!* (68) and *Hello Dolly!* (69). Films at Metro: *The Band Wagon* (53), *Seven Brides for Seven Brothers* (54), *It's Always Fair Weather* (acted only) (55), *Guys and Dolls* (55), *Merry Andrew* (also dir.) (58).

KINGSLEY, DOROTHY (1908-). American scriptwriter, former radio writer, who has made a lasting contribution to the musical genre. Films (mostly MGM productions) include *Bathing Beauty* (44), *Easy to Wed* (46), *Neptune's Daughter* (49), *Texas Carnival* (51), *Kiss Me Kate* (53), *Seven Brides for Seven Brothers* (54), *Jupiter's Darling* (55), *Pal Joey* (57), *Can Can* (60), *Pepe* (60), *Half a Sixpence* (67).

KOSTAL, IRWIN (1915-   ). Music arranger associated with several
Broadway productions before turning to films in the 60s. Musicals:
West Side Story (61), *Mary Poppins* (64), *The Sound Of Music*
(65), *A Funny Thing Happened On The Way To The Forum* (66),
Half A Sixpence (67), *Chitty Chitty Bang Bang* (68), *Bedknobs
And Broomsticks* (71), *The Blue Bird* (76), *Pete's Dragon* (77).

KOSTER, HENRY (1905-   ). Director of many Deanna Durbin pre-
war musicals at Universal. Later worked with Grable at Fox and
brought Rodgers and Hammerstein's *Flower Drum Song* to the
screen. Films: *Three Smart Girls* (37), *One Hundred Men and a
Girl* (37), *Three Smart Girls Grow Up* (38), *First Love* (39), *Spring
Parade* (40), *Music for Millions* (44), *Wabash Avenue* (50), *My
Blue Heaven* (50), *Flower Drum Song* (61).

LANG, WALTER (1896-1972). Veteran American director of many
Fox musicals. Guided Shirley Temple through the pre-war *The
Little Princess* (39) and worked with Grable on six occasions during
the 40s, i.e. *Tin Pan Alley* (40), *Moon Over Miami* (41), *Song of
the Islands* (42), *Coney Island* (43), *Mother Wore Tights* (47),
When My Baby Smiles at Me (48). Later entrusted with several
of the studio's big-budget CinemaScope musicals, including *There's
No Business Like Show Business* (54), *The King and I* (56) and
Can Can (60). Others: *Weekend in Havana* (41), *Greenwich Village*
(44), *State Fair* (45), *With a Song in My Heart* (52), *Call Me
Madam* (53).

LANZA, MARIO (1921-1959). Italian-American tenor who enjoyed a
considerable success as *The Great Caruso* in 1951. Formerly a
concert and opera star. Films: *That Midnight Kiss* (49), *The Toast
of New Orleans* (50), *Because You're Mine* (52), *The Student
Prince* (voice only) (54), *Serenade* (56), *For the First Time* (59).

LEHMAN, ERNEST (1915-   ). Writer-producer, mostly associated
with dramatic subjects early in his career — *Executive Suite*
(54), *The Sweet Smell Of Success* (57) and *North By Northwest*
(59 — but best known in the 60s for the musicals *West Side Story*
(61), *The Sound Of Music* (65) and *Hello Dolly!* (69).

LENNART, ISOBEL (1914-1971). American screenwriter, a specialist
in MGM musicals for many years. Towards the end of her career
associated with the Barbra Streisand hit *Funny Girl* (68). Scripts:
Anchors Aweigh (45), *It Happened In Brooklyn* (47), *Love Me
Or Leave Me* (55), *Meet Me In Las Vegas* (56), *Merry Andrew*
(58).

LEONARD, ROBERT Z. (1889-1968). MGM director, former stage actor and singer. Filmed the Academy Award winning *The Great Ziegfeld* in 1936 and several of the Jeanette MacDonald/Nelson Eddy operettas of the late 30s, i.e. *Maytime* (37), *The Girl of the Golden West* (38), *New Moon* (40). Others: *Marianne* (29), *In Gay Madrid* (30), *Dancing Lady* (33), *Peg O' My Heart* (33), *The Firefly* (37), *Ziegfeld Girl* (41), *In the Good Old Summertime* (49), *Nancy Goes to Rio* (50), *The Duchess of Idaho* (50), *Everything I Have Is Yours* (52).

LERNER, ALAN JAY (1918-). Lyricist and screenwriter, long associated with composer Frederick Loewe: *Brigadoon* (54), *Gigi* (58), *My Fair Lady* (64), *Camelot* (67), *Paint Your Wagon* (69). Also screenplay and lyrics for *Royal Wedding* (51), story and screenplay for *An American In Paris* (51), screenplay and lyrics for *On A Clear Day You Can See Forever* (70), and screenplay and lyrics for *The Little Prince* (74).

LEROY, MERVYN (1900-). A talented, now somewhat underrated director best known for his problem movies of the 30s, *I Am A Fugitive from a Chain Gang* (32), *They Won't Forget* (37), etc. The excellent *Gypsy* (62), an adaptation of the Broadway success, with Natalie Wood as Gypsy Rose Lee, is by far the best of his dozen musicals which include *Gold Diggers of 1933* (33), *Sweet Adeline* (35), *Lovely to Look At* (52), *Million Dollar Mermaid* (52) and *Rose Marie* (54).

LEVANT, OSCAR (1906-1972). American pianist/comedian seen frequently in Warner and Metro musicals during the 1947-52 period. Films: *Rhapsody in Blue* (45), *Romance on the High Seas* (48), *The Barkleys of Broadway* (49), *An American in Paris* (51), *The I Don't Care Girl* (53), *The Band Wagon* (53).

LEVEN, BORIS (c.1900-). Russian-born production designer, in Hollywood since the early 30s. Numerous set designs for musicals including *Alexander's Ragtime Band* (38), *The Shocking Miss Pilgrim* (47), *I Wonder Who's Kissing Her Now* (47), *West Side Story* (61), *The Sound Of Music* (65), *Star!* (68), *New York, New York* (77).

LOGAN, JOSHUA (1908-). American stage and screen director who has adapted several Broadway hits into film terms, e.g. *South Pacific* (58), *Camelot* (67), *Paint Your Wagon* (69).

LUBITSCH, ERNST (1892-1947). German director noted for his sophisticated sex comedies (see page 17) and the MacDonald/ Chevalier musicals he made at Paramount during the early 30s. Films: *The Love Parade* (29), *Monte Carlo* (30), *The Smiling Lieutenant* (31), *One Hour with You* (co-dir.) (32), *The Merry Widow* (34), *That Lady in Ermine* (48).

MACDONALD, JEANETTE (1901-1965). The first of the popular singing stars, Jeanette MacDonald shared in two enormously successful screen partnerships during the 30s and 40s, the first with Maurice Chevalier with whom she made four films, the second with Nelson Eddy who co-starred with her in eight musicals between 1935 and 1942. Films (with Chevalier): *The Love Parade* (29), *One Hour With You* (32), *Love Me Tonight* (32), *The Merry Widow* (34). Films (with Eddy): *Naughty Marietta* (35), *Rose Marie* (36), *Maytime* (37), *The Girl of the Golden West* (38), *Sweethearts* (38), *New Moon* (40), *Bitter Sweet* (40), *I Married an Angel* (42). Others: *The Vagabond King* (30), *Monte Carlo* (30), *The Firefly* (37), *Broadway Serenade* (39), *Follow the Boys* (44).

MACRAE, GORDON (1921-   ). Reliable singing performer, frequently seen in Warner musicals during the late 40s. Subsequently took the leads in more ambitious productions for Zinnemann (*Oklahoma!*) and Henry King (*Carousel*). Films: *Look for the Silver Lining* (49), *The Daughter of Rosie O'Grady* (50), *Tea for Two* (50), *West Point Story* (50), *On Moonlight Bay* (51), *By the Light of the Silvery Moon* (53). *The Desert Song* (53), *The Best Things in Life are Free* (56).

MAMOULIAN, ROUBEN (1897-   ). American director who gained fame with his revolutionary use of sound in such early talkies as *Underworld* (27), *Applause* (29) and not least *Love Me Tonight* (32), a film considered by many critics to be the most important of all the early musicals. Other works in the genre: *The Gay Desperado* (36), *High, Wide and Handsome* (37), *Summer Holiday* (48), *Silk Stockings* (57).

MERMAN, ETHEL (1909-   ). Broadway performer (*Annie Get Your Gun, Gypsy*, etc.), best known on the screen for her dynamic performance as the 'hostess with the mostest' in Walter Lang's *Call Me Madam* (53). Also: *Kid Millions* (34), *Anything Goes* (36), *Strike Me Pink* (36), *Alexander's Ragtime Band* (38), *Stage Door Canteen* (43), *There's No Business Like Show Business* (54).

MILLER, ANN (1919-   ). A brilliant American tap dancer whose best opportunities occurred at MGM after a long series of mediocre movies at Columbia. Outstanding routines: 'Shakin' The Blues

Away' in *Easter Parade* (48), 'Prehistoric Man' in *On the Town* (49) and 'Too Darn Hot' in *Kiss Me Kate* (53). Other musicals: *Texas Carnival* (51), *Two Tickets to Broadway* (51), *Lovely to Look At* (52), *Deep in my Heart* (54), *Hit the Deck* (55), *The Opposite Sex* (56).

MINNELLI, LIZA (1946-). Daughter of Vincente Minnelli and Judy Garland and it shows in every frame of her screen performances. Academy Award for her Berlin cabaret artist Sally Bowles in *Cabaret* (72); a brilliant rendering of the title song in *New York, New York*, Scorsese's homage to the big band era of the 40s. Also: *Lucky Lady* (76).

MINNELLI, VINCENTE (1910-). Perhaps the most inventive of all musical film-makers and a favourite director of both Kelly and Astaire. Won a deserved Oscar for his work on the charming *Gigi* (58), but generally considered to have achieved his best results on Garland's *Meet Me In St. Louis* (44) and *The Pirate* (48). Films: *Cabin in the Sky* (43), *I Dood It* (43), *Yolanda and the Thief* (45), *Ziegfeld Follies* (46), *An American In Paris* (51), *The Band Wagon* (53), *Brigadoon* (54), *Kismet* (55), *Bells are Ringing* (60), *On a Clear Day You Can See Forever* (70).

MUNSHIN, JULES (1913-1970). Metro dancer-comedian responsible for some of the more amusing sequences in *Take Me Out to the Ball Game* (49) and *On the Town* (49). Also: *Easter Parade* (48), *That Midnight Kiss* (49), *Silk Stockings* (57).

NELSON, GENE (1920-). American dancer who began as a skater with Sonja Henie. Several excellent routines at Warners but, like his co-star at the studio, Ray Bolger, generally overshadowed by the achievements of Kelly and Astaire at MGM. Main musicals: *I Wonder Who's Kissing Her Now?* (47), *The Daughter of Rosie O'Grady* (50), *Tea for Two* (50), *West Point Story* (50), *Lullaby of Broadway* (51), *Painting the Clouds with Sunshine* (51), *She's Working Her Way Through College* (52), *So This is Paris* (54), *Oklahoma!* (55).

NEWMAN, ALFRED (1901-1970). American composer and arranger. More than eighty musicals in the latter capacity, mostly at Fox. Major films in the genre: *Whoopee* (30), *The Kid From Spain* (32), *Roman Scandals* (33), *One Night of Love* (34), *Broadway Melody of 1936* (35), *Strike Me Pink* (36), *The Gay Desperado* (36), *Born to Dance* (36), *Goldwyn Follies* (38), *Alexander's Ragtime Band* (38), *Tin Pan Alley* (40), *That Night in Rio* (41), *Song of the Islands* (42), *Orchestra Wives* (42), *Coney Island* (43), *Sweet Rosie O'Grady* (43), *Pin-Up Girl* (44), *Diamond*

Horseshoe (45), *The Dolly Sisters* (45), *State Fair* (45), *When My Baby Smiles at Me* (48), *My Blue Heaven* (50), *With a Song in My Heart* (52), *Call Me Madam* (53), *There's No Business Like Show Business* (54), *Daddy Long Legs* (55), *Carousel* (56), *The King and I* (56), *South Pacific* (58), *Flower Drum Song* (61), *Camelot* (67).

OAKIE, JACK (1903-1978). American comedian-singer who lent support to many Paramount and Fox musical stars of the 30s and 40s, including Betty Grable, Alice Faye, John Payne, etc. Films include *Paramount on Parade* (30), *College Humour* (33), *The Big Broadcast of 1936* (35), *Tin Pan Alley* (40), *The Great American Broadcast* (41), *Song of the Islands* (42), *Hello 'Frisco Hello* (43), *Wintertime* (43), *When My Baby Smiles At Me* (48).

O'CONNOR, DONALD (1925-). American actor-dancer, a familiar name in musicals since the late 40s. Matched Kelly step-for-step and word-for-word in many of the routines in *Singin' In The Rain* (52). Also: *I Love Melvin* (53), *Call Me Madam* (53), *Walkin' My Baby Back Home* (53), *There's No Business Like Show Business* (54), *Anything Goes* (56), *That's Entertainment!* (74).

PALMER, ERNEST (1885-1978). One of Fox's top colour cameramen of the 40s. Films: *Tall Dark And Handsome* (41), *Weekend In Havana* (41), *Song Of The Islands* (42), *My Gal Sal* (42), *Springtime In The Rockies* (42), *Coney Island* (43), *Sweet Rosie O'Grady* (43), *Pin Up Girl* (44), *Diamond Horseshoe* (45), *The Dolly Sisters* (45), *Centennial Summer* (46), *Three Little Girls In Blue* (46), *I Wonder Who's Kissing Her Now?* (47).

PAN, HERMES (1910-). American choreographer on nearly fifty musicals, including several with Astaire and Rogers at RKO before the War. Main films: *Flying Down To Rio* (33), *The Gay Divorcee* (34), *Roberta* (35), *Top Hat* (35), *Follow The Fleet* (36), *Swing Time* (36), *Shall We Dance?* (37), *Damsel In Distress* (37), *That Night In Rio* (41), *My Gal Sal* (42), *Sweet Rosie O'Grady* (43), *Pin Up Girl* (44), *Diamond Horseshoe* (45), *Blue Skies* (46), *Three Little Words* (50), *Lovely To Look At* (52), *Kiss Me Kate* (53), *Hit The Deck* (55), *Silk Stockings* (57), *Pal Joey* (57), *Porgy And Bess* (59), *Flower Drum Song* (61), *My Fair Lady* (64), *Finian's Rainbow* (68), *Darling Lili* (70), *Lost Horizon* (73).

PARKS, LARRY (1914-1975). American actor best remembered for his portrayals of Al Jolson in Columbia's post-war hits *The Jolson Story* (46) and *Jolson Sings Again* (49). Also: *You Were Never Lovelier* (42), *Down To Earth* (47), *The Light Fantastic* (51), *Love Is Better Than Ever* (52).

PASTERNAK, JOE (1901-   ). Producer, long at MGM. Films mostly second string productions, but nearly all commercial successes, e.g. *Thousands Cheer* (43), *Anchors Aweigh* (45), *In The Good Old Summertime* (49), *The Duchess of Idaho* (50), *Summer Stock* (50), *The Great Caruso* (51), *Because You're Mine* (52), *The Student Prince* (54), *Hit the Deck* (55), *Billy Rose's Jumbo* (62).

PAYNE, JOHN (1912-   ). A regular leading man in Fox musicals. Films (several with Grable): *Tin Pan Alley* (40), *Star Dust* (40), *The Great American Broadcast* (41), *Sun Valley Serenade* (41), *Weekend in Havana* (41), *Footlight Serenade* (42), *Iceland* (42), *Springtime in the Rockies* (42), *Hello 'Frisco Hello* (43), *The Dolly Sisters* (45).

PORTER, COLE (1891-1964). Together with Berlin, Gershwin and Kern, one of the most important composer-lyricists of the 30s and 40s. Life story filmed in 1946 under the title *Night and Day* with Cary Grant in the leading role. Scores include *The Gay Divorcee* (34), *Born to Dance* (36), *Anything Goes* (36), *You'll Never Get Rich* (41), *The Pirate* (48), *Kiss Me Kate* (53), *High Society* (56), *Silk Stockings* (57), *Les Girls* (57), *Can Can* (60).

POWELL, DICK (1904-1963). The romantic singing lead in many Warner musicals of the 30s. Seven films with Ruby Keeler, i.e. *42nd Street* (33), *Footlight Parade* (33), *Gold Diggers of 1933* (33), *Dames* (34), *Flirtation Walk* (34), *Shipmates for Ever* (35), *Colleen* (36). Also: *Twenty Million Sweethearts* (34), *Wonder Bar* (34), *Thanks a Million* (35), *Gold Diggers of 1937* (36), *Hollywood Hotel* (37), *On the Avenue* (37), *Hard to Get* (38), *Star Spangled Rhythm* (42), *Riding High* (43).

POWELL, ELEANOR (1912-   ). MGM tap dancer, popular during the 1935-45 period. Films: *George White's Scandals Of 1935* (35), *Broadway Melody Of 1936* (35), *Born To Dance* (36), *Broadway Melody Of 1938* (37), *Rosalie* (37), *Broadway Melody Of 1940* (40), *Lady Be Good* (41), *I Dood It* (43), *Thousands Cheer* (43), *Duchess Of Idaho* (50).

POWELL, JANE (1928-   ). MGM singing star, best remembered for her 'Goin' Courtin'' and 'Wonderful, Wonderful Day' numbers in *Seven Brides for Seven Brothers* (54). Films: *A Date with Judy* (48), *Nancy Goes to Rio* (50), *Two Weeks with Love* (50), *Royal Wedding* (51), *Deep in my Heart* (54), *Hit the Deck* (55).

PREMINGER, OTTO (1906-   ). Austrian-born director whose two major musicals both starred all-coloured casts: the exhilarating *Carmen Jones* (54), an adaptation of Bizet's 'Carmen' with Dorothy Dandridge and Harry Belafonte, and *Porgy and Bess* (59), Goldwyn's lavish version of the Gershwin opera.

PRESLEY, ELVIS (1935-1977). 'Rock-and-roll' pop singer who appeared in over thirty films in his 15 year screen career. Debut in *Love Me Tender* in 1956. Also: *Jailhouse Rock* (57), *King Creole* (58), *Blue Hawaii* (61), *Kid Galahad* (62), *Girls! Girls! Girls!* (62), *Fun In Acapulco* (63), *It Happened At The World's Fair* (63), *Viva Las Vegas* (64), *Frankie And Johnny* (66), *Easy Come, Easy Go* (67), *The Trouble With Girls* (70), *Elvis — That's The Way It Is* (70).

PREVIN, ANDRE (1929-   ). Prominent composer-arranger. More than a dozen films in the latter capacity, including *Three Little Words* (50), *Kiss Me Kate* (53), *It's Always Fair Weather* (also comp.) (55), *Kismet* (55), *Silk Stockings* (57), *Gigi* (58), *Porgy And Bess* (59), *Bells Are Ringing* (60), *My Fair Lady* (64), *Thoroughly Modern Millie* (67), *Paint Your Wagon* (69), *Jesus Christ Superstar* (73).

PRINZ, LEROY (1895-   ). American choreographer who spent many years at Warners. Musicals include *Yankee Doodle Dandy* (42), *This is the Army* (43), *Rhapsody in Blue* (45), *Night and Day* (46), *Romance on the High Seas* (48), *My Dream is Yours* (49), *Tea for Two* (50), *Lullaby of Broadway* (51), *On Moonlight Bay* (51), *I'll See You in My Dreams* (52), *April in Paris* (52), *Calamity Jane* (53), *South Pacific* (58).

REYNOLDS, DEBBIE (1932-   ). One of MGM's musical 'finds' of the late 40s, a vivacious, energetic young performer who received her best opportunities with Kelly and O'Connor in *Singin' In The Rain* (52). Others: *Three Little Words* (50), *Two Weeks With Love* (50), *I Love Melvin* (53), *Give A Girl A Break* (53), *Hit The Deck* (55), *Say One For Me* (59), *The Unsinkable Molly Brown* (64), *The Singing Nun* (66), *That's Entertainment!* (74).

ROBBINS, JEROME (1918-   ). Broadway choreographer-director who won an Oscar for his work on *West Side Story* (61) which he co-directed with Robert Wise. Choreographed *The King and I* (56).

RODGERS, RICHARD (1901-   ). American composer who shared in two enormously successful musical partnerships, the first with Lorenz Hart, the second and most famous with Oscar Hammerstein II. Films containing Rodgers and Hart scores include *Love Me Tonight* (32), *Mississippi* (35), *Babes in Arms* (39), *Words and*

Music (48) and *Pal Joey* (57). Films containing Rodgers and Hammerstein scores: *State Fair* (45), *Oklahoma!* (55), *Carousel* (56), *The King and I* (56), *South Pacific,* (58), *Flower Drum Song* (61), *State Fair* (62), *The Sound of Music* (65).

ROGERS, GINGER (1911-). Red-headed musical star, Astaire's dancing partner in nine pre-war films at RKO and the post-war *The Barkleys of Broadway* (49) at MGM. Films with Astaire: *Flying Down to Rio* (33), *The Gay Divorcee* (34), *Roberta* (35), *Top Hat* (35), *Follow the Fleet* (36), *Swing Time* (36), *Shall We Dance?* (37), *Carefree* (38), *The Story of Vernon and Irene Castle* (39), *The Barkleys of Broadway* (49). Others: *42nd Street* (33), *Gold Diggers of 1933* (33), *Sitting Pretty* (33), *Lady in the Dark* (44).

ROONEY, MICKEY (1920-). Judy Garland's talented co-star in five of her early musicals: *Babes In Arms* (39), *Strike Up The Band* (40), *Babes On Broadway* (41), *Girl Crazy* (43), *Thousands Cheer* (43). After featuring in Mamoulian's underrated *Summer Holiday* (48) and appearing as Lorenz Hart in *Words And Music* (48), he left the musical scene to concentrate on more dramatic roles, mostly in crime movies. Guested recently in MGM's musical compilation *That's Entertainment!* (74).

ROSHER, CHARLES (1885-1974). British-born cameraman, long in Hollywood. A specialist in musicals after the war, he worked with Minnelli, Thorpe and most regularly George Sidney (four films) at MGM. Main musicals: *Kismet* (44), *Yolanda And The Thief* (45), *Ziegfeld Follies* (co-phot.) (46), *Fiesta* (47), *Words And Music* (co.phot.) (48), *On An Island With You* (48), *Neptune's Daughter* (49), *Annie Get Your Gun* (50), *Show Boat* (51), *Kiss Me Kate* (53), *Jupiter's Darling* (55).

ROSS, DIANA (1944-). Black Motown singer, formerly with The Supremes. Won an Oscar nomination for her portrayal of jazz singer Billie Holiday in *Lady Sings The Blues* (72); appeared as an updated — and grown up — Dorothy in Sidney Lumet's *The Wiz* (78).

ROSS, HERBERT (1927-). American director, former choreographer: *Carmen Jones* (54) (chor. only), *Doctor Dolittle* (67) (chor. only), *Funny Girl* (68) (chor. and dir. musical sequences). Made his debut as a director with the Leslie Bricusse musical *Goodbye Mr. Chips* (69). Has also filmed the Fanny Brice sequel *Funny Lady* (75) and explored backstage ambitions in the American ballet world in *The Turning Point* (77). Lately more active in the comedy genre (see page 20).

ROSSON, HAROLD (1895-   ). Celebrated Hollywood cameraman who photographed *On the Town* (49) and *Singin' in the Rain* (52) for Kelly and Donen. Also: *The Wizard of Oz* (39), *I Love Melvin* (53), *Dangerous when Wet* (53).

ROWLAND, ROY (1910-   ). American director of mainly second string musicals at MGM. The musical fantasy *The 5,000 Fingers of Dr. T* (53) which he filmed for Stanley Kramer at Columbia is well above the standard of his other work in the genre. Films: *Two Weeks with Love* (50), *Hit the Deck* (55), *Meet Me in Las Vegas* (56), *The Seven Hills of Rome* (57).

SANDRICH, MARK (1900-1945). Director of five of the pre-war Astaire/ Rogers musicals: *The Gay Divorcee* (34), *Top Hat* (35), *Follow the Fleet* (36), *Shall We Dance?* (37), *Carefree* (38). Later filmed *Holiday Inn* (42) with Astaire and Crosby at Paramount.

SHAMROY, LEON (1901-1974). Veteran Fox cameraman famed for his colour work. Over thirty musicals, including *Down Argentine Way* (co.phot.) (40), *Tin Pan Alley* (40), *That Night In Rio* (co.phot.) (41), *Moon Over Miami* (co-phot.) (41), *State Fair* (45), *On The Riviera* (51), *With A Song In My Heart* (52), *Call Me Madam* (53), *There's No Business Like Show Business* (54), *Daddy Long Legs* (55), *The King And I* (56), *The Best Things In Life Are Free* (56), *South Pacific* (58), *Porgy And Bess* (59), *What A Way To Go!* (64).

SHERMAN, RICHARD M. (1928-   ) and SHERMAN, ROBERT B. (1925-   ). American songwriting brothers, most of whose work has been for Disney — they won an Oscar for 'Chim Chim Cher-ee' in *Mary Poppins* (64) — although they have also contributed scores for two large-scale British musicals: *Chitty Chitty Bang Bang* (68) and *The Slipper And The Rose* (76). Major film scores: *The Happiest Millionaire* (67), *The Jungle Book* (67), *The One And Only Genuine, Original Family Band* (68), *The Aristocats* (70), *Bedknobs And Broomsticks* (71), *Snoopy, Come Home* (72), *Charlotte's Web* (73), *Tom Sawyer* (73), *Huckleberry Finn* (74).

SIDNEY, GEORGE (1911-   ). American director with several stage adaptations among his output, including the excellent *Kiss Me Kate* (53) and the much neglected *Pal Joey* (57). Also: *Thousands Cheer* (43), *Bathing Beauty* (44), *Anchors Aweigh* (45), *The Harvey Girls* (46), *Annie Get Your Gun* (50), *Show Boat* (51), *Jupiter's Darling* (55), *The Eddy Duchin Story* (56), *Pepe* (60), *Bye Bye Birdie* (63), *Half a Sixpence* (67).

SIEGEL, SOL C. (1903-   ). Distinguished American producer, associated with many commercially successful musicals at Paramount, Fox and Metro. Best known film in the genre: *High Society* (56), the musical remake of *The Philadelphia Story* with Bing Crosby, Grace Kelly and Frank Sinatra. Also: *Blue Skies* (46), *My Blue Heaven* (50), *Call Me Madam* (53), *Gentlemen Prefer Blondes* (53), *There's No Business Like Show Business* (54), *Les Girls* (57).

SILVERS, PHIL (1912-   ). American comedian who, together with Jack Oakie, provided many of the wisecracks in American musicals of the 40s. Films, mostly at Fox, include *Footlight Serenade* (42), *My Gal Sal* (42), *Coney Island* (43), *Cover Girl* (44), *Diamond Horseshoe* (45), *Summer Stock* (50), *Lucky Me* (54), *A Funny Thing Happened On The Way To The Forum* (66).

SINATRA, FRANK (1915-   ). Actor-crooner whose performance as the sailor buddy of Gene Kelly in *On The Town* (49), stands out from several routine musical roles at MGM. His Joey Evans in Sidney's underrated *Pal Joey* (57) remains the best of his later musical performances. Films: *Higher And Higher* (43), *Step Lively* (44), *Anchors Aweigh* (45), *Take Me Out To The Ball Game* (49), *Young At Heart* (54), *Guys And Dolls* (55), *High Society* (56), *Can Can* (60), *Robin And The Seven Hoods* (64), *That's Entertainment!* (74).

SKELTON, RED (1910-   ). MGM comedy star who also featured in several of the studio's musical entertainments. Played Harry Ruby opposite Fred Astaire's Bert Kalmar in *Three Little Words* (50). Also: *Lady Be Good* (41), *DuBarry Was a Lady* (43), *I Dood It* (43), *Thousands Cheer* (43), *Bathing Beauty* (44), *Ziegfeld Follies* (46), *Neptune's Daughter* (49), *Texas Carnival* (51), *Lovely to Look At* (52).

STOLL, GEORGE (1905-   ). MGM musical director who won an Oscar for his scoring of *Anchors Aweigh* (45). Sixty films in the genre including *Babes In Arms* (39), *Strike Up The Band* (40), *Ziegfeld Girl* (41), *Cabin In The Sky* (43), *Meet Me In St. Louis* (44), *Neptune's Daughter* (49), *The Duchess Of Idaho* (50), *I Love Melvin* (53), *Rose Marie* (54), *The Student Prince* (54), *Hit The Deck* (55), *Billy Rose's Jumbo* (62), *Viva Las Vegas* (64).

STOLOFF, MORRIS (1893-   ). Musical director, at Columbia for more than two decades. Academy Awards for *Cover Girl* (44), *The Jolson Story* (46) and *Song Without End* (60). Also: *You Were Never Lovelier* (42), *A Song to Remember* (45), *Down to Earth* (47), *Jolson Sings Again* (49), *The 5,000 Fingers of Dr. T* (53), *My Sister Eileen* (55), *The Eddy Duchin Story* (56), *Pal Joey* (57).

STRADLING, HARRY (1901-1970). One of the genre's most accomplished cameramen. Eighteen musicals, including several for Minnelli and Walters. Academy Award for *My Fair Lady* (64). Films: *Till the Clouds Roll By* (co-phot.) (46), *The Pirate* (48), *Easter Parade* (48), *Words and Music* (co-phot.) (48), *The Barkleys of Broadway* (49), *Guys and Dolls* (55), *The Pajama Game* (57), *Gypsy* (62), *Funny Girl* (68), *Hello Dolly!* (69), *On a Clear Day You Can See Forever* (70).

STREISAND, BARBRA (1942-). The foremost musical star of the decade, winning an Oscar first time out for her Fanny Brice in *Funny Girl* (68) (a role she repeated seven years later in *Funny Lady*) and bringing tremendous vigour — if inappropriate youth — to matchmaker Dolly Levi in *Hello Dolly!* (69). Turned Judy Garland's Vicki Lester role into a rock singer in an updated version of *A Star Is Born* (76). Also: *On A Clear Day You Can See Forever* (70). Notable as a comedienne.

TAMBLYN, RUSS (1934-). Acrobatic dancer who enjoyed a successful career at MGM during the 50s. Played Biff in the Wise/Robbins production of *West Side Story* (61). Films: *Seven Brides for Seven Brothers* (54), *Hit the Deck* (55), *Tom Thumb* (58).

TAUROG, NORMAN (1899-). Prolific Hollywood director, many routine comedies and musicals. Films in the latter category include the early Garland vehicles *Little Nellie Kelly* (40), *Presenting Lily Mars* (43), and *Girl Crazy* (43). Worked frequently with Elvis Presley during the 60s.

TEMPLE, SHIRLEY (1928-). Hollywood child star, enormously popular during the late 30s when she sang and danced her way through a long series of musicals at the Fox studio. Introduced such songs as 'On the Good Ship Lollipop' in *Bright Eyes* (34), 'Picture Me Without You' in *Dimples* (36), and 'Come and Get Your Happiness' in *Rebecca of Sunnybrook Farm* (38). Films include *Stand up and Cheer* (34), *Little Miss Marker* (34), *Curly Top* (35), *The Littlest Rebel* (35), *Captain January* (36), *Poor Little Rich Girl* (36), *Stowaway* (36), *Little Miss Broadway* (38), *Just Around the Corner* (38), *Young People* (40).

THORPE, RICHARD (1896-). American director who guided Esther Williams through several watery musicals of the 40s and helped turn Mario Lanza into a star in *The Great Caruso* (51). Films: *Thrill of a Romance* (45), *Fiesta* (47), *This Time for Keeps* (47), *On an Island with You* (48), *A Date with Judy* (48), *Three Little Words* (50), *The Student Prince* (54), *Jailhouse Rock* (57).

TRAVOLTA, JOHN (1954-). American actor/dancer who burst into the superstar bracket with two sensational musical successes in the late 70s — *Saturday Night Fever* (77) and *Grease* (78). Has brought 'dance' back to the screen musical which has been dominated by 'song' since the retirement of Astaire and Kelly.

VAN DYKE, W. S. (1889-1944). American director. Several MacDonald-Eddy operettas during the 30s, i.e. *Naughty Marietta* (35), *Rose Marie* (36), *Sweethearts* (38), *Bitter Sweet* (40), *I Married an Angel* (42).

VERA-ELLEN (1926-). After Cyd Charisse (see page 123) Astaire's most delightful dancing partner of the post-war years appearing with him in *Three Little Words* (50) and *Belle of New York* (52). Superb also with Kelly in the 'Slaughter on Tenth Avenue' sequence in *Words and Music* (48) and 'The Miss Turnstiles Ballet' in *On the Town* (49). Others: *Three Little Girls in Blue* (46), *Carnival in Costa Rica* (47), *Happy Go Lovely* (51), *Call Me Madam* (53), *White Christmas* (54).

WALTERS, CHARLES (1911-). A former dancer-choreographer who became one of the leading directors at MGM after the War. Films rarely up to the standard of those of Minnelli and Donen, but often possessing a charm that the musicals of the more established directors lacked, particularly *Good News* (his first directorial effort) (47), *The Barkleys of Broadway* (the film that re-united Astaire and Rogers after a ten year absence) (49) and *Summer Stock* (50) with Garland and Kelly. Films (as choreographer): *Girl Crazy* (43), *Meet Me in St. Louis* (44), *Summer Holiday* (48), Films (as director): *Easter Parade* (48), *Texas Carnival* (51), *Belle of New York* (52), *Dangerous When Wet* (also co-chor.) (53), *Lili* (also chor.) (53), *Easy to Love* (53), *High Society* (56), *Billy Rose's Jumbo* (62), *The Unsinkable Molly Brown* (64).

WILLIAMS, ESTHER (1921-). Glamorous swimming star of nearly twenty aqua-musicals at MGM. Like most other performers on the lot, contributed her own particular brand of entertainment to Minnelli's *Ziegfeld Follies* (46), but enjoyed perhaps her most successful role when she played the baseball manager of Kelly and Sinatra in *Take Me Out to the Ball Game* (49). Several films with Richard Thorpe: *Thrill of a Romance* (45), *Fiesta* (47), *This Time for Keeps* (47), *On an Island With You* (48). Also: *Bathing Beauty* (44), *Neptune's Daughter* (49), *The Duchess of Idaho* (50), *Texas Carnival* (51), *Million Dollar Mermaid* (52), *Dangerous When Wet* (53), *Easy to Love* (53), *Jupiter's Darling* (55).

WISE, ROBERT (1914-). American director noted for his classic low-budget horror movies at **RKO** in the 40s but whose Academy Awards came for his work in the musical genre i.e. *West Side Story* (61) (co-directed with Jerome Robbins) and *The Sound Of Music* (65). Also filmed the biography of Gertrude Lawrence, *Star!* (68).

ROMANCE

STELLA DALLAS   1925

This old-fashioned romance about a young girl from the 'wrong side of the tracks', who marries above her position and then sacrifices her happiness for that of her daughter, comes alive mainly because of the superlative direction of Henry King who, with this film, consolidated his position as one of the foremost directors in America. Acting and direction were not matched, however, in King Vidor's 1937 remake with Barbara Stanwyck. Most famous moment: the climactic scene when Stella, old and forgotten and unable to reveal herself, peers through the window at her daughter's wedding and is told to 'Move on' by a city cop.

Production Company:	United Artists
Production:	Samuel Goldwyn
Direction:	Henry King
Adaptation:	Frances Marion
from the novel by	
Olive Higgins Prouty	
Photography:	Arthur Edeson
Leading Players:	Ronald Colman, Belle Bennett, Lois Moran,
Alice Joyce, Douglas Fairbanks, Jr., Jean Hersholt, Vera Lewis	

SEVENTH HEAVEN   1927

Frank Borzage was in many people's eyes the most talented romantic director of them all, for he had the uncanny knack of taking the tritest of tales and turning them into something delicate and moving on the screen. This was particularly true of *Seventh Heaven*, a simple love story set at the beginning of the Great War. It was not the playing of Janet Gaynor and Charles Farrell, which was excellent, or even the music ('Diane' was the popular theme tune) that made the film work so well, but the direction of Borzage. Just how masterly this is can be seen more clearly when the film is compared with the 1937 remake, an inferior production that accentuates rather than overcomes the banalities of the plot.

Production Company:	Fox
Direction:	Frank Borzage
Screenplay:	Benjamin Glazer
from the play by Austin Strong	

Photography: Ernest Palmer and
                                  J. A. Valentine
Leading Players: Janet Gaynor, Charles Farrell, Ben Bard, David
   Butler, Marie Mosquini, Albert Gran, Gladys Brockwell, Emile
   Chautard, George Stone

QUEEN CHRISTINA   1933

Garbo's first and only film with Rouben Mamoulian, a tragic story of
a Swedish queen who renounces her kingdom after an ill-fated love
affair with the Spanish envoy (John Gilbert) to her Court. A superior
film to the more famous *Camille* and one that continues to improve with
the passing of time. The final close-up of Garbo's face as she stands at
the prow of the ship taking her into self-imposed exile is one of the most
beautiful and moving scenes in all American cinema.

Production Company: Metro-Goldwyn-Mayer
Direction: Rouben Mamoulian
Screenplay: H. M. Harwood and
                                 Salka Viertel
Dialogue: S. N. Behrman
Story: Salka Viertel and
                                 Margaret R. Levino
Photography: William Daniels
Music: Herbert Stothart
Leading Players: Greta Garbo, John Gilbert, Ian Keith, Lewis
   Stone, Elizabeth Young, C. Aubrey Smith, Reginald Owen

GONE WITH THE WIND   1939

Call it an epic, call it a war movie, call it what you will, but at the centre
of *Gone With The Wind* lies one of the most deeply felt romances in
movies — that between scheming Southern belle Scarlet O'Hara (Vivien
Leigh) and cavalier blockade runner (Clark Gable). That the pair spend
most of their time fighting each other rather than getting together
makes their affair all the more fascinating as it spreads itself contagiously over a four-hour canvas of Civil War drama. The stairs of the
Butler mansion figure in two key scenes: when Scarlett tumbles head-
long and loses her child and in an earlier sequence when a drunken
Gable picks up a struggling Miss Leigh, issues a dynamic ''This is one
night you're not going to lock me out of your bedroom'' and storms up
the stairs to glory!

Production: Selznick-International/
                                 Metro-Goldwyn-Mayer
Production: David O. Selznick
Direction: Victor Fleming
Screenplay: Sidney Howard
   based on the novel by
   Margaret Mitchell

Photography (Technicolor):	Ernest Haller and
	Ray Rennahan
Music:	Max Steiner

Leading Players: Clark Gable, Vivien Leigh, Olivia de Havilland, Leslie Howard, Hattie McDaniel, Thomas Mitchell, Ona Munson

Note: Filmed over 22 weeks, from January 26, 1939 to July 1.

WATERLOO BRIDGE   1940

A lush MGM tear-jerker, relating the tragic love affair of an army colonel (Robert Taylor) and the young ballet dancer (Vivien Leigh) he meets, marries and is forced to leave during the First World War. The tragic aftermath when the girl, believing her lover killed at the Front, turns to a living on the streets, is sheer melodrama, but the skill with which Mervyn LeRoy puts the story across, the gloss of Ruttenberg's camerawork and Cedric Gibbons' aristocratic English settings make it all enormously entertaining. The supporting cast includes, inevitably, Sir C. Aubrey Smith as an English duke and Maria Ouspenskaya as Miss Leigh's ballet mistress.

Production Company:	Metro-Goldwyn-Mayer
Direction:	Mervyn LeRoy
Screenplay:	S. N. Behrman
from the play by	Hans Rameau and
Robert E. Sherwood	George Froeschel
Photography:	Joseph Ruttenberg
Music:	Herbert Stothart

Leading Players: Robert Taylor, Vivien Leigh, Virginia Field, Maria Ouspenskaya, Steffie Dana, Lucile Watson, C. Aubrey Smith

RANDOM HARVEST   1942

A shell-shocked soldier (Ronald Colman) of World War I finds himself unable to remember his past and starts his life anew by marrying a young stage actress (Greer Garson). When he is injured in a car accident his memory returns and he reverts to his former life forgetting all about his wife and unborn child. This somewhat preposterous tale is derived from a novel by James Hilton, yet for all its clichés, stilted dialogue and amusing Hollywood attempts to recreate the typically English scene — cottages in the country, rose blossom round the door, etc. — it remains one of the most fondly remembered weepies of the war years.

Production Company:	Metro-Goldwyn-Mayer
Direction:	Mervyn LeRoy
Screenplay:	Claudine West,
from the novel by	George Froeschel and
James Hilton	Arthur Wimperis
Photography:	Joseph Ruttenberg
Music:	Herbert Stothart

Leading Players: Ronald Colman, Greer Garson, Philip Dorn,
Susan Peters, Henry Travers, Reginald Owen, Bramwell Fletcher,
Rhys Williams, Una O'Connor

Note: Filmed in Hollywood, May-July, 1942.

CASABLANCA   1943

Considered by many critics to be the most accomplished of all Hollywood romances, this melodrama about love and intrigue in Vichy-
occupied Casablanca shows what can be achieved in commercial cinema
when a class director and top flight cast come to grips with a well-written
screenplay. Everything about the film works, from the playing of the
principals right down to the nostalgic song 'As times goes by'. Perhaps
its only faults are that Peter Lorre as the fugitive Ugarte disappears
in the first reel and that Sydney Greenstreet's scenes as the shady
owner of the Blue Parrott Café are all too brief. Humphrey Bogart
plays the cynical owner of 'Rick's Place', Ingrid Bergman features as
his former love from Paris, Paul Henreid is an underground leader and
Claude Rains, superb as usual, is the chief of the Vichy police.

Production Company:	Warner Bros.
Production:	Hal. B. Wallis
Direction:	Michael Curtiz
Screenplay:	Julius J. Epstein,
based on 'Everybody Comes	Philip G. Epstein and
to Rick's', an unproduced	Howard Koch
play by Murray Burnett	
and Joan Alison.	
Photography:	Arthur Edeson
Music:	Max Steiner

Leading Players: Humphrey Bogart, Ingrid Bergman, Paul Henreid,
Claude Rains, Conrad Veidt, Sydney Greenstreet, Peter Lorre,
S. Z. Sakall

Note: Filmed in Hollywood, May-August, 1942. The parts made
famous by Bogart, Bergman and Henreid were originally scheduled
for Ronald Reagan, Ann Sheridan and Dennis Morgan.

THE MAN IN GREY   1943

Regency melodrama which began a series of novelettish romances at
the Gainsborough Studio during the 1943-47 period. An inferior production in many ways, and sometimes unintentionally hilarious, but
very popular with British audiences who needed this sort of escapist
fare to help them forget the air raids of World War II and the grim
austerity that followed. James Mason as a sadistic Marquis and
Margaret Lockwood as a scheming adventuress feature in the leading
roles. Margaret Kennedy and Leslie Arliss contributed the screenplay, which included such lines as: 'I don't think I can bear this. I can't!
I really can't!'

Production Company:	Gainsborough
Production:	Edward Black
Direction:	Leslie Arliss
Screenplay:	Margaret Kennedy and
based on a novel by	Leslie Arliss
Lady Eleanor Smith	
Photography:	Arthur Crabtree
Music:	Cedric Mallabey

Leading Players: James Mason, Margaret Lockwood, Phyllis Calvert, Stewart Granger, Helen Haye, Raymond Lovell, Nora Swinburne, Martita Hunt

Note: Filmed at Shepherd's Bush Studios, October-December, 1942.

FRENCHMAN'S CREEK   1945

Daphne du Maurier tale about the love affair between an aristocratic young English woman (Joan Fontaine) and a dashing 'Robin Hood' style French pirate (Arturo de Cordova) who spends most of his time plundering the Cornish coast during the latter part of the seventeenth century. Sheer nonsense, but like all films of its kind made palatable, indeed highly enjoyable, by the professional skill of those working behind the camera. In this case it is the settings of Hans Dreier and Ernst Fegte (AA), the sumptuous colour work of George Barnes and the music score of Victor Young that deserve to be singled out. Directed by Mitchell Leisen, one of the most underrated directors of the thirties and forties.

Production Company:	Paramount
Production and Direction:	Mitchell Leisen
Screenplay:	Talbot Jennings
based on the novel by	
Daphne du Maurier	
Photography (Technicolor):	George Barnes
Music:	Victor Young

Leading Players: Joan Fontaine, Arturo de Cordova, Basil Rathbone, Nigel Bruce, Cecil Kellaway, Ralph Forbes

Note: Filmed in Mendocino Co., 600 miles north of Hollywood, and at Paramount studios, June-October, 1943.

LETTER FROM AN UNKNOWN WOMAN   1948

An adolescent girl, living in Vienna at the turn-of-the-century, has a brief week-long love affair with a philandering pianist and later bears his child. Years later, when both she and her son have been fatally stricken with typhus, she writes him a letter, confessing her undying love. The pianist, to whom the woman was just another conquest, cannot even remember her name. This Max Ophuls film could so easily have been maudlin and sentimental; that it is not is due entirely to Ophuls' delicate handling and the genuine feeling with which he approached the story. It ranks as one of the most beautiful films in the romantic genre and was photographed by the great Franz Planer who shot the same director's pre-war *Liebelei*.

Production Company:	Universal International
Production:	John Houseman
Direction:	Max Ophuls
Screenplay:	Howard Koch
based on the story of the same name by Stefan Zweig	
Photography:	Franz Planer
Music:	Daniele Amfitheatrof

Leading Players: John Fontaine, Louis Jourdan, Mady Christians, Marcel Journet, Art Smith, Howard Freeman, John Good

Note: Filmed in Hollywood, September-November, 1947.

THE BLUE VEIL   1951

A moving portrait of a children's nurse (Jane Wyman) who after losing her own child at birth, devotes the rest of her life to looking after other people's babies. Not the long-suffering Miss Wyman's best-known film in the genre, but one of the most skilfully made, and a fine example of the work of German-born director Curtis Bernhardt who directed several of Hollywood's most accomplished soap operas of the forties and fifties. The supporting cast is headed by Charles Laughton as a middle-aged widower, Cyril Cusack as an Irish toyshop owner and Joan Blondell as a flashy musical comedy queen.

Production Company:	RKO Radio
Production:	Jerry Wald and Norman Krasna
Direction:	Curtis Bernhardt
Screenplay:	Norman Corwin
Story:	François Campaux
Photography:	Franz Planer

Leading Players: Jane Wyman, Charles Laughton, Joan Blondell, Richard Carlson, Agnes Moorehead, Don Taylor, Audrey Totter, Cyril Cusack, Everett Sloane

Note: Filmed in Hollywood, April-June, 1951.

A PLACE IN THE SUN   1951

This brilliant production with its huge close-ups, lingering dissolves and the plaintive melancholy of Franz Waxman's music score brings tragic romance to a maturity that has rarely been achieved in American cinema, either before or since. Montgomery Clift is a poor factory worker who is driven to murder when he finds himself inextricably involved with two women in different stratums of society — a plain, working girl (Shelley Winters) who carries his illegitimate child and a society beauty (Elizabeth Taylor) whose luxury world he craves for. Dreiser's 'An American Tragedy', on which the film is based, states categorically that the boy has no chance from the outset, that he is trapped by his environment and the rules of the society in which he lives. The film says the same but in more muted tones. George Stevens' direction has never been more assured, a fact duly recognised at the Oscar ceremonies.

Production Company:	Paramount
Production and Direction:	George Stevens
Screenplay:	Michael Wilson and
	Harry Brown
Photography:	William C. Mellor
Music:	Franz Waxman

Leading Players: Montgomery Clift, Elizabeth Taylor, Shelley Winters, Anne Revere, Raymond Burr, Herbert Heyes, Keefe Brasselle, Shepperd Strudwick

BREAKFAST AT TIFFANY'S   1961

Audrey Hepburn's dawn sorties (accompanied by Mancini's 'Moon River') to the deserted streets of New York to gaze at the jewellry in Tiffany's window conjure up more romantic memories than almost any other movie of the 60s. Miss Hepburn, as super-tramp Holly Golightly, pays Tiffany's a visit every time she has 'the mean reds' (her own peculiar equivalent of the blues) which is something this film never suffers from. It's romance, charm and tears all the way as Holly enjoys wild escapades in Manhattan and a love affair with the young writer living upstairs (George Peppard). Stylish and softened up considerably from Truman Capote's novella, it takes on a romantic air all its own and demands comparison with Paramount's most sophisticated successes of the 30s.

Production Company:	Paramount
Production:	Martin Jurow and
	Richard Shepherd
Direction:	Blake Edwards
Screenplay:	George Axelrod
from the novella by	
Truman Capote	
Photography (Technicolor):	Franz Planer
Music:	Henry Mancini

Leading Players: Audrey Hepburn, George Peppard, Patricia Neal, Mickey Rooney, Buddy Ebsen, Martin Balsam, John McGiver

RYAN'S DAUGHTER   1970

A film of exquisite beauty, *Ryan's Daughter* is set in a poverty-stricken Irish village just after the Easter Rising and centres on a headstrong young girl who arrives at a disillusioned maturity through her marriage to a middle-aged schoolteacher and a tragic love affair with a British

soldier. Robert Bolt's script is uneven and the playing often no more
than adequate, but director David Lean's handling and the lush camerawork (shades of Selznick in the silhouettes against sunset) make the
film one of the most unashamedly romantic dramas of recent times.
Sarah Miles features as the girl, Robert Mitchum as the schoolteacher
and Christopher Jones as the soldier. John Mills won an Academy
Award for his supporting portrayal of the mute village freak.

Production Company: Metro-Goldwyn-Mayer
Production: Anthony Havelock-Allan
Direction: David Lean
Original Screenplay: Robert Bolt
Photography (Metrocolor/70
    MM Super-Panavision):   Freddie Young
Music: Maurice Jarre
Leading Players: Robert Mitchum, Sarah Miles, Christopher
    Jones, Trevor Howard, John Mills, Leo McKern, Barry Foster

Note: Filmed on location in Ireland, March, 1969-March, 1970.

THE WAY WE WERE   1973

A movie which proves that romantic films don't necessarily have to
propound the theme 'love means never having to say you're sorry' (i.e.
Love Story). It's the tale of the on-off love affair between two opposites
— a young political activist (Barbra Streisand) who never once betrays
her principles, and an All-American boy (Robert Redford) who makes it
to the top via publishing and Hollywood before selling out in the
McCarthy era. Both survive but the romance, inevitably, falls to pieces.
The period covered is from the late 30s to the early 50s. The mood is
tender, nostalgic but never cloyingly sentimental. The reason is due not
only to the performances of the two leads but the sensitive direction
of Sydney Pollack and the music of Marvin Hamlisch which echoes
Casablanca in its theme of loss and regret.

Production Company: Columbia
Production: Ray Stark
Direction: Sydney Pollack
Screenplay: Arthur Laurents
    based on his own novel
Photography (Eastman Color/
    Panavision):   Harry Stradling Jr.
Music: Marvin Hamlisch
Leading Players: Barbra Streisand, Robert Redford, Bradford
    Dillman, Lois Chiles, Patrick O'Neal, Viveca Lindfors

BEHRMAN, S. N. (1893-   ). American playwright/scriptwriter associated with Salka Viertel on several Garbo films during the 30s,
e.g. *Queen Christina* (33), *Anna Karenina* (35), *Conquest* (37),
Two-Faced Woman (41). Also: *Liliom* (30), *Waterloo Bridge* (40).

BERGMAN, INGRID (1915-   ). "Where do the noses go?" asked this
famous Swedish actress as she prepared to kiss Gary Cooper in
Hemingway's *For Whom The Bell Tolls* (43). It took her but a few
seconds to find out and romance quickly blossomed in the midst
of the Spanish Civil War. Coop was just one of her leading men of
the 40s. Several others were also lucky enough to star opposite
Bergman's classical beauty i.e. Leslie Howard in *Intermezzo*
(39), Bogart in *Casablanca* (43) and Bing Crosby in Leo McCarey's
sentimental follow up to *Going My Way* — *The Bells Of St. Mary's*
(45). Also: *Adam Had Four Sons* (41), *Goodbye, Again* (61), *A
Walk In The Spring Rain* (70).

BERNHARDT, CURTIS (1899-   ). Bette Davis (twice), Barbara
Stanwyck, Joan Crawford and Jane Wyman all appeared in this
underrated director's movies which include the psychological
drama *Possessed* (47), the unjustly neglected *The Blue Veil* (51)
(see page 152) and *Interrupted Melody* (55) featuring Eleanor
Parker as Majorie Lawrence. Also: *Devotion* (46), *My Reputation*
(46), *A Stolen Life* (46), *Payment on Demand* (51), *Interrupted
Melody* (55), *Gaby* (56).

BORZAGE, FRANK (1893-1962). Former actor who turned to directing
in the early 20s and became famous for his handling of such
romantic dramas as *Seventh Heaven* (AA) (27) and *Street Angel*
(28), both starring Janet Gaynor. Won his second Academy Award
for his direction of *Bad Girl* (32). Major films: *History is Made at
Night* (37), *The Shining Hour* (38), *Three Comrades* (38), *Till We
Meet Again* (44), *I've Always Loved You* (46).

BOYER, CHARLES (1899-1978). Romantic French actor who became
one of the most popular performers on the American screen. His
Duke de Praslin in *All This And Heaven Too* (40) and Napoleon
Bonaparte in Clarence Brown's *Conquest* (37) belong with his

most famous characterizations in the genre. Peak period: 1937-46 when he worked with Borzage, Stahl, Litvak, Leisen and Goulding. Films: *Private Worlds* (35), *The Garden Of Allah* (36), *Mayerling* (36), *History Is Made At Night* (37), *Love Affair* (39), *When Tomorrow Comes* (39), *Back Street* (41), *Hold Back The Dawn* (41), *The Constant Nymph* (43), *Together Again* (44), *Cluny Brown* (46). Subsequent films, although still in suave romantic vein, were often in the comedy genre — *A Very Special Favour* (64), *How To Steal A Million* (66), *Barefoot In The Park* (67), *The April Fools* (69).

BRAZZI, ROSSANO (1916-   ). Italian actor, several films for Negulesco and Daves. Films: *Three Coins in the Fountain* (54), *Summertime* (*Summer Madness*) (55), *A Certain Smile* (58), *Count Your Blessings* (59), *Light in the Piazza* (62), *Rome Adventure* (62), *The Battle of the Villa Fiorita* (65).

BRENT, GEORGE (1904-1979). Irish-American leading man, a regular partner of Bette Davis at Warner Bros. during the 30s and 40s. Films include *So Big* (32), *The Painted Veil* (34), *Jezebel* (38), *Dark Victory* (39), *The Old Maid* (39), *Till We Meet Again* (40), *The Great Lie* (41), *In This Our Life* (42), *Tomorrow Is Forever* (46), *My Reputation* (46).

BROWN, CLARENCE (1890-   ). Greta Garbo's favourite director, seven films with the actress (all at MGM): *Flesh And The Devil* (27), *A Woman Of Affairs* (29), *Anna Christie* (30), *Romance* (30), *Inspiration* (31), *Anna Karenina* (35), *Conquest* (37), Also: *Letty Lynton* (32), *Sadie McKee* (34), *Chained* (34), *The Gorgeous Hussy* (36), *The White Cliffs Of Dover* (44), *To Please A Lady* (50).

CALVERT, PHYLLIS (1915-   ). British actress, exceedingly popular in the war and post-war periods when, together with Mason, Granger and Lockwood, she played in many of Gainsborough's romantic melodramas e.g. *The Man In Grey* (43), *Fanny By Gaslight* (44), *Madonna Of The Seven Moons* (44), *They Were Sisters* (45), *The Magic Bow* (46), *The Root Of All Evil* (47). More recently appeared in Daves' *The Battle Of The Villa Fiorita* (65) and on TV in the long running soap opera *Kate*.

CHATTERTON, RUTH (1893-1961). American stage and screen actress, famous for her portrayal of *Madame X* (29). Over twenty films during the 1928-39 period, among them *Charming Sinners* (29), *Sarah and Son* (30), *Unfaithful* (31), *The Magnificent Lie* (31), *Tomorrow and Tomorrow* (32), *Lady of Secrets* (36).

COLMAN, RONALD (1891-1959). British actor, at his best in romantic melodrama. Most famous role in the genre: the amnesiac soldier in LeRoy's *Random Harvest* (42). Films: *The White Sister* (23), *Romola* (24), *Tarnish* (24), *His Supreme Moment* (25), *The Dark Angel* (25), *Stella Dallas* (25), *The Magic Flame* (27), *The Unholy Garden* (31), *Cynara* (32).

COTTEN, JOSEPH (1905-   ). After beginning his screen career with Orson Welles (*Citizen Kane, The Magnificent Ambersons*), Cotten concentrated on a series of romantic movies for Selznick, partnering Jennifer Jones in *Since You Went Away* (44), *Love Letters* (45) and best of all, the haunting little fantasy *Portrait of Jennie* (48). Also: *I'll Be Seeing You* (45), *Beyond the Forest* (49), *September Affair* (50).

CRABTREE, ARTHUR (1900-   ). British director, former cameraman, best known for his work at Gainsborough. Films: (as cameraman) *The Man in Grey* (43). As director: *Madonna of the Seven Moons* (44), *They were Sisters* (45), *Caravan* (46).

CRAWFORD, JOAN (1904-1977). A screen sufferer if ever there was one, especially at Warners in the 40s, and although her career took in every kind of movie from musicals to westerns it was in melodramatic soap opera that Joan Crawford shone most effectively e.g. in *Humoresque* (46) as the wealthy dilettante obsessed with violinist John Garfield, *Possessed* (47) and *Daisy Kenyon* (47). Won an Oscar for her long suffering mom in *Mildred Pierce* (45). Films: *Possessed* (31), *Letty Lynton* (32), *Sadie McKee* (34), *Chained* (34), *Forsaking All Others* (35), *I Live My Life* (35), *The Gorgeous Hussy* (36), *The Bride Wore Red* (37), *Mannequin* (38), *The Shining Hour* (38), *Susan And God* (40), *A Woman's Face* (41), *When Ladies Meet* (41), *Possessed* (47), *Harriet Craig* (50), *Torch Song* (53), *Female On The Beach* (55).

CROMWELL, JOHN (1888-   ). One of the genre's leading directors and, like Stahl, Borzage and Sirk, a very much underrated film-maker. Notable work during the 40s on *Since You Went Away* (44), an affectionate study of American family life when the menfolk are away at war, and *The Enchanted Cottage* (45), a tender romance between a badly disfigured pilot and an unattractive girl whose deep and mutual love makes them appear beautiful in each other's eyes. Also: *Unfaithful* (31), *Silver Cord* (33), *Ann Vickers* (33), *If I Were Free* (33), *This Man Is Mine* (34), *Of Human Bondage* (34), *In Name Only* (39), *Anna And The King Of Siam* (46), *Night Song* (47).

DANIELS, WILLIAM (1895-1970). Cameraman on all but five of Greta

Garbo's American films. Pictures with Garbo: *The Torrent* (26), *Flesh and the Devil* (27), *Love* (27), *The Mysterious Lady* (28), *A Woman of Affairs* (29), *Wild Orchids* (29), *The Kiss* (29), *Anna Christie* (30), *Romance* (30), *Inspiration* (31), *Susan Lennox: Her Fall and Rise* (31), *Mata Hari* (32), *Grand Hotel* (32), *As You Desire Me* (32), *Queen Christina* (33), *The Painted Veil* (34), *Anna Karenina* (35), *Camille* (37), *Ninotchka* (39).

DAVES, DELMER (1904-1977). An excellent writer/director of westerns, Daves turned his hand to soap opera during the 60s when he made a long series of romantic melodramas with Troy Donahue, i.e. *A Summer Place* (59), *Parrish* (61), *Susan Slade* (61), *Rome Adventure* (62), *The Battle of the Villa Fiorita* (65).

DAVIS, BETTE (1908-   ). Warners' most famous exponent of romantic drama, particularly during the 1939-45 period when she made, among others, *Dark Victory* (as the dying heroine Judith Traherne) (39), *All This and Heaven Too* (40), *The Great Lie* (41) and *Now Voyager* (42). Starred opposite Charles Boyer, George Brent, Paul Henreid and Claude Rains and worked with most of the studio's top directors, e.g. Edmund Goulding, Anatole Litvak and Irving Rapper. Films in the genre: *So Big* (32), *Of Human Bondage* (34), *Dangerous* (35), *That Certain Woman* (37), *Jezebel* (38), *The Sisters* (38), *The Old Maid* (39) *Old Acquaintance* (43), *Mr. Skeffington* (44), *The Corn is Green* (45), *A Stolen Life* (46), *Deception* (46), *Winter Meeting* (48), *Beyond the Forest* (49), *Payment on Demand* (51).

DE HAVILLAND, OLIVIA (1916-). British-born actress who graduated from playing feminine leads in Errol Flynn swash-bucklers and westerns to more substantial roles for Litvak (*The Snake Pit*), Wyler (*The Heiress*), etc. Appeared in a few romantic dramas during the mid-40s, e.g. Mitchell Leisen's *Hold Back the Dawn* (41) and *To Each His Own* (46). Also played Melanie Hamilton in *Gone With the Wind* (39) and Charlotte Brontë in *Devotion* (46). Others: *My Cousin Rachel* (52), *That Lady* (55), *Light in the Piazza* (61).

DIETERLE, WILLIAM (1893-1972). German director, best remembered for the biographies he made at Warners during the 30s — *The Story of Louis Pasteur* (36), *The Life of Emile Zola* (37), *Juarez* (39), etc. His romantic movies, especially *Love Letters* (45) and the superb *Portrait of Jennie* (48) are no less skilful and like many of his films, have remained neglected in most critical appraisals of the 40s. Also: *I'll Be Seeing You* (45), *This Love of Ours* (45), *September Affair* (50).

DIETRICH, MARLENE (1902-   ). A goddess of the American cinema
during the 30s, Marlene Dietrich was taken to the US by Joseph
von Sternberg after causing a sensation as the night club singer
Lola in *The Blue Angel* (30). Her romantic dramas of the period
included *Morocco* (30), *Song of Songs* (33) and *Garden of Allah* (36).

DUNNE, IRENE (1904-   ). A favourite star of Hollywood soap opera
who appeared for nearly all the major directors — Stahl, Cromwell,
Brown — during the 30s and 40s. Most famous role in the genre:
the blind heroine in Stahl's *Magnificent Obsession* (35). Films:
Back Street (32), *Symphony of Six Million* (32), *The Silver Cord*
(33), *Ann Vickers* (33), *If I Were Free* (33), *This Man is Mine*
(34), *Love Affair* (39), *When Tomorrow Comes* (39), *Penny
Serenade* (41), *Unfinished Business* (41), *A Guy Named Joe* (43),
The White Cliffs of Dover (44), *Together Again* (44), *Anna And
The King Of Siam* (46).

FITZMAURICE, GEORGE (1885-1940). French-born director, several
romantic movies in Hollywood during the silent and early sound
periods, including Garbo's *Mata Hari* (32) and *As You Desire Me*
(32). Also: *The Dark Angel* (25), *Son of the Sheik* (26), *The Night
of Love* (27), *The Unholy Garden* (31).

FONTAINE, JOAN (1917-   ). American actress (sister of Olivia de
Havilland) whose mousy, shy, sometimes terrified heroines were
a key part of the 40s romantic scene. Hitchcock especially found
her timid quality to his liking when he cast her as the persecuted
heroines of *Rebecca* (40) and *Suspicion* (41) as did Ophuls in the
miniature classic *Letter From An Unknown Woman* (48). Leisen,
however, let her have her fling in *Frenchman's Creek* (45) when
she found adventurous romance with pirate Arturo De Cordova.
Also: *The Constant Nymph* (43), *Jane Eyre* (44), *From This Day
Forward* (46), *September Affair* (50), *Decameron Nights* (52),
Island In The Sun (56), *Until They Sail* (57), *A Certain Smile* (58),
Tender Is The Night (61).

FRANCIS, KAY (1903-   ). American actress who worked on numerous
occasions with Frank Borzage and John Cromwell. Films: *Trans-
gression* (31), *Cyanara* (32), *Doctor Monica* (34), *Give Me Your
Heart* (36), *My Bill* (38), *In Name Only* (39).

FRANKLIN, SIDNEY (1893-1972). Metro producer/director, very
active in the former capacity during the 40s when he guided many
of the studio's most expensive soap operas through production,
e.g. *Waterloo Bridge* (40), *Random Harvest* (42), *White Cliffs
of Dover* (44); earlier directed Norma Shearer in *Smilin' Through*

(32) and Merle Oberon in *The Dark Angel* (35). Directed both versions of *The Barretts Of Wimpole Street*, the first in 1934 with Fredric March, Norma Shearer and Charles Laughton, the second in 1957 with Bill Travers, Jennifer Jones and John Gielgud.

GABLE, CLARK, (1901-1960). 'Kiss me Scarlett. . .kiss me. . .just once' whispered Gable to Vivien Leigh halfway through *Gone With The Wind* (39). She did and a million women swooned. To this day Gable's Rhett Butler remains the personification of he-man sexuality. During the 30s and 40s it was simply a case of MGM's top female stars queueing up to play opposite 'The King'. Jean Harlow, Hedy Lamarr, Lana Turner and Greer Garson were just some who stood in line. Films: *A Free Soul* (31), *Susan Lennox: Her Rise And Fall* (32), *It Happened One Night* (34), *Manhattan Melodrama* (34), *Chained* (34), *Wife Versus Secretary* (36), *Love On The Run* (37), *Idiot's Delight* (39), *Comrade X* (40), *They Met In Bombay* (41), *Somewhere I'll Find You* (42), *Adventure* (45), *Homecoming* (48), *To Please A Lady* (50), *Never Let Me Go* (53), *But Not For Me* (59), *It Started In Naples* (59).

GARBO, GRETA (1905-   ). The undisputed queen of Hollywood from the late 20s when she starred in *Flesh and the Devil* (27) to her last film, *Two-faced Woman*, in 1941. Nearly all her films were romances of one kind or another and a few, such as *Queen Christina* (33) and *Camille* (37), belong with the best of their kind ever produced in Hollywood. Films: *The Torrent* (26), *The Temptress* (27), *Love* (27), *The Divine Woman* (28), *The Mysterious Lady* (28), *A Woman of Affairs* (29), *Wild Orchids* (29), *The Single Standard* (29), *The Kiss* (29), *Anna Christie* (30), *Romance* (30), *Inspiration* (31), *Susan Lennox: Her Fall and Rise* (31), *Mata Hari* (32), *Grand Hotel* (32), *As You Desire Me* (32), *The Painted Veil* (34), *Anna Karenina* (35), *Conquest* (37), *Ninotchka* (39).

GARMES, LEE (1898-1978). Distinguished American cameraman. Over 100 films, including *Since You Went Away* (44) for Cromwell and *Love Letters* (45) for Dieterle. Also: *Morocco* (30), *Smilin' Through* (32), *Gone With The Wind* (39) (co. phot.), *Lydia* (41), *The Searching Wind* (46), *My Foolish Heart* (49), *Our Very Own* (50).

GARSON, GREER (1908-   ). Red-headed Irish actress who enjoyed a highly successful career at MGM during the 40s, often rising above the limitations of her soap opera material. Her Edna Gladney, the founder of the Texas Children's Home and Aid Society, in *Blossoms In The Dust* (41) and actress wife of Ronald Colman in *Random Harvest* (42) are both exquisite performances. Films: *Goodbye Mr. Chips* (39) (debut as Donat's young wife), *When Ladies Meet* (41), *Mrs Miniver* (42), *Madame Curie* (43),

Mrs. Parkington (44), *Valley Of Decision* (45), *Adventure* (45), *Desire Me* (47), *The Miniver Story* (50), *Scandal At Scourie* (52), *Her Twelve Men* (54).

GAYNOR, JANET (1907-   ). A popular American star of the late silent and early sound periods when she enjoyed an eleven picture association with Charles Farrell and was directed by the great Frank Borzage in *Seventh Heaven* (27) and *Street Angel* (28). Films include *Lucky Star* (29), *Merely Mary Ann* (31), *The First Year* (32), *Tess of the Storm Country* (32), *Carolina* (34), *Change of Heart* (34), *Ladies in Love* (36), *The Young in Heart* (38). Retired after the latter film then made a brief appearance in *Bernadine* in 1957.

GILBERT, JOHN (1895-1936). Popular American actor of the silent era, Garbo's leading man in four movies, i.e. *Flesh and the Devil* (27), *Love* (27), *A Woman of Affairs* (29), and *Queen Christina* (33). Also: *Arabian Love* (22), *A California Romance* (23), *A Man's Mate* (24), *His Hour* (24), *La Bohéme* (26).

GISH, LILLIAN (1896-   ). America's best-loved heroine of the silent period, making several pictures for D. W. Griffith, including *Hearts of the World* (18), *Broken Blossoms* (19), *Way Down East* (20) and *Orphans of the Storm* (21), a French Revolution story co-starring her sister Dorothy. Also: *The White Sister* (23), *Romola* (24), *The Scarlet Letter* (26), *One Romantic Night* (30). Occasional appearances in recent years, e.g. *Portrait of Jennie* (48), *The Cobweb* (55), *The Comedians* (67).

GOULDING, EDMUND (1891-1951). British-born writer/director, former actor, in Hollywood from the early 20s. The Bette Davis vehicles *Dark Victory* (39), *The Old Maid* (39) and *The Great Lie* (41) are among the most distinguished of his dozen soap operas. Also: *Love* (27), *Riptide* (34), *The Flame Within* (35), *That Certain Woman* (37), *White Banners* (38), *Till We Meet Again* (40), *The Constant Nymph* (43), *Claudia* (43), *Of Human Bondage* (46).

GRANGER, STEWART (1913-   ). Dashing British actor, a regular member of the Gainsborough 'Repertory Company' during the 43/47 period. Films (many opposite James Mason, Margaret Lockwood, etc.) include *The Man in Grey* (43), *Love Story* (44), *Madonna of the Seven Moons* (44), *Fanny by Gaslight* (44), *Caravan* (46), *The Magic Bow* (as Paganini) (46).

HALLER, ERNEST (1896-1970). Celebrated American cameraman,

many Bette Davis movies during his career at Warners including *Dangerous* (35), *That Certain Woman* (37), *Jezebel* (38), *Dark Victory* (39), *All This And Heaven Too* (40), *In This Our Life* (42), *Mr. Skeffington* (44), *A Stolen Life* (46), *Deception* (46), *Winter Meeting* (48). Others: *Gone With The Wind* (39) (co-phot.), *Mildred Pierce* (45), *Devotion* (46), *Humoresque* (46), *The Unfaithful* (47).

HAYWARD, SUSAN (1918-1975). Susan Hayward suffered on screen almost as much as Joan Crawford, which is saying quite a lot. Her screen love affairs were hindered by a variety of mishaps including alcoholism — *Smash Up* (47), *I'll Cry Tomorrow* (55) — and physical accident — *With A Song In My Heart* (52). When she did at last win her deserved Oscar it was for a walk to the gas chamber in Robert Wise's *I Want To Live* (58). Soap operas: *And Now Tomorrow* (44), *They Won't Believe Me* (47), *The Lost Moment* (47), *My Foolish Heart* (49), *The Snows Of Kilimanjaro* (52), *A Woman Obsessed* (59), *Ada* (61), *Back Street* (61), *Stolen Hours* (63), *I Thank A Fool* (63).

HENREID, PAUL (1907-   ). Austrian actor who became one of the romantic idols of the 40s. Played opposite most of the top Warner stars of the period, including Bette Davis in *Now Voyager* (42), the film in which he performed his famous trick of lighting two cigarettes in his mouth at the same time. Films: *Casablanca* (43), *Devotion* (46), *Deception* (46), *Of Human Bondage* (46), *Song Of Love* (47).

HEPBURN, AUDREY (1929-   ). Few were able to resist the appeal of this elfin-like actress when she first burst on the scene in the early 50s as Wyler's runaway princess in *Roman Holiday* (53). Her prize in this first starring role was Gregory Peck and she has continued to snare leading men during the rest of her delightful career e.g. William Holden *and* Humphrey Bogart in *Sabrina* (54), Gary Cooper in *Love In The Afternoon* (57), Fred Astaire in *Funny Face* (57), George Peppard in *Breakfast At Tiffany's* (61). Others: *Green Mansions* (59), *Charade* (63), *Paris When It Sizzles* (64), *My Fair Lady* (64), *Two For The Road* (66).

HEPBURN, KATHARINE (1907-   ). A despairing wave from a carriage window as her train speeds from the Venice station, bringing to an end an all too brief middle-aged love affair with Rossano Brazzi. In these few seconds Katharine Hepburn established herself as one of the greatest screen actresses of the century and although she has enjoyed many supreme moments in other movies she has never quite equalled those final anguished seconds in Lean's *Summertime* (55). Also: *A Bill Of Divorcement* (32), *Alice Adams* (35), *Sylvia Scarlett* (35), *A Woman Rebels* (36), *Quality Street* (37), *Without Love* (45), *Song Of Love* (47), *The Rainmaker* (56).

HOWARD, LESLIE (1893-1943). British actor, seen regularly in Hollywood movies during the 30s. Most famous role: Ashley Wilkes in *Gone With the Wind* (39). Other films in the genre include *A Free Soul* (31), and *Smilin' Through* (32), both opposite Norma Shearer, *Of Human Bondage* (34) with Bette Davis and *Intermezzo* (39) with Ingrid Bergman.

HUNTER, ROSS (1916-   ). American producer who revived the genre during the 50s with lush remakes of *Magnificent Obsession* (54), *Imitation of Life* (59), *Back Street* (61) and *Madame X* (66). Also: *One Desire* (55), *All That Heaven Allows* (55), *There's Always Tomorrow* (56), *Interlude* (57).

JONES, JENNIFER (1919-   ). American actress, former wife of David O. Selznick, whose beach.scene romance with William Holden — she in white bathing suit, he muscular and handsome — caused tears and deep emotion among audiences of the mid-50s, especially when the soundtrack insisted that *Love Is A Many Splendoured Thing* (55). A frequent visitor to the genre in the 40s and 50s, Miss Jones excelled as the young girl spirit in love with struggling artist Joseph Cotten in *Portrait Of Jennie* (48). Films: *Since You Went Away* (44), *Love Letters* (45), *Cluny Brown* (46), *Madame Bovary* (49), *Carrie* (52), *Gone To Earth* (52), *Indiscretion* (54), *Good Morning Miss Dove* (55), *The Barretts Of Wimpole Street* (57), *A Farewell To Arms* (57), *Tender Is The Night* (61).

JOURDAN, LOUIS (1919-   ). Handsome, debonair French actor who carried on the suave Boyer tradition in Hollywood in the post-war years. Charmed a variety of actresses with his elegance and seductive manners including Joan Fontaine in *Letter From An Unknown Woman* (48) and *Decameron Nights* (52), Jennifer Jones in *Madame Bovary* (49) and Grace Kelly in *The Swan* (56). Also: *Bird Of Paradise* (50), *Three Coins In The Fountain* (54), *Gigi* (58), *The Best Of Everything* (59), *Can Can* (60), *The VIPs* (63).

KNOWLES, BERNARD (1900-   ). Another of the popular Gainsborough team of the mid-40s. A cameraman on *Love Story* (44) and later director of *A Place of One's Own* (45) and *The Magic Bow* (46).

KORNGOLD, ERICH WOLFGANG (1897-1957). The Warner Studio's leading composer of the 34/35 period. Films in the genre: *Anthony Adverse* (36), *The Private Lives Of Elizabeth And Essex* (39), *The Constant Nymph* (43), *Devotion* (46), *Deception* (46), *Of Human Bondage* (46).

LEAN, DAVID (1908-). As a film-maker, a man responsible for fewer films over a period of years (just 15 between 1942 and 1970) than any other major director but whose work has always borne the mark of quality, not least when he has portrayed, with extreme sensitivity, the tragic love affairs of the young — *Doctor Zhivago* (65) — and the middle-aged — *Brief Encounter* (46), *Summertime* (55). Also: *The Passionate Friends* (48), *Ryan's Daughter* (70).

LEIGH, VIVIEN (1913-1967). Like Susan Hayward, an exponent of doomed romance on screen, finishing up without Gable in *Gone With The Wind* (39), turning to prostitution in *Waterloo Bridge* (40), throwing herself beneath a train in *Anna Karenina* (48) and trying yet another suicide attempt in *The Deep Blue Sea* (55). Nonetheless several distinguished performances in the genre. Films: *A Yank At Oxford* (38), *Lady Hamilton* (41), *The Roman Spring Of Mrs. Stone* (61).

LEISEN, MITCHELL (1898-1972). A former set designer for DeMille, Leisen began directing whilst at Paramount and was responsible for two of the most enjoyable romances of the 40s in *Frenchman's Creek* (45) and *To Each His Own* (46), the former film being especially notable for the quality of its colour work. Also: *Hold Back the Dawn* (41), *Kitty* (45), *Golden Earrings* (47).

LEROY, MERVYN (1900-). Veteran American director who made his name with realistic social pictures at Warners during the 30s but who made an abrupt change of pace when he joined MGM in 1938. His two major soap operas — *Waterloo Bridge* (40) and *Random Harvest* (42) — were among the most accomplished made in Hollywood during the war period. Also: *Blossoms in the Dust* (41), *Madame Curie* (43), *Homecoming* (48).

LITVAK, ANATOLE (1902-1974). Russian-born director responsible for many soap operas during his early years in Hollywood; later turned to thrillers (see page 68) and war movies (see page 199). Films: *Mayerling* (36), *The Sisters* (38), *All This and Heaven Too* (40), *This Above All* (42), *Goodbye Again* (61).

LOCKWOOD, MARGARET (1916-). Gainsborough's leading 'wicked lady' of the mid-40s and one of Britain's top box-office stars of the decade. Films include *The Man in Grey* (43), *I'll Be Your Sweetheart* (44), *Love Story* (44), *A Place of One's Own* (45), *The Wicked Lady* (as Lady Skelton) (45), *Jassy* (47).

MASON, JAMES (1909-). British leading man who became something of a box-office phenomenon after his performance as the sadistic Marquis of Rohan in *The Man in Grey* (43). Appeared in several other Gainsborough romances including *The Wicked Lady* (45), with Margaret Lockwood, before moving to Hollywood in the late 40s. Films: *Fanny by Gaslight* (44), *A Place of One's Own* (45), *They Were Sisters* (45), *The Seventh Veil* (45), *Pandora and the Flying Dutchman* (51), *The Story of Three Loves* (53).

METTY, RUSSELL (1900-1978). Universal cameraman who provided some superb Technicolor for Douglas Sirk during the 50s. Films: *Magnificent Obsession* (54), *All That Heaven Allows* (55), *There's Always Tomorrow* (56), *Imitation of Life* (59), *By Love Possessed* (61), *Madame X* (66).

MONTGOMERY, ROBERT (1904-). American actor, a popular leading man of Joan Crawford, Greta Garbo and other leading actresses before the war. Romantic dramas include *Their Own Desire* (30), *The Divorcee* (30), *Inspiration* (31), *Letty Lynton* (32), *Riptide* (34), *Vanessa, Her Love Story* (35).

MOOREHEAD, AGNES (1906-1974). American actress often seen in supporting roles — nurses, life-long companions, rich relatives, etc., — in the romantic films of Jane Wyman and Greer Garson. Never quite matched her two debut performances for Orson Welles in *Citizen Kane* (41) and *The Magnificent Ambersons* (42). Films include: *Jane Eyre* (44), *Since You Went Away* (44), *Mrs. Parkington* (44), *Our Vines Have Tender Grapes* (45), *Johnny Belinda* (48), *The Blue Veil* (51), *Scandal At Scourie* (53), *Magnificent Obsession* (54), *All That Heaven Allows* (55), *The Swan* (56), *Jessica* (62).

NEGULESCO, JEAN (1900-). A Rumanian-born director who did much to keep the romantic genre alive during the 50s. Films: *Humoresque* (46), *Johnny Belinda* (48), *Scandal At Scourie* (53), *Three Coins In The Fountain* (54), *The Gift Of Love* (58), *A Certain Smile* (58), *Count Your Blessings* (59), *Jessica* (62), *The Pleasure Seekers* (65), *Hello-Goodbye* (70).

OBERON, MERLE (1911-). British actress, best remembered for her performance as Cathy in William Wyler's version of *Wuthering Heights* (39). Several films for Korda during the 30s. Films: *The Dark Angel* (35), *The Divorce of Lady X* (38), *Till We Meet Again* (40), *Lydia* (41), *This Love of Ours* (45), *Night Song* (47), *Twenty Four Hours of a Woman's Life* (52), *Desiree* (54).

ORRY-KELLY (1897-1964). Australian-born costume designer who dressed most of the Bette Davis pictures at Warners. Films: *Dangerous* (35), *That Certain Woman* (37), *Jezebel* (38), *The Old Maid* (39), *Dark Victory* (39), *The Letter* (40), *The Great Lie* (41), *Now Voyager* (42), *Old Acquaintance* (43), *Mr. Skeffington* (44), *The Corn is Green* (45), *A Stolen Life* (46).

PIDGEON, WALTER (1897-). One of Metro's biggest box-office stars of the war period. Eight films with Garson, including *Blossoms in the Dust* (41), *Mrs. Miniver* (42), *Madame Curie* (as Pierre Curie) (43), and *Mrs. Parkington* (44). Also: *Weekend at the Waldorf* (45), *The Secret Heart* (46), *Scandal at Scourie* (53), *The Last Time I Saw Paris* (54), *These Wilder Years* (56).

RAINS, CLAUDE (1890-1967). Polished British performer whose long Hollywood career took in three excellent Bette Davis movies, i.e. *Now Voyager* (42), *Mr. Skeffington* (44) and *Deception* (46). Also: *White Banners* (38), *Four Daughters* (38), *Casablanca* (43), *This Love of Ours* (45), *The Passionate Friends* (48).

RAPPER, IRVING (1898-). American director who did his most interesting work at Warners during the 40s. Three pictures with Bette Davis: *Now Voyager* (42), *The Corn is Green* (45), *Deception* (46).

REDFORD, ROBERT (1936-). Blond movie superstar possessed of all-American boyish good looks, a winning smile and not a little charm, all of which were displayed to full advantage in Pollack's tragic romance *The Way We Were* (73). Effective as Fitzgerald's doomed bootlegger *The Great Gatsby* (74) and the staid lawyer husband of a sex-charged Jane Fonda in *Barefoot In The Park* (67).

ROBINSON, CASEY (1903-). Hollywood screenwriter and producer; five Bette Davis soap operas, i.e. *Dark Victory* (39), *The Old Maid* (39), *All This and Heaven Too* (40), *Now Voyager* (42), *The Corn is Green* (45).

ROGERS, GINGER (1911-). An excellent musical comedy actress, Ginger Rogers also made a few ventures into the romantic genre during the 40s when she won an Oscar for her performance as *Kitty Foyle* (40), a girl from the wrong side of the tracks who loves well but unwisely. Also: *The Primrose Path* (40), *I'll Be Seeing You* (44), *Weekend At The Waldorf* (45), *Heartbeat* (46).

SHEARER, NORMA (1900-). Actress wife of producer Irving G.

Thalberg and the first lady of MGM before the War. Many films in the genre, including *The Trial of Mary Dugan* (29), *Their Own Desire* (30), *The Divorcee* (AA) (30), *Strangers May Kiss* (31), *Strange Interlude* (32), *Smilin' Through* (32), *Riptide* (34), *The Barretts of Wimpole Street* (34), *Her Cardboard Lover* (42).

SIRK, DOUGLAS (1900-). Danish director, in Hollywood during the 44-58 period when he filmed distinguished remakes of Stahl's pre-war weepies, *Magnificent Obsession* (54) and *Imitation of Life* (59). Others (all at Universal): *All I Desire* (53), *All That Heaven Allows* (55), *There's Always Tomorrow* (56), *Interlude* (57).

STAHL, JOHN M. (1886-1950). American director, long neglected because he worked in a less serious genre than many of Hollywood's more famous film makers. He was at his peak during the 30s when he guided Irene Dunne through *Back Street* (32) and *Magnificent Obsession* (35) and Claudette Colbert through *Imitation of Life* (34). Also: *Only Yesterday* (33), *When Tomorrow Comes* (39), *Leave Her to Heaven* (45).

STANWYCK, BARBARA (1907-). Apart from King Vidor's remake of *Stella Dallas* (37) in which she played the tragic heroine of the title, Stanwyck's romantic movies are generally less well known than those of other actresses of the period. Both Curtis Bernhardt's *My Reputation* (46) in which she featured as a young widow and Sirk's *All I Desire* (53) deserve wider recognition.

STEINER, MAX (1888-1972). One of the most talented composers ever to work in Hollywood, Steiner scored most of Bette Davis' movies of the 40s, winning an Academy Award for his music for *Now Voyager* (42) and an additional Oscar for *Since You Went Away* (44). Films: *A Bill Of Divorcement* (32), *Of Human Bondage* (34), *The Garden Of Allah* (36), *That Certain Woman* (37), *Jezebel* (38), *White Banners* (38), *The Sisters* (38), *Dark Victory* (39), *The Old Maid* (39), *Gone With The Wind* (39), *Intermezzo* (39), *All This And Heaven Too* (40), *The Letter* (40), *The Great Lie* (41), *In This Our Life* (42), *Casablanca* (43), *Mildred Pierce* (45), *The Corn Is Green* (45), *A Stolen Life* (46), *Tomorrow Is Forever* (46), *My Reputation* (46), *The Unfaithful* (47), *Winter Meeting* (48), *Johnny Belinda* (48), *Beyond The Forest* (49), *Close To My Heart* (51), *Marjorie Morningstar* (58), *A Summer Place* (59), *Parrish* (61), *Susan Slade* (61), *Rome Adventure* (62).

STOTHART, HERBERT (1885-1949). The leading composer at MGM for more than two decades. Scored all the studio's major soap operas, including Garbo's *Queen Christina* (33), *The Painted*

Veil (34) and *Camille* (37). Films: *The White Sister* (33), *Riptide* (34), *Chained* (34), *The Barretts of Wimpole Street* (34), *Vanessa, Her Love Story* (35), *Anna Karenina* (35), *Conquest* (37), *Waterloo Bridge* (40), *Blossoms in the Dust* (41), *Random Harvest* (42), *Madame Curie* (43), *The White Cliffs of Dover* (44), *Valley of Decision* (45), *If Winter Comes* (48).

SULLAVAN, MARGARET (1911-1960). Although she made only sixteen films in her career, Margaret Sullavan worked regularly in the romantic genre, giving excellent performances for John Stahl in *Only Yesterday* (33), Robert Stevenson in *Back Street* (41) and, not least, for Rudolph Mate as the dying housewife in *No Sad Songs for Me* (50). Others: *The Good Fairy* (35), *Three Comrades* (38), *The Shining Hour* (38), *Appointment with Love* (41).

TAYLOR, ELIZABETH (1932-   ). Romance (both on screen and off) has surrounded this British born actress since her love affair with her horse Pi in *National Velvet* (45). Her coming of age occurred in 1951 when she starred as Montgomery Clift's society love in George Stevens' classic *A Place In The Sun*. Films: *Rhapsody* (54), *The Last Time I Saw Paris* (54), *Raintree County* (57), *The VIPs* (63), *The Sandpiper* (65), *The Only Game In Town* (70), *Ash Wednesday* (73).

TAYLOR, ROBERT (1911-1969). Handsome American star likely to be best remembered for his romantic roles at MGM before the war, e.g. Armand in Cukor's *Camille* (37). Films: *Magnificent Obsession* (35), *The Gorgeous Hussy* (36), *Three Comrades* (38), *Waterloo Bridge* (40), *Her Cardboard Lover* (42).

TONE, FRANCHOT (1906-1969). American actor, at his peak during the 30s when he appeared in a long line of romantic dramas, mostly at MGM. Joan Crawford, Bette Davis and Margaret Sullavan all figured among his leading ladies. Main films: *Sadie McKee* (34), *No More Ladies* (35), *Dangerous* (35), *The Unguarded Hour* (35), *The Gorgeous Hussy* (36), *Between Two Women* (37), *Three Comrades* (38).

TURNER, LANA (1920-   ). A top star in romantic drama since the early 40s, Lana Turner enjoyed long careers at Metro and Universal where she appeared in Sirk's remake of *Imitation Of Life* (59) and also in *Madame X* (66). Other films in the genre: *Somewhere I'll Find You* (42), *Weekend At the Waldorf* (45), *Homecoming* (48), *A Life Of Her Own* (50), *The Flame And The Flesh* (54), *Diane* (55), *By Love Possessed* (61).

VALENTINO, RUDOLPH (1895-1926). Italian-American matinée idol of the 20s. Numerous performances as the great lover before his premature death in 1926. Films: *The Four Horsemen of the Apocalypse* (21), *Camille* (21), *The Sheik* (21), *Blood and Sand* (22), *Beyond the Rocks* (22), *Monsieur Beaucaire* (24), *The Eagle* (25), *Son of the Sheik* (26).

WAXMAN, FRANZ (1906-1967). German composer who made an outstanding contribution to the genre, especially at Warners, during the 40s. Main films: *Magnificent Obsession* (35), *Three Comrades* (38), *The Young In Heart* (38), *The Shining Hour* (38), *Old Acquaintance* (43), *Mr. Skeffington* (44), *Humoresque* (46), *Possessed* (47), *Nora Prentiss* (47), *The Blue Veil* (51), *A Place In The Sun* (51), *Phone Call From A Stranger* (52), *My Cousin Rachel* (52), *Miracle In The Rain* (56), *Love In The Afternoon* (57), *Sayonara* (57), *Count Your Blessings* (59), *Beloved Infidel* (59).

WILDER, BILLY (1906-). Romance in connection with this often acidly humorous director might seem a little wide of the mark but several of his films of the 50s betrayed a soft centre, reminiscent at times of Lubitsch with their charm, humour and surprising delicacy, i.e. *The Emperor Waltz* (47), *Sabrina* (54), *Love In The Afternoon* (57).

WYLER, WILLIAM (1902-). American director whose romantic movies, *Jezebel* (38) and *Wuthering Heights* (39), were both made during the pre-war period. His delightful *Roman Holiday* (53), made on location in Rome with Gregory Peck and Audrey Hepburn, almost qualifies for the genre with its charm and superb final sequence.

WYMAN, JANE (1914-). American actress mostly seen in routine leads before her Academy Award winning performance as the deaf mute farm girl *Johnny Belinda* (48), Thereafter specialized in superior tear-jerkers, e.g. *The Blue Veil* (51), *So Big* (53), *Magnificent Obsession* (54), *Lucy Gallant* (55), *All That Heaven Allows* (55), *Miracle in the Rain* (56).

YOUNG, ROBERT (1907-). American actor, a frequent performer in romantic drama during the pre-war and war periods. *Claudia* (43), its sequel *Claudia and David* (46), and *The Enchanted Cottage* (45) are perhaps his best remembered films in the genre. Joan Crawford, Laraine Day and Dorothy McGuire (three films) were among his leading ladies. Films: *The Right to Romance* (33), *Carolina* (34), *The Bride Wore Red* (37), *Three Comrades* (38), *The Shining Hour* (38), *The Trial of Mary Dugan* (41), *Journey for Margaret* (42), *Those Endearing Young Charms* (45).

YOUNG, VICTOR (1900-1956). American composer, long at Paramount. At his best when composing the lush, romantic themes for *Frenchman's Creek* (45), *Love Letters* (45) and *September Affair* (50). Also: *Hold Back The Dawn* (41), *For Whom The Bell Tolls* (43), *Kitty* (45), *To Each His Own* (46), *The Searching Wind* (46), *Golden Earrings* (47), *My Foolish Heart* (49), *Our Very Own* (50), *Payment On Demand* (51), *Three Coins In The Fountain* (54).

Romance, 1973 style. Barbra Streisand and Robert Redford in *The Way We Were*.

Clark Gable and Vivien Leigh sparring together in the classic *Gone With The Wind* (1939).

(Below)   Paul Newman and Steve McQueen involved in more serious business — saving lives in a skyscraper fire in *The Towering Inferno* (74).

The cause of all the trouble. The massive 138 storey tower block alight in *The Towering Inferno* (74).

Swashbuckling in medieval England. Robert Taylor swiftly disposing of Francis
De Wolffe in *Ivanhoe* (52).

Arab chieftain Sean Connery soothes the fears of white captive Candice Bergen
in *The Wind And The Lion* (75).

The grisly end for Ahab (Gregory Peck) in John Huston's exciting version of Melville's *Moby Dick* (56).

(Above and below)   A midnight swimmer finds herself cut in two by the monster shark in *Jaws* (75) and a group of young bathers suddenly find themselves faced with a similar hazard!

(Above) A happy Scrooge welcomes Christmas morning in Richard Williams'
Oscar-winning *A Christmas Carol* (72).

Martin Rosen's cartoon version of *Watership Down* (78).

EPICS

THE BIRTH OF A NATION   1915

The first American film of any real size and scope; a panoramic two-and-three-quarter hour story of the American Civil War from the early years of the conflict to the bitter aftermath. Based on 'The Clansman' by Thomas Dixon, the film is told from the Southern point of view (Griffith was bitterly accused of anti-negro bias) and includes all the major events of the war — the battles, the surrender of Lee, the sacking of Atlanta, Lincoln's assassination, the coming of the carpetbaggers and the rise of the Ku Klux Klan. Griffith's use of camera movement and his dynamic editing techniques ensure the film a permanent place in the history of the cinema and put it high on the short list of film masterpieces. After seeing the film President Woodrow Wilson remarked: "It is like writing history with lighting; my only regret is that it is so terribly true."

Production Company: Epoch Producing
                       Corporation
                       (D. W. Griffith)
Direction: D. W. Griffith
Screenplay: D. W. Griffith
   based on the novel and play 'The
   Clansman' by Thomas Dixon
Photography: G. W. Bitzer
                       assisted by Karl Brown
Music arranged by: Joseph Carl Breil and
                       D. W. Griffith
Leading Players: Lillian Gish, Mae Marsh, Henry Walthall, Miriam Cooper, Mary Alden, Ralph Lewis, George Seigmann, Walter Long, Robert Harron

Note: Griffith began filming in July, 1914, after spending some six weeks in rehearsal. He continued shooting until October, filming interiors at the Fine Arts Studio in Hollywood and the action scenes in the surrounding hills and valleys of Southern California. The movie was premiered in Los Angeles in February, 1915 under its original title *The Clansman*. A month later it was shown at The Liberty Theatre, New York as *The Birth of a Nation*. Among the players in the film who subsequently became famous were Donald Crisp, as General Lee, and Raoul Walsh, who featured as John Wilkes Booth.

INTOLERANCE   1916

Although well over fifty years old, this is still the greatest epic of them all, telling, in parallel action, four stories in different periods of history, all dealing with the theme of "Love's struggle and intolerance through the ages". The four stories — a modern story of the slums, the persecution and execution of Christ, the massacre of the Huguenots and the sacking of Babylon by Cyrus — were all shot without a script. In the original print which ran to 3 hours 25 minutes, each story had a basic colour tint, the modern story being filmed partly in amber, the Judean story in blue, the medieval French story in sepia and the Babylonian episode in grey-green. This last story contained some of the biggest sets ever constructed for a Hollywood film, the full-scale replica of Belshazzar's Empire City covering 254 acres and standing 200 feet tall. The film was originally shown with two intervals, one after the prologue and the other before the grand climax.

Production Company: Wark Producing Corporation
                             (D. W. Griffith)
Direction and Screenplay: D. W. Griffith
Photography: G. W. Bitzer and
                             Karl Brown
Assistant Direction: George Siegmann, W. S. Van Dyke,
                             Joseph Henaberry, Erich von
                             Stroheim, Edward Dillon and
                             Tod Browning
Leading Players: Mae Marsh, Fred Turner, Robert Harron, Sam de
   Grasse (Modern story); Howard Gaye, Lillian Langdon, Olga Grey,
   Bessie Love (Judean story), Margery Wilson, Eugene Pallette,
   Spottiswoode Aiken, Ruth Handforth (Medieval French story);
   Constance Talmadge, Elmer Clifton, Alfred Paget, Seena Owen,
   Carl Stockdale (Babylonian story)

Note: Griffith filmed *Intolerance* in the summer and autumn of 1915. Editing took just two months, a remarkable achievement considering the complexity of the work. The total budget was close to $2 million, a third of which was taken up by the Babylonian sequence. In the assault by Cyrus's armies on the walls of Babylon, 16,000 extras were seen on the screen at one time, one of the largest mass shots in the history of the cinema.

SAMSON AND DELILAH   1950

The first of the post-war epics and the film which set the pace for the genre during the fifties and sixties. Victor Mature plays the Danite strongman and Hedy Lamarr the Philistine temptress who eventually destroys him. Derisively described by one American critic as "the most expensive haircut in film history", the film is often crude and vulgar, but the elaborate spectacles — Samson's fight with a lion, his annihilation of an army with a jawbone of an ass and his destruction of the Temple of Gaza — are skilfully directed and remain in the memory long after the banalities of the screenplay have been forgotten.

Production Company:	Paramount
Production and Direction:	Cecil B. DeMille
Screenplay:	Jesse L. Lasky, Jun., and
based on a treatment by	Fredric M. Frank
Harold Lamb of the Bible Story	
and Vladimir Jabotinsky's	
novel 'Judge and Fool'	
Photography (Technicolor):	George Barnes
Music:	Victor Young

Leading Players: Victor Mature, Hedy Lamarr, George Sanders, Angela Lansbury, Henry Wilcoxon, Olive Deering, Fay Holden, Julia Faye, Russell Tamblyn

Note: Filmed at the Paramount Studios in Hollywood, October-December, 1949. The Temple of Gaza which occupied two of the Studio's sound stages was erected over a period of five months and was destroyed in just under two minutes.

WAR AND PEACE   1956

An uneven, occasionally impressive attempt by King Vidor to transfer Tolstoy's gigantic masterpiece to the screen. Inevitably it compares badly with the book (even at three-and-a-half hours only the bare bones of the story are presented), but the playing of Audrey Hepburn as Natasha, Herbert Lom as Napoleon and Oscar Homolka as General Kutzov often compensate for the limitations of the script. The spectacle in the second half, which includes the Battle of Borodino and the retreat from Moscow, is magnificently staged. Vidor worked on the film for a year-and-a-half and supervised the cutting, scoring, and every other aspect of the picture. Paramount later reduced the film to its final running time of 208 minutes.

Production Company:	Paramount
Production:	Dino de Laurentiis
Direction:	King Vidor
Screenplay:	Bridget Boland, Robert Westerby, King Vidor, Ivo Perilli, Mario Camerini and Ennio De Concini
From the novel by Tolstoy	
Photography (Technicolor/ VistaVision):	Jack Cardiff and Aldo Tonti
Music:	Nino Rota

Leading Players: Audrey Hepburn, Henry Fonda, Mel Ferrer, Vittorio Gassman, Herbert Lom, Oscar Homolka, Anita Ekberg, John Mills

Production note: Filmed in Italy, July-December, 1955.

THE TEN COMMANDMENTS   1956

DeMille's last film (his 70th) tells the story of Moses from the time he was found in the bullrushes to his receiving the Commandments on Mount Sinai. It is the longest and crudest of his epics, yet even allowing for the vulgarity of the screenplay and the ineptness of the playing, the spectacle remains. This cannot be faulted, for it is staged with a showman's flair and a supreme knowledge of cinema. The Exodus, which took ten days to film on location in Egypt, and the parting and closing of the Red Sea (shot in a studio tank in Hollywood) are especially brilliant and the photography of all four cameramen is outstanding.

Production Company:	Paramount
Production and Direction:	Cecil B. DeMille
Screenplay:	Aeneas MacKenzie,
from Dorothy Clarke Wilson's	Jesse L. Lasky, Jun.,
novel 'Prince of Egypt',	Jack Gariss and
Rev. J. H. Ingraham's novel	Fredric M. Frank
'Pillar of Fire' and Rev. G. E.	
Southon's 'On Eagle's Wings'	
Photography (Technicolor/	
VistaVision):	Loyal Griggs
Additional Photography:	J. Peverell Marley, John Warren
	and Wallace Kelley
Music:	Elmer Bernstein

Leading Players: Charlton Heston, Yul Brynner, Anne Baxter, Edward G. Robinson, Yvonne De Carlo, Debra Paget, John Derek, Sir Cedric Hardwicke, Nina Foch, Vincent Price, John Carradine

Note: Filmed on location in Egypt and the Sinai Peninsula, October-December, 1954; and at Paramount's Hollywood Studios, March-August, 1955.

BEN-HUR   1959

MGM's spectacular remake of Major General Lew Wallace's 'A Tale of the Christ', with Charlton Heston as the young Jew who is converted to Christianity and Stephen Boyd as his Roman enemy Messala. Notable for its literate dialogue (the screenplay is the work of at least six men although only Karl Tunberg is credited) and the action sequences of second unit directors Andrew Marton and Yakima Canutt, the film is marred only by its excessive length. The famous chariot race in the Circus Maximus took three months to shoot and runs to nine minutes on the screen.

Production Company:	Metro-Goldwyn-Mayer
Production:	Sam Zimbalist
Direction:	William Wyler
Screenplay:	Karl Tunberg
based on the novel by	
Lew Wallace	
Photography (Technicolor/	
MGM Camera 65):	Robert L. Surtees
Music:	Miklos Rozsa

Leading Players: Charlton Heston, Jack Hawkins, Stephen Boyd,
   Hugh Griffith, Martha Scott, Cathy O'Donnell, Haya Hayareet,
   Sam Jaffe, Finlay Currie, Frank Thring

Note: Filmed at the Cinecittà Studios in Rome, May, 1958-January,
   1959. A silent version of the novel, shot in 1925 and starring Ramon
   Novarro and Francis X. Bushman, was also filmed in Italy with
   additional scenes shot in Hollywood.

SPARTACUS   1960

One of the most intelligent epics of the sixties, this Stanley Kubrick
film is based on the novel by Howard Fast, and deals with an abortive
uprising of slaves in Rome in 73 B.C. The film is concerned with man's
struggle against oppression and, on occasion, particularly during the
scenes in the Roman Senate, it attains a standard of writing and performance only too rarely achieved in the genre. The single combat between
Spartacus (Kirk Douglas), armed with a short Thracian sword and a
negro slave armed with a trident and net, is the most impressive of the
action sequences. The opening credit titles, photographed in alternating
tints against Roman sculptures, were designed by Saul Bass.

Production Company:	Bryna/Universal
Production:	Edward Lewis
Direction:	Stanley Kubrick
Screenplay:	Dalton Trumbo
based on the novel by	
Howard Fast	
Photography (Technicolor/	
Super Technirama 70):	Russell Metty
Music:	Alex North

Leading Players: Kirk Douglas, Laurence Olivier, Jean Simmons,
   Charles Laughton, Peter Ustinov, John Gavin, Nina Foch, Herbert
   Lom, John Ireland, John Dall

Note: Filmed at the Universal Studio in Hollywood, on nearby
   locations in the San Fernando Valley, and on location in Spain,
   January-August, 1959.

EL CID   1961

A handsome film to look at, Anthony Mann's epic follows the adventures
of the legendary Castilian warrior El Cid who, in 11th century Spain,
united both the Moors and Christians under one King. The barely
competent playing is surmounted by the film's visual qualities. One
shot in particular, when the dead El Cid, complete in shining armour
and strapped to his white horse, rides out along the misty sea shore and
is lit suddenly by the first rays of the morning sun, is breathtakingly
beautiful.

Production Company:	Samuel Bronston/Dear Films
Production:	Samuel Bronston
Direction:	Anthony Mann
Screenplay:	Philip Yordan and
	Fredric M. Frank
Photography (Technicolor/	
Super Technirama 70):	Robert Krasker
Music:	Miklos Rozsa

Leading Players: Charlton Heston, Sophia Loren, Genevieve Page, Raf Vallone, John Fraser, Gary Raymond, Hurd Hatfield, Douglas Wilmer, Frank Thring

Note: Filmed on location in Spain, November, 1960-May, 1961. Eleventh-century castles in Burgos, Valladolid and Valem were used during the six month's shooting.

CLEOPATRA   1963

An indifferent spectacular about the Egyptian queen Cleopatra, and her life with Caesar and Mark Antony between 48 and 30 B.C. Out of five years preparation, ten months shooting and a budget of 37 million dollars, writer/director Joe Mankiewicz fashions two exciting moments of grandeur — Cleopatra's triumphant entry into Rome and her journey by Royal Barge to Tarsus. Not by any means a major epic, but of interest because it is probably the most famous 'bad luck' picture of all time and nearly brought the Fox studio to its knees. Heading the cast: Elizabeth Taylor (Cleopatra), Richard Burton (Mark Antony), Rex Harrison (Caesar).

Production Company:	Twentieth Century-Fox
Production:	Walter Wanger
Direction:	Joseph L. Mankiewicz
Screenplay:	Joseph L. Mankiewicz,
	Ranald MacDougall,
	Sidney Buchman
Photography (De Luxe/Todd AO):	Leon Shamroy
Music:	Alex North

Leading Players: Elizabeth Taylor, Richard Burton, Rex Harrison, Pamela Brown, George Cole, Hume Cronyn

Note: Cleopatra began shooting under Rouben Mamoulian's direction at Pinewood Studios, England, in September, 1960. Elizabeth Taylor's co-stars were Peter Finch (Caesar) and Stephen Boyd (Antony). The disasters that befell the film at this time included some appallingly cold weather and Miss Taylor's near-fatal illness, which lasted for several weeks. By January, 1961, only ten minutes of film had been shot at a cost of five million dollars. Mamoulian resigned and the film was scrapped. Shooting eventually restarted in Rome in September with Burton and Harrison as the new male stars and Mankiewicz as the new director. Filming continued, mostly at Cinecittà, until June 1962, bad weather again interfering with production. Additional scenes were later filmed in Egypt and Spain.

THE TOWERING INFERNO   1974

Studios became wary of investing in epics after *Cleopatra*. Those who did quickly got their fingers burnt. *The Greatest Story Ever Told, The Bible* and a handful of others proved to be expensive miscalculations and ancient times 'Hollywood style' was suddenly passé entertainment. In the 70s the epics of old have been replaced by disaster spectaculars in which earthquakes and tidal waves have rocked the screen and provided spectacle for a new generation. *The Towering Inferno* remains the most notable example of this new style entertainment if only because it tackles a problem that has brought disaster in real life — fire in a skyscraper office block. Its warnings about the constant need for safety checks, use of inferior wiring, cost trimming etc. are timely; its spectacle, as flames lick up to those trapped on the upper floors, devastating and its production values typical of Hollywood at its most accomplished. Steve McQueen leads the heroic rescue operations, Paul Newman is the unlucky designer/architect. Most terrifying moment: when doors are flung open to reveal a massive, unexpected wall of flame.

Production Company:	Twentieth Century-Fox/ Warner Bros.
Production:	Irwin Allen
Direction:	John Guillermin
Screenplay: based on the novels 'The Tower' by Richard Martin Stern and 'The Glass Inferno' by Thomas M. Scortia and Frank M. Robinson	Stirling Silliphant
Photography (DeLuxe/ Panavision):	Fred Koenekamp
Music:	John Williams

Leading Players: Steve McQueen, Paul Newman, William Holden, Faye Dunaway, Fred Astaire, Susan Blakely, Richard Chamberlain, Jennifer Jones, O. J. Simpson, Robert Vaughn

EPICS: WHO'S WHO

ALLEN, IRWIN (1916-). What DeMille was to spectaculars in the 40s and 50s and Bronston in the 60s so Allen is to the genre in the disaster conscious 70s. To date he has capsized an ocean liner in *The Poseidon Adventure* (72), set fire to a massive tower block in *The Towering Inferno* (74) and let loose an army of killer bees in *The Swarm* (78). And there is the promise of more to come! i.e. *Beyond The Poseidon Adventure* (79), *The Day The World Ended* (79).

BAKER, STANLEY (1927-1976). A Welsh actor who spent several years in spectaculars and routine thrillers before turning to more serious subjects with Joseph Losey. Epics include *Knights of the Round Table* (54), *Alexander the Great* (56), *Helen of Troy* (56), *Sodom and Gomorrah* (62).

BAUCHENS, ANNE (1882-1967). One of the best of Hollywood's long line of talented women editors, Anne Bauchens cut every DeMille film between 1918 and 1956, including both versions of *The Ten Commandments* (23) (56), *The King of Kings* (27) and *Samson and Delilah* (50). Also: *The Sign of the Cross* (32), *Cleopatra* (34), *The Crusades* (35).

BOYD, STEPHEN (1928-1977). Irish-born actor whose first 'epic' performance as Messala in *Ben Hur* (59) remained the best of his career. Other films in the genre included *The Fall Of The Roman Empire* (64), *Genghis Khan* (65), *The Bible* (66). In 1962 he was cast as Mark Antony in Mamoulian's abandoned British version of *Cleopatra*, the film that was eventually completed in 1963 with Elizabeth Taylor, Richard Burton and Rex Harrison in the leads.

BRONSTON, SAMUEL (1910-). Russian-born producer, in Hollywood for many years. Took over as 'epic king' after the death of DeMille in 1959, producing expensive spectaculars from his headquarters in Madrid, e.g. *King Of Kings* (61), *El Cid* (61), *55 Days At Peking* (63), *The Fall Of The Roman Empire* (64).

BRYNNER, YUL (1915-). Bald-headed Russian-American actor seen in several Hollywood epics since portraying Rameses II in DeMille's *The Ten Commandments*. Films: *Solomon and Sheba* (59), *Taras Bulba* (62), *Kings of the Sun* (63).

BURTON, RICHARD (1925-). Best-known for his Mark Antony in the ill-fated *Cleopatra* (63), Burton gave his finest epic performance several years earlier when he played the title role in Robert Rossen's *Alexander the Great* (56). His other major film in the genre was *The Robe* (53), the first feature to be photographed in CinemaScope.

CANUTT, YAKIMA (1895-). Second-unit director, former stunt man. With Andrew Marton shot the 9-minute chariot race in Wyler's *Ben-Hur* (59). Also filmed the second unit action sequences in *El Cid* (61), *The Fall Of The Roman Empire* (64), *Khartoum* (66).

CARDIFF, JACK (1914-). Britain's leading colour cameraman of the post-war period. Photographed *War and Peace* (56) for Vidor and *The Vikings* (58) for Fleischer; later directed *The Long Ships* (64).

CURRIE, FINLAY (1878-1968). Scottish character actor forever famous for his portrayal of the convict Magwitch in David Lean's *Great Expectations* (47). After playing Peter in LeRoy's *Quo Vadis* (51) he made regular appearances in Hollywood's epics: *Ben-Hur* (59), *The Tempest* (59), *Solomon And Sheba* (59), *Joseph And His Brethren* (60), *Francis Of Assisi* (61), *Cleopatra* (63), *The Fall Of The Roman Empire* (64).

CURTIS, TONY (1925-). Heroic leading man of several swashbucklers (see page 214) and epics of the 50s. Films: *The Vikings* (58), *Spartacus* (60), *Taras Bulba* (62).

DE LAURENTIIS, DINO (1919-). Italian producer associated with many Italian/American co-productions, e.g. *Ulysses* (55), *War And Peace* (56), *The Tempest* (59), *Barabbas* (62), *The Bible* (66), *Waterloo* (71), *King Kong* (76), *The Hurricane* (79).

DEMILLE, CECIL B. (1881-1959). The genre's most celebrated director, DeMille parted the Red Sea twice, burnt Rome and destroyed the Temple of Gaza during his 45-year career. A master showman and superb technician, he never once worked from an adequate script; if he had a masterpiece might have resulted. Spectaculars include *The Ten Commandments* (23), *King of Kings* (27), *The Sign of the Cross* (32), *Cleopatra* (34), *The Crusades* (35), *Samson and Delilah* (50), *The Ten Commandments* (56).

FRANK, FREDRIC M. (1911-1977). American screenwriter with long experience of writing for the genre. Several films for DeMille, including *Samson and Delilah* (50) and *The Ten Commandments* (56). Also *El Cid* (61) for Bronston.

GRIFFITH, D. W. (1880-1948). The first major film-maker of the American cinema, Griffith directed two of the most memorable epics of the silent screen in *The Birth of a Nation* (15) and *Intolerance* (16). Of his later works both *Orphans of the Storm* (22), a story of the French Revolution, and *America* (24) fall into the epic category.

HAYWARD, SUSAN (1918-1975). Spirited Brooklyn-born actress, best remembered for her tortured portrayals in the problem films *I'll Cry Tomorrow* (55) and *I Want to Live* (AA) (58). Three epics during the 50s: *David and Bathsheba* (51), *Demetrius and the Gladiators* (54), *The Conquerer* (56).

HESTON, CHARLTON (1924-   ). One of the great epic stars, Heston appeared regularly in the genre during the 50s and 60s appearing for DeMille in *The Ten Commandments* (as Moses) (56) and winning an Academy Award for his performance in the title role of Wyler's *Ben-Hur* (59). Others: *El Cid* (61), *55 Days At Peking* (63), *The War Lord* (65), *Khartoum* (as General Gordon) (66). More recently has figured prominently in the epic (i.e. disaster spectacular) revival, failing to cope with the after effects of a major Los Angeles earth tremor in *Earthquake* (74) but regaining confidence by successfully landing a damaged Boeing 747 in *Airport 75* (75).

IRELAND, JOHN (1914-   ). Canadian-born actor who made a big impression early in his career as the disillusioned reporter in *All the King's Men* (49). Later roles less rewarding. Epics: *Spartacus* (60), *55 Days at Peking* (63), *The Fall of the Roman Empire* (64).

KENNEDY, GEORGE (1925-   ). Oscar-winning actor (for *Cool Hand Luke*) who has become a regular performer on today's epic-disaster scene. As aviation engineer Joe Patroni he has dealt in turn with a plane blown half apart in *Airport* (70), a Boeing 747 that has collided in mid-air in *Airport 75* (75) and a luxury airliner that has sunk beneath the ocean in *Airport 77* (77). He was also round (as a cop) when the disastrous tremor struck Los Angeles in *Earthquake* (74) and reappears as Patroni in *Airport 79 — Concorde* (79).

KOPP, RUDOLPH. American composer. Three films for DeMille in the 30s: *The Sign of the Cross* (32), *Cleopatra* (34), *The Crusades* (35).

KRASKER, ROBERT (1913-). Oscar-winning British cameraman who photographed epics for Robert Rossen and Anthony Mann. Films: *Alexander the Great* (56), *El Cid* (61), *The Fall of the Roman Empire* (64).

LASKY, JESSE L. JUN. (1910-). Veteran Hollywood screenwriter, long associated with Cecil B. DeMille. Films in the genre include *Samson and Delilah* (50), *The Ten Commandments* (56), *John Paul Jones* (59).

LAUGHTON, CHARLES (1899-1962). Remarkable British actor who brought his talents to bear on recreating several historical characters for the screen — Henry VIII, Captain Bligh, Rembrandt etc. Leered effectively for DeMille as an effeminate Nero in *The Sign Of The Cross* (32) and as Herod drooled over Rita Hayworth in *Salome* (53); brought distinction to the role of the Roman senator Gracchus in *Spartacus* (60). In 1937 he appeared for von Sternberg in the unfinished *I Claudius*.

LOM, HERBERT (1917-). Czech actor, long in Britain. Played Napoleon in King Vidor's *War and Peace* (56). Also *The Big Fisherman* (as Herod Antipas) (59), *Spartacus* (60), *El Cid* (61).

LOREN, SOPHIA (1934-). Italian actress, in numerous American films since the mid-50s. Her two epics for Bronston — *El Cid* (61) and *The Fall of the Roman Empire* (64) — were preceded by *The Pride and the Passion* (57), an adaptation by Stanley Kramer of C. S. Forester's 'The Gun'.

MACPHERSON, JEANIE. DeMille's scenarist from the early silent days (1915) to 1930. Authored the scenarios for the first *The Ten Commandments* (23) and *The King of Kings* (27).

MANN, ANTHONY (1906-1967). Best-known for the series of westerns he directed in the 50s (see page 103), Mann turned to spectacle later in his career, producing in *El Cid* (61) the most beautiful of all post-war epics, and in *The Fall of the Roman Empire* (64), one of the most intelligent. In 1951 he directed the burning of Rome sequences in *Quo Vadis*.

MARLEY, J. PEVERELL (1901-1964). Veteran American cinematographer. Cameraman for DeMille on *The King of Kings* (27) and
on both versions of *The Ten Commandments* (23) (56).

MARTON, ANDREW (1904-   ). Hungarian-born director, best-known
for his second-unit work on contemporary American epics. Outstanding achievement: the 9-minute chariot race in *Ben-Hur*
(59). Also: *55 Days At Peking* (63), *Cleopatra* (63), *The Fall Of
The Roman Empire* (64).

MATURE, VICTOR (1915-   ). Rugged American leading man whose
performance as Samson in DeMille's *Samson and Delilah* (50)
led to many subsequent epic roles, including those in *The Robe*
(53), *Demetrius and the Gladiators* (54) and *The Egyptian*
(54).

MILNER, VICTOR (1893-   ). Paramount's leading cameraman of
the 30s. Eight films for DeMille, including *Cleopatra* (34) which
won him an Academy Award, and *The Crusades* (35).

PALANCE, JACK (1920-   ). One of Hollywood's most popular heavies,
a specialist in the genre since playing Attila the Hun in Sirk's
Sign Of The Pagan (54). Others: *The Silver Chalice* (54), *The
Mongols* (61), *Barabbas* (62), *Sword Of The Conqueror* (62), *The
Horsemen* (71).

REEVES, STEVE (1926-   ). A former Mr. World and Mr. Universe,
whose rippling muscles took care of most of the obstacles put in
his way during his long series of dubbed Italian epics of the 50s
and 60s. Heaved, panted and clichéd his way through the following:
Hercules (58), *Hercules Unchained* (59), *Goliath And The Bar-
barians* (59), *The Giant Of Marathon* (59), *The Last Days Of
Pompeii* (60), *The Trojan Horse* (62), *Duel Of The Titans* (63),
The Slave (63), *Sandokan The Great* (65).

ROZSA, MIKLOS (1907-   ). Celebrated Hungarian composer, in
Hollywood since the early 40s. Many epic scores since first
becoming associated with the genre in 1951. Films: *Quo Vadis*
(51), *Ben-Hur* (AA) (59), *King of Kings* (61), *El Cid* (61), *Sodom
and Gomorrah* (62).

SHAMROY, LEON (1901-1974). Talented American cameraman,
unequalled when working in colour. Lensed all the major Fox
epics of the post-war years, including *Cleopatra* (63), which won

him an Oscar for the best colour photography of the year. Also: *David And Bathsheba* (51), *The Robe* (53), *The Egyptian* (54).

SHARIF, OMAR (1932-). Egyptian actor who first rose to fame in David Lean's *Lawrence of Arabia*. Concentrated on several large-scale spectaculars during the 60s e.g. *The Fall of the Roman Empire* (64), *Genghis Khan* (65), *Doctor Zhivago* (65), *The Last Valley* (71), *The Horsemen* (71).

SILLIPHANT, STIRLING (1918-). American screenwriter who has achieved his best results in the crime genre (see page 75) but who of late has concentrated on scripting on a somewhat larger scale, drowning, burning and stinging to death well over twenty top Hollywood stars in the disaster spectaculars *The Poseidon Adventure* (72) (co-scripted), *The Towering Inferno* (74) (scripted) and *The Swarm* (78) (scripted).

SIMMONS, JEAN (1929-). British actress whose performance as the slave girl Varinia in Kubrick's *Spartacus* (60) remains one of the best of her Hollywood career. Appeared also in *The Robe* (53), opposite Richard Burton, and *The Egyptian* (54).

SURTEES, ROBERT L. (1906-). A leading American cameraman since 1944, Surtees photographed many of Metro's large-scale post-war productions, including the epics *Quo Vadis* (51) and *Ben-Hur* (59) winning an Academy Award for his work on the latter film.

THRING, FRANK. Australian actor who appeared as Pontius Pilate in Wyler's *Ben-Hur* (59). Other epics: *The Vikings* (58), *King of Kings* (as Herod Antipas) (61), *El Cid* (61).

TIOMKIN, DIMITRI (1899-). Prolific American composer whose work has embraced most film genres, particularly the western (see page 110). During the 50s and 60s scored several Hollywood spectaculars, including *Land of the Pharaohs* (55), *55 Days at Peking* (63), *The Fall of the Roman Empire* (64).

USTINOV, PETER (1921-). Talented actor/writer/director who first appeared in a Hollywood epic in 1951 when he played Nero in LeRoy's *Quo Vadis*. Later featured in *The Egyptian* (54) and as Batiatus, master of the gladiator school in Kubrick's *Spartacus* (60).

WAXMAN, FRANZ (1906-1967). Brilliant German-born composer whose epic scores were generally superior to the quality of the films themselves. Films: *The Silver Chalice* (54), *Demetrius And The Gladiators* (54), *The Story Of Ruth* (60), *Taras Bulba* (62).

WILCOXON, HENRY (1905-   ). Veteran British actor, a regular performer for DeMille between 1930 and 1956. Epics include *Cleopatra* (as Mark Antony) (34), *The Crusades* (35), *Samson And Delilah* (50), *The Ten Commandments* (56), *The War Lord* (65).

YORDAN, PHILIP (1913-   ). American screenwriter who brought an intelligence and high degree of literacy to the Hollywood spectacular. Worked for Bronston during the 60s, scripting two films for Nicholas Ray — *King of Kings* (61), *55 Days at Peking* (63) — and two for Anthony Mann — *El Cid* (61), *The Fall of the Roman Empire* (64).

YOUNG, WALDEMAR. American scriptwriter who worked regularly for DeMille during the 30s. Films: *The Sign of the Cross* (32), *The Crusades* (35).

WAR

ALL QUIET ON THE WESTERN FRONT   1930

No film has ever condemned war more impassionately than this one, which, like *The Grapes of Wrath* and *Citizen Kane*, is one of the enduring masterpieces of the American cinema. The story concerns a group of German youths who volunteer to serve their Fatherland during the 1st World War and are gradually disillusioned by the death, squalor and hunger they find at the Front. By the film's close all the soldiers, seen in the initial sequences as schoolboys in a classroom, have been killed. The battle scenes, notably a terrifying bayonet charge across the trenches, are unforgettable and the final sequence when a young infantryman (Lew Ayres) is shot while reaching for a butterfly is one of the most poetic in all cinema.

Production Company:	Universal
Direction:	Lewis Milestone
Production:	Carl Laemmle
Screenplay:	Dell Andrews,
	Maxwell Anderson
	and George Abbott

from the novel by
Erich Maria Remarque
Photography: Arthur Edeson
Leading Players: Lew Ayres, Louis Wolheim, John Wray, Owen Davis, Jun., Raymond Griffith, Slim Summerville, Ben Alexander

Note: Filmed (mainly in sequence) at the Universal Studio, Balboa and the Irving ranch nr. Hollywood. The butterfly scene was the brainchild of German cameraman Karl Freund who suggested it to Milestone after the film had been completed with a different ending. Milestone shot the scene, using his own hand, and cut it into the finished film.

A WALK IN THE SUN   1945

This is Milestone's homage to the ordinary guys who served in World War II. The 'walk in the sun' is that taken by a platoon of American infantrymen when they land on an Italian beachhead and march towards a German-occupied farm house. The actual mission is of little value, but it tests the men's nerves, emotions and fears as they soldier on towards their objective. The men — a cross-section of Americans including an understanding sergeant, an American-Italian machine gunner, a minister's son and a first aid man — perform no mock heroics. Some live and some die. At the final count the film is a series of vignettes graphically illustrating man's response to war and his desperate loneliness and bewilderment when participating in combat. "We've got a grandstand seat," says one of the soldiers during the long walk. "Only we can't see nothing. That's the trouble with war. You can't see nothing! You have to find the enemy by ear!"

Production Company:	Twentieth Century-Fox
Production and Direction:	Lewis Milestone
Screenplay:	Robert Rossen
from the novel by Harry Brown	
Photography:	Russell Harlan
Music:	Fredric Efrem

Leading Players: Dana Andrews, Richard Conte, Sterling Holloway, George Tyne, John Ireland, Herbert Rudley, Richard Benedict, Lloyd Bridges

TWELVE O'CLOCK HIGH   1949

A ruthless C.O. (Gregory Peck) takes over command of a shattered American bomber group stationed in England during the last war, restores their morale and turns them into an efficient fighting force once more at the expense of his own health. Recollected nostalgically by the station adjutant when he visits a deserted airfield after the war, the film concerns itself not with the physical side of war (there is only one combat sequence) but with its physical and psychological effects on the health of men. Beautifully performed by the all-male cast, especially Peck, who here gives perhaps the finest performance of his career.

Production Company:	Twentieth Century-Fox
Production:	Darryl F. Zanuck
Direction:	Henry King
Screenplay:	Sy Bartlett and
from their own novel	Beirne Lay, Jun.
Photography:	Leon Shamroy
Music:	Alfred Newman

Leading Players: Gregory Peck, Hugh Marlowe, Gary Merrill, Millard Mitchell, Dean Jagger, Paul Stewart

Note: Filmed in Hollywood, May-July, 1949.

THE WOODEN HORSE   1950

A film version of the famous escape from Stalag Luft III in 1943, when three British prisoners tunnelled their way to freedom, using a wooden vaulting horse to cover the underground passage dug daily during the physical exercise period in the camp. Up until the point of escape (about halfway through) the film has considerable tension, but the later sequences when the men make their way to Sweden and safety are more commonplace. Important none the less, for it was the first escape picture to come out of World War II and spawned several successors, e.g. *Albert R.N., The Colditz Story, Stalag 17, The Great Escape.*

Production Company: Wessex/London Films
Production: Ian Dalrymple
Direction: Jack Lee
Screenplay: Eric Williams
   from his own novel
Photography: G. Pennington Richards
Music: Clifton Parker
Leading Players: Leo Genn, David Tomlinson, Anthony Steel, David Greene, Peter Burton, Michael Goodliffe, Bryan Forbes

Note: Filmed on location in Germany near Soltau on Luneberg Heath and in England, September, 1949-January, 1950.

THE CRUEL SEA   1953

A long, restrained adaptation of Nicholas Monsarrat's best-selling novel about the lives of the crew serving on a corvette during the Battle of the Atlantic. The domestic scenes ashore now appear somewhat naïve, but the overall film, with its quiet authority and penetrating look at the physical hardships and loneliness of men at sea, has if anything improved with age and stands head and shoulders above the majority of Britain's flag-waving movies of the post-war era. Jack Hawkins, in his most accomplished service role, features as Captain Ericson.

Production Company: Ealing Studios
Production: Leslie Norman
Direction: Charles Frend
Screenplay: Eric Ambler
   from the novel by
   Nicholas Monsarrat
Photography: Gordon Dines
Music: Alan Rawsthorne
Leading Players: Jack Hawkins, Donald Sinden, John Stratton, Denholm Elliott, Stanley Baker, John Warner, Bruce Seton, Liam Redmond, Virginia McKenna

Note: Filmed at Ealing Studios, Portland Bill and Devonport in the summer and autumn of 1952.

A TIME OUT OF WAR   1954

The story of an unofficial truce between two Northern soldiers and one Confederate infantryman on a hot, drowsy afternoon during the American Civil War. For an hour the men talk and fish and exchange rations and tobacco. At the appointed time of five o'clock they return to their positions on either side of a shallow river, their guns at the ready. The film runs twenty-two minutes. It is not sentimental and never hammers its points home, but it speaks volumes about the absurdity of war and ranks among the best short films ever made.

Production Company:	Sanders Bros. Productions
Production:	Denis Sanders
Photography:	Terry Sanders
Assistant Director:	Rita Montgomery
Music:	Frank Hamilton
Leading Players:	Barry Atwater, Robert Sherry, Alan Cohen

Note: A Time out of War was made as a thesis project while Denis Sanders was working for his Master's degree in the Department of Theatre Arts, University of California. It was based on the little-known short story 'Pickets', written in the 1890s by Robert W. Chambers.

THE BRIDGE ON THE RIVER KWAI   1957

Apart from *In Which We Serve*, which he co-directed with Noel Coward, this is David Lean's only war film. It is a large, expensive piece of entertainment about the construction by British prisoners in 1943 of a bridge on the notorious Burma-Siam railway and of its subsequent destruction by an Allied sabotage unit. The film has dated more than most of its kind, but Alec Guinness's performance as the British colonel, who fails to see that by encouraging his men to build the bridge to the best of their ability he is collaborating with the enemy, is superb. Technically the production is magnificent, especially the bridge-blowing scene, at the end, but as the anti-war movie which it purports to be, it is not really in the same class as *Paths of Glory* released the same year.

Production Company:	Horizon/Columbia
Production:	Sam Spiegel
Direction:	David Lean
Screenplay:	Pierre Boulle
based on his own novel	
Photography (Technicolor):	Jack Hildyard
Music:	Malcolm Arnold
Leading Players:	Alec Guinness, William Holden, Jack Hawkins, Sessue Hayakawa, Geoffrey Horne, James Donald, Andre Morell, Peter Williams

Note: Filmed on location in Ceylon, October, 1956-April, 1957.

PATHS OF GLORY   1957

A study of corruption in the French Army during the First World War, centring on the court martial and execution of three innocent soldiers selected as scapegoats for the failure of a suicidal infantry attack on the Western Front. The film comes out against war and all it stands for and also finds time to cast a savage eye on the officers of the French High Command who put personal ambition before military strategy and the safety of their men. Technically outstanding — Kubrick makes brilliant use of the tracking shot during the infantry attack — and beautifully played from first to last by Kirk Douglas as the officer elected to defend the soldiers, Adolphe Menjou as the French Corps Commander and George Macready as a promotion-hungry general.

Production Company:	Bryna/United Artists
Production:	James B. Harris
Direction:	Stanley Kubrick
Screenplay:	Stanley Kubrick
based on the novel by	Calder Willingham and
Humphrey Cobb	Jim Thompson
Photography:	George Krause
Music:	Gerald Fried

Leading Players: Kirk Douglas, Ralph Meeker, Adolphe Menjou, George Macready, Wayne Morris, Richard Anderson

Note: Filmed on location in Germany, April-May, 1957.

BATTLE OF BRITAIN   1969

Large-scale version of the R.A.F.'s victory over the German Luftwaffe in the summer and autumn of 1940. Fictional stories are interwoven with factual episodes, resulting often in trite dialogue and stereotyped characterization, but whenever the factual events are presented the film is remarkably effective. Sir Laurence Olivier plays Air Chief Marshal Sir Hugh Dowding, Trevor Howard features as Air Vice-Marshal Keith Park and Michael Caine, Christopher Plummer and Robert Shaw appear as Battle of Britain pilots. The flying sequences are the film's main asset, and one sequence in particular when the noise of the planes and their gunfire is faded out and replaced by Walton's music is great cinema.

Production Company:	Spitfire Productions United Artists
Production:	Harry Saltzman and S. Benjamin Fisz
Direction:	Guy Hamilton
Screenplay:	James Kennaway and Wilfred Greatorex
based partly on the book 'The Narrow Margin' by Derek Wood and Derek Dempster	
Photography (Panavision/ Technicolor):	Freddie Young
Music:	Ron Goodwin and William Walton

Leading Players: Laurence Olivier, Robert Shaw, Christopher Plummer, Susannah York, Ian McShane, Michael Caine, Kenneth More, Trevor Howard, Patrick Wymark, Ralph Richardson

Note: Filmed in England and Spain, March-November, 1968. The English airfield locations were all authentic and included Duxford, Hawkinge, North Weald and Northolt. The Luftwaffe sequences were shot in Spain on Tablana airfield near Seville. Rex Harrison was originally scheduled for the role of Air Vice-Marshal Park but was replaced by Trevor Howard.

M-A-S-H   1970

This black, extremely funny comedy is set in a mobile army hospital during the Korean War and concerns three hell-raising army surgeons who keep their sanity only by completely disregarding army bureaucracy and joking to each other as they operate on the endless number of wounded men who come in from the Front. Described by some critics as showing 'the brutalizing effects of war' and others as nothing more than an irreverent 'Carry On in Korea', the film is not so much anti-war as anti-authority, which is perhaps the main reason why it was banned from U.S. Army and Airforce theatres. The only shots fired in the film are those fired from the starting gun during a hilarious football game between rival units.

Production Company:	Aspen/Twentieth Century-Fox
Production:	Ingo Preminger
Direction:	Robert Altman
Screenplay:	Ring Lardner, Jun.
based on the novel by Richard Hooker	
Photography (De Luxe/ Panavision):	Harold E. Stine
Music:	Johnny Mandel

Leading Players: Donald Sutherland, Elliott Gould, Tom Skerritt, Sally Kellerman, Robert Duvall, Jo Ann Pflug, Rene Auberjonois, Roger Bowen

Note: Filmed April-June, 1969.

PATTON: LUST FOR GLORY   1970

Franklin Schaffner's study of 'Blood and Guts' Patton, the controversial American general who, during World War II, forfeited command of the Seventh Army in Sicily because he slapped and accused of cowardice a soldier suffering from battle fatigue. Where the film succeeds so admirably is in its presentation of a *complete* portrait of a highly complex man, showing not only his arrogance, personal flamboyance (he wore a gun holster with two ivory-handled pistols) and less endearing characteristics, but also something of his delicacy and overriding passion for war. 'God help me, I love it,'' he says as he walks among the corpses after battle, ''I love it all.'' Among the finest screen biographies of recent times; George C. Scott won but refused the 1970 Academy Award for his performance in the leading role.

Production Company:	Twentieth Century-Fox
Production:	Frank McCarthy
Direction:	Franklin J. Schaffner
Screenplay:	Francis Ford Coppola
based on material from the	and Edmund H. North
books 'Patton: Ordeal and	
Triumph' by Ladislas Farago	
and 'A Soldier's Story' by	
Omar M. Bradley	
Photography (DeLuxe Color/	
Dimension 150):	Fred Koenekamp
Music:	Jerry Goldsmith

Leading Players: George C. Scott, Karl Malden (Omar M. Bradley), Michael Bates, Stephen Young, Michael Strong, Cary Loftin

Note: Patton had an eighteen-week shooting schedule (January-May, 1969) and was filmed in Spain (battle sequences), England, Morocco and Greece. Post production work was done in Hollywood. The film was named Best of the Year by the Academy of Motion Picture Arts and Sciences.

COMING HOME   1978

That Vietnam should raise its fearsome head in the late 70s, long after hostilities have ceased, comes as no surprise. It takes time for a scarred nation to lick its wounds. Yet the questions raised in this movie are the same as those raised on campuses in the late 60s. The film concentrates on the effects of the war on both men *and* women, on the problems they have to face during the conflict and after the war, when they have to come to terms with a new set of values. Jane Fonda is the focal point, a lonely wife who helps out in a veteran's hospital and finds herself caught between her physical passion for paralysed veteran Jon Voight and her loyalty to hawkish Marine Corps husband Bruce Dern. The attitudes are conflicting, the time (1968) faithfully recreated through a mosaic of songs by The Beatles, Bob Dylan, Mick Jagger etc. Not a shot is fired. One simply witnesses lives being transformed by an unseen horror. The final sequences as the tragically disturbed Dern sheds his uniform and medals and plunges naked into the sea is sobering and pessimistic in the extreme.

Production Company:	United Artists
Production:	Jerome Hellman
Direction:	Hal Ashby
Screenplay:	Waldo Salt and Robert C. Jones
Story:	Nancy Dowd
Photography (DeLuxe Color):	Haskell Wexler
Music:	Songs by The Beatles, Bob Dylan, Aretha Franklin, Mick Jagger, Simon and Garfunkel and others

Leading Players: Jane Fonda, Jon Voight, Bruce Dern, Robert Carradine, Penelope Milford, Robert Ginty

ADDISON, JOHN (1920-). British composer, in films since 1948. Several war movies during the 50s: *The Red Beret* (53), *Cockleshell Heroes* (55), *Reach For The Sky* (56), *I Was Monty's Double* (58), *Guns At Batasi* (64), *The Charge Of The Light Brigade* (68), *A Bridge Too Far* (77).

ALDRICH, ROBERT (1918-). Controversial American director of three savage war films: *Attack* (56), a story of cowardice and corruption in an American army unit during World War II, *The Dirty Dozen* (67) and *Too Late the Hero* (70).

ANDERSON, MICHAEL (1920-). British director, at his peak during the 50s when he filmed Mike Todd's super spectacle *Around The World In Eighty Days* (56) and the war films *The Dam Busters* (55) and *Yangtse Incident* (57). Also: *Operation Crossbow* (65), *Conduct Unbecoming* (75).

ANDREWS, DANA (1912-). Twentieth Century-Fox star who made numerous war movies for his studio. Best performance in the genre: Sergeant Tyne who takes command of the platoon in Milestone's *A Walk in the Sun* (45). Films: *Crash Dive* (43), *North Star* (43), *The Purple Heart* (44), *A Wing and a Prayer* (44), *The Best Years of Our Lives* (46), *The Frogmen* (51), *The Battle of the Bulge* (65), *In Harm's Way* (65), *The Devil's Brigade* (68).

ANDREWS, HARRY (1911-). British supporting player, excellent at portraying tough army types, e.g. the R.S.M. in Lumet's *The Hill* (65). Films: *A Hill In Korea* (56), *Ice Cold In Alex* (58), *Circle Of Deception* (60), *633 Squadron* (64), *Sands Of The Kalahari* (65), *Play Dirty* (68), *The Charge Of The Light Brigade* (68), *Battle Of Britain* (69), *Too Late The Hero* (70).

ARNOLD, MALCOLM (1921-). British composer, most famous for his adaptation of the Colonel Bogey march in Lean's *The Bridge on the River Kwai* (57) (AA). Also: *The Sea Shall Not Have Them* (54), *Dunkirk* (58), *Tunes of Glory* (60), *The Heroes of Telemark* (65).

ASQUITH, ANTHONY (1902-1968). British director whose *Way to the Stars* (45) is one of Britain's best remembered war movies of the 40s. Outstanding achievement in the genre: *Orders to Kill* (58), a bitter story of wartime espionage scripted by Paul Dehn. Also: *We Dive at Dawn* (43).

ATTENBOROUGH, RICHARD (1923-). One of the most talented of British actors, mostly seen in cowardly roles early in his career. More recently has directed the film version of Joan Littlewood's *Oh! What A Lovely War* (69), *Young Winston* (72) and *A Bridge Too Far* (77), the story of the Battle of Arnhem. Films (as actor): *In Which We Serve* (42), *Morning Departure* (50), *The Gift Horse* (52), *Dunkirk* (58), *Sea Of Sand* (58), *Danger Within* (59), *The Great Escape* (63), *Guns At Batasi* (64), *The Sand Pebbles* (66), *Conduct Unbecoming* (75).

BAKER, STANLEY (1927-1976). Welsh-born actor, in films since 1941. War pictures: *The Cruel Sea* (53), *The Red Beret* (53), *A Hill in Korea* (56), *Yesterday's Enemy* (59), *The Guns of Navarone* (61), *Sands of the Kalahari* (65), *The Last Grenade* (70).

BARTLETT, SY (1909-1978). American writer-producer. Films: *Twelve O'Clock High* (49), *Pork Chop Hill* (59), *A Gathering Of Eagles* (63), *In Enemy Country* (68), *Che!* (69).

BENDIX, WILLIAM (1906-1964). Likeable, Brooklyn-born actor, often seen as a tough but good-natured G.I. Films: *Wake Island* (42), *Guadalcanal Diary* (43), *A Bell for Adano* (45), *Submarine Command* (51), *Battle Stations* (56), *The Deep Six* (58).

BOGARDE, DIRK (1920-). Intelligent British actor, in several war movies early in his career. Excellent as the defending counsel of Tom Courtenay in Losey's *King And Country* (64) and Lt-Gen. Frederick 'Boy' Browning in *A Bridge Too Far* (77). Films: *Appointment In London* (52), *They Who Dare* (53), *The Sea Shall Not Have Them* (54), *Ill Met By Moonlight* (57), *The Password Is Courage* (62), *Oh! What A Lovely War* (69).

BROWN, HARRY (1917-). American novelist-screenwriter. Films: *The True Glory* (45), *A Walk in the Sun* (45), *Sands of Iwo Jima* (49), *Eight Iron Men* (52), *D-Day, the Sixth of June* (56), *Between Heaven and Hell* (56).

BURTON, RICHARD (1925-). In his very first year in Hollywood this Welsh born actor was thrown into the desert campaign against Mason's Rommel in *The Desert Rats* (53). He emerged victorious even though the film was below par for the course. Since then he has revisited the genre every five or six years, most recently as the mercenary commander out to rescue a deposed political leader in a central African state in *The Wild Geese* (78). Others: *Bitter Victory* (57), *The Longest Day* (62), *Where Eagles Dare* (69), *Raid On Rommel* (71), *Sergeant Steiner* (79).

BUTTOLPH, DAVID. Hollywood composer, associated with many war films, including Farrow's documentary-styled account of the conflict on *Wake Island* (42). Also: *Thunder Birds* (42), *Crash Dive* (43), *Submarine Command* (51), *PT 109* (63).

CAINE, MICHAEL (1933-). Top British star of the 60s. Appeared as one of the 'Few' in Hamilton's *Battle Of Britain* (69). Also: *A Hill In Korea* (56), *Play Dirty* (68), *Too Late The Hero* (70), *The Eagle Has Landed* (77), *A Bridge Too Far* (77).

CHALLIS, CHRISTOPHER (1919-). Ace British cameraman, active at the start of the post-war British self-glorification boom e.g. *Angels One Five* (52) and still going strong — *Force 10 From Navarone* (78). In between: *The Battle Of The River Plate* (56), *Ill Met By Moonlight* (57), *Sink The Bismarck* (60), *The Victors* (63).

CLIFT, MONTGOMERY (1920-1966). Sensitive American actor whose limited output (16 films in 18 years) included *The Search* (48), *From Here to Eternity* (as Robert E. Lee Prewitt) (53), *The Young Lions* (58) and *Judgment at Nuremberg* (61).

COOPER, GARY (1901-1961). American actor who appeared in many war pictures during his 35-year career; his performance as World War I hero Alvin C. York won him an Academy Award as best actor of 1941. Films include: *The Real Glory* (39), *Sergeant York* (41), *The Story of Dr. Wassell* (44), *Task Force* (49), *The Court-Martial of Billy Mitchell* (55).

DMYTRYK, EDWARD (1908-). American director, former editor, best known in the genre for his ambitious but ultimately disappointing version of Irwin Shaw's war novel *The Young Lions* (58). Also: *Hitler's Children* (43), *Behind The Rising Sun* (43), *Back To Bataan* (45), *Eight Iron Men* (52), *Anzio* (68).

DOUGLAS, KIRK (1916-). American actor most of whose war films are only routine; his defence counsel in Kubrick's *Paths of Glory* (57) is however a notable achievement in a brilliant film (see 188). Also: *Act of Love* (54), *The Hook* (63), *The Heroes of Telemark* (65), *In Harm's Way* (65), *Is Paris Burning?* (66).

FAIRCHILD, WILLIAM (1918-   ). British scriptwriter and director, very active in the genre during the 50s. Films: *Morning Departure* (screen) (50), *The Gift Horse* (screen) (52), *The Malta Story* (screen) (53), *The Silent Enemy* (screen and dir.) (58).

FARROW, JOHN (1904-1963). Australian-born director particularly at home with sea movies and, to a lesser degree, war pictures. The first of his war films, *Wake Island*, won him the New York Critics Award for best direction of 1942. Films: *The Commandos Strike At Dawn* (42), *The Hitler Gang* (44), *Submarine Command* (51), *The Sea Chase* (55).

FINCH, PETER (1916-1977). British actor, in Australia early in his career. War movies: *The Wooden Horse* (50), *A Town Like Alice* (56), *The Battle Of The River Plate* (as Hans Langsdorff, Captain of the 'Graf Spee') (56), *Operation Amsterdam* (57).

FLYNN, ERROL (1909-1959). Warner swashbuckling king who changed from costume drama to World War II adventures during the 40s. "Won the war" for America in the notorious *Objective, Burma!* (45), the film that was withdrawn from public showing in England because of its glorification of American's part in the Burma Campaign. Also: *Dive Bomber* (41), *Desperate Journey* (42), *Edge of Darkness* (43), *Northern Pursuit* (43), *Uncertain Glory* (44).

FONDA, HENRY (1905-   ). Distinguished American actor, more at ease in pioneer America than with an army rifle. Has usually played minor roles in large-scale war movies e.g. Brig. General Theodore Roosevelt in *The Longest Day* (62) and Admiral Chester Nimitz in *Midway* (76). Films: *The Immortal Sergeant* (43), *In Harm's Way* (65), *The Battle Of The Bulge* (65), *Too Late The Hero* (70).

FORBES, BRYAN (1926-). British actor/writer/director; several minor performances in British war films during the 50s. Films: *The Wooden Horse* (50), *Appointment in London* (52), *Cockleshell Heroes* (screen only) (55), *I Was Monty's Double* (also screen) (58), *Yesterday's Enemy* (59), *The Guns of Navarone* (61), *King Rat* (screen & dir.) (65).

FORD, GLENN (1916-). Another 'Mr. Dependable' American star in the William Holden-Gregory Peck mould. Featured as General Omar Bradley in *Is Paris Burning?* (66). War movies: *Flight Lieutenant* (42), *Destroyer* (43), *The Flying Missile* (50), *Torpedo Run* (58), *Midway* (66).

FORD, JOHN (1895-1973). Director of more good movies than any other American film-maker. Most accomplished war film: *They Were Expendable* (45), an account of how PT Boats were used in the Philippines during World War II. Also filmed the documentaries *The Battle Of Midway* (42), *Torpedo Squadron* (42), *December 7th* (43), *This Is Korea* (51). Other features: *The Lost Patrol* (34), *Submarine Patrol* (38), *What Price Glory* (52), *The Wings Of Eagles* (57).

FOREMAN, CARL (1914-). American writer/director/producer, based in England since the early 50s. His original screenplay for *The Men* (50), a story of paraplegics and their struggles to adjust to post-war society, remains his best work in the genre. Also: *The Guns Of Navarone* (screen and prod.) (61), *The Victors* (screen, prod., dir.) (63), *The Virgin Soldiers* (prod.) (69), *Young Winston* (screen and prod.) (72).

FREND, CHARLES (1909-1977). Ealing director of the notable *The Cruel Sea* (53). Several earlier wartime movies for the studio, including *The Big Blockade* (41), *The Foreman Went to France* (42) and *San Demetrio London* (43).

FRIEDHOFER, HUGO (1902-). American composer who won an Academy Award for his score of Wyler's *The Best Years Of Our Lives* (46). Films include *China Girl* (42), *A Wing And A Prayer* (44), *Three Came Home* (50), *Island In The Sky* (53), *Above And Beyond* (53), *Between Heaven And Hell* (56), *The Young Lions* (58), *In Love And War* (58), *Never So Few* (59), *The Secret Invasion* (64), *Von Richthofen And Brown* (71).

FULLER, SAMUEL (1916-). American writer/director, former newsman. War films: *The Steel Helmet* (50), *Fixed Bayonets* (51), *Hell And High Water* (54), *China Gate* (57), *Merrill's Marauders* (62), *The Big Red One* (79).

GILBERT, LEWIS (1920-). British director who handled two of the most popular war films of the 50s, i.e. *Reach For The Sky* (56) with Kenneth More as Douglas Bader and *Carve Her Name With Pride* (58), the story of resistance heroine Violette Szabo. Also: *Albert R.N.* (53), *The Sea Shall Not Have Them* (54), *Sink The Bismarck* (60), *The Seventh Dawn* (64), *Operation Daybreak* (76).

GOLDSMITH, JERRY. American composer, very active during the 60s, mostly at the Fox studio. His fine score for Schaffner's *Patton* (70), ranks with his best work in the genre. Films: *A Gathering Of Eagles* (63), *In Harm's Way* (65), *Von Ryan's Express* (65),

Morituri (65), *The Sand Pebbles* (66), *The Blue Max* (66), *Tora! Tora! Tora!* (70), *MacArthur* (77).

GOODWIN, RON (c.1930-   ). British composer of the popular score for *633 Squadron* (64). Also: *Operation Crossbow* (65), *Where Eagles Dare* (69), *Battle Of Britain* (69), *Force 10 From Navarone* (78).

GREGSON, JOHN (1919-1975). British performer, often seen in RAF and Naval roles during the 50s. Films: *Angels One Five* (52), *Above Us The Waves* (55), *The Battle Of The River Plate* (56), *Sea Of Sand* (58), *The Longest Day* (62), *The Night Of The Generals* (67).

GUFFEY, BURNETT (1905-   ). Columbia's leading cameraman of the 50s and 60s. Won an Academy Award for his work on Zinnemann's *From Here To Eternity* (53). Films include: *Battle Stations* (56), *The Mountain Road* (60), *Hell To Eternity* (60), *King Rat* (65).

GUILLERMIN, JOHN (1925-   ). British director with several war movies to his credit, including *The Blue Max* (66), a story of a young German flier and his attempts to win Germany's top decoration for air valour during World War I. Also: *I Was Monty's Double* (58), *Guns At Batasi* (64), *The Bridge At Remagen* (69). Has lately been more concerned with blazing tower blocks — *The Towering Inferno* and giant apes — *King Kong* (76).

HAMILTON, GUY (1922-   ). British director whose *Battle Of Britain* (69) ranks among the outstanding British war films of recent years. Others: *The Colditz Story* (54), *The Best Of Enemies* (61), *The Man In The Middle* (64), *Force 10 from Navarone* (78).

HARLAN, RUSSELL (1903-1974). American cameraman who shot Milestone's World War II classic *A Walk In The Sun* (45). Other war assignments include *Run Silent Run Deep* (58), *A Gathering Of Eagles* (63), *Tobruk* (67), *Darling Lili* (70).

HATHAWAY, HENRY (1898-   ). One of the industry's most accomplished professionals and a man who always directs his own second unit. His war films are somewhat few and far between but the biographical *Rommel, Desert Fox* (51) with James Mason in the title role, deserves more attention than it has so far received, especially for its long, history making pre-credit sequence of a commando raid. Others: *The Real Glory* (39), *China Girl* (42), *A Wing And A Prayer* (44), *Raid On Rommel* (71).

HAWKINS, JACK (1910-1973). Distinguished British actor often cast in Service roles during the 50s. Superb as Commander Ericson in *The Cruel Sea* (53). Films: *Angels One Five* (52), *The Malta Story* (53), *The Bridge On The River Kwai* (57), *The Two-Headed Spy* (58), *Guns At Batasi* (64), *Oh! What A Lovely War* (69), *Young Winston* (72).

HAWKS, HOWARD, (1896-1977). A major American film maker whose work covered all genres. War films: *The Dawn Patrol* (30), *Sergeant York* (41), *Air Force* (43), *Corvette K-225* (prod. only) (43).

HODIAK, JOHN (1914-1955). Capable American actor, seen in several war movies before his premature death in 1955. Appeared in King's underrated *A Bell for Adano* (45), a story of the day-to-day problems of the American military whilst occupying a small Sicilian town during World War II. Others: *Sunday Dinner for a Soldier* (44), *Homecoming* (48), *Command Decision* (48), *Battleground* (49), *Battle Zone* (52).

HOLDEN, WILLIAM (1918-). Top American star who won an Oscar for his portrayal of the cynical Sefton in Billy Wilder's prisoner-of-war movie *Stalag 17* (53). Several other films in the genre, mostly at Paramount: *Submarine Command* (51), *Force of Arms* (51), *The Bridges at Toko-Ri* (55), *The Bridge on the River Kwai* (57), *The Counterfeit Traitor* (62), *The Seventh Dawn* (64), *The Devil's Brigade* (68).

HOWARD, TREVOR (1916-). British actor, a cultured star of the 40s and 50s but these days only rarely receiving the roles he deserves. Appeared as Air Vice-Marshal Keith Park in Hamilton's *Battle Of Britain* (69). Also: *The Way Ahead* (44), *The Way To The Stars* (45), *Odette* (50), *The Gift Horse* (52), *Cockleshell Heroes* (55), *Man In The Middle* (63), *Operation Crossbow* (65), *Morituri* (65), *Von Ryan's Express* (65), *The Charge of The Light Brigade* (68) (as Lord Cardigan), *Conduct Unbecoming* (75), *Aces High* (76).

HUSTON, JOHN (1906-). American director whose early work includes a mutilated but none the less impressive version of Stephen Crane's Civil War classic *The Red Badge of Courage* (51). His three war documentaries — *Report from the Aleutians* (43), *The Battle of San Pietro* (44), *Let There be Light* (45) — are equally memorable.

JARRE, MAURICE (1924-). French composer best known for his long association with David Lean (*Lawrence of Arabia, Dr. Zhivago,* etc.) War films: *The Longest Day* (62), *The Train* (64), *Is Paris Burning?* (66).

KUBRICK, STANLEY (1928-). Among the most individual writer/directors of the post-war scene Kubrick, long domiciled in England, has trained his camera on war twice — in the savage *Paths Of Glory* (57) (see page 188) and the black comedy *Dr. Strangelove* (64) in which nuclear war and the dangers of that finger on the button are exposed, scorned and eventually ridiculed. Sterling Hayden is the maniacal American general whose actions bring the Russian Doomsday Weapon into operation, Slim Pickens an American pilot who whoops with delight as he plunges to earth astride an H-bomb and Vera Lynn sings the final 'We'll Meet Again' to the accompaniment of the billowing mushroom cloud. Top star though is Peter Sellers who appears in three roles — an R.A.F. officer, the President of the United States and the ominous German scientist of the film's title.

LANCASTER, BURT (1913-). American leading man, at his best in vigorous outdoor roles. War movies, which include *From Here To Eternity* (as Sergeant Warden) (53), also figure among his best work. Others: *Run Silent Run Deep* (58), *The Train* (64), *Castle Keep* (69), *Go Tell The Spartans* (78).

LAY, BEIRNE JUN. (1909-). American writer/producer usually associated with films of aviation, e.g. *Twelve O'Clock High* (49) which he co-scripted with Sy Bartlett and *Above And Beyond* (53). Also: *I Wanted Wings* (41), *Strategic Air Command* (55), *Toward The Unknown* (56), *The Gallant Hours* (60), *The Young And The Brave* (63).

LITVAK, ANATOLE (1902-1974). Russian-born director, in Hollywood from 1937. His war films, although uneven, include the ambitious *Decision Before Dawn* (51), a story of German P.o.W.s who are trained to spy for the Allies during the latter stages of World War II. During the war co-directed several of the 'Why We Fight' documentaries with Frank Capra. Films include the documentaries *The Nazis Strike* (42), *Divide And Conquer* (43), *The Battle Of China* (44), all with Capra, *Act Of Love* (54) and *The Night Of The Generals* (67).

MACDONALD, JOE (1906-1968). American cameraman, superb when working in monochrome, only adequate when filming in colour. Peak period the late 40s when he lensed several location thrillers for Twentieth Century-Fox (see page 69). Numerous war films for the same studio: *Sunday Dinner For A Soldier* (44), *What Price Glory* (52), *Hell And High Water* (54), *The Young Lions* (58), *The Gallant Hours* (60), *The Sand Pebbles* (66).

MALDEN, KARL (1914-   ). American actor often seen in Kazan movies. His war films include the Academy Award winning *Patton* (70) in which he played General Omar Bradley. Others: *Winged Victory* (44), *Halls Of Montezuma* (50), *Decision Before Dawn* (51), *Operation Secret* (52), *Take The High Ground!* (53), *Bombers B 52* (57), *Time Limit* (57) (directed).

MARVIN, LEE (1924-   ). American actor who has done much of his best work in the genre. Played the cynical Colonel Bartlett in Robert Aldrich's *Attack* (56) and the army major in charge of the same director's *Dirty Dozen* (67). Films: *Eight Iron Men* (52), *The Rack* (56), *Hell In The Pacific* (68), *Shout At The Devil* (76), *The Big Red One* (79).

MASON, JAMES (1909-   ). Suave British actor, in many American films since 1948. Played Field Marshal Rommel in *Rommel, Desert Fox* (51) and *The Desert Rats* (53). More recently — *The Blue Max* (66), *Cross Of Iron* (77), *The Passage* (79).

MAYES, WENDELL (1918-   ). American screenwriter, best work with Preminger — *Anatomy Of A Murder* (59), *Advise And Consent* (62), War Scripts: *The Enemy Below* (57), *The Hunters* (58), *In Harm's Way* (also Preminger) (65), *Von Ryan's Express* (65), *Go Tell The Spartans* (78).

MCQUEEN, STEVE (1932-   ). Top American star famous in the genre for his motorcycle dash for freedom in John Sturges' P.o.W. drama *The Great Escape* (63). Films: *Never So Few* (59), *Hell is for Heroes* (62), *The War Lover* (62), *The Sand Pebbles* (66).

MILESTONE, LEWIS (1895-   ). American director of *All Quiet On the Western Front* (30), the first and perhaps only masterpiece in the genre. Later filmed the poetic *A Walk in the Sun* (45), an account of the experiences of a platoon of Texas infantrymen during the Salerno landings in Italy in World War II. Other war films only routine: *Edge of Darkness* (43), *North Star* (43), *The Purple Heart* (44), *Halls of Montezuma* (50), *They Who Dare* (53), *Pork Chop Hill* (59).

MILLS, JOHN (1908-). A regular performer in British war films since playing an able seaman in the Lean/Coward production *In Which We Serve* in 1942. Has appeared in almost all ranks in all three Services. Films: *We Dive at Dawn* (43), *The Way to the Stars* (45), *Morning Departure* (50), *The Colditz Story* (54), *Above Us the Waves* (55), *Dunkirk* (58), *Ice Cold in Alex* (58), *I Was Monty's Double* (58), *Tunes of Glory* (60), *The Valiant* (62), *Operation Crossbow* (65), *King Rat* (65), *Oh! What a Lovely War* (as Field Marshal Sir Douglas Haig) (69), *Young Winston* (72).

MITCHUM, ROBERT (1917-). One of the top American stars to emerge during the post-war period. Major war films: Wellman's *The Story Of G.I. Joe* (45), a movie based on the writings of war correspondent Ernie Pyle, and *The Longest Day* (as Brig. General Norman Cota) (62). Also: *Thirty Seconds Over Tokyo* (44), *The Man In The Middle* (63), *Anzio* (68), *Midway* (76) (as Admiral Halsey), *Sergeant Steiner* (79).

MORE, KENNETH (1914-). British actor who starred as Douglas Bader in Lewis Gilbert's *Reach For The Sky* (56). Guest appearances in several large-scale war movies of the 60s including *The Longest Day* (62), *The Battle Of Britain* (69) and *Oh! What A Lovely War* (as Kaiser Wilhelm II) (69). Also: *Morning Departure* (50), *Sink The Bismarck* (60), *The Mercenaries* (67).

NEWMAN, ALFRED (1901-1970). Prolific Hollywood composer. War films: *China Girl* (42), *To The Shores Of Tripoli* (42), *The Purple Heart* (44), *Sunday Dinner For A Soldier* (44), *A Bell For Adano* (45), *Twelve O'Clock High* (49), *What Price Glory* (52), *Hell And High Water* (54), *The Counterfeit Traitor* (62); also the documentaries *The Battle Of Midway* (42) and *December 7th* (43).

NORTH, EDMUND H. (1911-). American scriptwriter whose screenplay for *Patton* (written in collaboration with Francis Ford Coppola) qualifies as one of the most penetrating and thought-provoking in the genre. Also: *Sink The Bismarck* (60), *Submarine X-1* (69).

OLIVIER, LAURENCE (1907-). Distinguished British stage and screen actor whose appearances in war films have usually been brief. Played Air Chief Marshal Sir Hugh Dowding in *Battle Of Britain* (69). Films: *The 49th Parallel* (41), *Oh! What A Lovely War* (69), *A Bridge Too Far* (77).

PARKER, CLIFTON (1905-). British composer whose music for the wartime documentary *Western Approaches* (44) is one of the best known scores in the genre. Many others including *The Wooden Horse* (50), *The Gift Horse* (52), *Sea of Sand* (58), *Sink the Bismarck* (60), *Circle of Deception* (61).

PECK, GREGORY (1916-   ). Leading American actor whose first major role in the genre — the martinet General Savage in King's *Twelve O'Clock High* — won him the New York Critics Award as best actor of 1950. Films: *Night People* (54), *Pork Chop Hill* (59), *The Guns of Navarone* (61), *Captain Newman M.D.* (63), *MacArthur* (77).

PECKINPAH, SAM (1926-   ). It seems strange that Peckinpah, who has dealt so effectively with violence in the old and new societies of America, should have visited the war scene but once, but at least his excursion into the genre has been memorable. Not for him Vietnam or Korea but a return to the carnage of World War II, specifically the Eastern front of Russia during the German retreat of 1943. The film: *Cross Of Iron* (77). The theme: the high command's own self-glorification at the expense of the lives of the men in the field. The result: a dramatic exposure of the futility of war, very nearly as effective as Milestone's *All Quiet On The Western Front* (30) and Kubrick's *Paths Of Glory* (57).

PIDGEON, WALTER (1897-   ). Canadian-born actor who spent most of his forty-year career at MGM. Usually played generals, colonels, etc. in the Studio's war movies. Films: *Flight Command* (40), *Command Decision* (48), *Men of the Fighting Lady* (54), *The Rack* (56).

PIROSH, ROBERT (1910-   ). American writer/director, a specialist in war movies since winning an Oscar for his original screenplay for *Battleground* in 1949. Also: *Go For Broke* (also directed) (51), *Hell is for Heroes* (62), *A Gathering of Eagles* (63).

PLUMMER, CHRISTOPHER (1927-   ). Canadian stage and screen actor who seemed to get a bit lost among the mountains of Austria and the music of Rodgers and Hammerstein in *The Sound Of Music* (65) but has since found more substantial roles in the war genre e.g. as Airforce pilots of World War I and II respectively in *Aces High* (76) and *Battle Of Britain* (69) and double spy Eddie Chapman in *Triple Cross* (66). Also: *The Night Of The Generals* (67), *Hanover Street* (79).

POWELL, MICHAEL (1905-   ). British writer/director/producer whose collaboration with Emeric Pressburger produced some notable British films (*A Matter Of Life And Death, The Red Shoes,* etc.) and several war pictures of somewhat uneven quality, i.e.

The 49th Parallel (41), *One Of Our Aircraft Is Missing* (42), *The Life And Death Of Colonel Blimp* (43), *The Battle Of The River Plate* (56), *Ill Met By Moonlight* (57).

REDGRAVE, MICHAEL (1908-   ). Distinguished British actor, superb as the boffin Dr. Barnes Wallis in the otherwise routine *The Dam Busters* (55). Also: *The Way to the Stars* (45), *The Captive Heart* (46), *The Sea Shall Not Have Them* (54), *The Hill* (65), *The Heroes of Telemark* (65), *Oh! What a Lovely War* (69).

ROBERTSON, CLIFF (1925-   ). Oscar-winning American actor. War films range from the ambitious *The Naked And The Dead* (58) to the commonplace *The Devil's Brigade* (68). Also: *P.T. 109* (63), *633 Squadron* (64), *Too Late The Hero* (70), *Midway* (76).

ROBSON, MARK (1913-1978). American director whose three war films — *The Bridges at Toko-Ri* (55), *Von Ryan's Express* (65), *The Lost Command* (66) — are undistinguished but whose earlier *Home Of The Brave* (49), a story of racial prejudice among G.I.'s in wartime and *Lights Out* (51), which showed the problems of a blinded war veteran returning to civilian life, are two of the best works in the genre.

ROSSON, HAROLD (1895-   ). American cameraman who did notable work for Huston on *The Red Badge Of Courage* (51). Also: *Flight Command* (40), *Thirty Seconds Over Tokyo* (44), *Command Decision* (48).

RYAN, ROBERT (1913-1973). One of America's most talented performers. War films include *The Longest Day* (62) in which he had a guest spot as Brig. General James M. Gavin. Others: *Bombardier* (43), *Behind the Rising Sun* (43), *Marine Raiders* (44), *Flying Leathernecks* (51), *Men In War* (57), *Battle Of The Bulge* (65), *The Dirty Dozen* (67), *Anzio* (68).

SEATON, GEORGE (1911-   ). American writer/director who began his career at Fox in the 40s with lightweight musical comedies then progressed to heavier themes e.g. the perils of being a double agent in wartime in the quite excellent — and factual — *The Counterfeit Traitor* (62) with William Holden and Lili Palmer. In 1950 he examined the early effects of the Cold War, via the Berlin Airlift, in the now rarely seen *The Big Lift*. Others: *The Proud And The Profane* (56), *The Hook* (63), *36 Hours* (64).

SINATRA, FRANK (1915-   ). American actor/singer whose performance as Maggio in Zinnemann's *From Here to Eternity* (53)
established him as a player of some distinction. Films: *Kings
Go Forth* (58), *Never So Few* (59), *Von Ryan's Express* (65).

STEINER, MAX (1888-1972). Austrian composer, long in America.
Many scores for war movies produced at the Warner studio, e.g.
The Dawn Patrol (38), *Dive Bomber* (41), *Captains Of The Clouds*
(42), *Desperate Journey* (42), *Fighter Squadron* (48), *Force Of
Arms* (51), *Operation Pacific* (51), *Battle Cry* (55), *Darby's
Rangers* (58).

TARADASH, DANIEL (1913-   ). American scriptwriter of long standing.
Few war movies among his work but included here for his Academy
Award winning screenplay of *From Here To Eternity* (53). Also:
Morituri (65), *Castle Keep* (69).

TAYLOR, ROBERT (1911-1969). A top Metro star for more than two
decades, excellent in *Above And Beyond* (53) as Colonel Paul
Tibbetts, the pilot responsible for dropping the first atomic bomb
on Hiroshima. Also: *Flight Command* (40), *Stand By For Action*
(43), *Bataan* (43), *Song Of Russia* (43), *D-Day The Sixth Of
June* (56).

TIOMKIN, DIMITRI (1899-   ). Hollywood composer who scored several
war documentaries made by Frank Capra and John Huston during
the 42-45 period, i.e. *Prelude To War* (42), *The Nazis Strike* (42),
Divide And Conquer (43), *Report From The Aleutians* (43), *Tunisian
Victory* (43), *The Battle Of China* (44), *The Battle Of San Pietro* (44),
Let There Be Light (45), *Know Your Enemy: Japan* (45), *Two
Down, One To Go* (45). Also: *Home Of The Brave* (49), *The Men*
(50), *Take The High Ground!* (53), *Cease Fire!* (53), *The Guns Of
Navarone* (61), *36 Hours* (65).

TODD, RICHARD (1919-   ). Capable British performer who gained
fame as the dying Scottish soldier in *The Hasty Heart* (49).
Portrayed Wing Commander Guy Gibson in *The Dam Busters*
(55) and later guested in *The Longest Day* (62). Films: *Yangtse
Incident* (57), *Danger Within* (59), *The Long, The Short And The
Tall* (61), *Operation Crossbow* (65).

WALSH, RAOUL (1892-   ). Veteran American director. Several war
adventures at Warners during the 40s, e.g. *Desperate Journey*
(42), *Background To Danger* (43), *Northern Pursuit* (43), *Uncertain
Glory* (44), *Objective Burma* (45) but best known for his silent

What Price Glory (26) and the more recent, under-valued *The Naked And The Dead* (58), Norman Mailer's harsh look at the relationships between officers and men during World War II combat in the Pacific.

WAXMAN, FRANZ (1906-1967). German composer in Hollywood from 1935. War movies: *Flight Command* (40), *Air Force* (43), *Destination Tokyo* (44), *Hotel Berlin* (45), *God Is My Co-Pilot* (45), *Objective Burma* (45), *Pride Of The Marines* (45), *Task Force* (49), *Decision Before Dawn* (51), *Stalag 17* (53), *Run Silent Run Deep* (58), *Lost Command* (66).

WAYNE, JOHN (1907-1979). Veteran American performer whose war films included John Ford's *They Were Expendable* (45) and *Wings Of Eagles* (as 'Spig' Wead) (57). Also: *Flying Tigers* (43), *The Fighting Seabees* (44), *Back To Bataan* (45), *Sands Of Iwo Jima* (49), *Flying Leathernecks* (51), *Operation Pacific* (51), *Jet Pilot* (52), *Island In The Sky* (53), *The Sea Chase* (55), *The Longest Day* (62), *In Harm's Way* (65), *The Green Berets* (also dir.) (68).

WELLMAN, WILLIAM A. (1896-1975). American director of several major war movies including *Wings* (27), the first film to win an Academy Award, *The Story of G.I. Joe* (45), an account of the war experiences of news correspondent Ernie Pyle, and *Battleground* (49), a reconstruction of the Battle of Bastogne. Other films in the genre: *Thunder Birds* (42), *Darby's Rangers* (58), *Lafayette Escadrille* (58).

WIDMARK, RICHARD (1915-   ). American actor, best-known for his tough guy parts (see page 77). War movies, mostly at the Fox studio, include *Halls of Montezuma* (50), *The Frogmen* (51), *Destination Gobi* (53), *Take the High Ground* (53), *Hell and High Water* (54), *Time Limit* (57), *The Bedford Incident* (65).

WISE, ROBERT (1914-   ). American director who has achieved his best results in the horror genre (see page 44). Of his four war films, *The Sand Pebbles* (66), a story of an American gunboat patrolling the Yangtse during the Twenties, is the most successful. Others: *The Desert Rats* (53), *Destination Gobi* (53), *Run Silent Run Deep* (58).

WYLER, WILLIAM (1902-   ). Major American director now retired, whose work is somewhat out of fashion with contemporary critics. His contribution to the war genre consists of two outstanding documentaries — *Memphis Belle* (44), *Thunderbolt* (45) — and

Sam Goldwyn's famous 'problem' movie *The Best Years Of Our Lives* (46), a story of three American war veterans and their attempts to readjust to small town civilian life.

YOUNG, TERENCE (1915-   ). British director who made the wartime documentary of Arnhem, *Theirs Is The Glory* (46). Later war films include *They Were Not Divided* (50), *The Red Beret* (53), *Triple Cross* (66).

ZANUCK, DARRYL F. (1902-   ). American producer, former script-writer, long at Twentieth Century-Fox. Responsible in recent years for the large-scale war movies *The Longest Day* (62) and *Tora! Tora! Tora!* (70). Others: *The Purple Heart* (44), *Winged Victory* (44), *Twelve O'Clock High* (49).

ZINNEMANN, FRED (1907-   ). Austrian-born director whose films in the genre have dealt primarily with the 'effects of war'. *The Search* (48), a story of homeless refugee children in post-war Germany remains his most distinguished work although it was for his direction of *From Here to Eternity* (53) that he won the first of his Oscars. Also: *The Seventh Cross* (44), *The Men* (50).

SWASHBUCKLERS

THE MARK OF ZORRO   1920

An historic film that established Douglas Fairbanks as the king of the silent swashbucklers. Adapted from Johnson McCulley's novel *The Curse of Capistrano*, it centres on the adventures of a young swordsman who returns home from Madrid to free nineteenth century California of tyrannical rule. The duelling was devised by Henry J. Uyttenhove and is among the most accomplished of the silent cinema. In 1925 Fairbanks starred in a two-hour sequel entitled *Don Q, Son of Zorro*. Donald Crisp directed and co-starred with Mary Astor.

Production:	Douglas Fairbanks Pictures Corporation/United Artists
Direction:	Fred Niblo
Photography:	William McGann and Harry Thorpe
Leading Players:	Douglas Fairbanks, Noah Beery, Charles Hill Mailes, Claire McDowell, Marguerite de la Motte, Robert McKim

Note: The Mark of Zorro has been remade twice, firstly by Rouben Mamoulian in 1940 and secondly by Walt Disney (under the title *The Sign of Zorro*) in 1960. Mamoulian's film contains an exciting four-minute duel between Tyrone Power and Basil Rathbone, the former player using the same duelling blade that Fairbanks had used twenty years earlier.

THE THREE MUSKETEERS   1921

Still the best version of Dumas' adventure classic of seventeenth century France. Fairbanks, sporting the famous moustache he grew especially for the film and retained for the rest of his life, features as the acrobatic D'Artagnan and Leon Barry (Athos), George Siegmann (Porthos) and Eugene Pallette (Aramis) appear as the musketeers. Fairbanks repeated his role six years later in *The Iron Mask*. Uyttenhove was in charge of the duels in *The Three Musketeers* and Fred Cavens handled the rapier routines in the sequel.

Production:	Douglas Fairbanks Pictures Corporation/United Artists
Direction:	Fred Niblo
Photography:	Arthur Edeson

Art Direction: Edward Langley
Leading Players: Douglas Fairbanks, Marguerite de la Motte,
    Barbara La Marr, Adolphe Menjou, Leon Barry, George Siegmann,
    Eugene Pallette

Note: Other versions of *The Three Musketeers* include a 1911 Edison
    production, a 1936 adaptation with Walter Abel, and a lavish 1948
    Technicolor production starring Gene Kelly (D'Artagnan), Van
    Heflin (Athos), Gig Young (Porthos) and Robert Coote (Aramis).
    Richard Lester also filmed the story in 1974.

SCARAMOUCHE   1923

Ramon Novarro consolidated his position as a leading swashbuckler
in this 1923 version of the Sabatini novel. The story is set against the
background of pre-revolutionary France and follows the exploits of a
French nobleman who turns politician, duellist and actor to avenge a
murdered friend. Novarro and Lewis Stone headed the cast just as they
had done a year earlier in *The Prisoner of Zenda*, but on this occasion
it was Novarro who played the heroic lead and Stone who appeared as
the villain. The duels were staged by Henry J. Uyttenhove.

Production: Metro Pictures
Direction: Rex Ingram
Screenplay: Willis Goldbeck
    from the novel by
    Rafael Sabatini
Photography: John B. Seitz
Leading Players: Ramon Novarro, Alice Terry, Lewis Stone, Lloyd
    Ingraham, Julia Swayne Gordon

Note: During the early Fifties *Scaramouche* was remade with Stewart
    Granger and Mel Ferrer in the leading roles. Although only
    moderately successful it contained an elaborately mounted six-
    and-a-half minute duel which remains one of the longest ever
    filmed.

THE PRISONER OF ZENDA   1937

A near perfect adaptation of Anthony Hope's Ruritanian romance,
this superbly produced (Selznick) movie features Ronald Colman as
an heroic Englishman who poses as a king in order to prevent a takeover of the throne. The script is wittier and more literate than most of
its kind and the climactic sabre duel is every bit as exciting as the
more famous Flynn/Rathbone encounter in the subsequent *The Adventures of Robin Hood*. As the rascally Rupert of Hentzau, Douglas
Fairbanks Jun. gave the first indications that he would follow in his
father's footsteps.

Production: Selznick/United Artists
Screenplay: John L. Balderston
Direction: John Cromwell

Additional Dialogue:	Donald Ogden Stewart
Adaptation:	Wells Root
from the novel by	
Anthony Hope	
Photography:	James Wong Howe
Art Direction:	Lyle Wheeler
Music:	Alfred Newman

Leading Players: Ronald Colman, Madeleine Carroll, Douglas Fairbanks, Jun., Mary Astor, C. Aubrey Smith, Raymond Massey, David Niven

Note: There have been at least four other versions of *The Prisoner of Zenda*, including the 1922 production starring Ramon Novarro and Lewis Stone, and the 1952 remake with Stewart Granger and James Mason. The 1922 picture was directed by Rex Ingram who took the unusual step of shooting two separate endings, one happy, one tragic, inviting exhibitors of the time to take their choice.

THE ADVENTURES OF ROBIN HOOD   1938

The Robin Hood legend has been filmed many times, but never as efficiently as in this Michael Curtiz/William Keighley production, which won Academy Awards for its composer, art director and editor. Errol Flynn appears as the twelfth century outlaw, Claude Rains as the scheming Prince John and Basil Rathbone as Sir Guy of Gisbourne. Such incidents as Robin's meeting with Little John on a log across a stream (filmed by Keighley) and his encounter with Friar Tuck were reconstructed on the screen for the first time. The famous duel between Flynn and Rathbone in Nottingham Castle was staged by Fred Cavens.

Production:	Warner Bros./First National
Direction:	Michael Curtiz and
	William Keighley
Screenplay:	Norman Reilly Raine and
	Seton I. Miller
based upon ancient Robin	
Hood legends	
Photography (Technicolor):	Sol Polito and
	Tony Gaudio
Art Direction:	Carl Jules Weyl
Music:	Erich Wolfgang Korngold
Editing:	Ralph Dawson

Leading Players: Errol Flynn, Olivia de Havilland, Basil Rathbone, Claude Rains, Patric Knowles, Eugene Pallette, Alan Hale, Melville Cooper

Note: There have been at least eight versions of the Robin Hood story, including the above-mentioned Flynn version, the large-scale 1922 epic with Douglas Fairbanks, and Walt Disney's more intimate 1952 movie with Richard Todd. Other versions include a 1912 three-reeler, a four-reel Thanhouser production starring William

Russell and *Men of Sherwood Forest* (1956) with Don Taylor. *The Bandit of Sherwood Forest* (1946) remains the best of the sequels.

THE SEA HAWK   1940

The last of the early Flynn vehicles, this swashbuckling adventure casts him as a Francis Drake-styled adventurer who plunders the coast of Spain in the days preceding the Armada. The brilliant Michael Curtiz (this was his final film in the genre) is in perfect control of his material and Sol Polito's monochrome photography is as handsome as any to be found in Hollywood movies during the early forties. As Elizabeth, Flora Robson repeats the role she first played in *Fire Over England.*

Production:	Warner Bros./First National
Direction:	Michael Curtiz
Original Screenplay:	Howard Koch and
	Seton I. Miller
Photography:	Sol Polito
Music:	Erich Wolfgang Korngold
Art Direction:	Anton Grot
Editing:	George Amy

Leading Players: Errol Flynn, Brenda Marshall, Claude Rains, Donald Crisp, Flora Robson, Alan Hale, Henry Daniell

THE BLACK SWAN   1942

Henry King's lively buccaneering movie (another Sabatini adaptation) is notable mainly for the excellence of the colour photography which won cameraman Leon Shamroy the first of his four Academy Awards. The story — about a 17th century adventurer (Tyrone Power) who helps the reformed buccaneer Sir Henry Morgan clear the piracy from the Jamaican seas — is told with a maximum of robust dialogue, fast-paced action and colourful characterization. Laird Cregar as Morgan and George Sanders as a villainous privateer stand out in the supporting cast.

Production:	Twentieth Century-Fox
Direction:	Henry King
Screenplay:	Ben Hecht and
from the novel by	Seton I. Miller
Rafael Sabatini	
Photography (Technicolor):	Leon Shamroy
Art Direction:	Richard Day and
	James Basevi
Music:	Alfred Newman
Editing:	Barbara McLean

Leading Players: Tyrone Power, Maureen O'Hara, Laird Cregar, Thomas Mitchell, George Sanders, Anthony Quinn, George Zucco

CYRANO DE BERGERAC   1950

Of all the swashbucklers made since the heyday of Douglas Fairbanks, this is the only one that has required any great acting ability from its leading player. As the long-nosed Gascon braggart who courts the woman he loves for another man, Jose Ferrer won a deserved Academy Award as best actor of 1950. Ferrer and other members of the cast were coached in the duelling sequences by the Fairbanks/Flynn instructor Fred Cavens who, on this occasion, was assisted by his son Albert Cavens. The film was based on Edmond Rostand's 1897 verse comedy. Ferrer's performance was a repeat of the one he gave on Broadway in 1946.

Production:	Stanley Kramer Productions/ United Artists
Direction:	Michael Gordon
Screenplay:	Carl Foreman
Photography:	Franz Planer
Music:	Dimitri Tiomkin

Leading Players: Jose Ferrer, Mala Powers, William Prince, Morris Carnovsky, Ralph Clanton, Lloyd Corrigan

IVANHOE   1952

The swashbuckler enjoyed a final flourish at MGM before it disappeared into relative obscurity in the late 50s and 60s. *Scaramouche* and *The Prisoner Of Zenda* were remade, both with Stewart Granger; Walter Scott's *Ivanhoe*, a blend of romance and pageantry in medieval England, selected as a vehicle for a fading Robert Taylor. The gamble worked and Taylor's stock soared to fresh heights. In *Ivanhoe* he features as the loyal Saxon knight Wilfred of Ivanhoe, a man faithful to King Richard and loved by two beautiful women — Saxon heiress Joan Fontaine and dark haired Jewess Elizabeth Taylor. Up against him is villain De Bois Guilbert (George Sanders) who is finally disposed of after a titanic battle with axe and mace. Full of splendidly staged action sequences including the storming of a Norman castle and containing some surprisingly sharp comments on anti-semitism during the period, the film stands as a testament to the no-nonsense professionalism of its veteran action director, Richard Thorpe.

Production Company:	Metro-Goldwyn-Mayer
Production:	Pandro S. Berman
Direction:	Richard Thorpe
Screenplay:	Noel Langley
adapted by Aeneas MacKenzie from the novel by Sir Walter Scott	
Photography (Technicolor):	F. A. Young
Music:	Miklos Rozsa

Leading Players: Robert Taylor, Elizabeth Taylor, Joan Fontaine, George Sanders, Emlyn Williams, Robert Douglas, Finlay Currie, Felix Aylmer

ROBIN AND MARIAN   1976

The re-emergence of the swashbuckling film in the 70s has been due largely to Richard Lester who has directed a series of exhilarating costumers including two *Musketeers* films. Lester has often been inclined to spoof the genre. In this film he does not. His cameras are bloodily realistic. *Robin And Marian* is simply a story of old age told in terms of costume drama. The legendary heroes are aged and creaky, their golden years long past. The mood is one of sadness, of men striving to accomplish what is now beyond them. The result is tragedy as Robin, sickened by the brutality of the Crusades, returns home to his now dilapidated Sherwood Forest to carry on his battle with the Sheriff of Nottingham (Robert Shaw). Both men eventually succumb, the sheriff in hand to hand combat, Robin from his wounds and a merciful poison administered by his beloved Marian — played with quiet dignity by Audrey Hepburn.

Production Company:	Columbia
Production:	Denis O'Dell
Direction:	Richard Lester
Screenplay:	James Goldman
Photography (Technicolor):	David Watkin
Music:	John Barry

Leading Players: Sean Connery, Audrey Hepburn, Robert Shaw, Richard Harris, Nicol Williamson, Denholm Elliott, Kenneth Haigh, Ronnie Barker

BARRYMORE, JOHN (1882-1942). Distinguished American stage and screen actor, brother of Ethel and Lionel Barrymore. Some fine swashbucklers among his early work, including Alan Crosland's *Don Juan* (26), an exhilarating adventure piece set in the court of the Borgias.

BEERY, NOAH (1884-1946). Actor brother of Wallace Beery, well-known in the swashbuckling genre for his duel with Douglas Fairbanks in *The Mark of Zorro* (20). Famous also for his villainous Sergeant Lejaune in Herbert Brenon's silent *Beau Geste* (26).

CAVENS, FRED. Belgian fencing master, in Hollywood from the early 20s. Coached Fairbanks, Flynn, Power and co. and staged the majority of screen duels between 1920 and 1950, including the Flynn/Rathbone duel in *The Adventures of Robin Hood* (38). In *Don Juan* (26) staged the silent screen's longest and most effective sword-fight. Main films: *Don Q, Son of Zorro* (25), *The Black Pirate* (26), *The Iron Mask* (29), *Captain Blood* (35), *The Sea Hawk* (40), *The Exile* (47), *Adventures of Don Juan* (49), *Sons of the Musketeers* (52).

CHAMBERLAIN, RICHARD (1935-). American actor whose classical good looks and distinguished speaking voice have made him a natural for hero roles in recent remakes of the Dumas classics. Appeared as a foppish Aramis in Lester's *The Three Musketeers (The Queen's Diamonds)* (74) and *The Four Musketeers (Revenge Of Milady)* (75), Edmond Dantes in *The Count Of Monte Cristo* (74) and Louis XIV in *The Man In The Iron Mask* (76).

CRISP, DONALD (1882-1974). British actor/director who filmed the two-hour Fairbanks epic, *Don Q, Son of Zorro* in 1925, and then appeared in supporting roles in several Warner swashbucklers of the 30s. Films (as actor) include *Mutiny on the Bounty* (35), *The Charge of the Light Brigade* (36), *The Private Lives of Elizabeth and Essex* (39), *The Sea Hawk* (40) and *Prince Valiant* (54).

CURRIE, FINLAY (1878-1968). A memorable if brief appearance as Billy Bones in the first reels of Disney's *Treasure Island* (50) paved the way for several swashbuckling roles by this lovable old Scottish character actor. A frequent companion of Messrs Power, Taylor, Wilde and company during the 50s. Films: *The Black Rose* (50), *Ivanhoe* (52), *Rob Roy* (53), *Treasure Of The Golden Condor* (53), *Beau Brummel* (54), *Captain Lightfoot* (55), *Dangerous Exile* (57), *Kidnapped* (60).

CURTIS, TONY (1925-   ). American leading man who began his career in double-feature swashbucklers at the Universal studio. Main films in the genre: *The Prince Who Was A Thief* (51), *Son Of Ali Baba* (52), *The Black Shield Of Falworth* (54), *The Purple Mask* (55), *The Vikings* (58), *The Count Of Monte Cristo* (74) (as Mondego).

CURTIZ, MICHAEL (1888-1962). Prolific and exceptionally gifted Hungarian-born director who worked for many years at the Warner studio. His five swashbucklers, all made with Flynn, are key films, especially *Captain Blood* (35) which reinstated the genre in the 30s and *The Adventures of Robin Hood* (38) which he co-directed with William Keighley. Others: *The Charge of the Light Brigade* (36), *The Private Lives of Elizabeth and Essex* (39) and *The Sea Hawk* (40).

DANIELL, HENRY (1894-1963). British supporting actor, in Hollywood from 1929. Frequently seen in villainous roles during the 1940-50 period. Duelled unsuccessfully with Errol Flynn in *The Sea Hawk* (40) and with Cornel Wilde in *The Bandit Of Sherwood Forest* (46). Others: *The Private Lives Of Elizabeth And Essex* (39), *Captain Kidd* (45), *The Exile* (47), *Siren Of Atlantis* (48), *Buccaneer's Girl* (50), *Diane* (55).

DE CARLO, YVONNE (1922-   ). American actress who became a swashbuckling heroine at Universal after the death of Maria Montez. Films (mostly double-features) include *Slave Girl* (47), *Buccaneer's Girl* (50), *The Desert Hawk* (50), and *Sea Devils* (53).

DEREK, JOHN (1926-   ). American actor who played heroic leads in several minor swashbucklers after the war. Main films: *Rogues of Sherwood Forest* (as the son of Robin Hood) (50), *Mask of the Avenger* (51), *Prince of Pirates* (53), *The Adventures of Hajji Baba* (54).

DOUGLAS, ROBERT (1909-). The natural successor to Basil
Rathbone as the leading villain in the genre, Douglas clashed with
Errol Flynn in *Adventures Of Don Juan* (49), Burt Lancaster in
The Flame And The Arrow (50) and Robert Taylor in *Ivanhoe*
(52), and appeared to notable effect as Prince Michael in Thorpe's
1952 remake of *The Prisoner Of Zenda*. Others: *Kim* (51), *Sons
Of The Musketeers* (52), *King Richard And The Crusaders* (54),
The Virgin Queen (55), *The Scarlet Coat* (55).

EDESON, ARTHUR (1891-1970). American cameraman. Three swashbucklers for Fairbanks in the 20s: *The Three Musketeers* (21),
Robin Hood (22), *The Thief of Bagdad* (24).

FAIRBANKS, DOUGLAS (1883-1939). The most famous of the silent
swashbuckling stars. Seven films in the genre between 1920
and 1929: *The Mark of Zorro* (20), *The Three Musketeers* (as
D'Artagnan) (21), *Robin Hood* (22), *The Thief of Bagdad* (24),
Don Q, Son of Zorro (25), *The Black Pirate* (26), *The Iron Mask*
(as D'Artagnan) (29).

FAIRBANKS, DOUGLAS Jun.(1909-). American actor who followed
his father into films as a dashing leading man. Best-known role:
Rupert of Hentzau in *The Prisoner of Zenda* (37). Main films:
The Corsican Brothers (41), *Sinbad the Sailor* (47), *The Exile* (47),
The Fighting O'Flynn (49).

FINCH, PETER (1916-1977). British actor (for many years in Australia)
who dabbled in costumers at the beginning of his career: *The
Story Of Robin Hood* (52) (as the Sheriff of Nottingham), *The
Warriors* (55). Featured as Alan Breck in Disney's version of
Kidnapped (60).

FLYNN, ERROL (1909-1959). The undisputed king of swashbucklers,
at his peak during the middle and late 30s when he appeared in
half-a-dozen cloak and sword adventures for Warner Bros.
Returned to the genre after the war but apart from *The Adventures
of Don Juan* (49), which had some isolated moments of vigour,
his later work was undistinguished. Main films: *Captain Blood*
(35), *The Charge of the Light Brigade* (36), *The Prince and the
Pauper* (37), *The Adventures of Robin Hood* (38), *The Private
Lives of Elizabeth and Essex* (39), *The Sea Hawk* (40), *The
Adventures of Don Juan* (49), *Kim* (51), *Adventures of Captain
Fabian* (51), *Against All Flags* (52), *The Master of Ballantrae*
(53), *Crossed Swords* (54), *The Warriors* (55).

GOMEZ, THOMAS (1905-1971). American supporting actor, in Hollywood from the early 40s. Several swashbucklers among his films, including *Captain from Castile* (47), *Kim* (51), *Anne of the Indies* (as Blackbeard) (51), *Adventures of Hajji Baba* (54).

GRANGER, STEWART (1913-   ). Romantic British star, a familiar swashbuckler in Hollywood during the early 50s. Main films: *Scaramouche* (52), *The Prisoner of Zenda* (as Rudolf Rassendyll) (52), *All the Brothers Were Valiant* (53), *Moonfleet* (55), *Swordsman of Siena* (62).

HALE, ALAN (1892-1950). Burly American character actor, often cast as a loyal-hearted henchman of Errol Flynn. Appeared as Little John on three occasions — *Robin Hood* (22), *Adventures of Robin Hood* (38), and *Rogues of Sherwood Forest* (50). Others: *The Prince and the Pauper* (37), *The Private Lives of Elizabeth and Essex* (39), *The Man in the Iron Mask* (39), *The Sea Hawk* (40), *The Adventures of Don Juan* (49).

HALL, JON (1913-   ). American leading man, co-starred in several Maria Montez vehicles during the early 40s: *Arabian Nights* (42), *Ali Baba And The Forty Thieves* (44), *Gypsy Wildcat* (44), *Sudan* (45), *Prince Of Thieves* (48), *The Mutineers* (49).

HAYWARD, LOUIS (1909-   ). American actor who played the dual role of Louis XIV and his twin brother Philippe in James Wale's remake of *The Man In The Iron Mask* (39). Also: *Son Of Monte Cristo* (40), *The Return Of Monte Cristo* (46), *The Black Arrow* (48), *Pirates Of Capri* (49), *The Fortunes Of Captain Blood* (50), *Dick Turpin's Ride* (51), *Lady In The Iron Mask* (52), *Captain Pirate* (52).

HENREID, PAUL (1907-   ). Best known for his romantic performances opposite Bette Davis and Ingrid Bergman (see page 162), Henreid turned to swashbucklers later in his career, appearing in Borzage's satirical *The Spanish Main* (45) and such lesser vehicles as *Last Of The Buccaneers* (50), *The Thief Of Damascus* (52), *Siren Of Bagdad* (53) and *Pirates Of Tripoli* (55).

HEREMANS, JEAN. Belgian fencing master who worked on several of Hollywood's post-war swashbucklers, including *Scaramouche* (52) for which he devised the 6 minute 30 second rapier routine between Stewart Granger and Mel Ferrer. Others: *The Three Musketeers* (48), *The Prisoner of Zenda* (52), *Prince Valiant* (54).

HUDSON, ROCK (1925-   ). A contract star at Universal during the 50s, Hudson appeared in several double-feature adventure movies before turning to comedy roles later in the decade (see page 14). His swashbucklers include *The Desert Hawk* (50), *Sea Devils* (53), *The Golden Blade* (53), *Captain Lightfoot* (55).

INGRAM, REX (1892-1950). American director, at his peak during the 20s when he directed Rudolph Valentino in *The Four Horsemen of the Apocalypse* (21) and guided Ramon Novarro to stardom in the swashbucklers *The Prisoner of Zenda* (22) and *Scaramouche* (23).

JOURDAN, LOUIS (1919-   ). Suave French leading man who has enjoyed the unique experience of playing both hero Edmond Dantes and villain De Villefort in *The Count Of Monte Cristo*, the former in a 1961 French version, the latter in David Greene's 1974 remake. Also: *Anne Of The Indies* (51), *Dangerous Exile* (57), *The Man In The Iron Mask* (76) (as D'Artagnan).

JUSTICE, JAMES ROBERTSON (1905-1975). Burly bewhiskered Scottish actor, often a dependable seaman quick with the 'Aye, aye sirs' in the swashbuckling 50s e.g. *Captain Horatio Hornblower* (51), *Anne Of The Indies* (51). Also a trio of costumers for Disney — *The Story Of Robin Hood* (52) (as Little John), *The Sword And The Rose* (53) (as Henry VIII), *Rob Roy* (53).

KORNGOLD, ERICH WOLFGANG (1897-1957). Distinguished Czech composer, with Warner Bros. during the 30s and 40s. At his best when scoring historical epics, e.g. *Captain Blood* (35), *The Prince and the Pauper* (37), *The Adventures of Robin Hood* (AA) (38), *The Private Lives of Elizabeth and Essex* (39), *The Sea Hawk* (40).

LANCASTER, BURT (1913-   ). Ex-circus performer who featured in two acrobatic swashbuckling roles early in his career: *The Flame and the Arrow* (50) and *The Crimson Pirate* (52).

LAURIE, PIPER (1932-   ). A regular co-star of Tony Curtis, Rock Hudson and other Universal stars of the early 50s, Piper Laurie later proved her acting ability with her performance as Paul Newman's crippled girl friend in *The Hustler* (61). Her swashbucklers (all double-features) include *The Prince Who Was a Thief* (51), *Son of Ali Baba* (52) and *The Golden Blade* (53).

LEIGH, JANET (1927-). One of those blonde American gals always in need of rescue no matter what the period of history — Revolutionary France (*Scaramouche*, 53), Medieval Britain (*The Black Shield Of Falworth*, 54), Arthurian England (*Prince Valiant,* 54). Even suffered at the hands of brutal Tenth Century Norsemen in *The Vikings* (58). Many films with former husband Tony Curtis.

LESTER, RICHARD (1932-). American director, long in Britain. Responsible for the brief swashbuckling revival of the early 70s — *The Three Musketeers* (*The Queen's Diamonds*) (74), *The Four Musketeers* (*Revenge Of Milady*) (75), *Royal Flash* (75), a spoof of *The Prisoner Of Zenda* and, best of all, *Robin And Marian* (76) a delicate, moving account of the final years of Robin Hood and his outlaw band.

MACREADY, GEORGE (1912-1973). A splendid swashbuckling villain, roles usually of the sly, cunning variety, similar to those played by Claude Rains in the pre-war period. Main films: *The Fighting Guardsman* (45), *The Bandit Of Sherwood Forest* (46), *The Return Of Monte Cristo* (46), *The Gallant Blade* (48), *The Black Arrow* (48), *The Swordsman* (48), *The Fortunes Of Captain Blood* (50), *The Desert Hawk* (50), *Rogues Of Sherwood Forest* (50), *The Golden Horde* (51), *Treasure Of The Golden Condor* (53), *The Golden Blade* (53).

MASON, JAMES (1909-). British actor, many films in Hollywood since 1948 including *The Prisoner of Zenda* (as Rupert of Hentzau) and *Prince Valiant* (54).

MEDINA, PATRICIA (1921-). A generous smile, dark shoulder-length hair and appealing eyes — qualities which made Miss Medina the most fought over heroine in swashbuckling history even if her films were, at best, no more than routine programmers. Numerous films with Louis Hayward, even an extraordinary excursion with Alan Ladd into medieval times in *The Black Knight* (54). Movies: *The Fortunes Of Captain Blood* (50), *The Magic Carpet* (51), *Dick Turpin's Ride* (51), *Captain Pirate* (52), *Lady In The Iron Mask* (52), *Siren Of Bagdad* (53), *Pirates Of Tripoli* (55).

METTY, RUSSELL (1906-1978). Distinguished American cameraman, long at Universal. Filmed several of the studio's swashbucklers in the early 50s: *Bagdad* (49), *Buccaneer's Girl* (50), *The Desert Hawk* (50), *The Golden Horde* (51), *Flame Of Araby* (51), *Yankee Buccaneer* (52), *Against All Flags* (53), *Veils Of Bagdad* (53).

MILLER, SETON I. (1902-1974). Hollywood scriptwriter with three quality swashbucklers to his credit — *The Adventures of Robin Hood* (38), *The Sea Hawk* (40), *The Black Swan* (42).

MONTEZ, MARIA (1918-1951). American actress, seen in several Eastern fantasies during the 40s. Now something of a cult figure. Films: *Arabian Nights* (42), *Ali Baba and the Forty Thieves* (44), *Gypsy Wildcat* (44), *Sudan* (45), *Pirates of Monterey* (47), *The Exile* (47), *Siren of Atlantis* (48).

NEWMAN, ALFRED (1901-1970). Prolific Hollywood composer whose scores include *The Prisoner of Zenda* (37) (52), *The Mark of Zorro* (40), *The Black Swan* (42) and *Captain from Castile* (47). The music for the latter film is among the most exhilarating ever composed for a costume adenture.

NEWTON, ROBERT (1905-1956). The most famous Long John Silver of them all, appearing twice in the role on screen — in *Treasure Island* (50) and *Long John Silver* (55) — as well as several times on television. Also rolled his eyeballs to great effect as Edward Teach in *Blackbeard The Pirate* (52).

NIBLO, FRED (1874-1948). A distinguished American director who guided Douglas Fairbanks through two of his early swashbucklers, *The Mark of Zorro* (20) and *The Three Musketeers* (21).

NOVARRO, RAMON (1899-1968). Mexican actor who rose to fame as Rupert of Hentzau in the silent version of *The Prisoner of Zenda* (22). Appeared also in *Scaramouche* (23) and the epic *Ben-Hur* (25).

O'HARA, MAUREEN (1920-   ). Red-headed Irish actress, a heroine of several swashbuckling movies in the post-war era. Main films: *The Black Swan* (42), *The Spanish Main* (45), *Sinbad The Sailor* (47), *Bagdad* (49), *Tripoli* (50), *Sons Of The Musketeers* (52), *Against All Flags* (52), *Flame Of Araby* (52).

POLITO, SOL (1894-1960). Distinguished American cameraman, with Warners for many years. Swashbucklers: *The Charge of the Light Brigade* (36), *The Prince and the Pauper* (37), *The Adventures of Robin Hood* (38) with Tony Gaudio, *The Private Lives of Elizabeth and Essex* (39), *The Sea Hawk* (40).

POWER, TYRONE (1913-1958). The Fox studio's answer to Errol Flynn. Several costume dramas during the 40s, notably *The Mark of Zorro* (40), for Rouben Mamoulian and *The Black Swan* (42) for Henry King. Others: *Son of Fury* (42), *Captain from Castile* (47), *Prince of Foxes* (49), *The Black Rose* (50).

QUINN, ANTHONY (1915-   ). Mexican-born actor who appeared in several small-scale swashbucklers during the middle period of his career, e.g. *The Black Swan* (42), *Sinbad The Sailor* (47), *Mask Of The Avenger* (51), *The Brigand* (52), *Against All Flags* (52). Directed the remake of DeMille's *The Buccaneer* (58).

RAINS, CLAUDE (1890-1967). British-born, soft-spoken villain of innumerable Hollywood movies. Main films in the genre: *The Prince and the Pauper* (37), *The Adventures of Robin Hood* (as Prince John) (38), *The Sea Hawk* (40).

RATHBONE, BASIL (1892-1967). One of the best-known of screen villains, Rathbone excelled in the swashbuckling genre and rarely used a double in his fencing scenes. In his heyday (The late 30s/ early 40s) he duelled with Errol Flynn in *Captain Blood* (35) and *The Adventures of Robin Hood* (38), and with Tyrone Power in *The Mark of Zorro* (40). Others: *If I Were King* (38), *Frenchman's Creek* (45), *The Court Jester* (56).

REED, OLIVER (1938-   ). Regular performer in Richard Lester's swashbuckling revival of the 70s. A notable Athos in *The Three Musketeers* (*The Queen's Diamonds*) (74) and *The Four Musketeers* (*Revenge Of Milady*) (75). Also: *The Sword Of Sherwood Forest* (60), *The Pirates Of Blood River* (62), *The Scarlet Blade* (63), *Royal Flash* (75), *The Prince And The Pauper* (77).

SANDERS, GEORGE (1906-1972). Like Rathbone, a master villain and invariably up against it in the swashbuckling stakes. Foolishly took on an in-form Ty Power in the pirate adventure *The Black Swan* (42) and showed equally poor judgement when battling with mace and axe with Robert Taylor in *Ivanhoe* (52). Also: *Son Of Monte Cristo* (40), *Son Of Fury* (42), *King Richard And The Crusaders* (54), *Moonfleet* (55), *The Scarlet Coat* (55), *The King's Thief* (55).

SEITZ, JOHN (1899-1979). Veteran American cameraman who photographed several films for Rex Ingram during the 20s, including *The Prisoner of Zenda* (22) and *Scaramouche* (23).

SHERMAN, GEORGE (1908-   ). Veteran American action director.

Several swashbucklers among his vast output including *The Bandit Of Sherwood Forest* (co-directed with Henry Levin), the film which gave new life to the genre after World War II. Films, mostly at Universal: *The Golden Horde* (51), *Against All Flags* (52), *Veils Of Bagdad* (53), *Son Of Robin Hood* (59), *The Wizard Of Bagdad* (60).

SIDNEY, GEORGE (1911-). Best-known for his musicals (see page 144), Sidney also filmed two lavish swashbucklers for MGM in the post-war period, i.e. *The Three Musketeers* (48) and *Scaramouche* (52).

SLEZAK, WALTER (1902-). Austrian-born character actor, usually seen in villainous roles. Swashbucklers include *The Spanish Main* (45) and *Sinbad the Sailor* (47). Appeared as Caribo in the musical fantasy *The Pirate* (48).

STEPHENSON, HENRY (1871-1956). British supporting actor, frequently cast as sympathetic lords, dukes, governors, etc., in Hollywood costume dramas of the 30s. Main films: *Captain Blood* (35), *The Charge of the Light Brigade* (36), *The Prince and the Pauper* (37), *The Private Lives of Elizabeth and Essex* (39).

TAYLOR, ROBERT (1911-1969). Leading MGM star of the 30s and 40s. Several epics and swashbucklers later in his career, notably *Ivanhoe* (52), *All the Brothers Were Valiant* (53), *Knights of the Round Table* (54), *The Adventures of Quentin Durward* (55).

THORPE, RICHARD (1896-). Veteran Hollywood director with a reputation for shooting in one take. Several films in the genre during the 50s. Best achievement: MGM's 1952 remake of *The Prisoner of Zenda*. Others: *Ivanhoe* (52), *All the Brothers Were Valiant* (53), *Knights of the Round Table* (54), *The Adventures of Quentin Durward* (55), *The Tartars* (62).

TODD, RICHARD (1919-). Disney's answer to a fading Errol Flynn in the early 50s, a stolid British actor who went nobly into action against a variety of historical tyrants. Disney costumers: *The Story Of Robin Hood* (52) (as the lead), *The Sword And The Rose* (53), *Rob Roy* (53). Also: *The Virgin Queen* (as Sir Walter Raleigh) (55).

UYTTENHOVE, HENRY J. Belgian fencing master and graduate of Belgium's famous Military Institute of Physical Education and Fencing. Staged several duels during the silent days, including those in *The Mark of Zorro* (20), *The Prisoner of Zenda* (22) and *Scaramouche* (23).

WALSH, RAOUL (1892-   ). Veteran American director with more than a hundred films to his credit, including *The Thief of Bagdad* (24). Later films in the genre include *Captain Horatio Hornblower* (51), *Blackbeard the Pirate* (52), *Sea Devils* (53).

WILDE, CORNEL (1915-   ). American leading man, a big success after the war as Robert, son of Robin Hood in *The Bandit Of Sherwood Forest* (46). Other films: *Sons Of The Musketeers* (52), *Treasure Of The Golden Condor* (53), *Star Of India* (54), *The Scarlet Coat* (55), *Omar Khayyam* (57), *Lancelot And Guinevere* (63), also produced and directed.

ADVENTURE

THE LIVES OF A BENGAL LANCER   1935

This film joins the talents of Gary Cooper, Henry Hathaway and camera-man Charles Lang in a lively adventure piece about service life in India at the turn of the century. The story hinges on three British officers of the 41st Bengal Lancers who become involved in a tribal uprising along the Northwest frontier. If the dialogue now seems unintentionally amusing it is more than compensated by Hathaway's splendid location work and by the climactic full-scale attack on a mountain fort, which remains one of the genre's most exciting set pieces. Cooper, Franchot Tone and Richard Cromwell play the heroic officers and Douglass Dumbrille features as the villain.

Production Company:	Paramount
Production:	Louis D. Lighton
Direction:	Henry Hathaway
Screenplay:	Waldemar Young,
	John L. Balderston,
	Achmed Abdullah
Adaptation:	Grover Jones,
	William Slavens McNutt
Photography:	Charles Lang
Music:	Milan Roder

Leading Players: Gary Cooper, Franchot Tone, Richard Cromwell, Sir Guy Standing, C. Aubrey Smith, Monte Blue, Kathleen Burke, Colin Tapley, Douglass Dumbrille, Akim Tamiroff

CHINA SEAS   1935

This stylish adventure piece represents Hollywood professionalism at its very best and is equally as effective today as it was forty-five years ago. Clark Gable plays a young sea captain in command of a ship carrying a cargo of gold from Hong Kong to Singapore. Also on board — some for the gold, others just for the fun of it — are seven of Metro's top stars of the period, including Lewis Stone as a broken-down ship's officer, Wallace Beery as a villainous trader, Jean Harlow as his moll and Rosalind Russell as a terribly nice English girl with "a charmin' little place down in Sussex with no end of huntin' and fishin'". Apart from Miss Russell's performance the film's main highlights are a spectacular typhoon and an attack by Chinese pirates.

Production Company:	Metro-Goldwyn-Mayer
Production:	Albert Lewin
Direction:	Tay Garnett
Screenplay:	Jules Furthman and
based on the novel by	James Keven McGuiness
Crosbie Garstin	
Photography:	Ray June
Music:	Herbert Stothart

Leading Players: Clark Gable, Jean Harlow, Wallace Beery, Lewis Stone, Rosalind Russell, Robert Benchley, Dudley Digges, C. Aubrey Smith

THE FOUR FEATHERS   1939

Rarely mentioned in film histories, this movie now leaves a somewhat unpleasant after-taste in its unashamed glorification of war, yet within the conventions of the adventure genre, it continues to hold a strange fascination. As a straightforward piece of hokum it works as well as any film in the pre-war period. Set on the eve of Kitchener's Sudan Campaign, it centres on a young Englishman who sets out to prove himself in Egypt after being branded a coward by his army comrades. John Clements brings conviction to the central role, although it is Ralph Richardson as the officer blinded by sunstroke in the desert (a brilliant scene) who takes most of the acting honours.

Production Company:	London Films Productions
Production:	Alexander Korda
Direction:	Zoltan Korda
Screenplay:	R. C. Sheriff
from the novel by	
A. E. W. Mason	
Photography (Technicolor):	Georges Perinal
Sudan Photography:	Osmond Borrodaile
Music:	Miklos Rozsa

Leading Players: John Clements, Ralph Richardson, C. Aubrey Smith, June Duprez, Allan Jeayes, Jack Allen, Donald Gray, Frederick Culler

GUNGA DIN   1939

Adapted from Rudyard Kipling's poem about a native water carrier, *Gunga Din* belongs to the pre-war golden era of Hollywood films when adventure stories were eagerly accepted and their often dubious morality rarely questioned by movie audiences. Cary Grant, Douglas Fairbanks, Jun. and Victor McLaglen play three swashbuckling soldiers who become personally involved in a massive Thuggee uprising, and Sam Jaffe evokes the necessary sympathy as Gunga Din. But this is, above all a director's film, and George Stevens, whilst never taking the story too seriously brings a tremendous vigour to the picture, especially to the battle scenes and the final moments when the wounded water carrier sounds the retreat and saves the regiment at the cost of his life.

Production Company:	RKO Radio
Production and Direction:	George Stevens
Screenplay:	Joel Sayre and
after an original story by	Fred Guiol
Ben Hecht and Charles	
MacArthur suggested by the	
Rudyard Kipling poem.	
Photography:	Joseph H. August
Music:	Alfred Newman

Leading Players: Cary Grant, Douglas Fairbanks, Jun., Victor McLaglen, Sam Jaffe, Eduardo Ciannelli, Joan Fontaine, Montague Love, Robert Coote

BEAU GESTE   1939

William Wellman's expert direction helps make this remake of P. C. Wren's adventure story of the Foreign Legion as effective as Herbert Brenon's silent version with Ronald Colman. If the 'Boy's Own Paper' view of heroism seems unacceptable in this modern age, the action scenes in the desert stand up well and the opening sequence showing the discovery of the deserted Fort Zinderneuf, manned only by dead Legionnaires, is still brilliantly effective. Gary Cooper, Ray Milland and Robert Preston play the three Geste brothers and Brian Donlevy features as Sergeant Markoff, 'the cruellest ruffian and the bravest soldier in the Legion'.

Production Company:	Paramount
Production and Direction:	William Wellman
Screenplay:	Robert Carson
based on the novel by	
Percival Christopher Wren	
Photography:	Theodor Sparkuhl and
	Archie Stout
Music:	Alfred Newman

Leading Players: Gary Cooper, Ray Milland, Robert Preston, Brian Donlevy, Susan Hayward, J. Carrol Naish, Albert Dekker, Broderick Crawford

20,000 LEAGUES UNDER THE SEA   1954

One of the Fifties' most enjoyable adventures, with James Mason as Jules Verne's society-hating genius, Captain Nemo, prowling the sea bed in his 19th-century submarine *Nautilus*, and being propelled by the dynamic force of the Universe. Mason's film without a doubt, but effective in most departments, not least in its breathtaking special effects which help make the battle between the submarine and a giant squid one of the screen's most spectacular highlights outside DeMille. Kirk Douglas as a harpooner, Paul Lukas as a French professor and Peter Lorre as his assistant also feature.

Production Company:	Walt Disney Prods.

Direction:	Richard Fleischer
Screenplay:	Earl Felton
from the novel by Jules Verne	
Photography (Technicolor/	
CinemaScope):	Franz Planer
Music:	Paul Smith

Leading Players: Kirk Douglas, James Mason, Paul Lukas, Peter Lorre, Robert J. Wilke, Carleton Young, Ted de Corsia

MOBY DICK   1956

From the moment Richard Basehart turns boldly to the camera and commands "Call me Ishmael", to the final sequence when a frenzied Gregory Peck (Ahab) roars "Thou damned whale" and thrusts his harpoon again and again into the plunging beast, this film sets the pulses racing both intellectually and emotionally. The fatalistic mood of Melville's great revenge novel is subtly caught by Huston's inspired direction, the final chase as the scarred Ahab perishes with the whale that has maimed him is more spectacular than Spielberg's subsequent shark hunt in *Jaws*. And if ever a movie looked right it is this one. The people of New Bedford, Massachusetts in the 1840s, the buildings and the sea scapes are photographed in muted Technicolor which brings to the film the look of an old whaling print. Leo Genn is Starbuck, Orson Welles Father Mapple and Frederick Ledebur the tattooed Queequeg.

Production Company:	Warner Bros.
Production:	John Huston
Direction:	John Huston
Screenplay:	John Huston
	and Ray Bradbury
from the novel by	
Herman Melville	
Photography (Technicolor):	Oswald Morris
Music:	Philip Stainton

Leading Players: Gregory Peck, Richard Basehart, Leo Genn, Orson Welles, Frederick Ledebur, Harry Andrews

Note: Filmed on location between July 1954 and February 1955 and at Elstree Studios. Locations included Youghal, County Cork (the New Bedford scenes), Fishguard, the Canary Isles, Madeira and the Azores where a camera crew spent several weeks on a whaling expedition. Moby Dick himself weighed several tons and measured 92 ft in length.

NORTH WEST FRONTIER   1959

The genre's favourite country and period — India at the turn of the century — is once again exploited to the full in this surprisingly success-ful revival of the adventure story. Kenneth More plays a British Army officer who takes a group of people on a perilous train journey across

India in order to save a six-year old prince from the Moslem hordes who have murdered his father. The film has everything, from ambushes, torn up rails, bridges blown by dynamite, to a fight on the top of a moving train, and includes one startlingly effective scene at an Indian border station when a baby is rescued from a train of massacred refugees. Director J. Lee Thompson has done subsequent work in the genre, but never anything as effective as this.

Production Company:	Rank
Production:	Marcel Hellman
Direction:	J. Lee Thompson
Screenplay:	Robin Estridge
Photography (Eastman Color):	Geoffrey Unsworth

Leading Players: Kenneth More, Lauren Bacall, Herbert Lom, Wilfrid Hyde White, I. S. Johar, Ursula Jeans

ZULU   1964

A film that is mainly remembered for one sequence — that in which thousands of Zulu warriors are at first heard, through the rhythmic beating of their drums, and then at last glimpsed in one astonishing shot as they appear across the horizon as far as the eye can see. The story, a true one, is set in South Africa in 1879 and tells how a small contingent of British troops successfully defends an isolated mission station against 4,000 Zulu warriors. The characterizations of the various soldier types are over-familiar and the first hour is slow moving, but the battle itself (it lasted for two days and resulted in eleven Victoria Crosses being awarded) is superbly staged. Stanley Baker, James Booth and Michael Caine appear as British soldiers and Jack Hawkins as a Swedish missionary.

Production Company:	Paramount
Production:	Stanley Baker and Cy Endfield
Direction:	Cy Endfield
Screenplay:	John Prebble and Cy Endfield
Photography (Technicolor):	Stephen Dade
Music:	John Barry

Leading Players: Stanley Baker, James Booth, Jack Hawkins, Ulla Jacobsson, Michael Caine, Nigel Green, Ivor Emmanuel, Paul Daneman

JAWS   1975

For many, *Jaws* is a horror movie. For others it is a terrifying thriller. But for most people it remains a straightforward adventure tale of the most basic kind as three men in a boat venture out to pit themselves against the monster shark that has been gobbling up holidaymakers along the Long Island beaches. Director Spielberg's frequent use of scenes filmed at water level adds considerably to the film's tension, as does the throbbing menace of John Williams' score. The sparing use of actual shark scenes (for most of the early reels the camera *is* the shark) is another plus factor which makes it all the more frightening when the 25ft monster does appear, especially when it leaps high alongside the frail craft and almost takes Roy Scheider's arm in one gulp! For two years the number one money-maker of all time.

Production Company:	Universal
Production:	Richard D. Zanuck
	and David Brown
Direction:	Steven Spielberg
Screenplay:	Peter Benchley and
	Carl Gottlieb
from the novel by	
Peter Benchley	
Photography (Technicolor/	
Panavision):	Bill Butler
Music:	John Williams

Leading Players: Roy Scheider, Robert Shaw, Richard Dreyfuss, Lorraine Gary, Murray Hamilton

THE WIND AND THE LION   1975

The possibility that adventure movies as a genre might cease with the advent of the American 'new wave' of the 70s is disproved by this work, made by one of the most talented of the younger set, John Milius. The movie, based on a true incident in Tangier in 1904 when a widowed American (Candice Bergen) was kidnapped with her children by a desert chieftain (Sean Connery), is both thought-provoking and exciting. The arab's ransom demand is for money, rifles and sovereignty for his people. The American reaction, influenced by the need of Theodore Roosevelt to find a strong vote-winning ploy for his presidential campaign, is to send the marines into Morocco. Glorious colour, a memorable Jerry Goldsmith score and a skilful portrait of Roosevelt by Brian Keith are just three of the film's virtues. Another is the sweep of its action scenes. Yet another is the tongue-in-cheek playing of Connery and Bergen. "I don't know who you are or what you want with us," screams the outraged Miss Bergen, eyeing her captor's tent with a more than interested glance. "But I will try with all the strength in me to kill you." A quizzical Connery simply raises an eyebrow: "Do you play checkers?" he asks sweetly.

Production Company:	Columbia/MGM
Production:	Herb Jaffe
Direction:	John Milius
Screenplay:	John Milius
Photography (Metrocolor/	
Panavision):	Billy Williams
Music:	Jerry Goldsmith

Leading Players: Sean Connery, Candice Bergen, Brian Keith, John Huston, Geoffrey Lewis

ADVENTURE: WHO'S WHO

ALLEN, IRWIN (1916-). American producer-director, most of whose adventure movies belong in the semi-fantasy category, e.g. *The Lost World* (60), *Voyage To The Bottom Of The Sea* (61), *Five Weeks In A Balloon* (62). Has recently been more involved in the popular spectacular disaster epics of the 70s, i.e. *The Poseidon Adventure* (72), *The Towering Inferno* (74) (co-directed), *The Swarm* (78) (produced and directed), *Beyond The Poseidon Adventure* (79) (produced and directed).

BEERY, WALLACE (1889-1949). Rugged, well-built American actor who played villains and sympathetic characters with equal assurance. His best period was the 30s when he appeared as Pancho Villa in *Viva Villa!* (34), Long John Silver in *Treasure Island* (34) and the trader James MacArdle in Garnett's *China Seas* (35). Earlier, during the 20s, he played Conan Doyle's Professor Challenger in *The Lost World* (25).

BORRODAILE, OSMOND (1892-). Canadian-born cameraman who shot many adventure movies for Korda during the pre-war period, e.g. *The Scarlet Pimpernel* (34), *Sanders of the River* (35), *Elephant Boy* (37), *The Four Feathers* (39). Later worked on Harry Watt's semi-documentary *The Overlanders* (46) and did the second unit work on *The Trap* (66).

BRYNNER, YUL (1915-). Bald-headed American actor, lately seen in several adventure pieces including *Escape From Zahrain* (62), *Kings of the Sun* (63), *Flight From Ashiya* (64), *The Long Duel* (67), *Villa Rides* (as Pancho Villa) (68).

CONNERY, SEAN (1930-). One of Connery's earliest roles was as a diamond hunting villain in *Tarzan's Greatest Adventure* (59). That was before Bond. Now that his 007 association has come to an end he has again ventured into the wide open spaces — as the Norwegian explorer Amundsen in *The Red Tent* (70), the heroic arab warlord in *The Wind And The Lion* (75) and Michael Caine's ambitious co-adventurer in Huston's version of the Kipling short story *The Man Who Would Be King* (75).

CONWAY, JACK (1887-1952). Front-rank MGM director of the 30s who handled the adventure movies *Viva Villa* (34) and *Boom Town* (40). Completed the second Weismuller Tarzan picture, *Tarzan and His Mate* (34), after Cedric Gibbons had been fired from the production.

COOPER, GARY (1901-1961). A favourite Hollywood hero for more than three decades. After his western roles (see page 92), his most enjoyable performances were in adventure pieces, such as DeMille's *Northwest Mounted Police* (40) and *Unconquered* (47), and Hathaway's Indian classic *Lives of a Bengal Lancer* (35). Others: *The General Died at Dawn* (36), *Souls at Sea* (37), *The Adventures of Marco Polo* (38), *Beau Geste* (39), *The Real Glory* (39), *Blowing Wild* (53), *The Wreck of the Mary Deare* (59).

DEMILLE, CECIL B. (1881-1959). Although he will always be remembered for his biblical spectaculars, DeMille invariably achieved his best results in the western and adventure genres. His most accomplished works in the latter category are *Reap the Wild Wind* (42), with its brilliantly filmed fight with a giant squid, and *Unconquered* (47), a pioneer story of the founding of Pittsburgh. Also: *Northwest Mounted Police* (40).

FAIRBANKS, DOUGLAS, JUN. (1909-   ). American actor who spent much of his career performing in swashbucklers (see page 215) and adventure movies. Films in the adventure genre include *Gunga Din* (39), *The Sun Never Sets* (39), *Rulers of the Sea* (39), *Green Hell* (40).

FARROW, JOHN (1904-1963). Underrated Australian writer/director with a strong liking for sea films, e.g. *Two Years Before the Mast* (46), *Botany Bay* (53), *The Sea Chase* (55), *John Paul Jones* (59). Also several actioners with Alan Ladd: *Calcutta* (47), *Beyond Glory* (48), etc.

FLEMING, RHONDA (1922-   ). People still talk of Cyd Charisse's legs but those of this lovely red-headed actress ran them very close. Rhonda Fleming's movies were never more than routine actioners, but even though the dialogue was banal and the sets strictly back lot Paramount, she was always worth gazing at and invariably made at least one token bathing suit or semi-clad appearance in each of her pictures. Films (many with John Payne, Forrest Tucker, Ronald Reagan, etc.): *The Eagle And The Hawk* (50), *The Last Outpost* (51), *Crosswinds* (51), *Hong Kong* (51), *Tropic Zone* (53), *Yankee Pasha* (54), *Jivaro* (54).

FORD, JOHN (1895-1973). A specialist in western movies (see page 96), Ford occasionally worked in the adventure genre, directing such widely diverse movies as *The Hurricane* (37), a South Seas drama with Dorothy Lamour, *Drums Along the Mohawk* (39), a story of the American War of Independence and *Mogambo* (53), a remake of *Red Dust* with Clark Gable and Ava Gardner. Also: *The Black Watch* (29), *Air Mail* (32), *The Adventures of Marco Polo* (a few sequences only) (38).

FOSTER, LEWIS R. (1899-1974). Oscar-winning writer (*Mr. Smith Goes To Washington*, 39) who aimed his sights a little lower when turning to direction. Responsible for most of the Pine-Thomas actioners at Paramount in the early 50s. Films: *Captain China* (50), *The Eagle And The Hawk* (50), *The Last Outpost* (51), *Passage West* (51), *Crosswinds* (51), *Hong Kong* (52), *Tropic Zone* (53), *Jamaica Run* (53).

GABLE, CLARK (1901-1960). Leading American actor, known for many years as 'The King of Hollywood'. Several enjoyable roles in the adventure genre, e.g. Fletcher Christian in *Mutiny on the Bounty* (35), Captain Alan Gaskell in *China Seas* (35), and big game hunter Vic Marswell in Ford's *Mogambo* (53). Others: *Call of the Wild* (35), *Test Pilot* (38), *Boom Town* (40), *Soldier of Fortune* (55), *Band of Angels* (57).

GODDARD, PAULETTE (1911-). A favourite DeMille heroine, excellent as the half-breed Louvette Corbeau in *Northwest Mounted Police* (40) and the tempestuous Loxi Claiborne in *Reap the Wild Wind* (42). Others: *The Forest Rangers* (42), *Unconquered* (47).

GRANGER, STEWART (1913-). Romantic British leading man who became a top MGM star of the early 50s. Played Allan Quartermain in *King Solomon's Mines* (50). Also: *The Wild North* (52), *All the Brothers were Valiant* (53), *Green Fire* (54), *Harry Black* (58), *The Last Safari* (67).

HARRIS, RICHARD (1932-). Rugged Irish actor, frequently seen in adventure yarns including several derived from the works of Alistair MacLean. A luckless crew member of Trevor Howard's 'Bounty' in Milestone's 62 remake. Films: *The Wreck Of The Mary Deare* (59), *The Guns Of Navarone* (61), *Mutiny On The Bounty* (62), *The Heroes Of Telemark* (65), *Hawaii* (66), *Man In The Wilderness* (71), *Orca — Killer Whale* (77), *Golden Rendezvous* (77).

HATHAWAY, HENRY (1898-). Veteran American director whose

Lives of a Bengal Lancer (35) is a classic among adventure films. Numerous other films in the genre, many of exceptional quality, e.g. *Trail of the Lonesome Pine* (36), *Souls at Sea* (37), *Spawn of the North* (38), *The Real Glory* (39), *Down to the Sea in Ships* (49), *White Witch Doctor* (53), *Legend of the Lost* (57), *The Last Safari* (67).

HAWKS, HOWARD (1896-1977). The recurring theme of man proving himself to himself frequently found this great director out-of-doors, not only in the West (see page 98) but also in varying parts of the globe i.e. South America where, in *Only Angels Have Wings* (39), a group of pilots run a dangerous air mail service over the Andes and in Africa (*Hatari!* 62) where John Wayne and co. round up wild animals for the world's zoos. Hawks also directed *Tiger Shark* (32) in which Edward G. Robinson lost a hand long before it became fashionable to be swallowed whole in *Jaws* (75). Others: *The Crowd Roars* (32), *Viva Villa!* (34) (co-directed), *Barbary Coast* (35), *Ceiling Zero* (35).

HAYWARD, SUSAN (1918-1975). Red-headed American actress whose high-charged, dynamic performances in *I'll Cry Tomorrow* (55), *I Want To Live* (58), etc. were interlaced with more straightforward roles in adventure movies. Films: *Beau Geste* (39), *The Forest Rangers* (42), *Reap The Wild Wind* (42), *Tulsa* (49), *White Witch Doctor* (53), *Soldier Of Fortune* (55), *Untamed* (55).

HERRMANN, BERNARD (1911-1975). Talented American composer, famous for his work with Welles and Hitchcock. His music for Henry King's adventure opus *King Of The Khyber Rifles* (54) brings a touch of quality to an otherwise banal film. Also: *White Witch Doctor* (53), *Beneath The Twelve Mile Reef* (53) and the adventure fantasies *The Seventh Voyage Of Sinbad* (58), *Journey To The Centre Of The Earth* (59), *Mysterious Island* (61), *Jason And The Argonauts* (63).

HESTON, CHARLTON (1924-   ). A Paramount contract player early in his career, Heston owed much of his early success to DeMille who cast him as the circus manager in *The Greatest Show On Earth* (52) and Moses in *The Ten Commandments* (56). During the same period he did his stint on the studio's adventure programmers, among them *The Naked Jungle* (54), *Secret Of The Incas* (54) and *The Far Horizons* (55). He later teamed effectively with Gary Cooper in *The Wreck Of The Mary Deare* (59) and more recently has starred in a remake of the Jack London story *Call Of The Wild* (72).

HUSTON, JOHN (1906-). Outdoor heroics, especially when the odds are heavily stacked against success, have invariably been a key part of this famous director's work, even though he began his career with the private-eye thriller *The Maltese Falcon* (41). Humphrey Bogart as one of three prospectors searching for gold in the Mexican hills in *The Treasure Of The Sierra Madre* (48), an obsessed Gregory Peck (as Ahab) hunting down Melville's great white whale *Moby Dick* (56) and Michael Caine and Sean Connery in *The Man Who Would Be King* (75) have all found thrilling adventure in his movies. So too did spinster missionary Katharine Hepburn in *The African Queen* (51) (again with Bogie) as she fought her way down an African river on an old tug boat in World War I.

JENNINGS, TALBOT. American screenwriter who brought his talents to bear on many notable adventure movies of the 30s, including *Mutiny on the Bounty* (35), *Spawn of the North* (38), *Rulers of the Sea* (39), *Northwest Passage* (40). Also *Escape to Burma* (55), *Pearl of the South Pacific* (55), *Untamed* (55).

JOYCE, BRENDA (1918-). American actress, former model. Numerous appearances as Tarzan's Jane, e.g. *Tarzan and the Amazons* (45), *Tarzan and the Leopard Woman* (46), *Tarzan and the Huntress* (47), *Tarzan and the Mermaids* (48), *Tarzan's Magic Fountain* (49).

KORDA, ZOLTAN (1895-1961). Hungarian director, responsible for most of the British adventure movies produced by brother Alexander during the 30s. Films: *Sanders of the River* (35), *Elephant Boy* (37), *The Drum* (38), *The Four Feathers* (39), *The Thief of Bagdad* (40).

LADD, ALAN (1913-1964). Best known for his tough guy roles, Alan Ladd became equally popular in westerns (see page 101) and adventure movies later in his career. Played the lead role in Farrow's version of Dana's sea epic *Two Years Before The Mast* (46). Also: *China* (43), *Calcutta* (47), *Wild Harvest* (47), *Beyond Glory* (48), *Botany Bay* (53), *Desert Legion* (53), *Saskatchewan* (54), *Hell Below Zero* (54).

LAMOUR, DOROTHY (1914-). American actress, famous for her sarong roles at Paramount. Later turned to comedy with Bob Hope and Bing Crosby. Adventure films: *The Jungle Princess* (36), *The Hurricane* (37), *Her Jungle Love* (38), *Spawn of the North* (38), *Typhoon* (40), *Aloma of the South Seas* (41), *Wild Harvest* (47).

LANG, CHARLES (1902-). Top Hollywood cameraman since the early 30s. Numerous adventure movies to his credit, including several at Paramount, where he worked under contract between 1929-52. Films include *Lives Of A Bengal Lancer* (35), *Souls At Sea* (37), *Spawn Of The North* (38)), *Sundown* (41), *The Forest Rangers* (42), *Rope Of Sand* (49), *Peking Express* (51).

LESSER, SOL (1890-). American producer, long associated with the Tarzan movies. Over fifteen Tarzan adventures since 1931, many with Johnny Weismuller, Lex Barker, Gordon Scott, etc.

LINCOLN, ELMO (1889-1952). The first screen Tarzan, Lincoln made his début in the role in 1918 in *Tarzan of the Apes* and later the same year appeared in a sequel, *Romance of Tarzan*. He appeared for the third and last time as the 'Ape Man' in 1921 when he starred in the 15-part serial *Adventures of Tarzan*. Twenty-seven years later he guested in a bit part as a jungle fisherman in *Tarzan's Magic Fountain* (48).

LLOYD, FRANK (1889-1960). Scottish-born director who spent a long and profitable career in Hollywood. His adventure movies represent his best work, especially *Mutiny on the Bounty* (35), which won him an Academy Award nomination. Others include: *Under Two Flags* (36), *If I Were King* (38), *Rulers of the Sea* (39).

MACLEAN, ALISTAIR (1922-). Best-selling adventure novelist, many of whose stories have been turned into financial blockbusters at the movie box-office: *The Guns Of Navarone* (61), *Ice Station Zebra* (68), *Where Eagles Dare* (69), *When Eight Bells Toll* (70), *Puppet On A Chain* (72), *Fear Is The Key* (72), *Caravan To Vacares* (75), *Breakheart Pass* (76), *Golden Rendezvous* (77), *Force 10 From Navarone* (78), *Bear Island* (79).

MAHIN, JOHN LEE (1907-). American screenwriter with several adventure movies among his credits — *Treasure Island* (34), *Boom Town* (40), *Down To The Sea In Ships* (49), *Mogambo* (53).

MARTON, ANDREW (1904-). Exceptionally talented film-maker and second-unit director whose best work has usually been in the latter category (see page 182), but who has also occasionally produced some interesting films as a fully fledged director, e.g. *King Solomon's Mines* (50) which he co-directed with Compton Bennett. Others: *The Wild North* (52), *Green Fire* (54), *Crack in the World* (65), *Africa Texas Style* (67).

MASON, JAMES (1909-   ). Mason's ventures into the genre have been rare but memorable and include Professor Oliver Lindenbrook in Jules Verne's *Journey to the Centre of the Earth* (59) and Captain Nemo in the same author's *Twenty Thousand Leagues Under the Sea* (54). He also featured to great effect as the Bligh-like skipper in John Farrow's *Botany Bay* (53).

MASSEY, RAYMOND (1896-   ). Canadian-born actor, best known for his television performances as Dr. Gillespie in the long-running *Dr. Kildare* series. His adventure movies, most of which were made during the 30s, include *The Scarlet Pimpernel* (as Chauvelin) (34), *Under the Red Robe* (37), *The Hurricane* (37), *The Drum* (38). In 1942 he appeared for DeMille in *Reap the Wild Wind* (as the salvage pirate King Cutler).

MCLAGLEN, VICTOR (1883-1959). Irish-born character actor, in Hollywood from the early 20s. Well used by George Stevens in *Gunga Din* (39) (see page 224). Others: *Beau Geste* (26), *The Black Watch* (29), *Under Two Flags* (36), *Fair Wind to Java* (53), *Sea Fury* (58).

MILLAND, RAY (1905-   ). A top Paramount star for many years, at his peak during the 40s when he appeared in several high quality movies for Wilder, Leisen and Farrow. His best roles in the adventure genre are his Captain Jack Stuart in DeMille's *Reap the Wild Wind* (42) and John Geste in Wellman's *Beau Geste* (39).

NEWMAN, ALFRED (1901-1970). American composer of numerous scores in the genre, including *The Call Of The Wild* (35), *Clive Of India* (35), *Slave Ship* (37), *The Hurricane* (37), *Trade Winds* (38), *Gunga Din* (39), *Drums Along The Mohawk* (39), *Beau Geste* (39), *The Real Glory* (39), *Hudson's Bay* (40).

O'SULLIVAN, MAUREEN (1911-   ). Irish-born actress who played Jane in several MGM Tarzan movies. Films (all opposite Johnny Weismuller): *Tarzan The Ape Man* (32), *Tarzan And His Mate* (34), *Tarzan Escapes* (36), *Tarzan Finds a Son* (39), *Tarzan's Secret Treasure* (41), *Tarzan's New York Adventure* (42).

OVERMAN, LYNNE (1887-1943). Paramount character actor, seen in numerous adventure movies towards the end of his career, including several for DeMille. Films include: *Her Jungle Love* (38), *Spawn of the North* (38), *Typhoon* (40), *Northwest Mounted Police* (40), *Reap the Wild Wind* (42), *The Forest Rangers* (42).

PAYNE, JOHN (1912-   ). Not exactly the best actor in the world but the rugged hero of innumerable Paramount adventures during the early 50s. Usually to be found tackling storms at sea, diving for sunken treasure in the Caribbean or hacking his way through South American banana plantations. Rhonda Fleming and Arlene Dahl were two leading ladies who frequently made things appear less arduous. Films: *Captain China* (50), *Tripoli* (50), *The Eagle And The Hawk* (50), *Passage West* (51), *Crosswinds* (51), *Caribbean* (52), *The Blazing Forest* (52), *Raiders Of The Seven Seas* (53), *The Vanquished* (53), *Hell's Island* (55).

PERINAL, GEORGES (1897-1965). French cameraman, long in Britain. Shot many adventure movies for Zoltan Korda, e.g. *Sanders of the River* (35), *Under the Red Robe* (37), *The Drum* (38), *The Four Feathers* (39), *The Thief of Bagdad* (AA) (40).

PINE, WILLIAM H. (1896-   ). American producer who worked as an associate to DeMille on *Northwest Mounted Police* (40), *Reap the Wild Wind* (42), etc., before teaming with fellow producer William C. Thomas. After the war turned out a long series of double-feature action dramas for Paramount, including *Captain China* (50), *Crosswinds* (51), *Hong Kong* (51), *The Blazing Forest* (52), *Tropic Zone* (53), *Jamaica Run* (53), *Sangaree* (53), *The Far Horizons* (55).

PRESTON, ROBERT (1917-   ). Broadway performer whose film parts (Harold Hill in *The Music Man* being the one exception) have rarely allowed him to display his full range of talents. Played Digby in *Beau Geste* (39), a mountie in DeMille's *Northwest Mounted Police* (40) and a salvage pirate in the same director's *Reap the Wild Wind* (42). Also *Typhoon* (40), *Wild Harvest* (47), *Tulsa* (49).

SABU (1924-1963). Indian child actor who began his career in Korda adventure movies of the late 30s. Films include: *Elephant Boy* (37), *The Drum* (38), *The Thief of Bagdad* (40), *The Jungle Book* (42), *Tangier* (46), *Man Eater of Kumaon* (48), *Song of India* (49), *Rampage* (63).

SHAW, ROBERT (1927-1978). A TV swashbuckler (*The Buccaneers*) who became both a distinguished actor and novelist, Shaw found himself back on the adventure/swashbuckling circuit just prior to his premature death, chasing sharks in *Jaws* (75), diving for buried treasure in *The Deep* (77) and repeating Gregory Peck's Major Mallory role in *Force 10 From Navarone* (78).

SURTEES, ROBERT L. (1906-   ). Surtees' fine camerawork was one of the most rewarding features of MGM movies during the 40s and 50s. A treble Academy Award winner for *King Solomon's Mines* (50), *The Bad And The Beautiful* (52) and *Ben-Hur* (59), he has also worked on such adventure epics as *The Wild North* (52), *Mogambo* (53), *Valley Of The Kings* (54) and *Mutiny On The Bounty* (62).

THORPE, RICHARD (1896-   ). Action director who took over the filming of *Tarzan Escapes* (36) from Jim McGay and John Farrow. Later directed the rest of Weismuller's MGM movies, i.e. *Tarzan Finds A Son* (39), *Tarzan's Secret Treasure* (41), *Tarzan's New York Adventure* (42). Numerous swashbucklers (see page 221) and actioners: *White Cargo* (42), *Malaya* (49), *The House Of The Seven Hawks* (59), *Killers Of Kilimanjaro* (60).

TRACY, SPENCER (1900-1967). Brilliant American actor whose most famous role in the genre was his Major Robert Rogers in King Vidor's *Northwest Passage* (40). Others: *Test Pilot* (38), *Stanley and Livingstone* (39), *Boom Town* (40), *Malaya* (49), *Plymouth Adventure* (52).

WALSH, RAOUL (1892-   ). Veteran American director with a penchant for fast-moving action pieces, especially those connected with the sea. Films: *Captain Horatio Hornblower* (51), *The World in His Arms* (52), *Sea Devils* (53), *Saskatchewan* (54), *Band of Angels* (57).

WAYNE, JOHN (1907-1979). American actor most often seen in westerns (see page 111), but equally effective in the adventure movies of DeMille, Ludwig, McLaglen, etc. Films: *Reap The Wild Wind* (42), *Tycoon* (47), *Wake Of The Red Witch* (48), *Big Jim McLain* (52), *The High And The Mighty* (54), *Blood Alley* (55), *Legend Of The Lost* (57), *Hatari* (62), *Hellfighters* (68).

WEISMULLER, JOHNNY (1904-   ). A former Olympic swimming champion who became the most famous of all screen Tarzans. Appeared in a dozen 'Ape Man' adventures between 1932 and 1948, six at MGM and a further half-a-dozen for Lesser at RKO. Films: *Tarzan the Ape Man* (32), *Tarzan and His Mate* (34), *Tarzan Escapes* (36), *Tarzan Finds a Son* (39), *Tarzan's Secret Treasure* (41), *Tarzan's New York Adventure* (42), *Tarzan Triumphs* (43), *Tarzan's Desert Mystery* (43), *Tarzan and the Amazons* (45), *Tarzan and the Leopard Woman* (46), *Tarzan and the Huntress* (47), *Tarzan and the Mermaids* (48).

WELLMAN, WILLIAM A. (1896-1975). Maverick director, similar in style to Hawks whose wide range of movie work took in war films, the Old West and straightforward action tales such as *Call Of The Wild* (35) and *Beau Geste* (39). Frequently displayed a penchant for films dealing with aviation: *Men With Wings* (38), *Gallant Journey* (46), *The High And The Mighty* (54). Also: *Reaching For The Sun* (41), *Island In The Sky* (52), *Track Of The Cat* (54), *Blood Alley* (55).

WILDE, CORNEL (1915-   ). Chopin in *A Song To Remember* (45) but more at home with swashbucklers (see page 222) and actioners, many of which he directed himself during the 60s. His *The Naked Prey* (66) the story of a white man being hunted through the jungle by African natives, is a notable achievement. Also: *California Conquest* (52), *Saadia* (53), *Hot Blood* (56), *Beyond Mombassa* (57), *Maracaibo* (58) (also directed), *Edge Of Eternity* (59), *Shark's Treasure* (75) (also directed), *The Norseman* (79).

YOUNG, VICTOR (1900-1956). American composer, scored all DeMille films between 1940 and 1952, including *Northwest Mounted Police* (40), *Reap The Wild Wind* (42), *Unconquered* (47). Also: *Ebb Tide* (37), *Moon Over Burma* (40), *Aloma Of The South Seas* (41), *The Forest Rangers* (42), *China* (43), *Two Years Before The Mast* (46), *Calcutta* (47), *Fair Wind To Java* (53), *Timberjack* (55).

ANIMATION

SNOW WHITE AND THE SEVEN DWARFS   1938

The film that began it all more than forty years ago, several years in the making, financed partly with borrowed money, but ultimately one of the classics of animated cinema. Adapted from the fairy story by the Brothers Grimm, it features some of Disney's most engaging cartoon work — the animals of the forest, the queen who turns herself into a hideous old crone, the magic mirror and the dwarfs themselves. If Snow White and her chocolate box prince now appear too sweet and treacly for modern tastes, they are the only aspects of the film which date. Still a unique entertainment. Hit songs: 'Heigh-Ho', 'Whistle While You Work', 'Someday My Prince Will Come'.

Production Company:	Walt Disney, released by RKO
Supervising Director:	David Hand
Sequence Directors:	Perce Pearce, William Cottrell, Larry Morey, Wilfred Jackson, Ben Sharpsteen
Supervising Animators:	Hamilton Luske, Fred Moore, Vladimir Tytla and Herman Ferguson
Music:	Frank Churchill, Leigh Harline and Paul Smith

Voices: Adriana Caselotti, Harry Stockwell, Lucille LaVerne, Scotty Mattraw, Roy Atwell, Pinto Colvig, Otis Harlan, Billy Gilbert, Moroni Olsen

FANTASIA   1940

Still the most ambitious feature length cartoon of all time. A massive undertaking by a then buoyant Disney to interpret eight widely differing pieces of classical music in cartoon terms, from the abstract visuals of Bach's 'Toccata and Fugue in D Minor' and a cheeky Mickey Mouse as 'The Sorcerer's Apprentice' to the enormous yellow-eyed demon demonstrating his power during Mussorgsky's 'Night On A Bare Mountain'. Other highlights: the prehistoric visions of 'The Rite Of Spring'; Chinese mushrooms dancing in 'The Nutcracker Suite' and the landscapes of Greek mythology in Beethoven's 'Pastoral Symphony'. Flawed, sometimes vulgar, more frequently inspired!

Production Company:	Walt Disney, released by RKO
Production Supervision:	Ben Sharpsteen
Story Direction:	Joe Grant and
	Dick Huemer
Narrative Introduction:	Deems Taylor
Musical Direction:	Edward H. Plumb

With Leopold Stokowski and the Philadelphia Orchestra

SONG OF THE SOUTH   1946

'Zip-a-dee Doo-Dah' sings a beaming James Baskett as Uncle Remus and suddenly his jovial black face is surrounded by cartoon birds and animals and he is walking through an animated countryside with 'blue-birds on his shoulder'. An historic moment and one that showed just what could be done by combining live action and animation techniques, even though Disney had already experimented to a certain extent in *The Three Caballeros* (45) as had Hanna and Barbera at MGM in *Anchors Aweigh* (45) when Gene Kelly danced with Jerry Mouse. The three animated Brer Rabbit stories in *Song Of The South* include 'The Tar Baby' and feature the characters Brer Rabbitt, Brer Fox and Brer Bear.

Production Company:	Walt Disney, released by RKO
Associate Producer:	Perce Pearce
Cartoon Direction:	Wilfred Jackson
Live Action Direction:	Harve Foster
Screenplay:	Dalton Raymond, Morton
	Grant and Maurice Rapf
Original story:	Dalton Raymond
based on 'Tales Of Uncle	
Remus' by Joel Chandler Harris	
Photography (Technicolor):	Gregg Toland
Cartoon Score:	Paul J. Smith
Live Action Score:	Daniele Amfitheatrof
Leading Players: Ruth Warrick, James Baskett, Bobby Driscoll,	
Luana Patten, Lucile Watson, Hattie McDaniel	

ANIMAL FARM   1954

George Orwell's political fable about some farm animals who drive out their drunken and inefficient farmer-master, only to find that the ruthless pig who led the revolution is every bit as unpleasant and domineering as their former boss. The message that absolute power corrupts absolutely ('All animals are equal but some are more equal than others') is put across with savage Swiftian irony, the animation is straightforward and the adaptation, minus a few subsidiary characters, faithful to the original. The first British full-length cartoon and the first to be aimed primarily at an adult audience. Produced and directed by the husband and wife team of John Halas and Joy Batchelor and sponsored by American producer Louis de Rochemont. British actor Maurice Denham supplies all the animal voices.

Production:	John Halas and Joy Batchelor for Louis de Rochemont
Direction:	John Halas and Joy Batchelor
Story Development:	Lothar Wolff, Borden Mace, Philip Stapp, John Halas, Joy Batchelor
Animation Direction (Technicolor):	John Reed
Music:	Matyas Seiber
Narration:	Gordon Heath
Voices of animals:	Maurice Denham

101 DALMATIANS   1961

In many ways the most inventive of Disney's post-war cartoons, adapted from the book by Dodie Smith and containing some of the master's most endearing animal creations since *Bambi*. The humans, too, are richly drawn — villainess Cruella de Ville, a cunning socialite who plans to turn fifteen Dalmatian pups into a fur coat and her two gormless sidekicks, burglars Jasper and Horace. Unlike Disney's classic adaptations of the 50s (*Peter Pan, Sleeping Beauty,* etc.) Brisk and unpretentious.

Production Company:	Walt Disney
Production Supervisor:	Ken Peterson
Direction:	Wolfgang Reitherman, Hamilton Luske and Clyde Geronimi
Story:	Bill Peet
based on the book 'The Hundred And One Dalmatians' by Dodie Smith	
Directing Animators:	Milt Kahl, Marc Davis, Oliver Johnston Jr, Franklin Thomas, John Lounsbery and Eric Larson
Music:	George Bruns

Voices: Rod Taylor, Lisa Davis, Cate Bauer, Ben Wright, Fred Warlock, J. Pat O'Malley, Betty Lou Gerson

THE JUNGLE BOOK   1967

The last feature cartoon made under Disney's personal supervision, a version of Rudyard Kipling's tale about a small boy, Mowgli, who is raised by wolves in the jungle and takes on the affectionate title of Man-Cub. Nowhere near as respectful an adaptation as *Pinocchio* but in its own way a highly engaging film with witty voice impersonations from George Sanders as the droll, menacing tiger Shere Khan and Phil Harris as Baloo the Bear. The animation displays little resemblance to the detailed backgrounds of Disney's other forest movie, *Bambi*, but with its delicate pastel shades and unsentimental approach the cartoon rates high among Disney's later films.

Production Company:	Walt Disney
Production:	Walt Disney
Direction:	Wolfgang Reitherman
Screenplay:	Larry Clemmons, Ralph Wright, Ken Anderson and Vance Gerry

based on the 'Mowgli' books
by Rudyard Kipling

Animation Direction:	Milt Kahl, Ollie Johnston, Frank Thomas, John Lounsbery
Music:	George Bruns
Songs:	Richard M. and Robert B. Sherman, Terry Gilkyson

Voices: Phil Harris, Sebastian Cabot, Louis Prima, George Sanders, Sterling Holloway, J. Pat O'Malley, Bruce Reitherman, Verna Felton and Clint Howard

YELLOW SUBMARINE   1968

The first full-length cartoon to come from a British studio since *Animal Farm*, but rather different in concept — a unique visual evocation of Beatles' themes, told with lively invention and a wide variety of animation styles. It's a case of The Beatles to the rescue as they journey in their submarine to save the people of Pepperland from the Blue Meanies, a group of nasties determined to rid the world of music and happiness. They win of course, but not before their magical mystery tour has thrown up all kinds of surrealist obstacles including kinky boot beasts, a teapot fish and a vacuum flask monster which sucks up everything then devours itself. Lively, controversial, uneven, rich in imagery — and both a commercial and artistic success!

Production Company:	King Features/Subafilms, distributed by United Artists
Production:	Al Brodax
Direction:	George Dunning
Screenplay:	Lee Minoff, Al Brodax, Jack Mendelsohn, Erich Segal
Story:	Lee Minoff

based on the song by John
Lennon and Paul McCartney

| Photography (DeLuxe Color): | John Williams |
| Music: | John Lennon and Paul McCartney |

Voices: John Clive, Geoffrey Hughes, Paul Angelus, Dick Emery, Lance Percival

A CHRISTMAS CAROL   1972

With some 30,000 drawings Richard Williams has succeeded where countless directors and actors have failed, namely in bringing Dickens' 'A Christmas Carol' to perfect life on screen. There is scarcely a blemish in this Oscar-winning little film. Williams is faithful both to the original text (all the words are Dickens' own) and the drawings of the period, using muted colours to heighten the realism. Genuinely eerie, especially when Scrooge is borne through the haunted night skies, and sometimes horrific (the appearance of Marley's ghost), the film is the result of meticulous research into the clothes, furniture and architecture of the time. It is also a perfect example of the animator's art and one of the definitive Dickens films.

Production Company:	Richard Williams Productions, sponsored by the Foundation for Full Service Banks
Production and Direction:	Richard Williams
Executive Producer:	Chuck Jones
Script:	Charles Dickens
Photography (Technicolor):	Roy Watford
Music, special effects:	Tristram Cary

Voices: Michael Redgrave (narration), Alastair Sim (Scrooge), Michael Horden (Marley)

WATERSHIP DOWN   1978

A faithful reconstruction of Richard Adams' bestselling novel about the adventures of a group of rabbits as they search for a new warren and try to escape the attentions of man. Exact and sometimes over meticulous animation, but the rabbit's eye view of the world comes across forcibly and the backgrounds are perfectly realised. Like *Animal Farm*, as much a film for adults as it is for children. The late John Hubley worked on the film as director before being replaced by his producer Martin Rosen. John Hurt voices the defiant Hazel, Richard Briers the young Fiver, Roy Kinnear is Pipkin and Ralph Richardson Chief Rabbit.

Production Company:	Nepenthe Productions
Direction:	Martin Rosen
Screenplay: based on the novel by Richard Adams	Martin Rosen
Animation Supervisor:	Philip Duncan
Animation Director:	Tony Guy
Music:	Angela Morley

Voices: John Hurt, Richard Briers, Michael Graham-Cox, John Bennett, Ralph Richardson, Roy Kinnear, Zero Mostel

ANIMATION: WHO'S WHO

AVERY, TEX (1908-). American animator, at Warners and MGM during the 30s, 40s and 50s where he perfected the 'destructive short cartoon' (sometimes called anarchistic) based on a string of violent but always humorous gags. Began making cartoons in 1930, working on *Aesop's Fables* with Charles Mintz and then on the *Oswald The Rabbit* series with Walter Lantz at Universal (1930-35). Made over 130 shorts, many featuring Porky Pig, Daffy Duck and Bugs Bunny. Created the doleful little hound Droopy in *Dumb-Hounded* (43). Won Oscar nominations for his cartoons *Detouring America* (39) and *A Wild Hare* (40) with Bugs Bunny.

BAKSHI, RALPH. Former Paramount animator who tired of "blowing up mice" and in the 70s turned to making animated features in the style of the underground press: *Fritz The Cat* (72), the story of a randy cat who enjoys a series of sex orgies, drug sessions, etc, *Heavy Traffic* (73), *Wizards* (77). Directed the ambitious two hour version of Tolkien's *The Lord Of The Rings* (78).

BASS, SAUL (1920-). American graphic designer who has done much notable work on film credit titles. Worked on the credits of some eight films for Otto Preminger who first commissioned him to design the titles for *Carmen Jones* in 1954. For the same director he made a jigsaw puzzle of a corpse in *Anatomy Of A Murder* (59) and took the lid off Washington in *Advise And Consent* (62). Other credit designs: the 'I' scratching itself in *The Seven Year Itch* (55), the spiralling into a woman's eye in *Vertigo* (58), the stalking black cat in *Walk On The Wild Side* (62) and the opening titles, parodying every film genre, in *That's Entertainment II* (76). Designed the murder sequence in Hitchcock's *Psycho* (60), won an Oscar for his short *Why Man Creates* in 1968 and turned director for the science-fiction drama *Phase IV* (73). Also: (credits) — *The Man With The Golden Arm* (55), *Around The World In Eighty Days* (56), *North By Northwest* (59), *Spartacus* (60), *Exodus* (60), *West Side Story* (61), *It's A Mad, Mad, Mad, Mad World* (63), *Seconds* (66).

BOSUSTOW, STEPHEN (1911-). The founder of the breakaway

animation company UPA in 1945, a company that produced new style cartoons with less realistic backgrounds than those of Walt Disney. Formerly with Walter Lantz and Disney, Bosustow created the bumbling, short sighted Mr. Magoo in *Ragtime Bear* (49) and was the recipient of numerous Oscars and nominations for his individual cartoon work during the 50s i.e. *Gerald McBoing-Boing* (50), *When Magoo Flew* (54), *Mr. Magoo's Puddle Jumper* (56) — all Oscar winners; *Robin Hoodlum* (48), *Magic Fluke* (49), *Trouble Indemnity* (50), *Rooty Toot Toot* (51), *Madeline* (52), *Pink And Blue Blues* (52), *Christopher Crumpet* (53). *The Tell Tale Heart* (53), *Gerald McBoing-Boing On Planet Moo* (56), *The Jaywalker* (56), *Trees And Jamaica Daddy* (57) — all nominees. In 1961 Bosustow left and sold his interest in the company to make travel and educational films. UPA continues with full-length features for TV and the cinema — *A Thousand And One Arabian Nights* (59), *Mister Magoo's Christmas Carol* (62), *Gay Purr-ee* (62), *Uncle Sam Magoo* (70).

DISNEY, WALT (1901-1966). The king of them all and founder of the largest animation studio in the world. Mickey Mouse, Donald Duck, Pluto, Goofy and the rest all emerged from his studio during the late 20s and 30s, each of them animated by such famous designers as Ub Iwerks, Hamilton Luske, Bill Tytla, Norman Ferguson, Wolfgang Reitherman, Art Babbitt, Grim Natwick and Milton Kahl. This same group, plus many others, also worked for Disney during his formative years in feature animation: *Snow White And The Seven Dwarfs* (38), *Pinocchio* (40), *Fantasia* (40), *Dumbo* (41), *Bambi* (42). Other feature length Disney cartoons: *Fun And Fancy Free* (47), *Melody Time* (48), *Ichabod And Mr. Toad* (49), *Cinderella* (50), *Alice In Wonderland* (51), *Peter Pan* (53), *Lady And The Tramp* (55), *Sleeping Beauty* (59), *101 Dalmatians* (61), *The Sword And The Stone* (63), *The Jungle Book* (67), *The Aristocats* (70), *Robin Hood* (73), *The Rescuers* (77). The Oscar winning shorts: *Flowers And Trees* (32), *Three Little Pigs* (33), *The Tortoise And The Hare* (34), *Three Orphan Kittens* (35), *Country Cousin* (36), *The Old Mill* (37), *Ferdinand The Bull* (38), *The Ugly Duckling* (39), *Lend A Paw* (41), *Der Fuehrer's Face* (42), *Toot, Whistle, Plunk And Boom* (53), *Winnie The Pooh And The Blustery Day* (68), *It's Tough To Be A Bird* (69).

DUNNING, GEORGE (1920-). Toronto-born animator who began his career with the National Film Board of Canada in 1943. Arrived in England in 1956 and has since been responsible for many individual, often surrealist-style cartoons, notably the controversial Beatles feature *Yellow Submarine* (68) (see page 242). Many sponsored films and TV commercials. Cinema films include *The Wardrobe* (59), *The Apple* (62), *The Everchanging Motor Car* (62), *The Flying Man* (62), *The Ladder* (68), *Moon Rock 10* (70), *Damon And The Mower* (71).

FLEISCHER, MAX (1889-1972). Austrian-born creator of the spinach eating Popeye and 30s cartoon vamp Betty Boop. First began working in cartoons (with his brother Dave) in the early 20s with *Out Of The Inkwell* (21) in which a character called Koko The Clown popped out of an ink bottle and got up to mischief in the real world around him. Made his first Popeye cartoon, *Popeye The Sailor*, in 1933 and for a time was the only animator to remotely rival Disney. His two feature length cartoons *Gulliver's Travels* (39) and *Mr. Bug Goes To Town* (40) were both financial failures, however, and for the rest of his career he reverted to the smaller, less ambitious world of the seven minute short cartoon.

FRELENG, FRIZ. American animator, long at Warners where he worked with fellow artists Tex Avery and Chuck Jones on the studio's 'Looney Tunes' and 'Merry Melodies' cartoons. Responsible for the characters of Sylvester and Tweetie Pie (the studio's answer to MGM's Tom and Jerry) and rakish, man-about-town mouse Speedy Gonzales. Now has his own production company with David De Patie and produces the Pink Panther cartoons for television. Oscars for the Warner shorts *Tweetie Pie* (47), *Speedy Gonzales* (55), *Birds Anonymous* (57) and *Knighty Knight Bugs* (58). Also for *The Pink Phink* (64).

HALAS, JOHN (1912-   ) and **BATCHELOR, JOY** (1914-   ). Husband and wife team who formed their own company in 1940, just four years after Hungarian-born Halas had first come to England in 1936. Responsible for the first full-length British cartoon feature, *Animal Farm* (54) (see page 240) and much work for TV both in the commercials and entertainment fields. Principal cinema shorts: *Magic Canvas* (51), *The Owl And The Pussycat* (53), *The History Of The Cinema* (56) and *Automania 2000* (63). In 1967 Joy Batchelor directed *Ruddigore*, a version of the Gilbert and Sullivan opera and in 1974 Halas animated *The Glorious Musketeers*, a TV version of the Alexandre Dumas classic.

HANNA, WILLIAM (1920-   ) and **BARBERA, JOSEPH** (1911-   ). The best known animators in the States and creators of the most famous cartoon twosome in movie history, Tom and Jerry — a pair who first appeared on screen in 1940 in *Puss Gets The Boot* (see Fred Quimby). Worked on between 100 and 200 cat and mouse cartoons at MGM until 1957 when they formed their own company and created several new characters for television, including Yogi Bear, Huckleberry Hound, Scooby Doo and the stone-age family The Flintstones. Several TV specials including *Jack And The Beanstalk* (67) and *Alice In Wonderland* (68) and animated features for the cinema: *Hey There, It's Yogi Bear* (64), *A Man Called Flintstone* (67), *Charlotte's Webb* (72).

HUBLEY, JOHN (1914-1977). American animator who worked for Disney on *Snow White And The Seven Dwarfs* (38), *Pinocchio* (40), *Fantasia* (40), *Dumbo* (41), etc. before moving to UPA in 1945 where he contributed to the first Magoo cartoon, *Ragtime Bear* (49) as well as *Fuddy Duddy Buddy* (49), another Magoo short and *Rooty Toot Toot* (51), a version of 'Frankie and Johnny'. With his wife Faith Hubley set up his own studio, Storyboard Inc, in the 50s producing a notable 53 minute feature *Of Stars And Men* (62) and numerous quality shorts i.e. *Adventures Of An Asterisk* (56), *Harlem Wednesday* (58), *The Tender Game* (58), *Children Of The Sun* (61), *The Hat* (64), *Windy Day* (68), *Of Men And Demons* (69), *Eggs* (71), *Voyage To Next* (74), *The Doonesbury Special* (77). Academy Awards for *Moonbird* (59), *The Hold* (62), and *Herb Alpert And The Tijuana Brass Double Feature* (66).

JONES, CHUCK (1915-   ). Veteran Hollywood animator/producer/director. Associated in recent years with feature length animation — *Gay Pur-ee* (62), *The Phantom Tollbooth* (70), *A Christmas Carol* (72) — but during the heyday of the short cartoon a prolific animator at Warners where he was responsible for over 200 cartoons. Bugs Bunny, Daffy Duck, The Road Runner (a mini Ostrich with the speed of an electric hare) figured among his many characters. Subsequently at MGM where he worked primarily on Tom and Jerry Cartoons (1963-67). Oscars for *For Scenti-mental Reasons* (49) a short featuring the amorous skunk Pepe le Pew and *The Dot And The Line* (65). Nominations: *Mouse Wreckers* (48), *From A To Z-Z-Z-Z* (53), *Beep Prepared* (61), *Now Hear This* (62).

LANTZ, WALTER (1900-   ). Pioneer American animator, associated with Universal since 1928 when he took over the studio's cartoon department and re-designed the Oswald Rabbit series begun by Disney. Chilly Willy and Andy Panda are two of his creations, although his most famous is the impish Woody Woodpecker who first made an appearance on screen in *Knock Knock* (40) and received star billing a year later in *Woody Woodpecker*. The bugle-like laugh heard at the beginning of each cartoon is that of Lantz's wife, Grace Stafford. The following Lantz-produced cartoons all received Oscar nominations: *The Merry Old Soul* (33), *Jolly Little Elves* (34), *Boogie Woogie Bugle Boy Of Company B* (41), *Juke Box Jamboree* (42), *The Dizzy Acrobat* (43), *Fish Fry* (44), *Poet And Peasant* (45), *Chopin's Musical Moments* (46), *Crazy Mixed Up Pup* (54), *The Legend Of Rock-A-Bye Point* (55).

MCLAREN, NORMAN (1914-   ). Scottish-born animator who made his first animated film, *Camera Makes Whoopee*, in 1935 and has worked at the National Film Board of Canada since the early 40s. Has subsequently proved to be an innovator of new techniques i.e. animating human actors, drawing directly on celluloid, animating cut out shapes etc. Many brilliant shorts including *Dots And Loops* (40), *Alouette* (44), *Hoppity Hop* (46), *Around Is Around* (51), *Neighbours* (52), *Two Bagatelles* (52), *Blinkity Blank* (54), *Lines Vertical* (60), *Pas de Deux* (68).

MELENDEZ, BILL. One of the most talented newcomers to American animation, a director who has transferred Schultz's comic strip 'Peanuts' — about a moon-faced little boy, Charlie Brown, and his endearing dog Snoopy — to both TV and cinema screens. Films: *A Boy Named Charlie Brown* (69), *Snoopy Come Home* (72), *Race For Your Life, Charlie Brown* (77), *Bon Voyage Charlie Brown* (79). Created the *Babar The Elephant* series on TV and more recently was responsible for the full-length cartoon *Dick Deadeye* (75), based on the drawings of Ronald Searle and inspired by the operas of Gilbert and Sullivan.

PAL, GEORGE (1908-   ). Hungarian-born producer, best known for his series of science-fiction films of the 50s, but who began his career in Holland and England (and then America) by designing puppet films linked and brought alive by animation techniques. His 'Puppetoon' series at Paramount in the early 40s frequently featured the character of a little black boy named Jasper and earned him a succession of Oscar nominations: *Rhythm In The Ranks* (41), *Tulips Shall Grow* (42), *The Five Hundred Hats Of Bartholomew Cubbins* (43), *And To Think I Saw It On Mulberry Street* (44), *Jasper And The Beanstalk* (45), *John Henry And The Inky Poo* (46), *Tubby The Tuba* (47).

QUIMBY, FRED (1886-1965). Producer of the long series of Tom and Jerry cartoons at MGM (see Hanna and Barbera) during the 40s and 50s. Worked at Fox before becoming manager of short subjects at Metro in 1926, a position he held until his retirement in 1956. Won eight Academy Awards in twelve years for Tom and Jerry shorts: *The Milky Way* (40), *Yankee Doodle Mouse* (43), *Mouse Trouble* (44), *Quiet Please* (45), *The Cat Concerto* (46), *The Little Orphan* (48), *Two Mouseketeers* (51), *Johann Mouse* (52). Oscar nominations for the same series — *Puss Gets The Boot* (40), *The Night Before Christmas* (41), *Dr. Jekyll And Mr. Mouse* (47), *Hatch Up Your Troubles* (49), *Jerry's Cousin* (50), *Touche, Pussy Cat* (54).

REITHERMAN, WOLFGANG. Disney's director of animation since *101 Dalmatians* (61). One of the original Disney crew from the 30s, he worked as an animator and designer on many of the pioneer features — *Snow White And The Seven Dwarfs* (38), *Pinocchio* (40), *Dumbo* (41) etc — before graduating to director status. Films as director: *101 Dalmatians* (61), *The Sword In The Stone* (63),

The Jungle Book (67), *The Aristocats* (70), *Robin Hood* (73), *The Rescuers* (77).

WILLIAMS, RICHARD (1933-). With his Oscar-winning 28-minute cartoon version of Dickens' *A Christmas Carol* (72) Canadian-born Richard Williams almost established himself as the second Disney. Long based in England he has been working for more than ten years on the yet-to-be-released Arabian Nights spectacular *The Thief And The Cobbler*, a film which promises to be a landmark in feature animation. He made his first cartoon, *The Little Island*, an abstract little piece about a conflict between Goodness, Truth and Beauty, in 1958 and has since divided his time between working on TV commercials and animating film credits i.e. *What's New Pussycat* (65), *A Funny Thing Happened On The Way To The Forum* (66), *The Charge Of The Light Brigade* (68), *The Pink Panther Strikes Again* (76). He recently completed a full length feature, *Raggedy Ann & Andy* (78), based on the stories by the late John Gruelle and following the adventures of two rag dolls when they leave their nursery to rescue an abducted French doll. Short films: *Lecture On Man* (62), *Love Me, Love Me, Love Me* (62), *The Dermis Probe* (65), *Sailor And The Devil* (68).

APPENDIX I

A CHECK LIST OF FAMOUS FILMS AND THEIR CAMERAMEN

These pages are intended as a guide to British and American films notable for their fine cinematography. The films are listed in alphabetical order with directors' names and release dates in parentheses. The cameramen are listed in the right-hand column. Films that have received Academy Award nominations for cinematography are marked with a *, Oscar winners with a †.

*Abe Lincoln in Illinois (Cromwell, 40)	James Wong Howe	B/W
Ace in the Hole (Wilder, 51)	Charles B. Lang	B/W
Adventures of a Young Man (Ritt, 62)	Lee Garmes	Col.
Adventures of Robin Hood (Curtiz/Keighley, 38)	Sol Polito and Tony Gaudio	Col.
The African Queen (Huston, 51)	Jack Cardiff	Col.
*Airport (Seaton, 70)	Ernest Laszlo	Col.
*Algiers (Cromwell, 38)	James Wong Howe	B/W
*All About Eve (Mankiewicz, 50)	Milton Krasner	B/W
*All Quiet on the Western Front (Milestone, 30)	Arthur Edeson	B/W
All That Money Can Buy (Dieterle, 41)	Joseph August	B/W
All The King's Men (Rossen, 49)	Burnett Guffey	B/W
All The President's Men (Pakula, 76)	Gordon Willis	Col.
America, America, (Kazan, 63)	Haskell Wexler	B/W
†An American in Paris (Minnelli, 51)	Alfred Gilks and John Alton	Col.
*Anatomy of a Murder (Preminger, 59)	Sam Leavitt	B/W
*Anchors Aweigh (Sidney, 45)	Robert Planck and Charles Boyle	Col.
The Andromeda Strain (Wise, 71)	Richard H. Kline	Col.
†Anna and the King of Siam (Cromwell, 46)	Arthur Miller	B/W
*Anna Christie (Brown, 30)	William Daniels	B/W
†Anthony Adverse (LeRoy, 36)	Tony Gaudio	B/W

An Unmarried Woman (Mazursky, 78)	Arthur J. Ornitz	Col.
*The Apartment (Wilder, 60)	Joseph LaShelle	B/W
†Around the World in 80 Days (Anderson, 56)	Lionel Lindon	Col.
*The Asphalt Jungle (Huston, 50)	Harold Rosson	B/W
Audrey Rose (Wise, 77)	Victor J. Kemper	Col.
*Baby Doll (Kazan, 56)	Boris Kaufman	B/W
†The Bad and the Beautiful (Minnelli, 52)	Robert Surtees	B/W
Bad Day At Black Rock (Sturges, 55)	William C. Mellor	Col.
The Barefoot Contessa (Mankiewicz, 54)	Jack Cardiff	Col.
†Barry Lindon (Kubrick, 75)	John Alcott	Col.
†Battleground (Wellman, 49)	Paul C. Vogel	B/W
*Becket (Glenville, 64)	Geoffrey Unsworth	Col.
†Ben-Hur (Wyler, 59)	Robert Surtees	Col.
The Best Years Of Our Lives (Wyler, 46)	Gregg Toland	B/W
The Big Clock (Farrow, 48)	John F. Seitz	B/W
The Big Country (Wyler, 58)	Franz Planer	Col.
*The Big Sky (Hawks, 52)	Russell Harlan	B/W
*Birdman of Alcatraz (Frankenheimer, 62)	Burnett Guffey	B/W
The Birds (Hitchcock, 63)	Robert Burks	Col.
*Blackboard Jungle (Brooks, 55)	Russell Harlan	B/W
†Black Narcissus (Powell/ Pressburger, 47)	Jack Cardiff	Col.
†The Black Swan (King, 42)	Leon Shamroy	Col.
Blithe Spirit (Lean, 45)	Ronald Neame	Col.
†Blood and Sand (Mamoulian, 41)	Ernest Palmer and Ray Rennahan	Col.
Body and Soul (Rossen, 47)	James Wong Howe	B/W
†Bonnie and Clyde (Penn, 67)	Burnett Guffey	Col.
Boomerang (Kazan, 47)	Norbert Brodine	B/W
†Bound For Glory (Ashby, 76)	Haskell Wexler	Col.
Breakfast at Tiffany's (Edwards, 61)	Franz Planer	Col.
The Breaking Point (Curtiz, 50)	Ted McCord	B/W
†The Bridge on the River Kwai (Lean, 57)	Jack Hildyard	Col.
A Bridge Too Far (Attenborough, 77)	Geoffrey Unsworth	Col.
Brief Encounter (Lean, 46)	Robert Krasker	B/W
*Broken Arrow (Daves, 50)	Ernest Palmer	Col.
†Butch Cassidy and The Sundance Kid (Hill, 69)	Conrad Hall	Col.
*Butterflies Are Free (Katselas, 72)	Charles B. Lang	Col.

†Cabaret (Fosse, 72)	Geoffrey Unsworth	Col.
Call Northside 777 (Hathaway, 48)	Joe MacDonald	B/W
Carnal Knowledge (Nichols, 71)	Guiseppe Rotunno	Col.
Carrie (Wyler, 52)	Victor Milner	B/W
Carrie (De Palma, 76)	Mario Tosi	Col.
*Casablanca (Curtiz, 43)	Arthur Edeson	B/W
*Champion (Robson, 49)	Franz Planer	B/W
*Cheyenne Autumn (Ford, 64)	William H. Clothier	Col.
*Chinatown (Polanski, 74)	John A. Alonzo	Col.
*Cimarron (Ruggles, 31)	Edward Cronjager	B/W
*Citizen Kane (Welles, 41)	Gregg Toland	B/W
†Cleopatra (DeMille, 34)	Victor Milner	B/W
†Cleopatra (Mankiewicz, 63)	Leon Shamroy	Col.
†Close Encounters Of The Third Kind (Spielberg, 77)	Vilmos Zsigmond	Col.
Coming Home (Ashby, 78)	Haskell Wexler	Col.
The Conversation (Coppola, 74)	Bill Butler	Col.
Convoy (Peckinpah, 78)	Harry Stradling Jr.	Col.
*Cover Girl (Vidor, 44)	Rudolph Mate and Allen M. Davey	Col.
Cross Of Iron (Peckinpah, 77)	John Coquillon	Col.
Cry The Beloved Country (Korda, 51)	Robert Krasker	B/W
Dark Victory (Goulding, 39)	Ernest Haller	B/W
*The Day Of The Locust (Schlesinger, 75)	Conrad Hall	Col.
†Days of Heaven (Malick, 78)	Nestor Almendros	Col.
*Dead End (Wyler, 37)	Gregg Toland	B/W
*Death of a Salesman (Benedek, 51)	Franz Planer	B/W
Death On The Nile (Guillermin, 78)	Jack Cardiff	Col.
*The Deer Hunter (Cimino, 78)	Vilmos Zsigmond	Col.
†The Defiant Ones (Kramer, 58)	Sam Leavitt	B/W
†The Diary of Anne Frank (Stevens, 59)	William C. Mellor	B/W
*Dr. Jekyll and Mr. Hyde (Mamoulian, 32)	Karl Struss	B/W
*Dr. Jekyll and Mr. Hyde (Fleming, 41)	Joseph Ruttenberg	B/W
†Doctor Zhivago (Lean, 65)	Freddie Young	Col.
*Double Indemnity (Wilder, 44)	John F. Seitz	Col.
Dracula (Browning, 31)	Karl Freund	B/W
Drums Along the Mohawk (Ford, 39)	Ray Rennahan and Bert Glennon	Col.
Duel in the Sun (Vidor, 46)	Lee Garmes, Harold Rosson and Ray Rennahan	Col.
*Earthquake (Robson, 74)	Philip Lathrop	Col.
East of Eden (Kazan, 55)	Ted McCord	Col.

*Executive Suite (Wise, 54)	George J. Folsey	B/W
*Exodus (Preminger, 60)	Sam Leavitt	Col.
*The Exorcist (Friedkin, 73)	Owen Roizman	Col.
Fahrenheit 451 (Truffaut, 66)	Nicolas Roeg	Col.
The Fallen Idol (Reed, 48)	Georges Perinal	B/W
†A Farewell to Arms (Borzage, 33)	Charles B. Lang	B/W
Far from the Madding Crowd (Schlesinger, 67)	Nicolas Roeg	Col.
†Fiddler on the Roof (Jewison, 71)	Oswald Morris	Col.
F.I.S.T. (Jewison, 78)	Laszlo Kovacs	Col.
*A Foreign Affair (Wilder, 48)	Charles B. Lang	B/W
*Foreign Correspondent (Hitchcock, 40)	Rudolph Mate	B/W
*For Whom the Bell Tolls (Wood, 43)	Ray Rennahan	Col.
Fourteen Hours (Hathaway, 51)	Joe MacDonald	B/W
Frankenstein (Whale, 31)	Arthur Edeson	B/W
*The French Connection (Friedkin, 71)	Owen Roizman	Col.
Frenchman's Creek (Leisen, 45)	George Barnes	Col.
Friendly Persuasion (Wyler, 56)	Ellsworth Fredericks	Col.
†From Here to Eternity (Zinnemann, 53)	Burnett Guffey	B/W
*Funny Face (Donen, 57)	Ray June	Col.
*Funny Girl (Wyler, 68)	Harry Stradling	Col.
*Funny Lady (Ross, 75)	James Wong Howe	Col.
*The Furies (Mann, 50)	Victor Milner	B/W
The Fury (De Palma, 78)	Richard H. Kline	Col.
*Gaslight (Cukor, 44)	Joseph Ruttenberg	B/W
*The General Died At Dawn (Milestone, 36)	Victor Milner	B/W
†Gigi (Minnelli, 58)	Joseph Ruttenberg	Col.
Gilda (Vidor, 46)	Rudolph Mate	B/W
The Go-Between (Losey)	Gerry Fisher	Col.
The Godfather (Coppola, 72)	Gordon Willis	Col.
The Godfather Part II (Coppola, 74)	Gordon Willis	Col.
†Gone With The Wind (Fleming, 39)	Ernest Haller and Ray Rennahan	Col.
†The Good Earth (Franklin, 37)	Karl Freund	B/W
*The Graduate (Nichols, 67)	Robert Surtees	Col.
The Grapes of Wrath (Ford, 40)	Gregg Toland	B/W
The Greatest Show on Earth (DeMille, 52)	George Barnes	Col.
*The Greatest Story Ever Told (Stevens, 65)	William C. Mellor and Loyal Griggs	Col.
†Great Expectations (Lean, 47)	Guy Green	B/W
The Great Gatsby (Clayton, 74)	Douglas Slocombe	Col.

The Great Waldo Pepper (Hill, 75)	Robert Surtees	Col.
†The Great Waltz (Duvivier, 38)	Joseph Ruttenberg	B/W
The Greengage Summer (Gilbert, 61)	Freddie Young	Col.
The Gunfighter (King, 50)	Arthur Miller	B/W
Hamlet (Olivier, 48)	Desmond Dickinson	B/W
*The Harder They Fall (Robson, 56)	Burnett Guffey	B/W
*Heaven Can Wait (Beatty/Henry, 78)	William A. Fraker	Col.
*The Heiress (Wyler, 49)	Leo Tover	B/W
Henry V (Olivier, 45)	Robert Krasker	Col.
High Noon (Zinnemann, 52)	Floyd Crosby	B/W
*The Hindenburg (Wise, 75)	Robert Surtees	Col.
Hobson's Choice (Lean, 54)	Jack Hildyard	B/W
Hombre (Ritt, 66)	James Wong Howe	Col.
†How Green Was My Valley (Ford, 41)	Arthur Miller	B/W
*How The West Was Won (Ford, Hathaway and Marshall, 63)	William Daniels, Milton Krasner, Charles B. Lang and Joseph LaShelle	Col.
†Hud (Ritt, 63)	James Wong Howe	B/W
Humoresque (Negulesco, 47)	Ernest Haller	B/W
The Hunchback of Notre Dame (Dieterle, 39)	Joseph August	B/W
†The Hustler (Rossen, 61)	Gene Shuftan	B/W
*In Cold Blood (Brooks, 67)	Conrad Hall	Col.
The Informer (Ford, 35)	Joseph August	B/W
*Inherit The Wind (Kramer, 60)	Ernest Laszlo	B/W
In the Heat of the Night (Jewison, 67)	Haskell Wexler	Col.
Intruder in the Dust (Brown, 49)	Robert Surtees	B/W
*I Remember Mama (Stevens, 48)	Nicholas Musuraca	B/W
*Islands in the Stream (Schaffner, 77)	Fred J. Koenekamp	Col.
It Always Rains on Sundays (Hamer, 47)	Douglas Slocombe	B/W
*I Want to Live (Wise, 58)	Lionel Lindon	B/W
Jaws (Spielberg, 75)	Bill Butler	Col.
Jesse James (King, 39)	George Barnes and W. Howard Greene	Col.
*Jezebel (Wyler, 38)	Ernest Haller	B/W
†Joan of Arc (Fleming, 48)	Joseph Valentine, William V. Skall and Winton C. Hoch	Col.
*Johnny Belinda (Negulesco, 48)	Ted McCord	B/W
*Judgment at Nuremberg (Kramer, 61)	Ernest Laszlo	B/W
*Julia (Zinnemann, 77)	Douglas Slocombe	Col.
*Julius Caesar (Mankiewicz, 53)	Joseph Ruttenberg	B/W

†King Solomon's Mines (Marton/Bennett, 50)	Robert Surtees	Col.
*King's Row (Wood, 42)	James Wong Howe	B/W
Klute (Pakula, 71)	Gordon Willis	Col.
*Lady in the Dark (Leisen, 44)	Ray Rennahan	Col.
*The Last Picture Show (Bogdanovich, 71)	Robert Surtees	B/W
The Last Tycoon (Kazan, 76)	Victor J. Kemper	Col.
†Laura (Preminger, 44)	Joseph LaShelle	B/W
†Lawrence of Arabia (Lean, 62)	Freddie Young	Col.
†Leave Her To Heaven (Stahl, 45)	Leon Shamroy	Col.
Left-Handed Gun (Penn, 58)	J. Peverell Marley	B/W
*Lenny (Fosse, 74)	Bruce Surtees	B/W
The Life and Death of Colonel Blimp (Powell/Pressburger, 43)	Georges Perinal	Col.
*Lili (Walters, 53)	Robert Planck	Col.
Little Big Man (Penn, 70)	Harry Stradling Jr.	B/W
The Little Foxes (Wyler, 41)	Gregg Toland	B/W
The Lodger (Brahm, 44)	Lucien Ballard	B/W
*Logan's Run (Anderson, 76)	Ernest Laszlo	Col.
Loneliness of the Long Distance Runner (Richardson, 62)	Walter Lassally	B/W
†The Longest Day (Zanuck, 62)	Jean Bourgoin, Henri Persin, Walter Wottitiz	B/W
The Long Voyage Home (Ford, 40)	Gregg Toland	B/W
*Looking for Mr. Goodbar (Brooks, 77)	William A. Fraker	Col.
*The Lost Weekend (Wilder, 45)	John F. Seitz	B/W
*Love with a Proper Stranger (Mulligan, 63)	Milton Krasner	B/W
*The Magnificent Ambersons (Welles, 42)	Stanley Cortez	B/W
The Magnificent Seven (Sturges, 60)	Charles B. Lang	Col.
Major Dundee (Peckinpah, 64)	Sam Leavitt	Col.
The Manchurian Candidate (Frankenheimer, 62)	Lionel Lindon	B/W
†A Man For All Seasons (Zinnemann, 66)	Ted Moore	Col.
The Man Who Fell To Earth (Roeg, 76)	Anthony Richmond	B/W
The Man Who Shot Liberty Valance (Ford, 62)	William H. Clothier	B/W
The Man Who Would Be King (Huston, 76)	Oswald Morris	Col.
Marathon Man (Schlesinger, 76)	Conrad Hall	Col.
The Mark of Zorro (Mamoulian, 40)	Arthur Miller	B/W

*Marty (Mann, 55)	Joseph LaShelle	B/W
Masque of the Red Death (Corman, 64)	Nicolas Roeg	Col.
A Matter of Life and Death (Powell/Pressburger, 46)	Jack Cardiff	Col.
*Meet Me in St. Louis (Minnelli, 44)	George J. Folsey	Col.
†A Midsummer Night's Dream (Dieterle/Reinhardt, 35)	Hal Mohr	B/W
*Mildred Pierce (Curtiz, 45)	Ernest Haller	B/W
Moby Dick (Huston, 56)	Oswald Morris	Col.
*Morocco (von Sternberg, 31)	Lee Garmes	B/W
Moulin Rouge (Huston, 52)	Oswald Morris	Col.
†Mrs. Miniver (Wyler, 42)	Joseph Ruttenberg	B/W
*Murder on the Orient Express (Lumet, 74)	Geoffrey Unsworth	Col.
My Darling Clementine (Ford, 46)	Joe MacDonald	B/W
†My Fair Lady (Cukor, 64)	Harry Stradling	Col.
†The Naked City (Dassin, 48)	William Daniels	B/W
*National Velvet (Brown, 45)	Leonard Smith	Col.
*Network, (Lumet, 76)	Owen Roizman	Col.
New York, New York (Scorsese, 77)	Laszlo Kovacs	Col.
*Nicholas And Alexandra (Schaffner, 71)	Freddie Young	Col.
Night of the Hunter (Laughton, 55)	Stanley Cortez	B/W
*Night of the Iguana (Huston, 64)	Gabriel Figueroa	B/W
North by Northwest (Hitchcock, 59)	Robert Burks	Col.
*North West Mounted Police (DeMille, 40)	Victor Milner and W. Howard Greene	Col.
*Northwest Passage (Vidor, 40)	Sidney Wagner and William V. Skall	Col.
Notorious (Hitchcock, 46)	Ted Tetzlaff	B/W
*The Nun's Story (Zinnemann, 59)	Franz Planer	Col.
Obsession (De Palma, 76)	Vilmos Zsigmond	Col.
Odd Man Out (Reed, 47)	Robert Krasker	B/W
*Oklahoma (Zinnemann, 55)	Robert Surtees	Col.
*The Old Man and the Sea (Sturges, 58)	James Wong Howe	Col.
*Oliver! (Reed, 68)	Oswald Morris	Col.
Oliver Twist (Lean, 48)	Guy Green	B/W
*One-Eyed Jacks (Brando, 61)	Charles B. Lang	Col.
*One Flew Over the Cuckoo's Nest (Forman, 75)	Haskell Wexler	Col.
*One, Two, Three (Wilder, 61)	Daniel Fapp	B/W
On The Town (Kelly/Donen, 49)	Harold Rosson	Col.
†On the Waterfront (Kazan, 54)	Boris Kaufman	B/W
An Outcast of the Islands (Reed, 52)	John Wilcox	B/W

Out of the Past (Tourneur, 47)	Nicholas Musuraca	B/W
The Overlanders (Watt, 46)	Osmond Borrodaile	B/W
The Ox-Bow Incident (Wellman, 43)	Arthur Miller	B/W
Pandora and the Flying Dutchman (Lewin, 50)	Jack Cardiff	Col.
Panic in the Streets (Kazan, 50)	Joe MacDonald	B/W
Paper Moon (Bogdanovich, 73)	Laszlo Kovacs	B/W
Papillon (Schaffner, 73)	Fred Koenekamp	Col.
*Patton (Schaffner, 70)	Fred Koenekamp	B/W
†The Phantom of the Opera (Lubin, 43)	Hal Mohr and W. Howard Greene	Col.
†The Picture of Dorian Gray (Lewin, 45)	Harry Stradling	B/W
The Pirate (Minnelli, 47)	Harry Stradling	Col.
†A Place in the Sun (Stevens, 51)	William C. Mellor	B/W
Planet of the Apes (Schaffner, 68)	Leon Shamroy	Col.
*Portrait of Jennie (Dieterle, 48)	Joseph August	B/W
*Prince of Foxes (King, 49)	Leon Shamroy	B/W
*Private Lives of Elizabeth and Essex (Curtiz, 39)	Sol Polito and W. Howard Greene	Col.
*The Professionals (Brooks, 66)	Conrad Hall	Col.
*Psycho (Hitchcock, 60)	John L. Russell	B/W
Queen Christina (Mamoulian, 33)	William Daniels	B/W
The Queen of Spades (Dickinson, 48)	Otto Heller	B/W
†The Quiet Man (Ford, 52)	Winton C. Hoch	Col.
Rancho Notorious (Lang, 52)	Hal Mohr	Col.
*Reap the Wild Wind (DeMille, 42)	Victor Milner and William V. Skall	Col.
*Rear Window (Hitchcock, 54)	Robert Burks	Col.
†Rebecca (Hitchcock, 40)	George Barnes	B/W
The Red Badge of Courage (Huston, 51)	Harold Rosson	B/W
Red River (Hawks, 48)	Russell Harlan	B/W
Richard III (Olivier, 55)	Otto Heller	Col.
Riot in Cell Block II (Siegel, 54)	Russell Harlan	B/W
Robinson Crusoe On Mars (Haskin, 64)	Winton C. Hoch	Col.
*Roman Holiday (Wyler, 53)	Franz Planer and Henri Alekan	B/W
†Romeo and Juliet (Zeffirelli, 68)	Pasqualino de Santis	Col.
†The Rose Tattoo (Mann, 55)	James Wong Howe	B/W
†Ryan's Daughter (Lean, 70)	Freddie Young	Col.

The Sailor Who Fell From Grace With The Sea (Carlino, 76)	Douglas Slocombe	Col.
*Same Time, Next Year (Mulligan, 78)	Robert Surtees	Col.
*Samson and Delilah (DeMille, 50)	George Barnes	Col.
Saturday Night and Sunday Morning (Reisz, 60)	Freddie Francis	B/W
The Scarlet Empress (von Sternberg, 34)	Bert Glennon	B/W
Scarlet Street (Lang, 45)	Milton Krasner	B/W
Scott of the Antarctic (Frend, 48)	Jack Cardiff, Osmond Borrodaile and Geoffrey Unsworth	Col.
The Sea Hawk (Curtiz, 40)	Sol Polito	B/W
The Searchers (Ford, 56)	Winton C. Hoch	Col.
*Seconds (Frankenheimer, 66)	James Wong Howe	B/W
The Set Up (Wise, 49)	Milton Krasner	B/W
*Seven Brides for Seven Brothers (Donen, 54)	George J. Folsey	Col.
Shampoo (Ashby, 75)	Laszlo Kovacs	Col.
†Shane (Stevens, 53)	Loyal Griggs	Col.
†Shanghai Express (von Sternberg, 32)	Lee Garmes	B/W
†She Wore a Yellow Ribbon (Ford, 49)	Winton C. Hoch	Col.
†Ship of Fools (Kramer, 65)	Ernest Laszlo	B/W
The Shout (Skolimowski, 78)	Mike Molloy	Col.
*Sign of the Cross (DeMille, 33)	Karl Struss	B/W
Singin' in the Rain (Kelly/Donen, 52)	Harold Rosson	Col.
The Snake Pit (Litvak, 48)	Leo Tover	B/W
*Snows of Kilimanjaro (King, 52)	Leon Shamroy	Col.
†Somebody Up There Likes Me (Wise, 56)	Joseph Ruttenberg	B/W
*Some Like it Hot (Wilder, 59)	Charles B. Lang	B/W
†The Song of Bernadette (King, 43)	Arthur Miller	B/W
†Sons and Lovers (Cardiff, 60)	Freddie Francis	B/W
The Sound Barrier (Lean, 52)	Jack Hildyard	B/W
*The Sound of Music (Wise, 65)	Ted McCord	Col.
†Spartacus (Kubrick, 60)	Russell Metty	Col.
*Spellbound (Hitchcock, 45)	George Barnes	B/W
The Spiral Staircase (Siodmak, 46)	Nicholas Musuraca	B/W
Splendour in the Grass (Kazan, 61)	Boris Kaufman	Col.
The Spy Who Loved Me (Gilbert, 77)	Claude Renoir	Col.
*Stagecoach (Ford, 39)	Bert Glennon	B/W
Stalag 17 (Wilder, 53)	Ernest Laszlo	B/W
A Star Is Born (Wellman, 37)	W. Howard Greene	Col.
A Star Is Born (Cukor, 54)	Sam Leavitt	Col.
*A Star Is Born (Pierson, 76)	Robert Surtees	Col.
Star Wars (Lucas, 77)	Gilbert Taylor	Col.
*The Sting (Hill, 73)	Robert Surtees	Col.
The Stranger (Welles, 46)	Russell Metty	B/W
*Strangers on a Train (Hitchcock, 51)	Robert Burks	B/W

*Street Angel (Borzage, 29)	Ernest Palmer	B/W
*A Streetcar Named Desire (Kazan, 51)	Harry Stradling	B/W
*Summer of '42 (Mulligan, 71)	Robert Surtees	Col.
Summertime (Lean, 55)	Jack Hildyard	Col.
†Sunrise (Murnau, 28)	Charles Rosher and Karl Struss	B/W
*Sunset Boulevard (Wilder, 50)	John Seitz	B/W
Sweet Smell of Success (Mackendrick, 57)	James Wong Howe	B/W
†Tabu (Flaherty/Murnau, 31)	Floyd Crosby	B/W
A Taste of Honey (Richardson, 61)	Walter Lassally	B/W
*The Ten Commandments (DeMille, 56)	Loyal Griggs	Col.
They Won't Forget (Le Roy, 37)	Arthur Edeson	B/W
†The Thief of Bagdad (Powell, 40)	Georges Perinal	Col.
The Thing From Another World (Nyby, 51)	Russell Harlan	B/W
†The Third Man (Reed, 49)	Robert Krasker	B/W
This Gun For Hire (Tuttle, 42)	John F. Seitz	B/W
This Happy Breed (Lean, 44)	Ronald Neame	Col.
This Sporting Life (Anderson, 63)	Denys Coop	B/W
†Three Coins in the Fountain (Negulesco, 54)	Milton Krasner	Col.
Three Days of the Condor (Pollack, 75)	Owen Roizman	Col.
†To Catch a Thief (Hitchcock, 55)	Robert Burks	Col.
*To Kill a Mockingbird (Mulligan, 62)	Russell Harlan	B/W
Tom Jones (Richardson, 63)	Walter Lassally	Col.
Touch of Evil (Welles, 58)	Russell Metty	B/W
†The Towering Inferno (Guillermin, 74)	Fred J. Koenekamp and Joseph Biroc	Col.
Trail of the Lonesome Pine (Hathaway, 36)	Robert C. Bruce and W. Howard Greene	Col.
*Travels With My Aunt (Cukor, 72)	Douglas Slocombe	Col.
The Trouble With Harry (Hitchcock, 56)	Robert Burks	Col.
True Grit (Hathaway, 69)	Lucien Ballard	Col.
*The Turning Point (Ross, 77)	Robert Surtees	Col.
Twelve O'Clock High (King, 49)	Leon Shamroy	B/W
20,000 Leagues Under The Sea (Fleischer, 54)	Franz Planer	Col.
Two Flags West (Wise, 50)	Leon Shamroy	B/W
*Two for the Seesaw (Wise, 62)	Ted McCord	B/W
2001: A Space Odyssey (Kubrick, 68)	Geoffrey Unsworth	Col.

Unconquered (DeMille, 47)	Ray Rennahan	Col.
Valentino (Russell, 77)	Peter Suschitzky	Col.
Vertigo (Hitchcock, 58)	Robert Burks	Col.
Viva Zapata (Kazan, 52)	Joe MacDonald	B/W
Wagonmaster (Ford, 50)	Bert Glennon and Archie Stout	B/W
The War Lord (Schaffner, 66)	Russell Metty	Col.
The War of the Worlds (Haskin, 53)	George Barnes	Col.
*The Way We Were (Pollack, 73)	Harry Stradling Jr.	Col.
†West Side Story (Wise/Robbins, 61)	Daniel L. Fapp	Col.
The Westerner (Wyler, 40)	Gregg Toland	B/W
*Whatever Happened to Baby Jane? (Aldrich, 62)	Ernest Haller	B/W
*When Worlds Collide (Mate, 51)	John Seitz and W. Howard Greene	Col.
†Who's Afraid of Virginia Woolf (Nichols, 66)	Haskell Wexler	B/W
The Wild Bunch (Peckinpah, 69)	Lucien Ballard	Col.
Will Penny (Gries, 67)	Lucien Ballard	Col.
†Wilson (King, 44)	Leon Shamroy	Col.
Winchester 73 (Anthony Mann, 50)	William Daniels	B/W
The Wind And The Lion (Milius, 75)	Bill Butler	Col.
Wings (Wellman, 27)	Harry Perry	B/W
*The Wiz (Lumet, 78)	Oswald Morris	Col.
The Woman In The Window (Lang, 44)	Milton Krasner	B/W
†Wuthering Heights (Wyler, 39)	Gregg Toland	B/W
†The Yearling (Brown, 46)	Charles Rosher, Leonard Smith and Arthur E. Arling	Col.
*The Young Lions (Dmytryk, 58)	Joe MacDonald	B/W
Young Mr. Lincoln (Ford, 39)	Bert Glennon	B/W
†Zorba the Greek (Cacoyannis, 64)	Walter Lassally	B/W

APPENDIX II

FAMOUS MUSIC SCORES: A CHECK LIST

The Director and release dates of films included in this list are shown in parentheses. The composers are listed in the right-hand column. Scores that have received Academy Award nominations are marked with a *, Oscar winners with a †.

Ace in the Hole (Wilder, 51)	Hugo Friedhofer
†Adventures of Robin Hood (Curtiz/Keighley, 38)	Erich Wolfgang Korngold
*The Agony and the Ecstasy (Reed, 65)	Alex North
*Airport (Seaton, 70)	Alfred Newman
*The Alamo (Wayne, 60)	Dimitri Tiomkin
*All About Eve (Mankiewicz, 50)	Alfred Newman
†All That Money Can Buy (Dieterle, 41)	Bernard Herrmann
All The President's Men (Pakula, 76)	David Grusin
*Anna and the King of Siam (Cromwell, 46)	Bernard Herrmann
*Anne of The Thousand Days (Jarrott, 69)	Georges Delerue
†Around the World in 80 Days (Anderson, 56)	Victor Young
*Becket (Glenville, 64)	Laurence Rosenthal
†Ben-Hur (Wyler, 59)	Miklos Rozsa
†The Best Years of Our Lives (Wyler, 46)	Hugo Friedhofer
*The Big Country (Wyler, 58)	Jerome Moross
*Bite The Bullet (Brooks, 75)	Alex North
*The Black Swan (King, 42)	Alfred Newman
Bobby Deerfield (Pollack, 77)	David Grusin
Bonnie and Clyde (Penn, 67)	Charles Strouse
†Born Free (Hill, 66)	John Barry
*The Boys From Brazil (Schaffner, 78)	Jerry Goldsmith
†Breakfast at Tiffany's (Edwards, 61)	Henry Mancini

†Bridge on the River Kwai (Lean, 57) Malcolm Arnold
A Bridge Too Far
  (Attenborough, 77) John Addison
†Butch Cassidy and the Sundance
  Kid (Hill, 69) Burt Bacharach

Captain Blood (Curtiz, 35) Erich Wolfgang Korngold
*Captain from Castile (King, 47) Alfred Newman
*Casablanca (Curtiz, 43) Max Steiner
*Champion (Robson, 49) Dimitri Tiomkin
*Charge of the Light Brigade
  (Curtiz, 36) Max Steiner
*Chinatown (Polanski, 74) Jerry Goldsmith
*Cinderella Liberty (Rydell, 73) John Williams
*Citizen Kane (Welles, 41) Bernard Herrmann
*Cleopatra (Mankiewicz, 63) Alex North
*Close Encounters Of The Third
  Kind (Spielberg, 77) John Williams
The Conversation (Coppola, 74) David Shire
*Cool Hand Luke (Rosenberg, 67) Lalo Schifrin
*Cromwell (Hughes, 70) Frank Cordell

*Dark Victory (Goulding, 39) Max Steiner
*Day of the Dolphin (Nichols, 73) Georges Delerue
Day of the Jackal (Zinnemann, 73) Georges Delerue
*Days of Heaven (Malick, 78) Ennio Morricone
*Death of a Salesman (Benedek, 51) Alex North
*The Diary of Anne Frank
  (Stevens, 59) Alfred Newman
Dirty Harry (Siegel, 71) Lalo Schifrin
*Dr. Jekyll and Mr. Hyde
  (Fleming, 41) Franz Waxman
†Doctor Zhivago (Lean, 65) Maurice Jarre
*Double Indemnity (Wilder, 44) Miklos Rozsa
†A Double Life (Cukor, 47) Miklos Rozsa
Duel in the Sun (Vidor, 46) Dimitri Tiomkin

*El Cid (Mann, 61) Miklos Rozsa
*Elmer Gantry (Brooks, 60) Andre Previn
*The Enchanted Cottage
  (Cromwell, 45) Roy Webb
†Exodus (Preminger, 60) Ernest Gold

Fahrenheit 451 (Truffaut, 66) Bernard Herrmann
*Fall of the Roman Empire
  (Mann, 64) Dimitri Tiomkin
Family Plot (Hitchcock, 76) John Williams
*Far from the Madding Crowd
  (Schlesinger, 67) Richard Rodney Bennett

*55 Days at Peking (Ray, 63)	Dimitri Tiomkin
*For Whom the Bell Tolls (Wood, 43)	Victor Young
*The Fox (Rydell, 68)	Lalo Schifrin
Frenchman's Creek (Leisen, 45)	Victor Young
Friendly Persuasion (Wyler, 56)	Dimitri Tiomkin
*From Here to Eternity (Zinnemann, 53)	George Duning
The Fury (De Palma, 78)	John Williams
*Genevieve (Cornelius, 53)	Larry Adler
*Giant (Stevens, 56)	Dimitri Tiomkin
The Godfather (Coppola, 72)	Nino Rota
†The Godfather Part II (Coppola, 74)	Nino Rota and Carmine Coppola
*Gone with the Wind (Fleming, 39)	Max Steiner
The Graduate (Nichols, 67)	Paul Simon
Great Expectations (Lean, 47)	Walter Goehr
The Great Northfield Minnesota Raid (Kaufman, 72)	David Grusin
The Great Waldo Pepper (Hill, 75)	Henry Mancini
*The Greatest Story Ever Told (Stevens, 65)	Alfred Newman
Gunfight at the O.K. Corral (Sturges, 57)	Dimitri Tiomkin
*Hamlet (Olivier, 48)	William Walton
*Hawaii (Hill, 66)	Elmer Bernstein
*Heaven Can Wait (Beatty/Henry, 78)	Dave Grusin
†The Heiress (Wyler, 49)	Aaron Copland
*Henry V (Olivier, 46)	William Walton
†The High and the Mighty (Wellman, 54)	Dimitri Tiomkin
†High Noon (Zinnemann, 52)	Dimitri Tiomkin
*Hold Back the Dawn (Leisen, 41)	Victor Young
*How Green was my Valley (Ford, 41)	Alfred Newman
*How the West Was Won (Ford, Hathaway, Marshall, 63)	Alfred Newman
*Humoresque (Negulesco, 46)	Franz Waxman
*The Hunchback of Notre Dame (Dieterle, 39)	Alfred Newman
*The Hurricane (Ford, 37)	Alfred Newman
The Hustler (Rossen, 61)	Kenyon Hopkins
*Images (Altman, 72)	John Williams
*I Married a Witch (Clair, 42)	Roy Webb
Islands In The Stream (Schaffner, 77)	Jerry Goldsmith
I Want to Live (Wise, 58)	John Mandel
*In Cold Blood (Brooks, 67)	Quincy Jones

*The Informer (Ford, 35)	Max Steiner
†Jaws (Spielberg, 75)	John Williams
*Jezebel (Wyler, 38)	Max Steiner
*Joan of Arc (Fleming, 48)	Hugo Friedhofer
*Johnny Belinda (Negulesco, 48)	Max Steiner
*Julia (Zinnemann, 77)	Georges Delerue
*Julius Caesar (Mankiewicz, 53)	Miklos Rozsa
Junior Bonner (Peckinpah, 72)	Jerry Fielding
The Killers (Siodmak, 46)	Miklos Rozsa
King Kong (Cooper/Schoedsack, 33)	Max Steiner
King Kong (Guillermin, 76)	John Barry
Klute (Pakula, 71)	Michael Small
†Lawrence of Arabia (Lean, 62)	Maurice Jarre
*The Letter (Wyler, 40)	Max Steiner
*The Life of Emile Zola (Dieterle, 37)	Max Steiner
*Life with Father (Curtiz, 47)	Max Steiner
†Lili (Walters, 53)	Bronislau Kaper
†Limelight (Chaplin, 52 — Oscar Awarded 72)	Charles Chaplin
†The Lion in Winter (Harvey, 68)	John Barry
*The Long Voyage Home (Ford, 40)	Richard Hageman
*Lost Horizon, Capra, 37)	Dimitri Tiomkin
*The Lost Patrol (Ford, 34)	Max Steiner
*The Lost Weekend (Wilder, 45)	Miklos Rozsa
†Love is a Many Splendoured Thing (King, 55)	Alfred Newman
*Love Letters (Dieterle, 45)	Victor Young
†Love Story (Hiller, 70)	Francis Lai
*Madame Curie (LeRoy, 43)	Herbert Stothart
The Magnificent Ambersons (Welles, 42)	Bernard Herrmann
*The Magnificent Seven (Sturges, 60)	Elmer Bernstein
A Man for All Seasons (Zinnemann, 66)	Georges Delerue
*The Man with the Golden Arm (Preminger, 55)	Elmer Bernstein
*The Mark of Zorro (Mamoulian, 40)	Alfred Newman
†Mary Poppins (Stevenson, 64)	Richard M. and Robert B. Sherman
*Mary Queen of Scots (Jarrott, 71)	John Barry

Midnight Cowboy (Sclesinger, 69)   John Barry
†Midnight Express (Parker, 78)   Giorgio Moroder
The Missouri Breaks (Penn, 76)   John Williams
*Mr. Smith Goes to Washington
    (Capra, 39)   Dimitri Tiomkin
Moulin Rouge (Huston, 52)   Georges Auric
*Murder on the Orient Express
    (Lumet, 74)   Richard Rodney Bennett
*Mutiny on the Bounty (Lloyd, 35)   Herbert Stothart
*Mutiny on the Bounty
    (Milestone, 62)   Bronislau Kaper

*Nicholas And Alexandra
    (Schaffner, 71)   Richard Rodney Bennett
North by Northwest (Hitchcock, 59)   Bernard Herrmann
*North West Mounted Police
    (DeMille, 40)   Victor Young
†Now Voyager (Rapper, 42)   Max Steiner
*The Nun's Story (Zinnemann, 59)   Franz Waxman

O Lucky Man (Anderson, 73)   Alan Price
*Obsession (De Palma, 76)   Bernard Herrmann
*Of Mice and Men (Milestone, 39)   Aaron Copland
†The Old Man and the Sea
    (Sturges, 58)   Dimitri Tiomkin
Oliver Twist (Lean, 48)   Arnold Bax
†The Omen (Donner, 76)   Jerry Goldsmith
*On The Waterfront (Kazan, 54)   Leonard Bernstein
*One Flew Over the Cuckoo's Nest
    (Forman, 75)   Jack Nitzsche
*Our Town (Wood, 40)   Aaron Copland
An Outcast of the Islands
    (Reed, 52)   Brian Easdale
*The Outlaw Josey Wales
    (Eastwood, 76)   Jerry Fielding

*Papillon (Schaffner, 73)   Jerry Goldsmith
*Patton (Schaffner, 70)   Jerry Goldsmith
*Picnic (Logan, 55)   George Duning
*The Pink Panther (Edwards, 64)   Henry Mancini
†A Place in the Sun (Stevens, 51)   Franz Waxman
*Planet of the Apes (Schaffner, 68)   Jerry Goldsmith
*The Poseidon Adventure
    (Neame, 72)   John Williams
*The Prisoner of Zenda
    (Cromwell, 37)   Alfred Newman
*Private Lives of Elizabeth and
    Essex (Curtiz, 39)   Erich Wolfgang Korngold
Psycho (Hitchcock, 60)   Bernard Herrmann

*Quo Vadis (LeRoy, 51)	Miklos Rozsa
*Raintree County (Dmytryk, 57)	Johnny Green
*Random Harvest (LeRoy, 42)	Herbert Stothart
*Rebecca (Hitchcock, 40)	Franz Waxman
Rebel Without a Cause (Ray, 55)	Leonard Rosenman
Red River (Hawks, 48)	Dimitri Tiomkin
†The Red Shoes	
(Powell/Pressburger, 48)	Brian Easdale
*The Reivers (Rydell, 69)	John Williams
Richard III (Olivier, 55)	William Walton
Rio Bravo (Hawks, 59)	Dimitri Tiomkin
Robin And Marian (Lester, 76)	John Barry
Room at the Top (Clayton, 59)	Mario Nascimbene
*The Rose Tattoo (Mann, 55)	Alex North
*Samson and Delilah (DeMille, 50)	Victor Young
Scott of the Antarctic (Frend, 48)	Vaughan Williams
*The Sea Hawk (Curtiz, 40)	Erich Wolfgang Korngold
The Searchers (Ford, 56)	Max Steiner
*Separate Tables (Mann, 58)	David Raksin
*Sergeant York (Hawks, 41)	Max Steiner
Shadow of a Doubt (Hitchcock, 43)	Dimitri Tiomkin
*Shaft (Parks, 71)	Isaac Hayes
Shane (Stevens, 53)	Victor Young
She Wore a Yellow Ribbon	
(Ford, 49)	Richard Hageman
†Since You Went Away	
(Cromwell, 44)	Max Steiner
*Sleuth (Mankiewicz, 72)	John Addison
*The Snake Pit (Litvak, 48)	Alfred Newman
Some Like it Hot (Wilder, 59)	Adolph Deutsch
†Song of Bernadette (King, 43)	Alfred Newman
The Sound Barrier (Lean, 52)	Malcolm Arnold
*Spartacus (Kubrick, 60)	Alex North
†Spellbound (Hitchcock, 45)	Miklos Rozsa
*The Spy Who Loved Me	
(Gilbert, 77)	Marvin Hamlisch
†Stagecoach (Ford, 39)	Richard Hageman, W. Franke Harling, John Leipold, Leo Shuken and Louis Gruenberg
†Star Wars (Lucas, 77)	John Williams
*Straw Dogs (Peckinpah, 71)	Jerry Fielding
*A Streetcar Named Desire	
(Kazan, 51)	Alex North
†Summer of '42 (Mulligan, 71)	Michel Legrand
†Sunset Boulevard (Wilder, 50)	Franz Waxman
*Superman (Donner, 78)	John Williams
*Suspicion (Hitchcock, 41)	Franz Waxman

A Taste of Honey (Richardson, 61)   John Addison
*Taxi Driver (Scorsese, 76)   Bernard Herrmann
The Third Man (Reed, 49)   Anton Karas
*The Thomas Crown Affair
   (Jewison, 68)   Michel Legrand
†Thoroughly Modern Millie
   (Hill, 67)   Elmer Bernstein
The Three Musketeers (Lester, 74)   Michel Legrand
*To Kill a Mockingbird
   (Mulligan, 62)   Elmer Bernstein
†Tom Jones (Richardson, 63)   John Addison
*A Touch of Class (Frank, 73)   John Cameron
*The Towering Inferno
   (Guillermin, 74)   John Williams

Vera Cruz (Aldrich, 54)   Hugo Friedhofer
Vertigo (Hitchcock, 58)   Bernard Herrmann
*Viva Zapata (Kazan, 52)   Alex North
*Voyage of the Damned
   (Rosenberg, 76)   Lalo Schifrin

*Waterloo Bridge (LeRoy, 40)   Herbert Stothart
The Way to the Stars (Asquith, 45)   Nicholas Brodzky
†The Way We Were (Pollack, 73)   Marvin Hamlisch
*Who's Afraid of Virginia Woolf?
   (Nichols, 66)   Alex North
*The Wild Bunch (Peckinpah, 69)   Jerry Fielding
*The Wind and the Lion
   (Milius, 75)   Jerry Goldsmith
*Wuthering Heights (Wyler, 39)   Alfred Newman

*The Young Lions (Dmytryk, 58)   Hugo Friedhofer

APPENDIX III

A selection of famous films derived from scenarios written directly for the screen. The names of the scriptwriters are listed in the second column. None of the films listed in this Appendix is adapted from novels or stage plays.

Ace in the Hole (1951)	Billy Wilder, Lesser Samuels and Walter Newman
Adam's Rib (1949)	Ruth Gordon and Garson Kanin
Alice Doesn't Live Here Anymore (1974)	Robert Getchell
America, America (1963)	Elia Kazan
American Graffiti (1973)	George Lucas, Gloria Katz and Willard Huyck
An American in Paris (1951)	Alan Jay Lerner
Annie Hall (1977)	Woody Allen and Marshall Brickman
An Unmarried Woman (1978)	Paul Mazursky
The Apartment (1960)	Billy Wilder and I. A. L. Diamond
The Bad News Bears (1976)	Bill Lancaster
The Band Wagon (1953)	Betty Comden and Adolph Green
The Barefoot Contessa (1954)	Joseph L. Mankiewicz
Battleground (1949)	Robert Pirosh
Blazing Saddles (1974)	Mel Brooks, Norman Steinberg, Andrew Bergman, Richard Pryor and Alan Unger
The Blue Dahlia (1946)	Raymond Chandler
The Blue Lamp (1949)	T. E. B. Clarke
Bob and Carol and Ted and Alice (1969)	Paul Mazursky and Larry Tucker
Body and Soul (1947)	Abraham Polonsky
Bonnie and Clyde (1967)	David Newman and Robert Benton
Butch Cassidy and the Sundance Kid (1969)	William Goldman
The Candidate (1972)	Jeremy Larner
Chinatown (1974)	Robert Towne
Citizen Kane (1941)	Herman J. Mankiewicz and Orson Welles
Coming Home (1978)	Waldo Salt and Robert C. Jones
The Conversation (1974)	Francis Ford Coppola
Darling (1965)	Frederic Raphael
The Deer Hunter (1978)	Michael Cimino, Deric Washburn, Louis Garfinkle and Quinn K. Redeker

The Defiant Ones (1958)	Nathan E. Douglas and Harold Jacob Smith
Dillinger (1974)	John Milius
Dog Day Afternoon (1975)	Frank Pierson
A Double Life (1947)	Ruth Gordon and Garson Kanin
Easy Rider (1969)	Peter Fonda, Dennis Hopper and Terry Southern
Faces (1968)	John Cassavetes
Five Easy Pieces (1970)	Adrien Joyce
Foreign Correspondent (1940)	Charles Bennett and Joan Harrison
The Front (1976)	Walter Bernstein
Funny Face (1957)	Leonard Gershe
Genevieve (1953)	William Rose
The Goddess (1958)	Paddy Chayefsky
The Goodbye Girl (1977)	Neil Simon
The Great Dictator (1940)	Charles Chaplin
The Great McGinty (1939)	Preston Sturges
The Great Waldo Pepper (1975)	William Goldman
Guess Who's Coming to Dinner? (1967)	William Rose
Gumshoe (1971)	Neville Smith
Hail the Conquering Hero (1944)	Preston Sturges
Harry And Tonto (1974)	Paul Mazursky and Josh Greenfeld
High Anxiety (1977)	Mel Brooks, Ron Clark, Rudy DeLuca and Barry Levinson
The Hospital (1971)	Paddy Chayefsky
Hue and Cry (1947)	T. E. B. Clarke
Interiors (1978)	Woody Allen
In Which We Serve (1942)	Noel Coward
It's a Mad, Mad, Mad, Mad World (1963)	William and Tania Rose
Kind Hearts and Coronets (1949)	Robert Hamer and John Dighton
Klute (1971)	Andy and Dave Lewis
The Ladykillers (1955)	William Rose
Lady Sings The Blues (1972)	Terence McCloy, Chris Clark, and Suzanne DePasse
The Late Show (1977)	Robert Benton
The Lavender Hill Mob (1951)	T. E. B. Clarke
Love Story (1970)	Erich Segal
The Man in the White Suit (1951)	Roger MacDougall, John Dighton and Alexander Mackendrick
The Marrying Kind (1952)	Ruth Gordon and Garson Kanin
A Matter of Life and Death (1946)	Michael Powell and Emeric Pressburger
The Men (1950)	Carl Foreman
The Miracle of Morgan's Creek (1944)	Preston Sturges
Monsieur Verdoux (1947)	Charles Chaplin
Murder By Death (1976)	Neil Simon
My Little Chickadee (1940)	Mae West and W. C. Fields

The Naked City (1948)	Albert Maltz and Malvin Wald
Network (1976)	Paddy Chayefsky
New York, New York (1977)	Earl Mac Rauch and Mardick Martin
North by Northwest (1959)	Ernest Lehman
Notorious (1946)	Ben Hecht
No Way Out (1950)	Joseph L. Mankiewicz and Lesser Samuels
The Overlanders (1946)	Harry Watt
The Palm Beach Story (1942)	Preston Sturges
Panic in the Streets (1950)	Edward and Edna Anhalt
Passport to Pimlico (1948)	T. E. B. Clarke
Pat and Mike (1952)	Ruth Gordon and Garson Kanin
The Red Shoes (1948)	Emeric Pressburger
Riot in Cell Block 11 (1954)	Richard Collins
Robin and Marian (1976)	James Goldman
Rocky (1976)	Sylvester Stallone
The St. Valentine's Day Massacre (1957)	Howard Browne
Save The Tiger (1973)	Steve Shagan
The Search (1948)	Richard Schweizer and David Wechsler
Shampoo (1975)	Robert Towne
Sleeper (1973)	Woody Allen and Marshall Brickman
The Sound Barrier (1952)	Terence Rattigan
Splendour in the Grass (1961)	William Inge
A Star is Born (1937)	Alan Campbell, Robert Carson Dorothy Parker
Star Wars (1977)	George Lucas
The Sting (1973)	David S. Ward
Sullivan's Travels (1942)	Preston Sturges
Summer of '42 (1971)	Herman Raucher
Sunday, Bloody Sunday (1971)	Penelope Gilliatt
Sunset Boulevard (1950)	Billy Wilder, Charles Brackett and D. M. Marshman Jun.
Taxi Driver (1976)	Paul Schrader
The Third Man (1949)	Graham Greene
A Touch of Class (1973)	Melvin Frank and Jack Rose
The Turning Point (1977)	Arthur Laurents
Two for the Road (1967)	Frederic Raphael
Viva Zapata (1952)	John Steinbeck
The Way to the Stars (1945)	Terence Rattigan
The Wild Bunch (1969)	Walon Green and Sam Peckinpah
The Wind and the Lion (1975)	John Milius
Woman of the Year (1942)	Michael Kanin and Ring Lardner Jun.
Young Frankenstein (1974)	Gene Wilder and Mel Brooks
Young Winston (1972)	Carl Foreman

APPENDIX IV

ART DIRECTORS: A CHECK LIST

All films are listed alphabetically. Directors' names and release dates are in parenthesis. Art Directors are listed in the right hand column. Films that have received Academy Award nominations for art direction are marked with a *, Oscar winners with a †.

Ace in the Hole (Wilder, 51)	Hal Pereira and Earl Hedrick	B/W
Adam's Rib (Cukor, 49)	Cedric Gibbons and William Ferrari	B/W
*The Adventures Of Don Juan (Sherman, 49)	Edward Carrere	Col.
†The Adventures Of Robin Hood (Curtiz, Keighley, 38)	Carl J. Weyl	Col.
*The Adventures Of Tom Sawyer (Taurog, 38)	Lyle Wheeler	Col.
*The Agony And The Ecstasy (Reed, 65)	John De Cuir and Jack Martin Smith	Col.
*Airport (Seaton, 70)	Alexander Golitzen and Preston Ames	Col.
*All About Eve (Mankiewicz, 50)	Lyle Wheeler and George W. Davis	B/W
†All The President's Men (Pakula, 76)	George Jenkins	Col.
†An American In Paris (Minnelli, 51)	Cedric Gibbons and Preston Ames	Col.
*The Andromeda Strain (Wise, 71)	Boris Leven and William Tuntke	Col.
†Anna And The King Of Siam (Cromwell, 46)	Lyle Wheeler and William Darling	B/W
Anna Karenina (Duvivier, 48)	Andre Andrejew	B/W
*Anne Of The Thousand Days (Jarrott, 69)	Maurice Carter and Lionel Couch	Col.
*Annie Get Your Gun (Sidney, 50)	Cedric Gibbons and Paul Groesse	Col.
†The Apartment (Wilder, 60)	Alexander Trauner	B/W
*Around The World In Eighty Days (Anderson, 56)	James W. Sullivan and Ken Adam	Col.
*Arrowsmith (Ford, 32)	Richard Day	B/W

*Auntie Mame (Da Costa, 58)	Malcolm Bert	Col.
†The Bad And The Beautiful (Minnelli, 52)	Cedric Gibbons and Edward Carfagno	B/W
The Band Wagon (Minnelli, 53)	Cedric Gibbons and Preston Ames	Col.
The Barkleys Of Broadway (Walters, 49)	Cedric Gibbons and Edward Carfagno	Col.
†Barry Lyndon (Kubrick, 75)	Ken Adam and Roy Walker	Col.
*Beau Geste (Wellman, 39)	Hans Dreier and Robert Odell	B/W
*Becket (Glenville, 64)	John Bryan and Maurice Carter	Col.
*Bell, Book And Candle (Quine, 58)	Cary Odell	Col.
†Ben-Hur (Wyler, 59)	William A. Horning and Edward Carfagno	Col.
The Best Years Of Our Lives (Wyler, 46)	George Jenkins and Perry Ferguson	B/W
†Black Narcissus (Powell, Pressburger, 47)	Alfred Junge	Col.
Black Sunday (Frankenheimer, 77)	Walter Tyler	Col.
Blithe Spirit (Lean, 45)	C. P. Norman	Col.
*Blood And Sand (Mamoulian, 41)	Richard Day and Joseph C. Wright	Col.
†Blood On The Sun (Lloyd, 45)	Wiard Ihnen	B/W
†Blossoms In The Dust (LeRoy, 41)	Cedric Gibbons and Urie McCleary	Col.
Bluebeard's Eighth Wife (Lubitsch, 38)	Hans Dreier and Robert Usher	B/W
*Breakfast At Tiffany's (Edwards, 61)	Hal Pereira and Roland Anderson	Col.
†Cabaret (Fosse, 72)	Rolf Zehetbauer and Jurgen Kiebach	Col.
Cabin In The Sky (Minnelli, 43)	Cedric Gibbons and Leonid Vasian	B/W
*Caesar And Cleopatra (Pascal, 46)	John Bryan	Col.
*California Suite (Ross, 78)	Albert Brenner	Col.
†Camelot (Logan, 67)	John Truscott and Edward Carrere	Col.
Camille (Cukor, 37)	Cedric Gibbons and Frederic Hope	B/W
Captain Horatio Hornblower (Walsh, 51)	Tom Morahan	Col.
*The Cardinal (Preminger, 63)	Lyle Wheeler	Col.
*Carrie (Wyler, 52)	Hal Pereira and Roland Anderson	B/W
†Cavalcade (Lloyd, 33)	William S. Darling	B/W

*Chinatown (Polanski, 74)	Richard Sylbert and	
	W. Stewart Campbell	Col.
†Cimarron (Ruggles, 31)	Max Ree	B/W
Citizen Kane (Welles, 41)	Van Nest Polglase and	
	Perry Ferguson	B/W
City Lights (Chaplin, 31)	Charles D. Hall	B/W
†Cleopatra (Mankiewicz, 63)	John DeCuir, Jack Martin Smith,	
	Hilyard Brown, Herman	
	Blumenthal, Elven Webb,	
	Maurice Pelling and	
	Boris Juraga	Col.
A Clockwork Orange (Kubrick, 71)	John Barry	Col.
*Close Encounters Of The Third		
Kind (Spielberg, 77)	Joe Alves, Dan Lomino	Col.
*The Country Girl	Hal Pereira and	
(Seaton, 54)	Roland Anderson	B/W
*Cover Girl (Vidor, 44)	Lionel Banks and	
	Cary Odell	Col.
†The Dark Angel (Franklin, 35)	Richard Day	B/W
Darling (Schlesinger, 65)	Ray Simm	B/W
‡David And Bathsheba (King, 51)	Lyle Wheeler and	
	George W. Davis	Col.
David Copperfield (Cukor, 35)	Cedric Gibbons	B/W
The Day Of The Locust		
(Schlesinger, 75)	Richard MacDonald	Col.
*Days Of Wine And Roses		
(Edwards, 62)	Joseph Wright	B/W
*Dead End (Wyler, 37)	Richard Day	B/W
Death On The Nile		
(Guillermin, 78)	Peter Murton	Col.
Desire (Borzage, 36)	Hans Dreier and	
	Robert Usher	B/W
*Destination Moon (Pichel, 50)	Ernst Fegte	Col.
†The Diary Of Anne Frank	Lyle Wheeler and	
(Stevens, 59)	George W. Davis	B/W
†Doctor Zhivago (Lean, 65)	John Box and	
	Terence Marsh	Col.
†Dodsworth (Wyler, 36)	Richard Day	B/W
Double Indemnity (Wilder, 44)	Hans Dreier and	
	Hal Pereira	B/W
*Down Argentine Way	Richard Day and	
(Cummings, 40)	Joseph C. Wright	Col.
Dr. Jekyll and Mr. Hyde		
(Mamoulian, 32)	Hans Dreier	B/W
Dr. Jekyll And Mr. Hyde	Cedric Gibbons and	
(Fleming, 41)	Daniel B. Cathcart	B/W
*Earthquake (Robson, 74)	Alexander Golitzen and	
	E. Preston Ames	Col.

Easter Parade (Walters, 48)	Cedric Gibbons and	
	Jack Martin Smith	Col.
*El Cid (Anthony Mann, 61)	Veniero Colasanti and	
	John Moore	Col.
Equus (Lumet, 77)	Tony Walton	Col.
*Executive Suite (Wise, 54)	Cedric Gibbons and	
	Edward Carfagno	B/W
*The Exorcist (Friedkin, 73)	Bill Malley	Col.
Fahrenheit 451 (Truffaut, 66)	Tony Walton	Col.
The Fallen Idol (Reed, 48)	Vincent Korda and	
	James Sawyer	B/W
†Fantastic Voyage (Fleischer, 66)	Jack Martin Smith and	
	Dale Hennesy	Col.
*A Farewell To Arms	Hans Dreier and	
(Borzage, 33)	Roland Anderson	B/W
Far From The Madding Crowd		
(Schlesinger, 67)	Richard MacDonald	Col.
*Fiddler On The Roof	Robert Boyle and	
(Jewison, 71)	Michael Stringer	Col.
Five Fingers (Mankiewicz, 52)	Lyle Wheeler and	
	George W. Davis	B/W
*Foreign Correspondent		
(Hitchcock, 40)	Alexander Golitzen	B/W
*For Whom The Bell Tolls	Hans Dreier and	
(Wood, 43)	Haldane Douglas	Col.
The Four Feathers		
(Zoltan Korda, 39)	Vincent Korda	Col.
*Fourteen Hours (Hathaway, 51)	Lyle R. Wheeler and	
	Leland Fuller	B/W
*The Foxes Of Harrow (Stahl, 47)	Lyle Wheeler and	
	Maurice Ransford	B/W
†Frenchman's Creek (Leisen, 45)	Hans Dreier and	
	Ernst Fegte	Col.
From Here To Eternity		
(Zinnemann, 53)	Cary Odell	B/W
*Funny Face (Donen, 57)	Hal Pereira and	
	George W. Davis	Col.
Funny Girl (Wyler, 68)	Gene Callahan	Col.
Funny Lady (Ross, 75)	George Jenkins	Col.
*The Gang's All Here	James Basevi and	
(Berkeley, 43)	Joseph C. Wright	Col.
†Gaslight (Cukor, 44)	Cedric Gibbons and	
	William Ferrari	B/W
*The Gay Divorcee	Van Nest Polglase and	
(Sandrich, 34)	Carroll Clark	B/W
*Giant (Stevens, 56)	Boris Leven	Col.
†Gigi (Minnelli, 58)	William A. Horning and	
	Preston Ames	Col.

Gilda (Vidor, 46)	Stephen Goosson and Van Nest Polglase	B/W
The Godfather (Coppola, 72)	Dean Tavoularis	Col.
†The Godfather Part II (Coppola, 74)	Richard Sylbert and W. Stewart Campbell	Col.
Goldfinger (Hamilton, 64)	Ken Adam	Col.
†Gone With The Wind (Fleming, 39)	Lyle Wheeler	Col.
*The Greatest Story Ever Told (Stevens, 65)	Richard Day, William Creber and David Hall	Col.
†Great Expectations (Lean, 47)	John Bryan	B/W
The Great Gatsby (Clayton, 74)	John Box	Col.
The Great McGinty (Sturges, 40)	Hans Dreier and Earl Hedrick	B/W
*The Great Ziegfeld (Leonard, 36)	Cedric Gibbons and Eddie Imazu	B/W
*Guess Who's Coming To Dinner (Kramer, 67)	Robert Clatworthy	Col.
*Guys and Dolls (Mankiewicz, 55)	Oliver Smith and Joseph C. Wright	Col.
Hail The Conquering Hero (Sturges, 44)	Hans Dreier and Haldane Douglas	B/W
†Hamlet (Olivier, 48)	Roger K. Furse	B/W
The Harvey Girls (Sidney, 46)	Cedric Gibbons and William Ferrari	Col.
Heaven Can Wait (Lubitsch, 43)	James Basevi and Leland Fuller	Col.
†Heaven Can Wait (Beatty/Henry, 78)	Paul Sylbert and Edwin O'Donovan	Col.
†The Heiress (Wyler, 49)	John Meehan and Harry Horner	B/W
†Hello Dolly! (Kelly, 69)	John De Cuir, Jack Martin Smith and Herman Blumenthal	Col.
*Henry V (Olivier, 46)	Paul Sheriff and Carmen Dillon	Col.
*The Hindenburg (Wise, 75)	Edward Carfagno	Col.
Hobson's Choice (Lean, 54)	Wilfred Shingleton	B/W
†How Green Was My Valley (Ford, 41)	Richard Day and Nathan Juran	B/W
*Hud (Ritt, 63)	Hal Pereira and Tambi Larsen	B/W
†The Hustler (Rossen, 61)	Harry Horner	B/W
*Inside Daisy Clover (Mulligan, 65)	Robert Clatworthy	Col.
*Interiors (Allen, 78)	Mel Bourne	Col.
Islands In The Stream (Schaffner, 77)	William J. Creber	Col.
Jesus Christ, Superstar (Jewison, 73)	Richard MacDonald	Col.
Jezebel (Wyler, 38)	Robert Haas	B/W

*Joan Of Arc (Fleming, 48)	Richard Day	Col.
*Johnny Belinda (Negulesco, 48)	Robert Haas	B/W
*Journey To The Centre Of The Earth (Levin, 59)	Lyle Wheeler, Franz Bachelin and Herman Blumenthal	Col.
*Judgment At Nuremberg (Kramer, 61)	Rudolph Sternad	B/W
Julia (Zinnemann, 77)	Gene Callahan, Willy Holt and Carmen Dillon	Col.
†Julius Caesar (Mankiewicz, 53)	Cedric Gibbons and Edward Carfagno	B/W
A Kid For Two Farthings (Reed, 55)	Wilfred Shingleton	Col.
Kind Hearts And Coronets (Hamer, 49)	William Kellner	B/W
†The King And I (Lang, 56)	Lyle Wheeler and John DeCuir	Col.
*Kitty (Leisen, 46)	Hans Dreier and Walter Tyler	B/W
*Knights Of The Round Table (Thorpe, 53)	Alfred Junge and Hans Peters	Col.
The Lady Eve (Sturges, 41)	Hans Dreier and Ernst Fegte	B/W
*Lady In The Dark (Leisen, 44)	Hans Dreier and Raoul Pene de Bois	Col.
The Ladykillers (Mackendrick, 56)	Jim Morahan	Col.
*The Last Tycoon (Kazan, 76)	Gene Callahan and Jack Collis	Col.
*Laura (Preminger, 44)	Lyle Wheeler and Leland Fuller	B/W
†Lawrence Of Arabia (Lean, 62)	John Box and John Stoll	Col.
*Les Girls (Cukor, 57)	William A. Horning and Gene Allen	Col.
The Letter (Wyler, 40)	Carl Jules Weyl	B/W
*The Life Of Emile Zola (Dieterle, 37)	Anton Grot	B/W
*Life With Father (Curtiz, 47)	Robert M. Haas	Col.
*Lili (Walters, 53)	Cedric Gibbons and Paul Groesse	Col.
*The Little Foxes (Wyler, 41)	Stephen Goosson	B/W
†Little Women (LeRoy, 49)	Cedric Gibbons and Paul Groesse	Col.
*Lives Of A Bengal Lancer (Hathaway, 35)	Hans Dreier and Roland Anderson	B/W
The Lodger (Brahm, 44)	James Basevi and John Ewing	B/W
*Logan's Run (Anderson, 76)	Dale Hennesy	Col.

†Lost Horizon (Capra, 37)	Stephen Goosson	B/W
The Lost Weekend (Wilder, 45)	Hans Dreier and	
	Earl Hedrick	B/W
*Love Affair (McCarey, 39)	Van Nest Polglase and	
	Al Herman	B/W
Love In The Afternoon (Wilder, 57)	Alexander Trauner	B/W
*Love Is A Many Splendoured	Lyle Wheeler and	
Thing (King, 55)	George W. Davis	Col.
Love Me Tonight (Mamoulian, 32)	Hans Dreier	B/W
*Lust For Life (Minnelli, 56)	Cedric Gibbons, Hans Peters	
	and Preston Ames	Col.
*Madame Bovary (Minnelli, 49)	Cedric Gibbons and	
	Jack Martin Smith	B/W
*Madame Curie (LeRoy, 43)	Cedric Gibbons and	
	Paul Groesse	B/W
Madeleine (Lean, 50)	John Bryan	B/W
The Magnificent Ambersons		
(Welles, 42)	Mark Lee Kirk	B/W
Mame (Saks, 74)	Robert F. Boyle	Col.
*The Man Who Would Be King	Alexander Trauner and	
(Huston, 75)	Tony Inglis	Col.
Marathon Man (Schlesinger, 76)	Richard MacDonald	Col.
The Mark Of Zorro	Richard Day and	
(Mamoulian, 40)	Joseph C. Wright	B/W
*Marty (Delbert Mann, 55)	Edward S. Haworth and	
	Walter Simonds	B/W
*Mary Poppins (Stevenson, 64)	Carroll Clark and	
	William H. Tuntke	Col.
*Mary, Queen of Scots	Terence Marsh and	
(Jarrott, 71)	Robert Cartwright	Col.
Meet Me In St. Louis	Cedric Gibbons, Lemuel Ayers	
(Minnelli, 44)	and Jack Martin Smith	Col.
†The Merry Widow (Lubitsch, 34)	Cedric Gibbons and	
	Frederic Hope	B/W
Midnight (Leisen, 39)	Hans Dreier and	
	Robert Usher	B/W
The Miracle Of Morgan's Creek	Hans Dreier and	
(Sturges, 44)	Ernst Fegte	B/W
Moby Dick (Huston, 56)	Ralph Brinton	Col.
Modern Times (Chaplin, 36)	Charles D. Hall	B/W
*The Molly Maguires (Ritt, 70)	Tambi Larsen	Col.
*Morocco (von Sternberg, 31)	Hans Dreier	B/W
†Moulin Rouge (Huston, 52)	Paul Sheriff	Col.
*Mr. Smith Goes To Washington		
(Capra, 39)	Lionel Banks	B/W
Murder On The Orient Express		
(Lumet, 74)	Tony Walton	Col.
*The Music Man (Da Costa, 62)	Paul Groesse	Col.
*Mutiny On The Bounty	George W. Davis and	
(Milestone, 62)	J. McMillan Johnson	Col.

*My Cousin Rachel (Koster, 52)	Lyle Wheeler and John De Cuir	B/W
†My Fair Lady (Cukor, 64)	Gene Allen and Cecil Beaton	Col.
†My Gal Sal (Cummings, 42)	Richard Day and Joseph C. Wright	Col.
*National Velvet (Brown, 45)	Cedric Gibbons and Urie McCleary	Col.
New York, New York (Scorsese, 77)	Boris Leven	
†Nicholas And Alexandra (Schaffner, 71)	John Box, Ernest Archer, Jack A. Maxsted and Gil Parrondo	Col.
Ninotchka (Lubitsch, 39)	Cedric Gibbons and Randall Duell	B/W
*North By Northwest (Hitchcock, 59)	William A. Horning, Robert Boyle and Merrill Pye	Col.
*North West Mounted Police (DeMille, 40)	Hans Dreier and Roland Anderson	Col.
Notorious (Hitchcock, 46)	Albert S. D'Agostino and Carroll Clark	B/W
Odd Man Out (Reed, 47)	Ralph Brinton	B/W
†Oliver! (Reed, 68)	John Box and Terence Marsh	Col.
Oliver Twist (Lean, 48)	John Bryan	B/W
On The Town (Kelly/Donen, 49)	Cedric Gibbons and Jack Martin Smith	Col.
†On The Waterfront (Kazan, 54)	Richard Day	B/W
The Other Side Of Midnight (Jarrott, 77)	John DeCuir	Col.
Outcast Of The Islands (Reed, 52)	Vincent Korda	B/W
*Pal Joey (Sidney, 57)	Walter Holscher	Col.
The Palm Beach Story (Sturges, 42)	Hans Dreier and Ernst Fegte	B/W
Pandora And The Flying Dutchman (Lewin, 51)	John Bryan	Col.
Papillon (Schaffner, 73)	Anthony Masters	Col.
†Patton (Schaffner, 70)	Urie McCleary and Gil Parrondo	Col.
†The Phantom Of The Opera (Lubin, 43)	Alexander Golitzen and John B. Goodman	Col.
Phase IV (Bass, 73)	John Barry	Col.
The Philadelphia Story (Cukor, 40)	Cedric Gibbons and Wade B. Rubottom	B/W
†Picnic (Logan, 55)	William Flannery and Jo Mielziner	Col.
*The Picture Of Dorian Gray (Lewin, 45)	Cedric Gibbons and Hans Peters	B/W

*Pillow Talk (Gordon, 59)	Richard H. Riedel	Col.
The Pirate (Minnelli, 48)	Cedric Gibbons and Jack Martin Smith	Col.
†Pride And Prejudice (Leonard, 40)	Cedric Gibbons and Paul Groesse	B/W
*The Prisoner Of Zenda (Cromwell, 37)	Lyle Wheeler	B/W
The Private Life Of Sherlock Holmes (Wilder, 70)	Alexander Trauner	Col.
*The Private Lives Of Elizabeth And Essex (Curtiz, 39)	Anton Grot	Col.
*Psycho (Hitchcock, 60)	Joseph Hurley and Robert Clatworthy	B/W
*Quo Vadis (LeRoy, 51)	Cedric Gibbons, William A. Horning and Edward Carfagno	Col.
*The Rains Came (Brown, 39)	William S. Darling and George Dudley	B/W
*Raintree County (Dmytryk, 57)	William A. Horning and Urie McCleary	Col.
*Random Harvest (LeRoy, 42)	Cedric Gibbons and Randall Duell	B/W
*The Razor's Edge (Goulding, 46)	Richard Day and Nathan Juran	B/W
*Reap The Wild Wind (DeMille, 42)	Hans Dreier and Roland Anderson	Col.
*Rebecca (Hitchcock, 40)	Lyle Wheeler	B/W
†The Red Shoes (Powell/Pressburger, 48)	Hein Heckroth	Col.
†The Robe (Koster, 53)	Lyle Wheeler and George W. Davis	Col.
Robin And Marian (Lester, 76)	Michael Stringer	Col.
*Roman Holiday (Wyler, 53)	Hal Pereira and Walter Tyler	B/W
*Romeo And Juliet (Cukor, 36)	Cedric Gibbons and Frederic Hope	B/W
†The Rose Tattoo (Daniel Mann, 55)	Hal Pereira and Tambi Larsen	B/W
*Sabrina (Wilder, 54)	Hal Pereira and Walter Tyler	B/W
The Sailor Who Fell From Grace With The Sea (Carlino, 76)	Ted Haworth	Col.
†Samson And Delilah (DeMille, 50)	Hans Dreier and Walter Tyler	Col.
*The Sand Pebbles (Wise, 66)	Boris Leven	Col.

†Sayonara (Logan, 57) — Ted Haworth — Col.

*Scrooge (Neame, 70) — Terry Marsh and Bob Cartwright — Col.

*The Sea Hawk (Curtiz, 40) — Anton Grot — B/W

*Seven Days In May (Frankenheimer, 64) — Cary Odell — B/W

*Shampoo (Ashby, 75) — Richard Sylbert and W. Stewart Campbell — Col.

†Ship Of Fools (Kramer, 65) — Robert Clatworthy — B/W

*Since You Went Away (Cromwell, 44) — Mark Lee Kirk — B/W

Slaughterhouse Five (Hill, 72) — Henry Bumstead — Col.

*The Snows Of Kilimanjaro (King, 52) — Lyle Wheeler and John De Cuir — Col.

†Somebody Up There Likes Me (Wise, 56) — Cedric Gibbons and Malcolm F. Brown — B/W

*Some Like It Hot (Wilder, 59) — Ted Haworth — B/W

†The Song Of Bernadette (King, 43) — James Basevi and William S. Darling — B/W

*Sons And Lovers (Cardiff, 60) — Tom Morahan — B/W

*The Sound Of Music (Wise, 65) — Boris Leven — Col.

†Spartacus (Kubrick, 60) — Alexander Golitzen and Eric Orbom — Col.

*The Spy Who Came In From The Cold (Ritt, 65) — Hal Pereira and Tambi Larsen — B/W

*The Spy Who Loved Me (Gilbert, 77) — Ken Adam — Col.

*Star! (Wise, 68) — Boris Leven — Col.

*A Star Is Born (Cukor, 54) — Malcolm Bert, Gene Allen and Irene Sharaff — Col.

†Star Wars (Lucas, 77) — John Barry, Norman Reynolds and Leslie Dilley — Col.

†The Sting (Hill, 73) — Henry Bumstead — Col.

†A Streetcar Named Desire (Kazan, 51) — Richard Day — B/W

†Sunset Boulevard (Wilder, 50) — Hans Dreier and John Meehan — B/W

*The Sunshine Boys (Ross, 75) — Albert Brenner — Col.

*Sweet Charity (Fosse, 69) — Alexander Golitzen and George C. Webb — Col.

*The Tales Of Hoffman (Powell/Pressburger, 51) — Hein Heckroth — Col.

*The Talk Of The Town (Stevens, 42) — Lionel Banks and Rudolph Sternad — B/W

*The Taming Of The Shrew (Zeffirelli, 67) — Renzo Mongiardino, John DeCuir, Elven Webb and Guiseppe Mariani — Col.

*The Ten Commandments (DeMille, 56) — Hal Pereira, Walter Tyler and Albert Nozaki — Col.

*That Touch Of Mink (Delbert Mann, 62)	Alexander Golitzen and Robert Clatworthy	Col.
*They Shoot Horses Don't They (Pollack, 69)	Harry Horner	Col.
†The Thief Of Bagdad (Powell, Berger and Whelan, 40)	Vincent Korda	Col.
†This Above All (Litvak, 42)	Richard Day and Joseph C. Wright	B/W
*Thoroughly Modern Millie (Hill, 67)	Alexander Golitzen and George C. Webb	Col.
The Three Musketeers (Lester, 74)	Brian Eatwell	Col.
*Titanic (Negulesco, 53)	Lyle Wheeler and Maurice Ransford	B/W
*To Catch A Thief (Hitchcock, 55)	Hal Pereira and Joseph McMillan Johnson	Col.
†To Kill A Mockingbird (Mulligan, 62)	Alexander Golitzen and Henry Bumstead	B/W
*Tom Jones (Richardson, 63)	Ralph Brinton and Ted Marshall	Col.
*Top Hat (Sandrich, 35)	Carroll Clark and Van Nest Polglase	B/W
*The Towering Inferno (Guillermin, 74)	William Creber and Ward Preston	Col.
*Travels With My Aunt (Cukor, 72)	John Box, Gil Parrondo and Robert W. Laing	Col.
*The Turning Point (Ross, 77)	Albert Brenner	Col.
†20,000 Leagues Under The Sea (Fleischer, 54)	John Meehan	Col.
*2001: A Space Odyssey (Kubrick, 68)	Tony Masters, Harry Lange and Ernie Archer	Col.
Valentino (Russell, 77)	Philip Harrison	Col.
*Vertigo (Hitchcock, 58)	Hal Pereira and Henry Bumstead	Col.
*Viva Zapata (Kazan, 52)	Lyle Wheeler and Leland Fuller	B/W
*The Way We Were (Pollack, 73)	Stephen Grimes	Col.
†West Side Story (Wise, 61)	Boris Leven	Col.
†Who's Afraid Of Virginia Woolf (Nichols, 66)	Richard Sylbert	B/W
†Wilson (King, 44)	Wiard Ihnen	Col.
The Wind And The Lion (Milius, 75)	Gil Parrondo	Col.
*The Wiz (Lumet, 78)	Tony Walton and Philip Rosenberg	Col.
*The Wizard Of Oz (Fleming, 39)	Cedric Gibbons and William A. Horning	Col.
*Wuthering Heights (Wyler, 39)	James Basevi	B/W

†The Yearling (Brown, 46)	Cedric Gibbons and Paul Groesse	Col.
*Young Bess (Sidney, 53)	Cedric Gibbons and Urie McCleary	Col.
Young Frankenstein (Brooks, 74)	Dale Hennesy	B/W
Young Mr. Lincoln (Ford, 39)	Richard Day and Mark Lee Kirk	B/W

APPENDIX V

COSTUME DESIGNERS: A CHECK LIST

All films are listed alphabetically. Directors' names and release dates are in parentheses. Costume Designers are listed in the right hand column. Films that have received Academy Award nominations for costume design are marked with a *, Oscar winners with a †. (*Note:* Academy Awards in the costume design category did not begin until 1948).

Film	Designer	Type
*The Actress (Cukor, 53)	Walter Plunkett	B/W
†The Adventures Of Don Juan (Sherman, 49)	Leah Rhodes, Travilla and Marjorie Best	Col.
The Adventures Of Robin Hood (Curtiz, Keighley, 38)	Milo Anderson	Col.
*The Agony And The Ecstasy (Reed, 65)	Vittorio Nino Novarese	Col.
Alexander's Ragtime Band (King, 38)	Gwen Wakeling	B/W
†All About Eve (Mankiewicz, 50)	Edith Head and Charles LeMaire	B/W
All That Money Can Buy (Dieterle, 41)	Edward Stevenson	B/W
*An Affair To Remember (McCarey, 57)	Charles LeMaire	Col.
†An American In Paris (Minnelli, 51)	Orry-Kelly, Walter Plunkett and Irene Sharaff	Col.
An Ideal Husband (Korda, 48)	Cecil Beaton	B/W
Anna Karenina (Brown, 35)	Adrian	B/W
Anna Karenina (Duvivier, 48)	Cecil Beaton	B/W
†Anne Of The Thousand Days (Jarrott, 69)	Margaret Furse	Col.
Arabesque (Donen, 66)	Christian Dior	Col.
*Around The World In Eighty Days (Anderson, 56)	Miles White	Col.
Ask Any Girl (Walters, 59)	Helen Rose	Col.
*Back Street (Miller, 61)	Jean Louis	Col.
†The Bad And The Beautiful (Minnelli, 52)	Helen Rose	B/W

*The Band Wagon (Minnelli, 53)	Mary Ann Nyberg	Col.
Barefoot In The Park (Saks, 67)	Edith Head	Col.
The Barkleys Of Broadway (Walters, 49)	Irene and Valles	Col.
The Barretts Of Wimpole Street (Franklin, 34)	Adrian	B/W
†Barry Lyndon (Kubrick, 75)	Ulla-Britt Soderlund and Milena Canonero	Col.
*Becket (Glenville, 64)	Margaret Furse	Col.
*Bell, Book And Candle (Quine, 58)	Jean Louis	Col.
†Ben-Hur (Wyler, 59)	Elizabeth Haffenden	Col.
The Best Years Of Our Lives (Wyler, 46)	Irene Sharaff	B/W
Blood And Sand (Mamoulian, 41)	Travis Banton	Col.
Blossoms In The Dust (LeRoy, 41)	Adrian and Gile Steele	Col.
The Blue Max (Guillermin, 66)	John Furness	Col.
*Bonnie And Clyde (Penn, 67)	Theadora Van Runkle	Col.
*Born Yesterday (Cukor, 50)	Jean Louis	B/W
*Bound For Glory (Ashby, 76)	William Theiss	Col.
The Boy Friend (Russell, 72)	Shirely Russell	Col.
Breakfast At Tiffany's (Edwards, 61)	Edith Head, Hubert De Givenchy and Pauline Trigere	Col.
*Brigadoon (Minnelli, 54)	Irene Sharaff	Col.
The Brothers Karamazov (Brooks, 58)	Walter Plunkett	Col.
Cabaret (Fosse, 72)	Charlotte Fleming	Col.
*Call Me Madam (Lang, 53)	Irene Sharaff	Col.
†Camelot (Logan, 67)	John Truscott	Col.
Camille (Cukor, 36)	Adrian	B/W
Captain From Castile (King, 47)	Charles LeMaire	Col.
*Carrie (Wyler, 52)	Edith Head	B/W
Casablanca (Curtiz, 43)	Orry-Kelly	B/W
Cat On A Hot Tin Roof (Brooks, 58)	Helen Rose	Col.
Charade (Donen, 63)	Hubert de Givenchy	Col.
The Charge Of The Light Brigade (Richardson, 68)	David Walker	Col.
*Chinatown (Polanski, 74)	Anthea Sylbert	Col.
Citizen Kane (Welles, 41)	Edward Stevenson	B/W
†Cleopatra (Mankiewicz, 63)	Irene Sharaff, Vittorio Nino Novarese and Renie	Col.
Cover Girl (Vidor, 44)	Travis Banton, Gwen Wakeling and Muriel King	Col.
†Cromwell (Hughes, 70)	Vittorio Nino Novarese	Col.
Cyrano de Bergerac (Gordon, 50)	Dorothy Jeakins	B/W
*Daisy Miller (Bogdanovich, 74)	John Furness	Col.
†Darling (Schlesinger, 65)	Julie Harris	B/W
*David And Bathsheba (King, 51)	Charles LeMaire and Edward Stevenson	Col.

The Day Of The Locust (Schlesinger, 75)	Ann Roth	Col.
†Death On The Nile (Guillermin, 78)	Anthony Powell	Col.
*The Diary Of Anne Frank (Stevens, 59)	Charles LeMaire and Mary Wills	B/W
Dinner At Eight (Cukor, 33)	Adrian	B/W
Dragonwyck (Mankiewicz, 46)	Rene Hubert	B/W
Dr. Jekyll And Mr. Hyde (Mamoulian, 32)	Travis Banton	B/W
Dr. Jekyll And Mr. Hyde (Fleming, 41)	Adrian and Gile Steele	B/W
†Dr. Zhivago (Lean, 65)	Phyllis Dalton	Col.
Duel In The Sun (Vidor, 46)	Walter Plunkett	Col.
Easter Parade (Walters, 48)	Irene and Valles	Col.
*Executive Suite (Wise, 54)	Helen Rose	B/W
†The Facts Of Life (Frank, 60)	Edith Head and Edward Stevenson	B/W
Family Plot (Hitchcock, 76)	Edith Head	Col.
Far From The Madding Crowd (Schlesinger, 67)	Alan Barrett	Col.
Father Of The Bride (Minnelli, 50)	Walter Plunkett and Helen Rose	B/W
Fiddler On The Roof (Jewison, 71)	Elizabeth Haffenden and Joan Bridge	Col.
Fire Over England (Howard, 37)	Rene Hubert	B/W
The 5,000 Fingers Of Dr. T (Rowland, 53)	Jean Louis	Col.
*Flower Drum Song (Koster, 61)	Irene Sharaff	Col.
The Four Feathers (Zoltan Korda, 39)	Rene Hubert and Godfrey Brennan	Col.
The Four Horsemen Of The Apocalypse (Minnelli, 61)	Walter Plunkett, Orry-Kelly and Rene Hubert	Col.
*From Here To Eternity (Zinnemann, 53)	Jean Louis	B/W
*Funny Face (Donen, 57)	Edith Head and Hubert de Givenchy	Col.
Funny Girl (Wyler, 68)	Irene Sharaff	Col.
*Funny Lady (Ross, 75)	Ray Aghayan and Bob Mackie	Col.
*Gambit (Neame, 66)	Jean Louis	Col.
Gaslight (Cukor, 44)	Irene and Marion Herwood Keyes	B/W
Gentlemen Prefer Blondes (Hawks, 53)	Charles LeMaire and Travilla	Col.
*Giant (Stevens, 56)	Moss Mabray and Marjorie Best	Col.

.†Gigi (Minnelli, 58)	Cecil Beaton	Col.
Gilda (Vidor, 46)	Jean Louis	B/W
The Go-Between (Losey, 71)	John Furness	Col.
*The Godfather (Coppola, 72)	Anna Hill Johnstone	Col.
*The Godfather Part II (Coppola, 74)	Theadora Van Runkle	Col.
Gone With The Wind (Fleming, 39)	Walter Plunkett	Col.
Goodbye Mr. Chips (Ross, 69)	Julie Harris	Col.
*The Greatest Show On Earth (DeMille, 52)	Edith Head, Dorothy Jeakins and Miles White	Col.
*The Greatest Story Ever Told (Stevens, 65)	Vittorio Nino Novarese and Marjorie Best	Col.
Great Expectations (Lean, 47)	Margaret Furse and Sophie Harris	B/W
†The Great Gatsby (Clayton, 74)	Theoni V. Aldredge	Col.
The Great Waldo Pepper (Hill, 75)	Edith Head	Col.
The Great Waltz (Duvivier, 38)	Adrian	B/W
The Great Ziegfeld (Leonard, 36)	Adrian	B/W
The Group (Lumet, 65)	Anna Hill Johnstone	Col.
Guess Who's Coming To Dinner? (Kramer, 67)	Jean Louis	Col.
Gunga Din (Stevens, 39)	Edward Stevenson	B/W
*Guys And Dolls (Mankiewicz, 55)	Irene Sharaff	Col.
*Gypsy (LeRoy, 62)	Orry-Kelly	Col.
Half A Sixpence (Sidney, 67)	Elizabeth Haffenden and Joan Bridge	Col.
†Hamlet (Olivier, 48)	Roger K. Furse	B/W
*Hans Christian Andersen (Vidor, 52)	Clave, Mary Wills and Karinska	Col.
*Hawaii (Hill, 66)	Dorothy Jeakins	Col.
Heaven Can Wait (Lubitsch, 43)	Rene Hubert	Col.
†The Heiress (Wyler, 49)	Edith Head and Gile Steele	B/W
*Hello, Dolly! (Kelly, 69)	Irene Sharaff	Col.
Henry V (Olivier, 46)	Roger Furse and Margaret Furse	Col.
High Society (Walters, 56)	Helen Rose	Col.
The Hindenburg (Wise, 76)	Dorothy Jeakins	Col.
The Hireling (Bridges, 73)	Phyllis Dalton	Col.
*How The West Was Won (Ford, Hathaway, Marshall, 62)	Walter Plunkett	Col.
*How To Marry A Millionaire (Negulesco, 53)	Charles LeMaire and Travilla	Col.
The Hunchback Of Notre Dame (Dieterle, 39)	Walter Plunkett	B/W
†I'll Cry Tomorrow (Daniel Mann, 55)	Helen Rose	B/W
Imitation Of Life (Sirk, 59)	Jean Louis and Bill Thomas	Col.

The Importance Of Being Earnest (Asquith, 52)	Beatrice Dawson	Col.
*Inside Daisy Clover (Mulligan, 65)	Edith Head and Bill Thomas	Col.
I Remember Mama (Stevens, 48)	Edward Stevenson and Gile Steele	B/W
Isadora (Reisz, 69)	Ruth Myers	Col.
It's A Mad, Mad, Mad, Mad World (Kramer, 63)	Bill Thomas	Col.
It's A Wonderful Life (Capra, 46)	Edward Stevenson	B/W
Jane Eyre (Stevenson, 44)	Rene Hubert	B/W
Jesus Christ, Superstar (Jewison, 73)	Yvonne Blake	Col.
Jezebel (Wyler, 38)	Orry-Kelly	B/W
†Joan Of Arc (Fleming, 48)	Dorothy Jeakins and Karinska	Col.
The Jolson Story (Green, 46)	Jean Louis	Col.
Juarez (Dieterle, 39)	Orry-Kelly	B/W
*Julia (Zinnemann, 77)	Anthea Sylbert	Col.
Kind Hearts And Coronets (Hamer, 49)	Anthony Mendleson	B/W
†The King And I (Lang, 56)	Irene Sharaff	Col.
Kings Row (Wood, 42)	Orry-Kelly	B/W
Kiss Me Kate (Sidney, 53)	Walter Plunkett	Col.
Lady In The Dark (Leisen, 44)	Raoul Pene du Bois, Edith Head, Mitchell Leisen and Babs Wilomez	Col.
The Ladykillers (Mackendrick, 55)	Anthony Mendleson	Col.
The Lavender Hill Mob (Crichton, 51)	Anthony Mendleson	B/W
Lawrence Of Arabia (Lean, 62)	Phyllis Dalton	Col.
†Les Girls (Cukor, 57)	Orry-Kelly	Col.
The Letter (Wyler, 40)	Orry-Kelly	B/W
A Letter To Three Wives (Mankiewicz, 49)	Charles LeMaire and Kay Nelson	B/W
The Life Of Emile Zola (Dieterle, 37)	Milo Anderson	B/w
Life With Father (Curtiz, 47)	Milo Anderson	Col.
*The Lion In Winter (Harvey, 68)	Margaret Furse	Col.
The Little Foxes (Wyler, 41)	Orry-Kelly	B/W
Lives Of A Bengal Lancer (Hathaway, 35)	Travis Banton	B/W
The Lodger (Brahm, 44)	Rene Hubert	B/W
Logan's Run (Anderson, 76)	Bill Thomas	Col.
Lord Jim (Brooks, 65)	Phyllis Dalton	Col.

Love In The Afternoon (Wilder, 57)	Hubert de Givenchy	B/W
†Love Is A Many Splendoured Thing (King, 55)	Charles LeMaire	Col.
*Love With The Proper Stranger (Mulligan, 63)	Edith Head	B/W
Madeleine (Lean, 50)	Margaret Furse	B/W
†A Man For All Seasons (Zinnemann, 66)	Elizabeth Haffenden and Joan Bridge	Col.
The Man In The White Suit (Mackendrick, 51)	Anthony Mendleson	B/W
*The Man Who Would Be King (Huston, 75)	Edith Head	Col.
The Mark Of Zorro (Mamoulian, 40)	Travis Banton	B/W
*Mary Poppins (Stevenson, 64)	Tony Walton	Col.
*Mary, Queen Of Scots (Jarrott, 71)	Margaret Furse	Col.
Meet Me In St. Louis (Minnelli, 44)	Irene and Irene Sharaff	Col.
*The Merry Widow (Bernhardt, 52)	Helen Rose and Gile Steele	Col.
*The Miracle Worker (Penn, 62)	Ruth Morley	B/W
Moby Dick (Huston, 56)	Elizabeth Haffenden	Col.
Morocco (von Sternberg, 30)	Travis Banton	B/W
†Moulin Rouge (Huston, 52)	Marcel Vertes	Col.
Mrs. Parkington (Garnett, 44)	Irene, Valles and Marion Herwood Keyes	B/W
*The Mudlark (Negulesco, 51)	Edward Stevenson and Margaret Furse	B/W
*Murder On The Orient Express (Lumet, 74)	Tony Walton	Col.
The Music Lovers (Russell, 71)	Shirley Russell	Col.
*The Music Man (Da Costa, 62)	Dorothy Jeakins	Col.
*My Cousin Rachel (Koster, 52)	Charles LeMaire and Dorothy Jeakins	B/W
†My Fair Lady (Cukor, 64)	Cecil Beaton	Col.
National Velvet (Brown, 45)	Irene, Valles and Kay Dean	Col.
New York, New York (Scorsese, 77)	Theodora Van Runkle	Col.
†Nicholas And Alexandra (Schaffner, 71)	Yvonne Blake and Antonio Castillo	Col.
†The Night Of The Iguana (Huston, 64)	Dorothy Jeakins	B/W
Notorious (Hitchcock, 46)	Edith Head	B/W
Oh! What A Lovely War (Attenborough, 69)	Anthony Mendleson	Col.

*Oliver! (Reed, 68)	Phyllis Dalton	Col.
Oliver Twist (Lean, 48)	Margaret Furse	B/W
On The Town (Kelly/Donen, 49)	Helen Rose	Col.
*The Other Side Of Midnight (Jarrott, 77)	Irene Sharaff	Col.
*Pal Joey (Sidney, 57)	Jean Louis	Col.
Pandora And The Flying Dutchman (Lewin, 51)	Beatrice Dawson and Julia Squire	Col.
Papillon (Schaffner, 73)	Anthony Powell	Col.
*The Pickwick Papers (Langley, 55)	Beatrice Dawson	B/W
The Picture Of Dorian Gray (Lewin, 45)	Irene, Valles and Marion Herwood Keyes	B/W
Pillow Talk (Gordon, 59)	Jean Louis	Col.
The Pirate (Minnelli, 48)	Irene and Tom Keogh	Col.
†A Place In The Sun (Stevens, 51)	Edith Head	B/W
*Planet Of The Apes (Schaffner, 68)	Morton Hack	Col.
*Porgy And Bess (Preminger, 59)	Irene Sharaff	Col.
Portrait Of Jennie (Dieterle, 48)	Lucinda Ballard and Anna Hill Johnstone	B/W
*Prince Of Foxes (King, 49)	Vittorio Nino Novarese	B/W
The Private Life Of Sherlock Holmes (Wilder, 70)	Julie Harris	Col.
The Private Lives Of Elizabeth And Essex (Curtiz, 39)	Orry-Kelly	Col.
The Pumpkin Eater (Clayton, 64)	Motley	B/W
*Quo Vadis (LeRoy, 51)	Herschel McCoy	Col.
*Raintree County (Dmytryk, 57)	Walter Plunkett	Col.
†The Robe (Koster, 53)	Charles LeMaire and Emile Santiago	Col.
†Roman Holiday (Wyler, 53)	Edith Head	B/W
Romeo And Juliet (Cukor, 36)	Adrian	B/W
†Romeo And Juliet (Zeffirelli, 68)	Danilo Donati	Col.
Rosemary's Baby (Polanski, 68)	Anthea Sylbert	Col.
*The Rose Tattoo (Daniel Mann, 55)	Edith Head	B/W
Ryan's Daughter (Lean, 70)	Jocelyn Richards	Col.
†Sabrina (Wilder, 54)	Edith Head	B/W
†Samson And Delilah (DeMille, 50)	Edith Head, Dorothy Jeakins, Eloise Jenssen, Gile Steele and Gwen Wakeling	Col.
The Scarlet Empress (von Sternberg, 34)	Travis Banton	B/W
*Scrooge (Neame, 70)	Margaret Furse	Col.
The Sea Hawk (Curtiz, 40)	Orry-Kelly	B/W

Send Me No Flowers (Jewison, 64)	Jean Louis	Col.
*The Seven Per Cent Solution (Ross, 76)	Alan Barrett	Col.
Shampoo (Ashby, 75)	Anthea Sylbert	Col.
Shanghai Express (von Sternberg, 32)	Travis Banton	B/W
*Ship Of Fools (Kubrick, 65)	Bill Thomas and Jean Louis	B/W
The Sign Of The Cross (DeMille, 32)	Travis Banton	B/W
Singin' In The Rain (Kelly/Donen, 52)	Walter Plunkett	Col.
The Snows Of Kilimanjaro (King, 52)	Charles LeMaire	Col.
†The Solid Gold Cadillac (Quine, 56)	Jean Louis	B/W
†Some Like It Hot (Wilder, 59)	Orry-Kelly	B/W
The Song Of Bernadette (King, 43)	Rene Hubert	B/W
A Song To Remember (Vidor, 45)	Walter Plunkett and Travis Banton	Col.
*The Sound Of Music (Wise, 65)	Dorothy Jeakins	Col.
†Spartacus (Kubrick, 60)	Valles and Bill Thomas	Col.
Splendour In The Grass (Kazan, 61)	Anna Hill Johnstone	Col.
*Star! (Wise, 68)	Donald Brooks	Col.
*A Star Is Born (Cukor, 54)	Jean Louis, Mary Ann Nyberg and Irene Sharaff	Col.
†Star Wars (Lucas, 77)	John Mollo	Col.
†The Sting (Hill, 73)	Edith Head	Col.
The Story Of Louis Pasteur (Dieterle, 35)	Milo Anderson	B/W
Strangers On A Train (Hitchcock, 51)	Leah Rhodes	B/W
*A Streetcar Named Desire (Kazan, 51)	Lucinda Ballard	B/W
Sunset Boulevard (Wilder, 50)	Edith Head	B/W
The Swan (Vidor, 56)	Helen Rose	Col.
*Sweet Charity (Fosse, 69)	Edith Head	Col.
A Tale Of Two Cities (Conway, 35)	Dolly Tree	B/W
Tales Of Beatrix Potter (Mills, 71)	Christine Edzard	Col.
*The Tales Of Hoffmann (Powell/Pressburger, 51)	Hein Heckroth	Col.
*The Taming Of The Shrew (Zeffirelli, 67)	Irene Sharaff and Danilo Donati	Col.
*The Ten Commandments (DeMille, 56)	Edith Head, Ralph Jester, John Jensen, Dorothy Jeakins and Arnold Friberg	Col.
The Tender Trap (Walters, 55)	Helen Rose	Col.
*There's No Business Like Show Business (Lang, 54)	Charles LeMaire, Travilla and Miles White	Col.

*They Shoot Horses, Don't They? (Pollack, 69)	Donfeld	Col.
The Thomas Crown Affair (Jewison, 68)	Theadora Van Runkle	Col.
*Thoroughly Modern Millie (Hill, 67)	Jean Louis	Col.
Those Magnificent Men In Their Flying Machines (Annakin, 65)	Osbert Lancaster and Dinah Greet	Col.
The Three Musketeers (Lester, 74)	Yvonne Blake	Col.
*To Catch A Thief (Hitchcock, 55)	Edith Head	Col.
Topaz (Hitchcock, 69)	Edith Head	Col.
†Travels With My Aunt (Cukor, 72)	Anthony Powell	Col.
Unconquered (DeMille, 47)	Gwen Wakeling	Col.
Under Capricorn (Hitchcock, 49)	Roger Furse	Col.
Valentino (Russell, 77)	Shirley Russell	Col.
Valley Of Decision (Garnett, 45)	Irene, Marion Herwood Keyes	B/W
Viva Zapata! (Kazan, 52)	Charles LeMaire and Travilla	B/W
Waltz Of The Toreadors (Guillermin, 61)	Beatrice Dawson	Col.
Waterloo (Bondarchuk, 70)	Maria De Matteis	Col.
Waterloo Bridge (LeRoy, 40)	Adrian and Gile Steele	B/W
*The Way We Were (Pollack, 73)	Dorothy Jeakins and Moss Mabry	Col.
†West Side Story (Wise/Robbins, 61)	Irene Sharaff	Col.
*What A Way To Go! (Lee Thompson, 64)	Edith Head and Moss Mabry	Col.
†Whatever Happened To Baby Jane? (Aldrich, 62)	Norma Koch	B/W
†Who's Afraid Of Virginia Woolf? (Nichols, 66)	Irene Sharaff	B/W
Wilson (King, 44)	Rene Hubert	Col.
The Wind And The Lion (Milius, 75)	Richard E. LaMotte	Col.
Witness For The Prosecution (Wilder, 57)	Edith Head	B/W
*The Wiz (Lumet, 78)	Tony Walton	Col.
Woman Of The Year (Stevens, 42)	Adrian	B/W
Women In Love (Russell, 70)	Shirley Russell	Col.
†The Wonderful World Of The Brothers Grimm (Levin, 62)	Mary Wills	Col.
Yankee Doodle Dandy (Curtiz, 42)	Milo Anderson	B/W
The Yellow Rolls Royce (Asquith, 64)	Anthony Mendleson	Col.

*Young Bess (Sidney, 53)	Walter Plunkett	Col.
Young Frankenstein (Brooks, 74)	Dorothy Jeakins	B/W
Ziegfeld Follies (Minnelli, 45)	Irene, Helen Rose and Irene Sharaff	Col.
Ziegfeld Girl (Leonard, 41)	Adrian	B/W

APPENDIX VI

FILM EDITORS: A CHECK LIST

All films are listed alphabetically. Director's names and release dates are in parenthesis. Editors are listed in the right hand column. Films that have received Academy Award nominations for editing are marked with a *, Oscar winners with a †.

Accident (Losey, 67)	Reginald Beck
Ace In The Hole (Wilder, 51)	Doane Harrison and Arthur Schmidt
Act Of Violence (Zinnemann, 48)	Conrad A. Nervig
†The Adventures Of Robin Hood (Curtiz/Keighley, 38)	Ralph Dawson
†Air Force (Hawks, 43)	George Amy
*Airport (Seaton, 70)	Stuart Gilmore
*All About Eve (Mankiewicz, 50)	Barbara McLean
All That Money Can Buy (Dieterle, 41)	Robert Wise
*All The King's Men (Rossen, 49)	Robert Parrish and Al Clark
*All The President's Men (Pakula, 76)	Robert L. Wolfe
*American Graffiti (Lucas, 73)	Verna Fields and Marcia Lucas
*An American In Paris (Minnelli, 51)	Adrienna Fazan
*Anatomy Of A Murder (Preminger, 59)	Louis R. Loeffler
*The Andromeda Strain (Wise, 71)	Stuart Gilmore and John W. Holmes
†Anthony Adverse (LeRoy, 36)	Ralph Dawson
†The Apartment (Wilder, 60)	Daniel Mandell
†Around The World In Eighty Days (Anderson, 56)	Gene Ruggiero and Paul Weatherwax
The Bad And The Beautiful (Minnelli, 52)	Conrad A. Nervig
The Barefoot Contessa (Mankiewicz, 54)	William Hornbeck
*Battleground (Wellman, 49)	John Dunning
*Becket (Glenville, 64)	Anne V. Coates
†Ben-Hur (Wyler, 59)	Ralph E. Winters and John Dunning
†The Best Years Of Our Lives (Wyler, 46)	Daniel Mandell
The Birds (Hitchcock, 63)	George Tomasini

*Blackboard Jungle (Brooks, 55)	Ferris Webster
The Blue Lamp (Dearden, 50)	Peter Tanner
†Body And Soul (Rossen, 47)	Francis Lyon and
	Robert Parrish
Bonnie And Clyde (Penn, 67)	Dede Allen
*Bound For Glory (Ashby, 76)	Robert Jones and
	Pembroke J. Herring
*The Boys From Brazil (Schaffner, 78)	Robert E. Swink
†The Bridge On The River Kwai (Lean, 57)	Peter Taylor
†Bullitt (Yates, 68)	Frank P. Keller
†Cabaret (Fosse, 72)	David Bretherton
Camelot (Logan, 67)	Folmar Blangsted
Camille (Cukor, 37)	Margaret Booth
*Captains Courageous (Fleming, 37)	Elmo Vernon
Carrie (DePalma, 76)	Paul Hirsch
*Casablanca (Curtiz, 43)	Owen Marks
Cat On A Hot Tin Roof (Brooks, 58)	Ferris Webster
†Champion (Robson, 49)	Harry Gerstad
*Chinatown (Polanski, 74)	Sam O'Steen
*Citizen Kane (Welles, 41)	Robert Wise
*Cleopatra (DeMille, 34)	Anne Bauchens
*Cleopatra (Mankiewicz, 63)	Dorothy Spencer
*A Clockwork Orange (Kubrick, 71)	Bill Butler
*Close Encounters Of The Third Kind	
(Spielberg, 77)	Michael Kahn
*Come Back Little Sheba (Daniel Mann, 52)	Warren Low
*Coming Home (Ashby, 78)	Don Zimmerman
Compulsion (Fleischer, 59)	William Reynolds
Cool Hand Luke (Rosenberg, 67)	Sam O'Steen
Cross Of Iron (Peckinpah, 77)	Tony Lawson and Mike Ellis
The Cruel Sea (Frend, 53)	Peter Tanner
*David Copperfield (Cukor, 35)	Robert J. Kern
*The Day Of The Jackal (Zinnemann, 73)	Ralph Kemplen
The Day The Earth Stood Still (Wise, 51)	William Reynolds
Dead End (Wyler, 37)	Daniel Mandell
*Decision Before Dawn (Litvak, 51)	Dorothy Spencer
†The Deer Hunter (Cimino, 78)	Peter Zinner
*The Defiant Ones (Kramer, 58)	Frederic Knudtson
*Deliverance (Boorman, 72)	Tom Priestly
The Diary Of Anne Frank (Stevens, 59)	Robert W. Swink, William
	Mace and David Bretherton
*The Dirty Dozen (Aldrich, 67)	Michael Luciano
*Dog Day Afternoon (Lumet, 75)	Dede Allen
Double Indemnity (Wilder, 44)	Doane Harrison
A Double Life (Cukor, 47)	Robert Parrish
Dr. Strangelove (Kubrick, 64)	Anthony Harvey
*Doctor Zhivago (Lean, 65)	Norman Savage
Duel In The Sun (Vidor, 46)	Hal C. Kern, William Ziegler,
	John D. Faure and
	Charles Freeman

*Earthquake (Robson, 74)	Dorothy Spencer
East Of Eden (Kazan, 55)	Owen Marks
†Eskimo (Van Dyke, 34)	Conrad Nervig
Executive Suite (Wise, 54)	Ralph Winters
*The Exorcist (Friedkin, 73)	Jordan Leondopoulos and Bud Smith
*Fantastic Voyage (Fleischer, 66)	William B. Murphy
Fat City (Huston, 72)	Margaret Booth
Father Of The Bride (Minnelli, 50)	Ferris Webster
Fiddler On The Roof (Jewison, 71)	Antony Gibbs
Foreign Correspondent (Hitchcock, 40)	Dorothy Spencer and Otho Lovering
Fourteen Hours (Hathaway, 51)	Dorothy Spencer
†The French Connection (Friedkin, 71)	Jerry Greenberg
†From Here To Eternity (Zinnemann, 53)	William Lyon
The Front Page (Wilder, 74)	Ralph E. Winters
*Funny Girl (Wyler, 68)	Robert Swink, Maury Winetrobe and William Sand
Gaslight (Cukor, 44)	Ralph E. Winters
*Gentleman's Agreement (Kazan, 47)	Harmon Jones
The Getaway (Peckinpah, 72)	Robert Wolfe
*Giant (Stevens, 56)	William Hornbeck, Philip W. Anderson and Fred Bohanan
†Gigi (Minnelli, 58)	Adrienne Fazan
The Go-Between (Losey, 71)	Reginald Beck
*The Godfather (Coppola, 72)	William Reynolds and Peter Zinner
The Godfather Part II (Coppola, 74)	Peter Zinner, Barry Malkin and Richard Marks
†Gone With The Wind (Fleming, 39)	Hal C. Kern and James E. Newcom
The Graduate (Nichols, 67)	Sam O'Steen
†Grand Prix (Frankenheimer, 66)	Frederic Steinkamp, Henry Berman, Stewart Linder and Frank Santillo
*The Grapes Of Wrath (Ford, 40)	Robert E. Simpson
*The Great Escape (Sturges, 63)	Ferris Webster
*The Greatest Show On Earth (DeMille, 52)	Anne Bauchens
The Great Northfield Minnesota Raid (Kaufman, 72)	Douglas Stewart
The Great Waldo Pepper (Hill, 75)	William Reynolds
*Guess Who's Coming To Dinner? (Kramer, 67)	Robert C. Jones
*Gunfight At The O.K. Corral (Sturges, 57)	Warren Low
The Gunfighter (King, 50)	Barbara McLean
The Heiress (Wyler, 49)	William Hornbeck

*Hello, Dolly! (Kelly, 69)	William Reynolds
†High Noon (Zinnemann, 52)	Elmo Williams and Harry Gerstad
Hobson's Choice (Lean, 54)	Peter Taylor
The Horse's Mouth (Neame, 59)	Anne V. Coates
House Of Wax (de Toth, 53)	Rudi Fehr
*How Green Was My Valley (Ford, 41)	James B. Clark
†How The West Was Won (Ford, Hathaway, Marshall, 63)	Harold F. Kress
Humoresque (Negulesco, 47)	Rudi Fehr
The Hunchback Of Notre Dame (Dieterle, 39)	William Hamilton and Robert Wise
The Hustler (Rossen, 61)	Dede Allen
*I Want To Live (Wise, 58)	William Hornbeck
*The Informer (Ford, 35)	George Hively
*Inherit The Wind (Kramer, 60)	Frederic Knudtson
†In The Heat Of The Night (Jewison, 67)	Hal Ashby
Islands In The Stream (Schaffner, 77)	Robert Swink
*It's A Wonderful Life (Capra, 46)	William Hornbeck
†Jaws (Spielberg, 75)	Verna Fields
Jeremiah Johnson (Pollack, 72)	Thomas Stanford
Jesus Christ Superstar (Jewison, 73)	Antony Gibbs
*The Jolson Story (Green, 46)	William Lyon
Juarez (Dieterle, 39)	Warren Low
*Judgment At Nuremberg (Kramer, 61)	Frederic Knudtson
*Julia (Zinnemann, 77)	Walter Murch and Marcel Durham
Key Largo (Huston, 48)	Rudi Fehr
*The Killers (Siodmak, 46)	Arthur Hilton
Kind Hearts And Coronets (Hamer, 49)	Peter Tanner
†King Solomon's Mines (Bennett, Marton, 50)	Ralph E. Winters and Conrad A. Nervig
Kiss Me Kate (Sidney, 53)	Ralph E. Winters
The Lady From Shanghai (Welles, 48)	Viola Lawrence
The Last Detail (Ashby, 73)	Robert C. Jones
The Lavender Hill Mob (Crichton, 51)	Seth Holt
†Lawrence Of Arabia (Lean, 62)	Anne V. Coates
The Left-Handed Gun (Penn, 58)	Folmar Blangsted
Lenny (Fosse, 74)	Alan Heim
*The Letter (Wyler, 40)	Warren Low
The Life Of Emile Zola (Dieterle, 37)	Warren Low
Lili (Walters, 53)	Ferris Webster
Little Big Man (Penn, 70)	Dede Allen

*The Little Foxes (Wyler, 41)	Daniel Mandell
*Lives Of A Bengal Lancer (Hathaway, 35)	Ellsworth Hoagland
Looking For Mr. Goodbar (Brooks, 77)	George Grenville
†Lost Horizon (Capra, 37)	Gene Havlick and Gene Milford
*The Lost Weekend (Wilder, 45)	Doane Harrison
Lust For Life (Minnelli, 56)	Adrienne Fazan
The Magnificent Ambersons (Welles, 42)	Robert Wise
The Magnificent Seven (Sturges, 60)	Ferris Webster
*The Manchurian Candidate (Frankenheimer, 62)	Ferris Webster
A Man For All Seasons (Zinnemann, 66)	Ralph Kemplen
The Man Who Would Be King (Huston, 75)	Russell Lloyd
†Mary Poppins (Stevenson, 64)	Cotton Warburton
*M.A.S.H. (Altman, 70)	Danford B. Greene
*Midnight Cowboy (Schlesinger, 69)	Hugh A. Robertson
*Midnight Express (Parker, 78)	Gerry Hambling
†A Midsummer Night's Dream (Reinhardt, Dieterle, 35)	Ralph Dawson
The Misfits (Huston, 61)	George Tomasini
*Moulin Rouge (Huston, 52)	Ralph Kemplen
*Mrs. Miniver (Wyler, 42)	Harold F. Kress
Murder On The Orient Express (Lumet, 74)	Anne V. Coates
*The Music Man (Da Costa, 62)	William Ziegler
*Mutiny On The Bounty (Lloyd, 35)	Margaret Booth
My Darling Clementine (Ford, 46)	Dorothy Spencer
*My Fair Lady (Cukor, 64)	William Ziegler
†The Naked City (Dassin, 48)	Paul Weatherwax
†National Velvet (Brown, 45)	Robert J. Kern
*Network (Lumet, 76)	Alan Heim
*North By Northwest (Hitchcock, 59)	George Tomasini
†North West Mounted Police (DeMille, 40)	Anne Bauchens
Now Voyager (Rapper, 42)	Warren Low
*The Nun's Story (Zinnemann, 59)	Walter Thompson
Obsession (DePalma, 76)	Paul Hirsch
*The Odd Couple (Saks, 68)	Frank Bracht
*Odd Man Out (Reed, 47)	Fergus McDonnell
*Oliver! (Reed, 68)	Ralph Kemplen
*One Flew Over The Cuckoo's Nest (Forman, 75)	Richard Chew, Lynzee Klingman and Sheldon Kahn
One, Two, Three (Wilder, 61)	Daniel Mandell
*On The Beach (Kramer, 59)	Frederic Knudtson
On The Town (Kelly, Donen, 49)	Ralph E. Winters
†On The Waterfront (Kazan, 54)	Gene Milford
Our Man In Havana (Reed, 60)	Bert Bates
Outcast Of The Islands (Reed, 52)	Bert Bates
The Outlaw Josey Wales (Eastwood, 76)	Ferris Webster

Paper Moon (Bogdanovich, 73)	Verna Fields
Papillon (Schaffner, 73)	Robert Swink
†Patton (Schaffner, 70)	Hugh S. Fowler
†Picnic (Logan, 55)	Charles Nelson and William A. Lyon
The Picture Of Dorian Gray (Lewin, 45)	Ferris Webster
†A Place In The Sun (Stevens, 51)	William Hornbeck
The Plainsman (DeMille, 37)	Anne Bauchens
Planet Of The Apes (Schaffner, 68)	Hugh S. Fowler
Possessed (Bernhardt, 47)	Rudi Fehr
†The Pride Of The Yankees (Wood, 42)	Daniel Mandell
The Private Life Of Sherlock Holmes (Wilder, 70)	Ernest Walter
Psycho (Hitchcock, 60)	George Tomasini
Pursued (Walsh, 47)	Christian Nyby
Rachel, Rachel (Newman, 68)	Dede Allen
Reap The Wild Wind (DeMille, 42)	Anne Bauchens
Rear Window (Hitchcock, 54)	George Tomasini
*Rebecca (Hitchcock, 40)	Hal C. Kern
Rebel Without A Cause (Ray, 55)	William Ziegler
*Red River (Hawks, 48)	Christian Nyby
*The Red Shoes (Powell/Pressburger, 48)	Reginald Mills
Rio Bravo (Hawks, 59)	Folmar Blangsted
†Rocky (Avildsen, 76)	Richard Halsey and Scott Conrad
*Roman Holiday (Wyler, 53)	Robert Swink
Room At The Top (Clayton, 59)	Ralph Kemplen
Rosemary's Baby (Polanski, 68)	Sam O'Steen and Robert Wyman
*The Rose Tattoo (Daniel Mann, 55)	Warren Low
The Sailor Who Fell From Grace With The Sea (Carlino, 76)	Antony Gibbs
Saturday Night And Sunday Morning (Reisz, 60)	Seth Holt
Saturday Night Fever (Badham, 77)	David Rawlins
Seconds (Frankenheimer, 66)	Ferris Webster and David Newhouse
†Sergeant York (Hawks, 41)	William Holmes
Serpico (Lumet, 73)	Dede Allen and Richard Marks
The Servant (Losey, 63)	Reginald Mills
*Seven Brides For Seven Brothers (Donen, 54)	Ralph E. Winters
Shampoo (Ashby, 75)	Robert C. Jones
Singin' In The Rain (Donen/Kelly, 52)	Adrienne Fazan
Slaughterhouse-Five (Hill, 72)	Dede Allen
The Snake Pit (Litvak, 48)	Dorothy Spencer
The Snows Of Kilimanjaro (King, 52)	Barbara McLean

*Somebody Up There Likes Me (Wise, 56) Albert Akst
*The Song Of Bernadette (King, 43) Barbara McLean
 Sorry, Wrong Number (Litvak, 48) Warren Low
†The Sound Of Music (Wise, 65) William Reynolds
*Spartacus (Kubrick, 60) Robert Lawrence
 Spellbound (Hitchcock, 45) Hal C. Kern
 The Spy Who Came In From The Cold
  (Ritt, 65) Anthony Harvey
*Stagecoach (Ford, 39) Otho Lovering
    and Dorothy Spencer
 Stalag 17 (Wilder, 53) George Tomasini
 A Star Is Born (Cukor, 54) Folmar Blangsted
 A Star Is Born (Pierson, 76) Peter Zinner
†Star Wars (Lucas, 77) Paul Hirsch, Marcia Lucas
    and Richard Chew
†The Sting (Hill, 73) William Reynolds
 Summertime (Lean, 55) Peter Taylor
*Summer Of '42 (Mulligan, 71) Folmar Blangsted
*Sunset Boulevard (Wilder, 50) Arthur Schmidt and
    Doane Harrison
*Superman (Donner, 78) Stuart Baird

*The Talk Of The Town (Stevens, 42) Otto Meyer
 Taxi Driver (Scorsese, 76) Tom Rolf and Melvin Shapiro
*The Ten Commandments (DeMille, 56) Anne Bauchens
*They Shoot Horses Don't They (Pollack, 69) Frederic Steinkamp
*The Third Man (Reed, 49) Oswald Hafenrichter
*Three Days Of The Condor (Pollack, 75) Frederic Steinkamp
 Three Strangers (Negulesco, 46) George Amy
 Topaz (Hitchcock, 69) William Ziegler
†The Towering Inferno (Guillermin, 74) Harold F. Kress
    and Carl Kress
 The Treasure Of The Sierra Madre
  (Huston, 48) Owen Marks
 Tunes Of Glory (Neame, 60) Anne V. Coates
*The Turning Point (Ross, 77) William Reynolds
 Twelve O'Clock High (King, 49) Barbara McLean
*20,000 Leagues Under The Sea
  (Fleischer, 54) Elmo Williams

 Union Pacific (DeMille, 39) Anne Bauchens

 Valentino (Russell, 77) Stuart Baird
 Vertigo (Hitchcock, 58) George Tomasini
 Viva Zapata (Kazan, 52) Barbara McLean

 The War Of The Worlds (Haskin, 53) Everett Douglas

†West Side Story (Wise/Robbins, 61)   Thomas Stanford
  The Whisperers (Forbes, 67)   Anthony Harvey
  White Heat (Walsh, 49)   Owen Marks
  Who's Afraid Of Virginia Woolf
      (Nichols, 66)   Sam O'Steen
†Wilson (King, 44)   Barbara McLean
  The Window (Tetzlaff, 49)   Frederic Knudtson
  Witness For The Prosecution (Wilder, 57) Daniel Mandell
  Wuthering Heights (Wyler, 39)   Daniel Mandell

  Yankee Doodle Dandy (Curtiz, 42)   George Amy
  The Yearling (Brown, 46)   Harold F. Kress

APPENDIX VII

ACADEMY AWARDS

A list of the major Oscars presented by the Academy of Motion Picture Arts and Sciences in Hollywood, from 1927 to the present day.

1927/28
Production   WINGS (Paramount)
Actor   Emil Jannings in *The Way of All Flesh* and *The Last Command*
Actress   Janet Gaynor in *Seventh Heaven, Street Angel* and *Sunrise*
Direction   Frank Borzage for *Seventh Heaven*

1928/29
Production   THE BROADWAY MELODY (MGM)
Actor   Warner Baxter in *In Old Arizona*
Actress   Mary Pickford in *Coquette*
Direction   Frank Lloyd for *The Divine Lady*

1929/30
Production   ALL QUIET ON THE WESTERN FRONT (Universal)
Actor   George Arliss in *Disraeli*
Actress   Norma Shearer in *The Divorcee*
Direction   Lewis Milestone for *All Quiet on the Western Front*

1930/31
Production   CIMARRON (RKO Radio)
Actor   Lionel Barrymore in *A Free Soul*
Actress   Marie Dressler in *Min and Bill*
Direction   Norman Taurog for *Skippy*

1931/32
Production   GRAND HOTEL (MGM)
Actor   Fredric March in *Dr. Jekyll and Mr. Hyde* and Wallace Beery in *The Champ*
Actress   Helen Hayes in *The Sin of Madelon Claudet*
Direction   Frank Borzage for *Bad Girl*

1932/33
Production   CAVALCADE (Fox)

Actor	Charles Laughton in *The Private Life of Henry VIII*
Actress	Katharine Hepburn in *Morning Glory*
Direction	Frank Lloyd for *Cavalcade*

1934

Production	IT HAPPENED ONE NIGHT (Columbia)
Actor	Clark Gable in *It Happened One Night*
Actress	Claudette Colbert in *It Happened One Night*
Direction	Frank Capra for *It Happened One Night*

1935

Production	MUTINY ON THE BOUNTY (MGM)
Actor	Victor McLaglen in *The Informer*
Actress	Bette Davis in *Dangerous*
Direction	John Ford for *The Informer*

1936

Production	THE GREAT ZIEGFELD (MGM)
Actor	Paul Muni in *The Story of Louis Pasteur*
Actress	Luise Rainer in *The Great Ziegfeld*
Direction	Frank Capra for *Mr. Deeds Goes to Town*

1937

Production	THE LIFE OF EMILE ZOLA (Warner Bros.)
Actor	Spencer Tracy in *Captains Courageous*
Actress	Luise Rainer in *The Good Earth*
Direction	Leo McCarey for *The Awful Truth*

1938

Production	YOU CAN'T TAKE IT WITH YOU (Columbia)
Actor	Spencer Tracy in *Boy's Town*
Actress	Bette Davis in *Jezebel*
Direction	Frank Capra for *You Can't Take it With You*

1939

Production	GONE WITH THE WIND (Selznick-MGM)
Actor	Robert Donat in *Goodbye Mr. Chips*
Actress	Vivien Leigh in *Gone With the Wind*
Direction	Victor Fleming for *Gone With the Wind*

1940

Production	REBECCA (Selznick-United Artists)
Actor	James Stewart in *The Philadelphia Story*
Actress	Ginger Rogers in *Kitty Foyle*
Direction	John Ford for *The Grapes of Wrath*

1941

Production	HOW GREEN WAS MY VALLEY (20th Century-Fox)
Actor	Gary Cooper in *Sergeant York*
Actress	Joan Fontaine in *Suspicion*
Direction	John Ford for *How Green Was My Valley*

1942

Production   MRS. MINIVER (MGM)
Actor   James Cagney in *Yankee Doodle Dandy*
Actress   Greer Garson in *Mrs. Miniver*
Direction   William Wyler for *Mrs. Miniver*

1943

Production   CASABLANCA (Warner Bros.)
Actor   Paul Lukas in *Watch on the Rhine*
Actress   Jennifer Jones in *The Song of Bernadette*
Direction   Michael Curtiz for *Casablanca*

1944

Production   GOING MY WAY (Paramount)
Actor   Bing Crosby in *Going My Way*
Actress   Ingrid Bergman in *Gaslight*
Direction   Leo McCarey for *Going My Way*

1945

Production   THE LOST WEEKEND (Paramount)
Actor   Ray Milland in *The Lost Weekend*
Actress   Joan Crawford in *Mildred Pierce*
Direction   Billy Wilder for *The Lost Weekend*

1946

Production   THE BEST YEARS OF OUR LIVES (Goldwyn-RKO Radio)
Actor   Fredric March in *The Best Years of Our Lives*
Actress   Olivia de Havilland in *To Each His Own*
Direction   William Wyler for *The Best Years of Our Lives*

1947

Production   GENTLEMAN'S AGREEMENT (20th Century-Fox)
Actor   Ronald Colman in *A Double Life*
Actress   Loretta Young in *The Farmer's Daughter*
Direction   Elia Kazan for *Gentleman's Agreement*

1948

Production   HAMLET (Two-Cities)
Actor   Laurence Olivier in *Hamlet*
Actress   Jane Wyman in *Johnny Belinda*
Direction   John Huston for *The Treasure of the Sierra Madre*

1949

Production   ALL THE KING'S MEN (Columbia)
Actor   Broderick Crawford in *All the King's Men*
Actress   Olivia de Havilland in *The Heiress*
Direction   Joseph L. Mankiewicz for *A Letter to Three Wives*

1950

Production   ALL ABOUT EVE (20th Century-Fox)
Actor   Jose Ferrer in *Cyrano de Bergerac*

Actress　　　　Judy Holliday in *Born Yesterday*
Direction　　　Joseph L. Mankiewicz for *All About Eve*

1951
Production　　AN AMERICAN IN PARIS (MGM)
Actor　　　　Humphrey Bogart in *The African Queen*
Actress　　　　Vivien Leigh in *A Streetcar Named Desire*
Direction　　　George Stevens for *A Place in the Sun*

1952
Production　　THE GREATEST SHOW ON EARTH (Paramount)
Actor　　　　Gary Cooper in *High Noon*
Actress　　　　Shirley Booth in *Come Back, Little Sheba*
Direction　　　John Ford for *The Quiet Man*

1953
Production　　FROM HERE TO ETERNITY (Columbia)
Actor　　　　William Holden in *Stalag 17*
Actress　　　　Audrey Hepburn in *Roman Holiday*
Direction　　　Fred Zinnemann for *From Here to Eternity*

1954
Production　　ON THE WATERFRONT (Columbia)
Actor　　　　Marlon Brando in *On the Waterfront*
Actress　　　　Grace Kelly in *The Country Girl*
Direction　　　Elia Kazan for *On the Waterfront*

1955
Production　　MARTY (United Artists)
Actor　　　　Ernest Borgnine in *Marty*
Actress　　　　Anna Magnani in *The Rose Tattoo*
Direction　　　Delbert Mann for *Marty*

1956
Production　　AROUND THE WORLD IN 80 DAYS (Todd-United Artists)
Actor　　　　Yul Brynner in *The King and I*
Actress　　　　Ingrid Bergman in *Anastasia*
Direction　　　George Stevens for *Giant*

1957
Production　　THE BRIDGE ON THE RIVER KWAI (Columbia)
Actor　　　　Alec Guinness in *The Bridge on the River Kwai*
Actress　　　　Joanne Woodward in *The Three Faces of Eve*
Direction　　　David Lean for *The Bridge on the River Kwai*

1958
Production　　GIGI (MGM)
Actor　　　　David Niven in *Separate Tables*
Actress　　　　Susan Hayward in *I Want to Live*
Direction　　　Vincente Minnelli for *Gigi*

1959
Production   BEN-HUR (MGM)
Actor   Charlton Heston in *Ben Hur*
Actress   Simone Signoret in *Room At The Top*
Direction   William Wyler for *Ben-Hur*

1960
Production   THE APARTMENT (Mirisch-United Artists)
Actor   Burt Lancaster in *Elmer Gantry*
Actress   Elizabeth Taylor in *Butterfield 8*
Direction   Billy Wilder for *The Apartment*

1961
Production   WEST SIDE STORY (Mirisch-United Artists)
Actor   Maximilian Schell in *Judgment At Nuremberg*
Actress   Sophia Loren in *Two Women*
Direction   Robert Wise and Jerome Robbins for *West Side Story*

1962
Production   LAWRENCE OF ARABIA (Columbia)
Actor   Gregory Peck in *To Kill a Mockingbird*
Actress   Anne Bancroft in *The Miracle Worker*
Direction   David Lean for *Lawrence of Arabia*

1963
Production   TOM JONES (Woodfall-United Artists)
Actor   Sidney Poitier in *Lilies of the Field*
Actress   Patricia Neal in *Hud*
Direction   Tony Richardson for *Tom Jones*

1964
Production   MY FAIR LADY (Warner Bros.)
Actor   Rex Harrison in *My Fair Lady*
Actress   Julie Andrews in *Mary Poppins*
Direction   George Cukor for *My Fair Lady*

1965
Production   THE SOUND OF MUSIC (20th Century-Fox)
Actor   Lee Marvin in *Cat Ballou*
Actress   Julie Christie in *Darling*
Direction   Robert Wise for *The Sound of Music*

1966
Production   A MAN FOR ALL SEASONS (Columbia)
Actor   Paul Scofield in *A Man for All Seasons*
Actress   Elizabeth Taylor in *Who's Afraid of Virginia Woolf?*
Direction   Fred Zinnemann for *A Man for All Seasons*

1967
Production   IN THE HEAT OF THE NIGHT (Mirisch-United
                  Artists

Actor	Rod Steiger in *In The Heat of the Night*
Actress	Katharine Hepburn in *Guess Who's Coming to Dinner?*
Direction	Mike Nichols for *The Graduate*

1968

Production	OLIVER! (Columbia)
Actor	Cliff Robertson in *Charly*
Actress	Katharine Hepburn in *The Lion in Winter* and Barbra Streisand in *Funny Girl*
Direction	Carol Reed for *Oliver*

1969

Production	MIDNIGHT COWBOY (United Artists)
Actor	John Wayne in *True Grit*
Actress	Maggie Smith in *The Prime of Miss Jean Brodie*
Direction	John Schlesinger for *Midnight Cowboy*

1970

Production	PATTON (20th Century-Fox)
Actor	George C. Scott in *Patton*
Actress	Glenda Jackson in *Women in Love*
Direction	Franklin Schaffner for *Patton*

1971

Production	THE FRENCH CONNECTION (20th Century-Fox)
Actor	Gene Hackman in *The French Connection*
Actress	Jane Fonda in *Klute*
Direction	William Friedkin for *The French Connection*

1972

Production	THE GODFATHER (Paramount)
Actor	Marlon Brando in *The Godfather*
Actress	Liza Minnelli in *Cabaret*
Direction	Bob Fosse for *Cabaret*

1973

Production	THE STING (Universal)
Actor	Jack Lemmon in *Save The Tiger*
Actress	Glenda Jackson in *A Touch Of Class*
Direction	George Roy Hill for *The Sting*

1974

Production	THE GODFATHER PART II (Paramount)
Actor	Art Carney in *Harry And Tonto*
Actress	Ellen Burstyn in *Alice Doesn't Live Here Anymore*
Direction	Francis Ford Coppola for *The Godfather Part II*

1975

Production	ONE FLEW OVER THE CUCKOO'S NEST (United Artists)

Actor	Jack Nicholson in *One Flew Over The Cuckoo's Nest*
Actress	Louise Fletcher in *One Flew Over The Cuckoo's Nest*
Direction	Milos Forman for *One Flew Over The Cuckoo's Nest*

1976

Production	ROCKY (United Artists)
Actor	Peter Finch in *Network*
Actress	Faye Dunaway in *Network*
Direction	John Avildsen for *Rocky*

1977

Production	ANNIE HALL (United Artists)
Actor	Richard Dreyfuss in *The Goodbye Girl*
Actress	Diane Keaton in *Annie Hall*
Direction	Woody Allen for *Annie Hall*

1978

PRODUCTION	THE DEER HUNTER (Universal)
Actor	Jon Voight in *Coming Home*
Actress	Jane Fonda in *Coming Home*
Direction	Michael Cimino for *The Deer Hunter*

INDEX

FEATURED FILMS

WHO'S WHO